THE MEMORIAL HALL

THESE HUNDRED YEARS

A HISTORY OF THE CONGREGATIONAL UNION OF ENGLAND AND WALES, 1831-1931

BY

ALBERT PEEL, M.A., Litt.D., B.Litt.

Editor of

The Congregational Quarterly and *The Transactions of the Congregational Historical Society*

LONDON:

CONGREGATIONAL UNION OF ENGLAND AND WALES

MEMORIAL HALL, E.C.4

1931.

First Published 1931.

PRINTED IN GREAT BRITAIN BY S. TINSLEY & CO., LTD., LONDON, E.C. 2.

TO THE

CONGREGATIONAL CHURCHES

AT

GREAT HARWOOD, LANCASHIRE,

AND

CLAPTON PARK, LONDON,

WHOSE PATIENCE, LOYALTY, AND TRUST
HAVE ENABLED THEIR MINISTER
TO SERVE THE
WIDER FELLOWSHIP OF
THE CONGREGATIONAL CHURCHES.

PREFACE.

THE Introduction printed within states the aim of this volume. Here it is only for me to say a word about the method that has been followed in writing it, and to express my thanks for help received.

The arrangement of the volume was not decided upon without much anxious thought. For a long time I planned to untangle the story and trace the different threads from the beginning to the end, taking the ministry—its training, recognition, maintenance, superannuation—and devoting a chapter to it, and so with all the important phases of the subject. But in practice I found the strands so interwoven that I had to revert to the chronological method with its obvious disadvantages. The difficulty has been to keep everything in proportion and yet to get in details essential to accuracy. I hope that the wood is not too often obscured by the trees.

The Histories of Bogue and Bennett, Waddington, and Dale, have been of great service for the periods they cover, though, of course, the *Congregational Year Books* have formed the basis on which the history has had to be built. The Official Minutes of the Union are so bald and lifeless as often to be useless and sometimes misleading.

In the main my effort has been to supplement, test, and, where necessary, correct, the official record with unofficial printed accounts in periodicals, and, in the later period, with verbal statements from those who played a part in the events concerned. Especially valuable for the last fifty years have been the memoranda supplied by Mr. Gerard Ford.

Oral tradition, I have found, is far from trustworthy. Sometimes quite contradictory accounts of an incident have been given me by those who took part in it; sometimes printed and oral descriptions have been in conflict. When this is the case it is to be regretted that so often manuscript evidence that would have been invaluable has been thoughtlessly destroyed. All Hannay's letter-books some miscreant threw away, while at some time or other vandals have been at work in the Memorial Hall on portraits, books, and MSS. Congregationalism has still a good deal to learn in the way of treasuring both its history and the materials for it.

To the Congregational Library I have turned again and again. Few Congregationalists realize what a store-house it is, and without it this book could not have been written. I am greatly indebted to its officials and to the officials of the Congregational Union, who have readily helped one who has been a continual source of trouble for many months. Many Departmental Secretaries of the Union, past and present, and others have furnished me with information for which I am grateful. To Dr. F. J. Powicke, now the doyen of Congregational historians, who read the MS., and made many useful suggestions, my best thanks are due, as they are to Dr. S. M. Berry, the Rev. W. L. Lee, and Mr. S. J. Dickins, all of whom read the book in MS. or in proof. To veterans who have allowed me to draw on their memories, and to some of them and to authorities who have read sections about which they have first-hand knowledge I am grateful, too, and also to those who have assisted me in research, typing, and proof-reading.

None of these is responsible for any errors the book contains. It would be folly to hope that they are missing in a book of this size, full of facts and figures. I ask pardon for them in advance, merely saying that I have done my best, and that there is nothing "set down in malice". I wish that it had been possible to breathe life into some of the facts relating to Constitution and Committees which had to find a place, but that I found beyond me.

I am indebted to all who have helped me with photographs : to my keen regret I have been unable to obtain one of the first Congregational Library or of Joshua Wilson, who had most right of all to appear.

Perhaps I may be allowed to say that this volume could not have been written without the loyalty and sacrifice of my wife and daughter. They have seen very little of me for six months, and then it has been when my home has been littered with attractive looking volumes like the *Congregational Year Books!*

1st May, 1931.   ALBERT PEEL.

CONTENTS

LIST OF ILLUSTRATIONS.

INTRODUCTION.

THE task of writing a History of the Congregational Union is one that imposes many restraints and demands great self-control. It has to be remembered constantly that a history of the Congregational Union is not a history of Congregationalism, and that many interesting matters pertinent to the latter must be ruled out of the former.

The Congregationalism of the hundred years, 1831 to 1931, contains scores of interesting personalities on whose characters and achievements it would be pleasant to dwell, but this History can only glance at them in so far as they are concerned with the Union. A great many biographies have had to be read, from which a huge amount of commentary on the life of the denomination has been drawn, but only a modicum, left after repeated siftings—that which touches the organized life of the churches—has been used. The trend of theological thought in the denomination is a study in itself; the writer of this History must turn his back resolutely on it, except when and where it affects the life of the Union. There are individual churches with striking stories, County Unions with rapidly growing activities, movements in thought and worship, and experiments in church life, all deserving of study; but these can only be used as they provide the atmosphere in which the development at the centre can be rightly discerned.

Restraint has had to be exercised, too, in another way. This volume aims at providing the facts regarding the Congregational Union rather than at giving a complete interpretation of them. To furnish as fully and as accurately as possible the material on which such an interpretation must be based, has been the aim throughout; the commentary on it has been deliberately left to a later date, and, maybe, to other hands.

One or two points must be made, however, in introducing the History proper. It is impossible to discuss a Union of Congregational Churches without understanding what

A

Congregational Churches are, and appreciating the principles by which their members have been guided. Congregationalism did not begin in 1831, but 1800 years before. When Jesus went about preaching and teaching He left in His train men and women whose hearts He had touched, who believed on Him, and naturally wished to gather for worship, fellowship, and service with others who had heard Him gladly. These little groups were the first Independent Churches, conscious, in their meetings, of the presence of their Master, and of the might and power He gave. After His death, when the Gospel began to be preached in lands beyond Palestine, similar groups gathered, equally conscious of the presence of their Lord —now the Risen Lord.

One striking fact about these early churches has often been overlooked. They were independent in that they acknowledged no Head but Christ Himself, but the intensity of their love for Him gave them a strong sense of attachment to, and of communion with, each other. He was the One Vine of which they were all branches, and the same Life flowed through them all. They were independent, and yet they belonged to the one church, holy, catholic, apostolic. They had all the blessings of freedom and yet they knew all the joys of fellowship.

This is not the place to describe how the simplicity of the life of these early churches was rapidly destroyed by the growth of elaborate organization, how their witness was buried beneath imposing and impressive hierarchical structures. With renewed access to the Scriptures in the 16th century the pristine beauty and simplicity of the church life of the first century were revealed : immediately, especially in England, some Christian believers determined to model their own church life upon it, and, despite ban and persecution, began to gather in groups for fellowship. As they grew in number, their problem was how to retain both the independence they cherished and the fellowship with each other that they knew was equally dear to the heart of their Lord and equally necessary to the life of their churches.

In local Associations they first endeavoured to solve their riddle, which was made no easier by the growing complexity of society after the Industrial Revolution. This, with the growth of cities, and the changed means of transit and communication, made the problem increasingly urgent. Could Independent Churches so co-operate as to give to one another all possible help, and the full advantage of the fact that they were *one,* with the same Lord, the same faith, the same message, the same work, and yet preserve in each of them that sense of independence, of immediate access to Him who met with them, and whose presence made them the Church Catholic when and where they met, and competent for all their duties and responsibilities?

It is that primary question which the Congregational Union of England and Wales was, and is, an attempt to answer.

" We must have increased centralization to make our work and witness effective."

" We cannot have increased centralization without losing our *raison d'être* and forsaking our distinctive principle."

These two cries have been constantly raised through the century. It is the old paradox : "If anything is to live, it must be organized; and yet organization kills it". The pages that follow provide the evidence to show how far Congregationalism in the last hundred years has managed to resolve that paradox.

I. THE MOVEMENT FOR ASSOCIATION.

THE beginnings of the movement for a union between Congregationalists in this country are by no means easy to trace. Some intercourse between ministers and congregations had, of course, been a common feature from the first. Sometimes, indeed, groups as far apart as Norwich and Yarmouth had belonged to the same church. But there had been nothing in the way of a synodical system or any systematized organization, although Congregationalists had on occasion met together for various purposes. In 1658 in consultation they set forth the Savoy Declaration, stating the things they believed, though the Preface aptly reveals both their unity in spirit and their lack of associated life.

> We confess that from the first, every, or at least the generality of our Churches, have been in a maner like so many Ships (though holding forth the same general colours) lancht singly, and sailing apart and alone in the vast Ocean of these tumultuating times, and they exposed to every wind of Doctrine, under no other conduct then the Word and Spirit, and their particular Elders and principal Brethren, without Associations among our selves, or so much as holding out common lights to others, whereby to know where we were.
>
> But yet whilest we thus confess to our own shame this neglect, let all acknowledge, that God hath ordered it for His high and greater glory, in that His singular care and power should have so watcht over each of these, as that all should be found to have steered their course by the same Chart, and to have been bound for one and the same Port, and that upon this general search now made, that the same holy and blessed Truths of all sorts, which are currant and warrantable amongst all the other Churches of Christ in the world, should be found to be our Lading.

In 1691 Independents and Presbyterians joined in the well-intentioned but short-lived "Happy Union", one of the objects of which was to discover the whereabouts and means of livelihood of ministers ejected in 1662, of students for the ministry in need of monetary aid, and of places where congregations had met, were meeting, or were likely to meet. Under this Union a Common Fund was established, from which grants were made.

After the disruption of the Fund eleven churches in London formed the Congregational Fund Board in 1695, raising funds by an annual collection in order to assist poorer ministers in the country and students for the ministry, the Fund being managed by the pastors and messengers of the contributing churches.

The London Board of Congregational Ministers was formed in 1727 "to take cognisance of everything affecting the interests of that Denomination, and of religion in general", and three years later the "Monthly Exercise of Congregational Ministers and Churches in the Metropolis" was started.

Doddridge, during his short but active life, encouraged the formation of Associations, though he did not limit them to his own denomination. After visiting the "Associations of Protestant Dissenting Ministers in Norfolk and Suffolk" in 1741, he wrote a letter in which he urged : —

> that neighbouring ministers, in one part of our land and another, especially in this country, should enter into associations, to strengthen the hands of each other by united consultations and prayer : and that meetings of ministers might, by some obvious regulations, be made more extensively useful than they often are : in which view it was farther proposed, with unanimous approbation, that these meetings should be held at certain periodical times :—That each member of the association should endeavour, if possible, to be present, studying to order his affairs so, as to guard against unnecessary hindrances :— That public worship should begin and end sooner than it commonly has done on these occasions :—That each pastor preach at these assemblies in his turn :—That the minister of the place determine who shall be employed in prayer :— That after a moderate repast, to be managed with as little trouble and expense as may be, an hour or two in the afternoon be spent in religious conference and prayer, and in taking into consideration, merely as a friendly council, and without the least pretence to any right of authoritative decision, the concerns of any brother, or any society which may be brought before us for our advice :—And finally, that every member of the association shall consider it as an additional obligation upon him, to endeavour to be, so far as he justly and honourably can, a friend and guardian to the reputation, comfort, and usefulness of all his brethren in the christian ministry near or remote, of whatever part and denomination.

Into the further purposes of these Associations Doddridge did not go, except to indicate that they should control the entrance into the Ministry by examining students and giving certificates of approbation to be signed by all the Associated Ministers present at the General Meeting.

It was not until the latter half of the eighteenth century, however, that anything in the way of Congregational Unions began to crystallize out in any number[1]. At that time County or District Associations began to be formed, with more or less definite constitutions, until almost every county in the South, so Bogue and Bennett tell us, had its Association with regular meetings, "the Independents, formerly the most tardy", being now "the most strenuous and active" in these united gatherings, so that it is to them "that the praise of County Associations and of the vigorous efforts to do good by these means, is due in the highest degree".

These Independent Associations vary considerably in form and in purpose. Some of them incorporated nearly all the churches in their areas, others comparatively few. Some consisted of ministers only, and existed in the main for fellowship and counsel, perhaps being something akin both to Elizabethan "prophesyings" and to modern "fraternals". Other Associations contained both ministers and churches, while occasionally a previously-formed ministerial society continued side by side with an organization including the churches. Thus, the Ministerial Association in Essex was started in 1776 for "Christian fellowship, conversation, and public worship among its members", while in 1793 a County Congregational Union was formed which contained both pastors and churches associated for Home Missionary objects[2].

1 Browne's *History of Congregationalism in Norfolk and Suffolk,* pp. 187-189, 200-205, offers excellent illustrations of the development and variety of " Union " theory and practice.

2 This is the explanation of some apparent contradictions in the *History* below. It was probably the Ministerial Association that was said to approve the Union in 1831, and Essex is not included in the 8 Associations " not yet in union with us " in 1833. Yet at Birmingham, in 1839, Burls says that the Essex Union, of which he is Secretary, " has not yet joined the National Union."

The names of most of the Associations suggest that the general aim was that of evangelization. Thus the Wiltshire and East Somerset Association of ministers and churches, formed in 1797, was "designed to promote mutual edification by Christian and ministerial intercourse, and to diffuse plans for the spread of the Gospel". The Lancashire Union was established in 1806 "to promote the spread of the Gospel" in the county, and the Hertfordshire Union in 1810 for "the diffusion of religious knowledge through the towns and villages of Herts."

The Evangelical Revival was largely responsible for turning the minds of Christians, impressed with the need for evangelization both abroad and at home, in the direction of union. In 1793 the *Evangelical Magazine* was started under the editorship of the Rev. John Eyre, an Evangelical clergyman of Hackney, who was largely responsible for bringing the London Missionary Society to birth. Eyre died in 1803 at the age of forty-nine, having done a remarkable work, the value and importance of which have never been adequately recognized.

How union in service at home and abroad were related may be gathered from the affairs of the Warwickshire "Association of Ministers for the Spread of the Gospel both at Home and Abroad", recorded in Minutes printed in the *Memoirs of the Rev. George Burder*[1], who was to become Eyre's successor, both as editor of the *Evangelical Magazine* and as Secretary of the London Missionary Society.

Formed in 1793, this Association in the same year debated the duties of Christians in regard to the spread of the Gospel. They agreed that every means should be employed both at home and abroad, and recommended the establishment of a fund for this purpose, Dr. Edward Williams of Birmingham being asked to write a circular letter. This letter, considered, by the way, at six o'clock one August morning, was sent to other Associations requesting their concurrence. In January, 1794, it was

---

[1] By his son, Dr. H. F. Burder, of Hackney, one of the Provisional Committee which prepared the "Plan of Union" in 1831.

decided to engage two itinerant ministers in the county. In September of the same year Williams wrote to the *Evangelical Magazine,* on behalf of the Association, approving David Bogue's letter in a previous issue in which he recommended Independents to unite in sending missionaries abroad.   He went on to express the Warwickshire Association's readiness to share in the work.   At the same time it was resolved to spend £5 in tracts to be distributed by the itinerant preachers.   In the next year three representatives, one of whom was Burder, were sent as delegates to London to the meeting to promote the Missionary Society.   Bogue's appeal proved irresistible. He had pointed out that Independents alone were idle : the Church of England, the Kirk of Scotland, the Moravians, the Methodists, and the Baptists had all formed Societies for the propagation of the Gospel abroad : the Independents alone had taken no action.   The London Missionary Society was thus formed, and almost immediately the Warwickshire Independents were found hard at work taking collections and securing missionary candidates.

And just as they were sharing in the duty of evangelization at home and abroad, even so John Eyre, nine days after the sailing of the *Duff* with missionaries for the South Seas, was travelling to Hampshire with the first agent of the Itinerant Society he had recently formed.   Hampshire is an excellent illustration of the way in which concern for the heathen afar off revived the effort "to rescue from perdition the heathen at home".   The Hampshire ministers had had an Association for some time, and in 1796 it was reported to them that

> a gentleman in London (I believe Mr. Welch) from the time of the missionary meeting in September, 1795, had thought that, as we are desirous of sending the Gospel to the heathen, we should likewise be solicitous of sending it to the towns and villages where it is not preached, and that if two suitable persons could be found who would itinerate for that purpose in Hampshire, he would defray all their expenses.

The ministers undertook to " seek for two suitable

persons, and to render them all the assistance in their power". In April, 1797, at James Bennett's ordination at Romsey, Bogue "called a meeting of the ministers and brethren present to take into consideration a plan for spreading the Gospel through every part of Hampshire", and they

> resolved to form themselves into a society for that purpose . . . From this time, the propagation of the Gospel at home became the grand object of the Hampshire Association, which had long existed as a friendly meeting of the Independent ministers of the county, to promote kind intercourse among the different churches.

The Treasurer of the Evangelical Society (founded in 1776) that was fostering many of these Home Missionary efforts, was Thomas Wilson[1], and in 1797 it is interesting to find him, like John Eyre, "up to the eyes" in both home and foreign missionary enterprise at the same time. Indeed, throughout the movement for the establishment of a Congregational Union the lead was taken by those Congregationalists who were already engaged in united effort in the management of the London Missionary Society. So much was this the case that Josiah Conder, writing in the *Eclectic Review*[2] in 1837, and replying to attacks on the Union, argues that the London Missionary Society and the Baptist Missionary Society are substantially Congregational and Baptist Unions. His words deserve extended quotation :

> In engaging in the work of foreign missions, we have learned, as it were, the lesson of Christianity afresh ; and the Church has gained strength in the very act of bracing herself for exertion. So completely has the missionary spirit now blended itself with dissenting institutions that it may be regarded as the vital principle of Dissent, the decay of which would inevitably be followed by the decline and wasting away, or falling to pieces, of the denomination which should be deprived of it. And it is this spirit which more especially constitutes the churches of each denomination one body, operating as a principle of cohesion, or "bond of peace". Yet, instead of making each sect more sectarian, it has done more to promote a catholic inter-

1 See below, p. 46.

2 p. 181.

communion of different sects than all the forms of concord, or plans of comprehension, that were ever devised.

For many years the annual meetings of the several missionary societies have exhibited the heart-cheering spectacle of a metropolitan convocation of each denomination; convened, not to decree articles of faith, not to adjust, by a usurped authority, intestine controversies, not to issue canons of excommunication, but to concert or sanction plans for the propagation of the faith of Christ. The London Missionary Society (though not strictly confined to the denomination) has been substantially a Congregational Union, and the Baptist Missionary Society a Baptist Union; and out of these annual assemblies or convocations, the Unions appear to have naturally arisen.

The Independents, then, were working together for foreign missions. Through their County Associations and in undenominational Societies they were engaged in Home Missions. But these by no means included all their united efforts in the years that preceded the Union. In organizations like the "Christian Instruction Associations", to take another example, they were actively employed, and were learning the value of co-operative effort.

These Societies consisted, in the main, of members of churches, and their aim was to visit and instruct the masses of the people alike in cities and in villages, to hold prayer meetings, deliver tracts, *etc.* The *Congregational Magazine* of 1831, in giving an account of the work of the London Christian Instruction Societies, and especially of those connected with Independent Churches, reported that 800 Independents were engaged in the work, 150 prayer meetings being held each week. A list of the churches concerned is given. It shows, for example, that Claremont Chapel had 60 visitors, who called on 1,627 families and conducted nine prayer meetings, while the churches of Hackney, Homerton, Clapton, and Bethnal Green formed one Association, with 90 visitors, calling on 2,494 families, and holding 16 prayer meetings. The Parent Society in London, anxious to promote similar Societies throughout the country, promised to make grants of tracts, and prepared a circular, asking for information about the population, the number and denomination of the places of worship, the number of Sunday Schools and children, the denomination of the church applying for aid, how many members of the congregation were willing to serve as. visitors, and how many families it was proposed to visit, whether there were any village preaching stations connected with the church, and how they were supplied, whether there were any persons willing to loan tracts to such villages, and whether the local Association would adopt the rules of the parent body.

In 1819 the Home Missionary Society was begun by London laymen, headed by Thomas Thompson. Undenominational at first, it followed the path of other Societies in becoming largely Independent, and in training Independents to work together. It functioned largely where County Associations did not exist or were weak. By 1830 it had 28 stations in 15 counties, its 28 missionaries holding services in 172 villages, where they had 75 Sunday schools.

It will have been observed that in most of these organizations the Independents were working hand in hand with Christians of other denominations. In many cases members of the Church of England shared with Methodists and Protestant Dissenters an intense evangelical faith. For a time, say in the last years of the eighteenth century and the first years of the nineteenth, it seemed as if the burning passion for the souls of men at home and abroad might weld into one body very diverse elements. Thus Anglicans and Nonconformists started the *Evangelical Magazine,* founded the London Missionary Society and the British and Foreign Bible Society, and joined together in many an Itinerant and Home Missionary Society. And even when the Anglicans withdrew, as they soon did from the London Missionary Society, there were many enterprises in which the Protestant Dissenters still stood side by side. Together they worked for the removal of civil and religious disabilities, and the long campaign for the repeal of the Test and Corporation Acts, ending victoriously in 1828, was but the most prominent of their achievements.

All this co-operation, excellent in many ways, nevertheless served to check for a time the movement for a *Congre-*

gational Union. To many it seemed as if any Union that should be formed should be of all Protestant Dissenters—Presbyterians and Baptists as well as Independents, and not of Independents only. The Baptists, however, formed their own Union, and as time went on the management of both the *Evangelical Magazine* and the London Missionary Society came more and more into the hands of the Independents. But when proposals for any united action between Independents alone were made, there was, invariably a loud outcry from those who feared that such action would separate them from other Evangelicals. A conspicuous example of this was seen when, in 1818, it was proposed to establish the *Congregational Magazine*. This project deserves attention, for the journal was duly started, and it did much to prepare the way for the Union, while the discussion in regard to it reveals very clearly the two views, and raises one or two points frequently cropping up in the Union's subsequent history. In the Congregational Library is a bundle of letters in which ministers in different parts of the country reply to requests that they should support the magazine. It will be seen that while most of them agree that a denominational periodical is a desideratum, some express doubt and hesitation. A Committee, ministerial and lay, with John Hooper as Chairman, Richard Bowden as Secretary, and Joshua Wilson as Treasurer, was responsible for starting the paper, a monthly, with the name *The London Christian Instructor or The Congregational Magazine*. They circularized the ministers, apparently inviting them to become shareholders at two guineas a share.

The Rev. R. Elliott, of Devizes, writes giving the names of those prepared to take and back the magazine, but reporting a suggestion about the title :

> Should the word "London" be a part of it—you know the jealousy of the country gentlemen with regard to you London dons—and as this is intended to be a very general concern it might perhaps be as well to leave this word out? Individually I do not care a button about it and it may not be worth while to say anything upon the subject—that must be referred to your superior wisdom.

In January, 1818, a reminder was sent to those who had not replied to the first circular. Among the letters in response is one from Penryn, which says the writer had decided to pass the first communication by "not in contemptuous but respectful silence". He has, however, informed Mr. Turnbull[1] that he

> had some doubts whether the publication was at all required, in fact; while both its Title, and its price, appeared to me particularly objectionable.
>
> The appropriation of the proceeds of the work will probably tend to make it somewhat popular—and had the price been suited to the circumstances of the great majority of Persons *of that denomination for which it is professedly designed* . . then, and in that case, according to my views, a much fairer prospect might be entertained of ultimate success. As far however as it is the means of doing good, I shall rejoice.

From Shrewsbury comes a letter expressing the concern of the writer and others for the interests of the *Evangelical Magazine,* "which, though it has no particular claim to literary excellence, is a valuable publication, and has been eminently useful". He would welcome the undertaking but for the idea of "rivalship and consequent injury" to the *Evangelical,* and says the "History of the Churches" in the different counties, a suggested feature of the magazine, would be useful, but he prays that "the spirit of strife or illwill, of pride or political disaffection, may never defile your pages".

From Wigan comes the same objection, especially as the conductors of the *Evangelical* "for the most part belong to the Congregational Denomination". Nevertheless, the writer sends two guineas, the amount of one share, and says 12 or 15 copies will be purchased by his people.

From Stourbridge comes a grumbling letter, the minister having received *two* circulars, which suggests "great negligence"! He will do what he can, but all his leisure time

> is taken up with the *Country Magazine, or Fireside Companion,* published once a fortnight, price 3d., and of which

[1] See below, p. 16.

we circulate 1,200 numbers. I derive no emolument from the sale, but I am satisfied to labour gratuitously, as I know it has been very useful in this neighbourhood. It does not indeed contain much original matter, but it is within the reach of the poor, and is at least new to them.

The minister at Deptford says that if the design is to assert, explain, and defend the principles of Independency, he approves,

for I doubt not but a very great majority in our respective congregations are entirely unacquainted with the principles of Dissent, and I verily believe that much of the disorder and contention which occurs in Congregational Churches arises from a want of understanding that mode of Government which they profess to adopt.

T. P. Bull, of Newport Pagnell, subsequently Chairman of the Union, approves,

for though the *Evangelical Mag.* has been eminently useful and one cannot but wish for its continued prosperity, yet it does not appear by any means to render your work unnecessary. Something seemed wanting to unite more closely the energies of our own denomination and I cannot but hope your publication may be the means of accomplishing this as well as other desirable objects.

John Nelson Goulty, of Henley, is unfavourable, having been

accustomed to think it an honour to the Denomination of Independent Churches that they had no specific organ of intelligence. *The Congregational Magazine,* in my view, therefore, breathes a feeling of party, and though I am most conscientiously and decidedly an Independent Dissenter and by no means ashamed of that preference, I do not think we are called upon in this age of harmony to advocate so publicly and so professedly an exclusive party. The invisible church and its holy interests are, I think, paramount to every visible form of it : and I feel unwilling to disturb that state of growing unanimity which appears to be hastening some great change not only in the moral character of the world, but also in the existing forms of Christian profession. Perhaps I am mistaken, and we ought not to be so quiet and inactive, but at present I must beg to decline any professed connexion with the *London Christian Instructor;* and I sincerely hope it will not widen the breach which has been so painfully made by the *Eclectic Review* in the manner of expressing its sentiments. I believe we feel this effect much more in the country than can be experienced in Town. We are regarded with so much jealousy and suspected of being, if we had opportunity to show it, as violent, *etc., etc.,* as the *Eclectic* reviewers.

Despite these misgivings, which were reiterated many times before the establishment of the Union, the *Congregational Magazine* was successfully floated, many of those taking part in its management being movers in the project for the Union ten to twelve years later. The lot of the journal was similar to that of many which were to follow it in future years, although, in one series and another, it survived until 1850. Its management may be seen from a letter from George Redford, one of the editors, in 1819, in which he speaks of

> "having the whole business of the Magazine upon my hands" and approves the plan "of making up the February and April numbers out of the *waste*".

He goes on :

> I totally disapprove of any public meeting of the subscribers to the Magazine, as we can receive no sort of aid and only waste our time and our money and hear a number of ignorant persons deliver their contrary and worthless opinions. *I* see no end to be answered by it—and of course shall discourage it by my absence. It remains for the Committee to take what steps they think proper—I think it is a great pity that another meeting of the Committee is called for Monday—as thus a great expense is incurred, when more money is wanted upon the literary department of the undertaking.

A printed circular was sent out in August, 1820, signed by Joseph Turnbull, George Redford, and Thomas Fisher, the three Editors, asking for support for "the only periodical publication which professedly defends Congregational principles" at a time "when unwearied and systematic attempts are made to disseminate influences hostile to primitive Christianity and genuine religious liberty". The *Congregational Magazine* is said to have "risen to considerable respectability", and a journal of its kind is imperative in consequence of the "difficulty of imparting instruction from the pulpit, upon our peculiar views as Dissenters, with the consequent ignorance of many who are growing

GEORGE REDFORD

BENJAMIN HANBURY

up in our Societies, or coming among us from other professions of Christianity, or from the world".

With the circular was sent a questionnaire of far too ambitious a kind, its range perhaps suggesting why statistics were so difficult to obtain, but significant in that it anticipates one of the reasons urged for the formation of a Union. It reads:—

The Editors of the *Congregational Magazine* will be much obliged to——for answers to the following Enquiries respecting the state of Dissenters in the County of ——.

I. A list of the Dissenting Congregations—Independent, Baptist, and Unitarian.

II. A list of the officiating and accredited Ministers, *ditto, ditto, ditto*.

III. The probable number of stated hearers, *ditto, ditto, ditto*.

IV. In what state is each Denomination—stationary, progressive, or declining?

V. If a County Association or Associations; the names, plans, times and places of meeting, names of officers, *etc., etc.*

VI. If any public Benevolent Societies—*e.g.,* Widows' or Ministers' Fund, County or District Itinerancy, Missionary or Tract Society, Sunday School Union, *etc.;* please state the plans, *etc.,* as above.

VII. Are there any apparent and remarkable effects of the zeal and piety of former Ministers of note in your county; or the same of private individuals? Have you any anecdotes of such which will be pleasing and useful?

VIII. Can you give any historical notices of the *past* state of Dissenters in your county? If so, please state them, as well as any antiquities respecting particular churches, ministers, or places, which you may be able to furnish. Your remarks on the *relative state* of Dissenters in your county will be particularly acceptable, *i.e.,* their *present* state in general as related to the *past;* and their relative state to each other, as consisting of different denominations.

IX. What is the state of religious liberty in your county? Please communicate any interesting facts on this head.

X. Are any Students for the Ministry educated in your county? If there are, how are they supported, by

B

whom, and where are they educated? What have been the effects of those academical Institutions in your county or neighbouring parts? *etc., etc.*

XI. Any other particulars respecting the past or present state of Dissenters in your county, as to the progress or decline of morals and piety; the character and effects of the doctrine preached; the state of church discipline, *etc., etc.*, will be very acceptable.

XII. If you can give any particulars respecting the state of other Dissenters not mentioned above—*e.g.*, Methodists, Moravians, *etc., etc.*, in your county, it would be desirable.

The financial struggle of the journal may be gauged from a vigorous, letter from the Rev. N. Sloper in 1820. He complains that £400 to £500 has been contributed by shareholders, the editors and managers are honorary, and yet at the end of the second year the journal is over £120 to the bad ! If, with these advantages, the *Congregational Magazine* cannot succeed, how do other magazines pay ? When are the shareholders going to see anything of their money ? Surely by this time there should have been profits for the benevolent purposes suggested. There is mismanagement somewhere, while the best friends of the magazine are of the opinion that it does not improve in interest or literary merit. The intelligence from America promised a year and a half ago has not yet appeared and the statistics are most unsatisfactory.

Despite this slashing attack the journal kept its head above water, and its existence probably was of major importance in determining the success of the Union proposals in 1830-31, whereas all previous efforts had failed. To those efforts attention must now be turned, once we have seen what the Independent churches of the time were like.

II.   THE INDEPENDENT CHURCHES, 1800—1830.

IT remains now to get some idea of these churches that were preparing to unite, their number, the kind of people of whom they were composed, their ministry—how far it was educated and how it was maintained—their prevailing theology and ecclesiastical outlook, their relationship to other Protestant Dissenters, to the Methodists, and to the Anglican Church.

What were these Independent Churches like, and how many of them were there?   These are questions much easier to ask than to answer.   When it is seen how difficult the Union found it to obtain statistics long after it was a "going concern"—it is well to remember once for all that it proved impossible to secure the number of Church members for the *Year Book* until 1899—no surprise will be expressed at the tentative and hesitating figures of pre-Union days.   It is unnecessary here to do more than mention the figures given at different times in the eighteenth century.   Two serious attempts were made, by Daniel Neal at the beginning of George I's reign, and by Josiah Thompson, a Baptist, in 1772.   Even from their figures, however, it is not always easy to get the truth, as Presbyterians and Independents are often put together.   In 1716 there were probably 380 Independent congregations in England and Wales, not more than one-sixth of which had meeting-houses.   The number of congregations increased slowly for some time, but after the Evangelical Revival the increase was much more rapid.   Independents profited in a considerable measure from the Arian Movement, for, while in 1772 it could be reported that not a single Independent congregation had turned Arian, there had been a steady influx into Independency of orthodox Presbyterians.   In 1716 the Independents, though more than the Baptists, were nothing like so many or so influential as the Presbyterians, but by 1772 they were in the majority, while in 1811 the Presbyterian congregations are

estimated at 252 only and the Independents at 799.   As
Halévy[1] well says :

> The history of the Dissenting bodies at the opening of
> the nineteenth century is the relation of an uninterrupted
> series of victories won by the Independents and Baptists,
> who had remained orthodox, over the Presbyterians who
> had gone over to Unitarianism.

He quotes the *Protestant Dissenters' Magazine* to show
that in London in 1796 there were 15 Presbyterian congregations, 33 Independent, 18 Baptist, and 30 Methodist.

In 1827 the *Congregational Magazine's* attempt at
statistics puts the number of Independent congregations at
1,203, and in 1829 at 1,289, though in a list county by
county, in that year, the total is 1,665, which figure (mistakenly 1,663) is referred to in the *Congregational
Magazine* for 1836, where the following totals of churches
in England and Wales are given :—

Roman Catholics	...	...	...	416
Presbyterians	...	...	...	197
Independents	...	...	...	1,840
Baptists	...	...	...	1,201
Calvinistic Methodists	...	...	...	427
Wesleyan Methodists	...	...	...	2,818
Other Methodists	...	...	...	666
Quakers	...	...	...	396
Home Missionary and other stations	...			453
				8,414
Episcopal Churches and Chapels		...		11,825

This superiority is borne out by Bennett's statement in
1833 that the Independents had a greater number of congregations than the other two denominations, and thus
formed the largest body of English Dissenters[2].

[1] *England in 1815*, I, 368.

[2] The comparative figures may be of interest, though some objection
was made to them :—

	Presbyt.	Indep.	Bapt.
1812	252	799	532
1827	204	1203	805
1829	258	1289 (? 1665)	888
1836	197	1840	1201

If we have difficulty in finding the number of churches, still harder is it to discover the number of members. Even in the forties all kinds of wild estimates were made, but it is clear now that they were little more than guesses.

The nature of the congregations had been largely influenced by the Methodist movement. Previously the Independents had been inclined to be proud of the intellectual standing of their members : an educated ministry had attracted intelligent people, and it was probably truer in 1691 than when Dale said it in 1891

> that the special mission of Congregationalism was to discipline to the highest intellectual and ethical perfection those never likely to be reached by such organizations as the Salvation Army.

Dale went on to point out that

> the Congregationalists of the Commonwealth times had many of the qualities of an intellectual aristocracy ; and for many generations Congregationalists were accustomed to assert the claims of the intellect in religion far more earnestly than other evangelical churches.

In the first quarter of the nineteenth century there were still many city congregations with men of education, wealth, and social standing. City merchants, legal luminaries, and men of the type of Robert Browning's father, were by no means uncommon. Samuel Favell, Treasurer of "the Dissenters' Grammar School, Mill Hill", and Deacon of the Camberwell Church, who died in 1830, may be taken as an example. Favell was as prominent in the life of the City of London as he was in the life of the religious community to which he belonged. Master of the Clothworkers' Company and member of the Common Council, he advocated the formation of the Guildhall Library, while by his casting vote the decision to build London Bridge was taken. When he retired, just before his death, the Lord Mayor, 12 Aldermen, and 218 Common Councillors presented him with "a superb piece of plate". This was the type of man Independency was still able to produce, active and respected in the life of the city, supporting projects like the University of London, on the one hand, and like the London Missionary Society and the British and Foreign Bible Society, on the other, standing alike for civil and religious liberty and for personal integrity and business ability.

Nevertheless, it is no doubt true to say that in the years preceding the foundation of the Union while the Independents had been rapidly gaining among the masses they had been losing in the higher and middle ranks of society. Their congregations were no longer producing learned or eminent men to the same extent, and already the cry had begun to be heard that "rarely are young men of liberal education and good family found to enter the Dissenting ministry".

True, the Independents had gained a good many people of means and social position from the Presbyterians, but they were few compared with the inrush of "common people" who had gladly heard the message of Christ during the Revival. Thousands of these, whose hearts the Lord had touched, had never given a thought to methods of Church government, but, in Walter Wilson's[1] words, they "subsided into Independent churches". First through the preaching of Whitefield, then by means of village preaching and Sunday Schools, the Independent congregations had been largely increased, and their nature in some measure changed.

This it was that roused the ire of Walter Wilson, the author of *The History and Antiquities of Dissenting Churches and Meeting Houses in London,* a compilation that has been invaluable to ecclesiastical historians. Published in 1814, this work contained a violent attack on the Independents for forsaking their principles, an attack renewed by him with even greater vigour in 1831 in an anonymous pamphlet (By "One of the Laity") entitled *Remarks Upon the Present State of the Dissenting Interest. With Hints for its Improvement by means of a Consolidated Union.* Wilson held that more than half the people who were called Dissenters were not Dissenters at

---

[1] Not to be confused with Thomas or Joshua Wilson. See below, *passim.*

all—they had the name but not the substance. What with the decline of spiritual religion among the Presbyterians, and the invasion by Methodism, the religion of excitement, the "Dissenting Interest" (to us Independency) was in a bad way.

It was, so to speak, being crucified between two thieves —indifference and enthusiasm. In 1814 he said that

> the Presbyterians have either deserted to the world, or sunk under the influence of a lukewarm ministry; and the Independents have gone over in a body to the Methodists. Indifference and enthusiasm have thinned the ranks of the old stock, and those who remain behind are lost in the crowd of modern religionists.

The result of all this, so Wilson said in 1831, was that, with a few exceptions in London, all the well-educated people had been driven away. Ignorance and poverty were no crime, but they had put stumbling-blocks in the way of the middle and upper classes, who had left Independency not merely because they were surrounded by rustics, but also because ministerial standards had so deteriorated that the pastors were often fit company only for rustics! There were now many illiterate ministers, who despised learning, interpreted the Scriptures by imagination rather than by sound scholarship, did not understand the principles of Dissent, and made no attempt to administer discipline. Further, students who were mere boys were allowed to preach, and the intellectual standard was once more lowered.

How far are these charges justified? It was no doubt true that the intensity of religious emotion during the Revival had led into the ministry men unfitted for it. It was by no means an uncommon practice to send a youth with absolutely no education to an Academy for a brief course of training, and after a short time he had no difficulty in getting an invitation to a pastorate if he had a flow of words. It was no doubt true also that some of the lay preachers, who often had merely shown a little promise in teaching in a Sunday School, were more zealous than learned. In his *John Angell James*, Dale describes the influence of the "shorter course" seminaries established by the Calvinistic Methodists and Evangelical Dissenters, and thus sums up the result :

> It lowered . . . the standard of general knowledge among Dissenters, so that to the superior information of the old Dissenting congregations, which were often assemblies of divines, succeeded the comparative ignorance of the Methodistic societies.

Nevertheless, writing in 1808, Bogue and Bennett could thus describe the Independent Churches and their ministry :

> Their original principles, both in doctrine and discipline, they still retain; and it may be confidently asserted, that no one class of ministers, in any ecclesiastical body of Protestants in the world, are more united in their religious sentiments. They now form the largest body among English Dissenters; and no denomination can boast of so great a number of ministers who preach the gospel in purity. As a body, none are more judicious. Men of very profound learning among them are not numerous. They have no sinecures, by means of which scholars can spend their years in uninterrupted literary pursuits. They are all men of action, and their studies are blended with the labours of the pulpit, and the care of a congregation. At the same time, there are fewer of them ignorant of theology than in any other body. The generality possess that portion of knowledge of the truths of sacred Scripture, and of those things which may be called the peculiar science of ministers of the gospel, which qualifies them for the duties of their office. To the honour of the younger ministers, it may be mentioned that there never was a greater spirit of improvement, nor a more eager desire to acquire knowledge.

And in 1831, in a lengthy reply to Wilson, Josiah Conder stated that the illiterates in the ministry were "a small and decreasing proportion", and that "half-educated ministers, pulpit fops, beardless pedants, and rhapsodists" were very rare. The Independent ministry, he admitted, was not all that it ought to be, but its superiority was recognized both by Episcopalians and Presbyterians. No Congregational Church could have a minister placed over it so unqualified as a large proportion of incumbents, while the demand of the Academies that students should have a real religious experience was of supreme value. What distinguished the Independent students from Episcopalian and Presbyterian was that, in Conder's words, they were "well grounded in religious knowledge before they enter upon a course of academic training. . . Hence the *steadiness* of religious sentiment which is so conspicuous among orthodox Dissenters". Heresies did not arise among them because ministers had religious knowledge. Further, the academic training was prolonged : the course at Homerton was six years, and in many other Academies four or five.

This seems a fairly conclusive reply, and it will be borne out by an examination of the Academies, which still played a large part in the life of the churches. Some of them were now of a fair age and, as Conder pointed out, gave a thorough training. Others were more recent, and sometimes had a shorter course. Finally were those of a preparatory type, and the private Academies, run by pastors who welcomed students into their homes.

Thus, while due notice must be taken of Wilson's words, the weight of the evidence seems to be on the other side. No doubt Independency suffered a sea-change during the Methodist Revival; but it is an utter exaggeration to say that it was denuded of well-educated people and that its congregations were henceforth composed of rustics ministered to by those little better equipped than themselves. The names of the ministers who took a prominent part in the early history of the Union would suffice in themselves to rebut the charge of illiteracy, while a few figures showing the amounts raised by Independent congregations in the year 1829-30 will speak for themselves. The income of the London Missionary Society for that year was £48,226, of which £37,376 was from "Donations, Subscriptions, and Collections" (in the main from Independents); that of the Home Missionary Society was £4,700[1].

The fact is, of course, that the Independent congregations were of vastly different kinds. Scattered up and down the country were many new meeting-houses, built when congregations were still unable to maintain their

---

1 No doubt, too, the Independents played their part in raising £84,892 for the British & Foreign Bible Society, £24,793 for the Religious Tract Society, £6,328 for the Sunday School Union, and £1,066 for the Christian Instruction Society.

pastors, and only to be paid for as and when these pastors could visit London—or perhaps Manchester or Liverpool —and solicit contributions from wealthy men, or, perchance, be allowed to preach to and obtain a collection from well-to-do congregations. That such congregations existed may be deduced from some of the collections made in London churches in 1831 for the suffering peasantry in the West of Ireland. New Court (Dr. Winter) collected £51, Weigh House (Thomas Binney) £59, Hackney (Dr. Burder) £67, Pentonville, Claremont (J. Blackburn) £90, Walworth (G. Clayton) £102, and Stepney (Dr. Fletcher) £116.

It is often in these wealthier churches that we find abundant evidence that even at the beginning of the nineteenth century comfort and respectability were so pronounced a feature that they prevented active and aggressive service for the Kingdom. Dale describes the churches of the time of J. A. James's youth as being "paralyzed by respectability and dullness", and the student reads so often that gatherings of Congregationalists were composed of "respectable gentlemen" that he becomes thoroughly tired of the sight of the expression. It was an excellent thing that the Evangelical Revival brought into Congregationalism men and women from the farm and factory, the street and the shop : otherwise its respectability would have killed it.

It remained, of course, very serious and sedate. When a writer, discussing the formation of the Union, ventured on a little mild humour, the *Congregational Magazine* solemnly and ponderously rebuked him, remarking : "We consider ridicule and jest as ill-adapted to such serious subjects as those before us".

A few words more must be said about the ministry. How did the churches maintain their ministers ? The differences in intellectual equipment just noted were reflected in the stipends paid. Some of the ministers in the cities had private means and came from good families. Others had large stipends, varying from £300 to £700. The *Congregational Magazine* for 1830 puts the average stipend at about £100, which means that many ministers had much less than that. Halévy, speaking of 1815, says[1] that there were men with £60, £40, and even £30, and that, while salaries and wages had in some measure followed the rise of prices, stipends in some cases had even been reduced. There were some charitable funds to aid aged and infirm men, but not of any considerable amount.

It is unnecessary here to say anything about the theology of the Independents at this time, as that must be discussed when the Declaration of Faith and Order is considered.   The founders of the Union generally spoke of themselves as "moderate Calvinists" ; to us the stress seems to fall on the adjective rather than the noun, for the influence of Wesley had undermined rigid Calvinism far more than most Independents were as yet prepared to admit.

Two things stand out pre-eminently in the Independent witness of this time :

1. The absolute confidence with which it was insisted that the Independent view of the Church was based on the Scriptures.   This we shall see repeatedly. Because the Bible was the Inspired Word, and because it was there written plainly for these Independents that the Apostolic Churches were neither Presbyterian nor Episcopal but Independent, they felt on sure ground.

2. The insistence on the Voluntary Principle, with its denial of the system of Establishment. It is hard to read ourselves back into the atmosphere of violent hostility between the Establishment and the Dissenting communities.   The bitterness was such that Thomas Binney could speak of the Established Church as "a great national evil", while clergy and magistrates (and the clergyman was often magistrate too) did not conceal their delight when village preachers were brutally treated, or when from the tower of the church stones and rotten eggs were

---

1 *England in 1815*, I. 357.

showered on an itinerant evangelist. When all the power of the State was at the call of a fox-hunting, hard-drinking, irresponsible clergy, and when persecution was the lot of those who tried to do the work the clergy left undone, the vehemence of the controversy of the time can be understood.

The strength of the opposition to the association of the State with religion received a striking illustration in the early days of 1832. Cholera was rapidly spreading, and the country was in a very disturbed state politically. J. A. James and G. Redford proposed a day of humiliation and prayer, saying :

> Public affairs are in a state of extreme agitation ; commerce, as well as trade of all kinds, is at a low ebb ; the fatal pestilence, like a destroying angel, has set its foot upon our shores, and pauses only till the Almighty Sovereign shall seal its commission. Infidelity vaunteth itself at the corners of the streets, and in the markets ; crimes unexampled have been brought to light ; violence has been rampant in our cities ; wasting and destruction have entered into all our borders ; the Church languishes, its vintage faileth.

The project was taken up at the London Board, and arrangements made for 16th Feb. to be observed as the day. This was postponed when a National Fast Day, with a general suspension of business, was announced, and vigorous were the protests of Protestant Nonconformity against allowing any State action or arrangement to interfere with the Nonconformist Churches.

The numerous periodicals representing the Establishment kept up a violent and virulent attack on the Dissenters. In the words of an Independent in 1833 :

> They have been for years playing upon us with all their might, and almost without intermission ; yet the moment they hear a shot from our batteries they shout, "What a malicious and uncharitable set these Sectaries are ; let us *exterminate* them !".

In general, it may be said that Independency was saved by the Evangelical Revival from the lukewarmness and indifference to religious doctrines that had ruined Presbyterianism, while its intellectual tradition and its belief in a "learned ministry" prevented the churches from being swept away on the tide of emotional religion. In the main they were amazingly united in doctrine and in practice, and yet there was little sense of denominational loyalty. Wilson in 1814 made much of the fact that while Methodists and General and Particular Baptists had their periodical publication the Independents "either had not sufficient means or sufficient zeal to support one"; and when this reproach was removed by the establishment of the *Congregational Magazine* in 1818, we have seen that some Congregationalists doubted whether it was not better to stick to the *Evangelical*. As a matter of fact, what was happening was that the churches were being so moved by fervent zeal for the evangelization of mankind that their thoughts turned but rarely to questions of polity. Churches now had their prayer-meetings open to all; they sent their members preaching into all the villages round about; as Dale said, in writing his *History of Congregationalism* :

> It would probably have been almost as difficult in 1820 to find a Congregational Church without a body of lay-preachers as it would be now to find a Congregational Church without a Sunday School.

To win men for Christ at home and abroad—on that the eyes of these Independents were fixed, rather than on their own "interest" and their distinctive principles. And for this great end they were willing to co-operate with men whose views were far removed from theirs. For this especially Walter Wilson blamed them, for throwing

> all their weight into the hands of nondescript persons who are more remarkable for their religious zeal than for its judicious application; and who divert their energies to the execution of schemes as wild in their nature as they are unproductive of benefit.

Here it was that Wilson launched his bolt on those so "liberal" that they thought it bigotry to avow one's principles, and deemed the Calamys, Bradburys, and Robinsons bigoted and lacking in missionary spirit, using the oft-quoted words :

> It is true, they did not beat up a crusade in the religious world for the wild purpose of proselyting the savage

hottentot, or the untutored islander, but they conducted
plans of instruction for the rising generation of their countrymen, which turned to infinitely better account. Let the
reader look back to the life of Mr. Ratcliffe, a Presbyterian
minister, recorded in the present volume, and let him
compare his labours with those of the host of missionaries,
transported at a vast expense to the Pacific Ocean ; and if
he is at all acquainted with the process of the human mind,
he will be able to judge correctly as to which was the most
productive field for usefulness, and whose labours were the
more rational. The immense sums that have been consumed
in equipping missionaries to the South Seas, without any
useful result, would have civilized all the inhabitants in the
vast parish of St. Giles's, and have provided them with
food, clothing, and religious instruction for the remainder
of their lives.

Wilson fumed in vain. The Independents were to prove
that they could unite with other Christians in all manner
of evangelistic activity and yet unite with one another and
proclaim their own principles.

III. UNSUCCESSFUL ATTEMPTS AT UNION.

As far back as in 1806 a definite attempt had been made "to roll away the reproach which had too long attached to the churches of this denomination—that they were a disjointed, disorganized aggregation, a mere rope of sand without connexion or continuity". The *Evangelical Magazine* outlined the need in this paragraph :

> The want of a General Union among the Congregational or Independent churches in Great Britain has been long felt and lamented; and wherever this subject has engaged the serious attention of ministers and others, a conviction of its vast importance has prevailed. It is perceived that by the sanction and aid of such a Union, were it wisely and firmly established, such great objects as the following might be more easily and extensively promoted : Newly-raised congregations might receive pecuniary assistance, until they should be able to maintain a settled minister; advice might be given to such congregations, as to the proper manner of making deeds of trust, and other difficulties attending the establishment of new interests; encouragement might be afforded to young men possessing gifts for the ministry, in order to their being introduced, at a proper time, into our evangelical academies; a mode might be adopted for a free communication between the County Associations and that formed by the regular churches in the metropolis; an Annual Conference might be held in London, and the other principal cities in the kingdom. That these and other interesting objects connected with the spread and support of the gospel may be fully considered and discussed, a Meeting will be held at St. Paul's Coffee-House, on Saturday morning, in the Missionary Week, 17th May, 1806, at Ten o'clock.

This meeting was duly held, and it was unanimously resolved that a Union was desirable, and the ministers of the London Board, "together with some other gentlemen", were asked to form a plan. This group reported in the following year, when a "numerous and respectable meeting of ministers and lay gentlemen both of London and the country" agreed to the plan and appointed a committee. In 1808 it was reported that several ministers and churches had approved the plan, and Thomas Wilson says, "We are likely to get on in the Congregational Union". But the Committee expressed regret that there was much mis-apprehension, and announced they did not consider the plan perfect and would welcome suggestions for improvement. It was further decided to have the Plan printed and circulated. In this year a sermon was preached before the members and friends of the Union by Dr. Williams, formerly of Birmingham, now of Rotherham College, and in the following year a similar sermon "appropriate to the occasion" was preached by David Bogue at Mr. Wall's meeting-house, Moorfields, the audience being " very respectable and attentive; and great concern for the interests of this important institution was manifested". The day after Bogue's sermon, at seven in the morning, the members and friends of the Union again assembled, new members were admitted, and "much interesting con-versation was had on the nature, objects, and advantages of the Union". In 1810 the sermon was preached by Robert Winter, and was subsequently printed with the " Plan of the Union ".

Meanwhile the Union had attempted to begin its work, its Committee, which met monthly, tackling the thorny problem of "chapel cases". It is difficult to realize in 1931 what chapel cases were, for it is extremely hard to put our-selves back into the religious life of the period. It was a time of chapel building, without any Chapel Building Society or anything of that kind. While "star preachers" came to London to preach sermons in order to raise money for missionary and charitable Societies, the ordinary pastor came to raise money for the chapel which had been built to house his congregation. This led to all kinds of trouble, some of them not without humour, as when a Liverpool minister wrote to one of his deacons acknowledging having preached in a black gown to a London congregation. He thought this conduct would excite some disagreeable sur-prise in Liverpool, but explained that it was when

> he was in London to collect for the payment of the chapel, and as he had obtained larger contributions from the

[*Photo: Russell*]   SIDNEY M. BERRY

ALGERNON WELLS

Calvinistic Methodists than from the Independents, he thought it lawful and prudent to humour their prejudice and preach to them in the vestment they liked to behold.

The system, it is easy to imagine, led to all kinds of abuses, and in January, 1809, the Committee recommended that congregations desiring the sanction of the Union for cases "for which they desired to collect in town" should write and get their approval before sending up their ministers or others to collect for them. The Committee can scarcely have understood on what delicate ground they were treading, for not merely the individual church but also the County Association would be quick to assume that this new organization was unduly interfering. Later in the year the Committee did suggest the advisability of establishing County Committees for the purpose of considering these "petitionary cases" before they were sent up to London, but they did not seem to have realized the wisdom of asking the co-operation of local Associations. No matter how sensible the suggestions, it can easily be imagined with what feelings Independent congregations in the country would read :—

The Committee deem it necessary to state, that every place of worship for which public benevolence is solicited, must be vested in the hands of Trustees, before their recommendation can be given. They have, likewise, to request that all cases, in favour of which their sanction may be desired, be transmitted to one of their Secretaries (the Rev. T. Hill, Homerton, near London; or the Rev. Charles Buck, Primrose Street, Bishopsgate Street, London) that they may be duly examined, and the parties informed of the result, in order that no obstacle may, on this account, be opposed to the bearer of the case on his arrival in town.

The following Resolutions have been proposed and adopted by the Committee of the Congregational Union.

That no Petitionary Case shall be signed by this Committee, until it shall have been considered at two successive Monthly Meetings. It is, therefore, requested that no Minister, or other Person deputed by a Congregation, come up to town to collect, until the case has been fully considered by the Committee, and the result communicated by one of the Secretaries : That it is expected that before any case is circulated in London, application for assistance be made in the neighbouring congregations.

c

This tactless beginning was probably one of the main reasons for the Union's failure. The ministers of Lancashire, where an Association for preserving a ministerial roll had been formed in 1786, and where one or two itinerant evangelists were employed, had become convinced of the need of union, and in 1806 had passed a resolution saying that "a General Union in order to promote the spread of the Gospel seems highly desirable". If the London Committee had seized on this, and London and the North had worked together, especially seeing they had the powerful support of David Bogue from Hampshire, a General Union might have been brought to birth some twenty years before 1831. As it was, Lancashire formed a strong County Union while the General Union languished and died.

Other causes contributed to the failure. George Burder thus referred to this abortive attempt :

> An ineffectual effort was made by me and others to produce an union of Independent ministers, in order to promote the cause of truth and religion. Many meetings were held, and papers printed; but the influential ministers held back, and the matter was dropped, much to the injury of the cause of religion, especially among the Independents. I told them other denominations would reap the advantage of our want of union, and we should suffer. Future ministers will, I hope, be wiser.

Possibly, too, some Independents were afraid of being labelled as revolutionaries, and Jacobins. Associations of any kind were suspect by the Government : who could say that political conspiracies and seditious plans were not being hatched in all these societies? Two illustrations might be given of the way in which a Tory churchman and a barrister regarded the growth of Dissenting churches and organizations. At the turn of the century, Samuel Horsley, Bishop of Rochester (afterwards St. Asaph) thus fulminated in his Visitation Charges :

> Still the operations of the evening are going on—still going on by stratagem. The stratagem still a pretence of reformation ; but the reformation, the very reverse of what was before attempted. Instead of divesting religion of its

mysteries, and reducing it to a mere philosophy in speculation, and to a mere morality in practice, the plan is now *to
affect a great zeal for orthodoxy;* to make great pretensions to an extraordinary measure of the Holy Spirit's
influence; to alienate the minds of the people from the
Established clergy, by representing them as sordid world-
lings; without any concern about the souls of men; indifferent to the religion which they ought to teach, and to
which the laity are attached; and destitute of the Spirit of
God. *In many parts of the kingdom new conventicles have
been opened in great number, and congregations formed of
one knows not what denomination.* The pastor is often, in
appearance at least, an illiterate peasant, or mechanic. The
congregation is visited occasionally by preachers from a
distance. Sunday Schools are opened in connexion with
these conventicles. There is much reason to suspect that
the expenses of these schools and conventicles are defrayed
by *Associations,* formed in different places for the
preachers, and schoolmasters are observed to engage in
expenses for the support and advancement of their institutions, to which, if we may judge from appearance, their
own means must be altogether inadequate. The poor are
even bribed by small pecuniary gifts from time to time,
to send their children to these schools of, they know not
what, rather than to those connected with the Established
Church, in which they would be bred in the principles of
true religion and loyalty. It is very remarkable that these
new congregations of nondescripts have been mostly formed
since the Jacobins have been laid under the restraint of
those two most salutary Statutes, commonly known by the
names of the Sedition and the Treason Bill—*a circumstance
which gives much ground for suspicion that sedition and
Atheism are the real objects of these institutions, rather
than religion.* Indeed, in some places, this is known to
be the case. In one topic the teachers of all these congregations agree: abuse of the Established clergy, as negligent
of their flocks, cold in their preaching, and destitute of
the Spirit. In this they are joined by persons of a very
different cast; whom a candour, of which they, on their
part, set but a poor example, is unwilling to suspect of any
ill-design; though it is difficult to acquit them of the imputation of an indiscretion in their zeal, which, in its consequences may be productive of mischief very remote, I believe, from their intentions. It is a dreadful aggravation
of the dangers of the present crisis in this country, that
persons of real piety should, without knowing it, be lend-
ing their aid to the common enemy, and making themselves
accomplices in a conspiracy against the Lord and against

His Christ. The Jacobins of this country, I very much fear, are, at this moment, making a tool of Methodism, just as the illuminées of Bavaria made a tool of freemasonry; while the real Methodist, like the real freemason, is kept in utter ignorance of the wicked enterprise the counterfeit has in hand.

What measures it may become the wisdom of the legislature to adopt to stop the growing evil, is a point on which I shall not touch in this assembly.

This, however, was quite mild compared with the language to which the barrister, James Sedgwick, was moved, a few years later, when the attempt to form a General Union was made. In 1808 he went to the trouble of publishing a pamphlet in which he printed the names of the County Associations, the dates of their meetings, and the names of their preachers, with those of the Officers and Committee of the General Union, and argued that these were proof of a widespread conspiracy :

> It is surely a most illegal, as well as insulting, violation of the spirit of the British Constitution, that any class or order of men in the kingdom should *dare* to erect themselves into a society for the purpose of exterminating doctrines which in *their* judgments are unsound, and introducing—by means of agents and emissaries—a certain system of religious belief, which they arrogantly pronounce to be the only true faith. If those who assumed this sort of sovereignty were men of vigorous intellect and profound learning, the evil, for it would even then be an evil, would be lessened. But when its casuists, in a far greater part, are blockheads, tainted with the mania of preaching, without a single requisite that should fit them for that high and important destination—when disdaining the usual means of acquiring a subsistence by honest industry—turn religion into a trade, and, like the quack professors in other sciences, live on that credulity of the ignorant upon which impostors for ever feed and fatten. When we behold this new order of ecclesiastics that thus obtrudes itself amongst us—consisting not of an enlightened, liberal, well-educated, moderate clergy, but of a bloated race of lay priests, propagating with importunate and unceasing zeal doctrines drawn not from that gospel which is the pure fountain of light and life, but from the absurd and irrational Institutes of John Calvin, imbibed at second-hand from an Assembly's Catechism—can we see this and not ask ourselves, are these upstart, untaught mechanics to be our

dictators? Are these foolish fanatics, who follow one another blindfolded, are they to be our infallible guides? . . . The aspect of things demands that we should speak out. It is not a time for complimenting and coquetting. Elsewhere, and at another period, these may be suitable; but here, and at this season, they would be sadly out of question. It is wise to take precaution while the wind whispers—it may be too late when it roars.

The feeling of the upper classes against associations of any kind which gathered together people other than themselves is well illustrated by the comments, of the *St. James' Chronicle* on the London Mechanics' Institution in 1825.

A scheme more completely adapted for the destruction of this empire could not have been invented by the author of evil himself than that which the depraved ambition of some men, the vanity of others, and the supineness of a third and more important class, has so nearly perfected.

With this kind of feeling very general the Dissenters were fearful of being accused of sedition, and were anxious to turn aside the accusation that their assemblies harboured conspiracies against the State.

It is well to remember that the limit of freedom sanctioned by the Toleration Act did not include the right of churches to organize themselves into Associations.

How strong was the fear of the Dissenters of being accused of sedition, may be seen in a letter of Josiah Conder, one of the foremost Congregational laymen, and Editor and Proprietor of the *Eclectic Review,* whom nobody would suspect of cowardice. John Foster had submitted an article on Benjamin Franklin to Conder for the *Eclectic.* He replied that he simply dare not print the article because of its commendation of some of the principles for which Franklin stood. The discussion that ensued between Foster and Conder is extremely good : Foster pokes fun at Conder's fears, and especially at his suggested deletion of a paragraph about William Cobbett.

In spite of everything, however, the impulse to union remained and grew apace. In 1816 the ministers and other members of the Independent Churches in the counties of Nottingham, Leicester, and Derby prepared and sent to the *Evangelical Magazine* a plan for a General Union of

Independent Churches. The plan is based on the idea that the advantages of union must be local and obvious, or the churches concerned would grow indifferent. The country must, therefore, be divided into small districts, which will make the running of the Union inexpensive and tend to convenience. Adequate publicity must also be secured. The Scheme, which is printed in detail, outlines 20 districts having their Annual Meetings on the same day. The churches are to be represented by the pastor and two messengers, the Committee being equally divided between ministerial and lay. A public meeting is to be held at each assembly. District No. 16 (Middlesex, Herts. and Essex), is to nominate the General Secretary, and District Secretaries are to keep him informed of their activities. Every church is to subscribe by means of annual subscriptions, collections, or "penny a week societies". A small portion of the income is to be set apart for new schemes, the rest being used for promoting the cause of religion among Independents. It is estimated that an income of £365 may be expected in each district, and the following specimen of how it might be employed is given[1] :

	£
To accumulating funds for general purposes	20
To Funds for aged ministers, widows and orphans	10
To Itinerants to labour in the Districts	100
To Religious Tracts for Itinerants to distribute	5
To an Academy	10
To liquidate a debt on Chapels at A, B & C (£50 each)	150
To fit up a place for Worship in Village D, E, F, and G (£5 each)	20
To supplies for new Congregations at H	30
To Schools for poor ministers' children	10
To Exhibitions in any case of extraordinary distress	5
To Sundries	5
	£365

The objections to the Plan, including the one that existing Associations were not uniform with the districts suggested, were stated and met. Arrangements were out-

[1] To the nearest pound.

lined for a general depository for records in each district, and it was urged that chapel building would be forwarded by a regular and efficient plan under this Scheme, for "petitionary cases" were not so well supported as formerly, and there was strong objection to ministers begging all over the country.   In the preamble, the plan states :

> Every person, who has been attentive to the state of the different denominations in England, must have observed that there is a less perfect union among the Independent or Congregational churches, than among other bodies of Christians ; and that, in proportion to their number and influence, the Independents have not shewn the same attention to the interests of their body as other denominations have done.   There is a visible, perhaps criminal, want of union and system among the Independents ; nor can they secure the most efficient employment of their means for doing good, while this state of things continues . . . .

> . . . while there is no other denomination which does so little for their own body exclusively as the Independents, it may fairly be doubted, whether there is any class of Christians who do more for the interests of other communities than they have done . . .

> . . . this want of union and co-operation . . . is, at least in part, to be attributed to an unreasonable jealousy lest a closer union of our churches should, at some indefinably distant period, lead to a sort of hierarchial power and domination amongst us . . .

> . . . some persons seem to have taken up an opinion that it is utterly impossible to bring the Independents into a closer union ; surely, no physical cause can be assigned for such an idea ; nor is there any thing in our religious views, or the constitution of our churches, to prevent the same degree of union which exists among other classes of British Christians.

> There is some reason to fear that the above opinion has been strengthened by the failure of a late *attempt to effect a more general and explicit union among the churches of the Congregational order.* But it should be remembered, the value of an object remains the same, though a proposed plan to obtain it may have failed.   Such failure is no just cause to abandon the object, though it should lead us to revise the plan, and to adopt more likely means . . .

> How much more good might the great body of Independents have done, if some regular system had been laid

down and observed, to excite, concentrate, and direct their energies, but for about a century and a half they have acted in a desultory manner, without union, without plan !

The advisability of union was continually kept before the notice of the churches in the decade before 1830. John Angell James's *Christian Fellowship; or the Church Members' Guide,* which, first published in 1822, quickly went through many editions, urges the value of union for the spread of the Gospel.

Many objects of vast importance to the spread of the gospel in the world can be accomplished by the *union* of churches which cannot be effected without it. Union is power. Places of worship may be opened, the faithful ministry of the word introduced, and churches planted in dark benighted villages; while all the grand and noble institutions organized to save a perishing world, may by this means receive additional support. United fires brighten each other's blaze, and increase each other's intensity; and thus the association of churches enkindles each other's zeal, and provokes one another to love and to good works. Nor is *zeal* the only Christian virtue promoted by such unions; brotherly *love* is cherished and excited. The presence of messengers from other churches at the annual meetings of our societies, produces a friendly feeling and brotherly interest, not unlike that which a family experiences when gathered together at their Christmas party.

In reviewing the book the *Eclectic Review* contends that "Independence . . . is a means in order to an end, a right in order to a duty—the end being the purity and spirituality of the particular association, the duty union with the whole body". Union need not be sectarian, but it would make Independents recognize the value of their principles, which are "the principles of Christianity consistently followed out in practice, the only principles on which the evangelization of the world can consistently proceed". A Congregational Union, "founded on unity of theological sentiment and an attachment to common principles", would be of advantage in proclaiming distinctly to the world that "as Congregationalists, holding the faith of the New Testament and of the Reformers, we are one body, though acknowledging no monarchial, prelatical, or synodical head".

In the same year John Morison, of Chelsea, soon to

begin an Editorship of the *Evangelical Magazine* which
lasted 30 years, published his Monthly Lecture, "On
the best Methods of promoting an effective Union among
Congregational Churches, without infringing on their
Independence", in which he says:

> Whenever our zeal for independency makes us feel as
> if we had no concern, or but little concern, in the spiritual
> prosperity of other similar societies; when we congratulate
> ourselves on the successful ministry, the crowded pews, the
> ample funds, the general harmony of our own sanctuary,
> and can at the same time witness, with obvious indifference,
> a declining, poor, or even dying church, at our very door,
> this argues a lamentable destitution of a primitive spirit.
> While we contend that there is nothing in the New Testa-
> ment to warrant the erection of a national church, com-
> posed of so many dioceses, or of so many presbyteries,
> we at the same time feel satisfied, that there existed among
> all the apostolic churches (though complete in themselves,
> in point of government), an unbroken sympathy of fellow-
> ship; such a sympathy as that if *"one member suffered
> all the members suffered with it; or, if one member was
> honoured, all the members rejoiced with it"*.

Again the *Eclectic Review* takes the opportunity to
press the need of union, saying that many who think a
Union desirable conceive it to be visionary and impracticable, especially as previous schemes, have met with no
support. The apparent want of unity is due to the fact that
Congregationalists are the representatives, rather than the
descendants, of the old orthodox Dissenters, consisting
for the most part of those who are Dissenters from a preference for an evangelical ministry and on the broad principles of religious liberty rather than from a preference for
a form of Church government. The old *esprit de corps,*
jealousy for the honour of the churches, and hereditary
attachment to modes and tenets ecclesiastical, had disappeared. Nevertheless, the absence of unity was more
external and formal than real.

> A greater unanimity of doctrine than prevails among the
> Congregational Dissenters of this Kingdom is never likely
> to be realized on earth. Their mode of worship is almost
> as uniform as if it were settled by a rubric or by an Act of
> Parliament.

What the Union should and should not be is then summarily stated :

> We have endeavoured to shew what it must not be; not a Union for the purpose of ecclesiastical jurisdiction,—an associate synod or general assembly, or dictatorial conference; not a junta of ministers, a Board for trying cases, or examining trusts, or doing what would be much better done by a solicitor; not a political association, with civil rights and civil injuries ever in its mouth; not a Union with large disposable funds, whether for building, or for charitable purposes; nor a Court of Arches for ecclesiastical offences. We do better, even as we are, than we should do with such an apparatus. But the measures we plead for, are such as should, in the first place, ascertain and consolidate the Union that already exists in the Congregational body—secure the more public recognition of the essential unity of the body—promote the local means of advancing the association of the churches—and create a *religious* feeling in favour of the object, on the true and proper ground, that it is connected with our most solemn obligations as disciples of Christ.

In 1826 the ministers of the *Monthly Exercise*[1], an institution already nearly a century old, circulated among the churches a letter signed by the Revs. James Stratten (Chairman) and John Blackburn (Secretary *pro tem.*) suggesting the establishment of the "London Congregational Union" for

> the promotion of the interests of religion, in connexion with the Congregational Churches of London and its vicinity, on such principles as accord with the constitution and rights of Independent Churches.

It said that the constitution of the Congregational Churches was truly liberal and unsectarian, especially in the Metropolis, and that they co-operated in all efforts for the diffusion of Evangelical religion. The direct interests of these churches, however, and the principles which supply

---

[1] The *Congregational Magazine* of 1832, in giving a list of the Exercise's lecturers and subjects for the year, says : "Many of our readers will learn with satisfaction that it is strongly recommended that tavern dinners be altogether discontinued, and that sandwiches or other convenient and moderate refreshments be provided in the schoolroom or vestries of the places of meeting, by which a great loss of time as well as needless expenditure will be obviated, and a better opportunity be afforded for serious and fraternal conference".

the vigour and efficiency which mark their operations, were comparatively neglected.

Any cause, however remotely connected with the promotion of Evangelical Religion, at once meets with support; but *the adoption of practicable measures for increasing and strengthening the Churches of our own faith and order, by a zealous and affectionate co-operation* has never yet been *sufficiently regarded* as the immediate and imperative duty of the Churches of London and its vicinity.

The proposed Union will not interfere with the Society for Christian Instruction, or with itinerant preachers, or Sabbath School teachers in the villages around the Metropolis.

Nor is it intended to establish a GENERAL Congregational Union, such as was proposed many years ago, and was not acted upon because of the suspicions which it excited in various parts of the country, and because, by aiming at *too much,* it affected nothing. Still less is it designed to adopt any measures, which may, *directly* or *indirectly,* interfere with the *rights and government* of the *separate* Churches that may be incorporated in this Association. The INDEPENDENCY of *each church* it most distinctly recognizes as an essential principle in the constitution of the Union itself; and to guard against the possibility of misconception, or the suspicion of its being a *ministerial* Union, that might lead to synodical jurisdiction, it proposes that double the number of those who are not ministers shall constitute the general body, to which the Committee shall be responsible; that such body itself shall be constituted by the annual appointment of the respective Churches, and that no measures to be adopted by the Union shall respect the *interior* regulation of the Churches themselves.

The Scheme is recommended on these grounds:

1. Because the number of Congregational Churches in London is far too small.

2. Many surrounding villages have no Congregational Churches.

3. Churches have become weak and ministers have abandoned stations through inadequate provision. The Union could interpose timely aid.

4. Ministers have to teach in schools when they might be itinerating. A small addition to their resources would make such secular engagements unnecessary.

5. The Union is based on the same principles as the many County Associations which have been so successful.

6. "The Academical Institutions connected with the London Congregational Churches will furnish obvious facilities for carrying some of the proposed objects, of the Union into effect; and provision for Sabbath School operation might, in various ways, be rendered subservient to the same general object".

7. The Union will derive great advantage from the continued existence, *etc.*, of the Monthly Meetings; it will provide a channel for Christian benevolence, especially for the richer members, bring the churches closer together, and refute the common charge against Congregationalism "that it separates and insulates our respective societies instead of combining their forces into one mighty agency against the united powers of darkness".

The regulations adopted included provision for an annual subscription from each church, a committee of twelve ministers, and twelve laymen, and two Secretaries, one to be a layman.

IV. ON THE STOCKS, 1830—1831.

WHEN the London Union was formed, the ministers were careful to say that they did not design a movement of national character. Experience rapidly changed their views. In May, 1830, a meeting of ministers and laymen from different parts of the country further ventilated the project, and a Provisional Committee was formed. In that month, a country minister urged the necessity in a letter in the *Congregational Magazine* arguing that union would show to adversaries that unity in faith and practice was more than a name. It would ensure, too, a better acquaintance with the denomination in all parts of England, a greater sympathy with weak churches, a general plan for chapel building without the evil of debts, and "the nuisance of begging by *Preachers of the Gospel* !". It would also promote the wider extension of Congregational principles. He went on to say that the Roman Catholics near where he lived were making "great, united, and persevering efforts", that the "Clergy of the Endowed Church" were trying in every possible way to stop the "progress of Dissent", even bribing children to desert the Independent Sunday Schools by the distribution of "Bonnets, Tippets, Bibles, and Prayer Books". Without infringing on the independency of the churches, he believed that their strength could be

> formed into one phalanx of scriptural churches, zealous ministers, devoted laymen; united by the bonds of a common faith, and advocating those great principles which are intimately connected with the existence and diffusion of civil and religious liberty throughout the world.

The Independents had the *unity* of the Spirit without Creeds, Confessions, or Acts of Parliament, and he hoped that the month of May would see the "choice spirits", lay and clerical, who come to London, discussing the whole problem.

A good deal of correspondence, much of which is summarized in the *Congregational Magazine,* took place, all sorts of suggestions being made as to the purposes and constitution of the Union. As the discussion proceeded, it became merged with the discussion of a proposal for a Congregational Library. One writer, probably John Blackburn, now the Editor, suggested

> to those gentlemen who are interested in promoting a *general union,* and in the *foundation of a library,* whether it would not greatly increase the interest of each if *their plans were united.* The same machinery would serve to bring both into operation, and the library would be a place of convocation, and a depository for archives, and would give the General Congregational Union "a local habitation and a name".

It was perhaps the formation of the London Union which had given impetus to this project for a library and denominational building, the realization of which did much to prepare the way for the establishment of a national Union. Once more the promoters were men actively associated with Congregational missionary enterprise at home and abroad. Pre-eminent among them were Thomas Wilson, whose optimism about the embryo Union in 1808 proved unfounded, and his son Joshua, to both of whom Congregationalism owes a debt that it has too swiftly forgotten. Thomas Wilson (1764—1843) retired from business at the early age of 34, in order to devote his life to the service of the Kingdom of God. His special interest was in Hoxton (afterwards Highbury) Academy, of which he was Treasurer, but every field of Congregational life experienced his beneficent and thoughtful activity. He was one of the first Directors of the London Missionary Society and subsequently its treasurer, and one of the earliest patrons of the Home Missionary Society. In chapel building he was always to the fore, and dozens of chapels in London and in the country were built largely by means of his generosity. He had a wide knowledge of men in the ministry, and often secured their introduction to the congregations whose chapels he had helped to build. Frequently such men were to be found engaged with him in denominational enterprises, foremost among them John Blackburn, of Claremont Chapel, whose words have just been quoted. Joshua was a worthy son of his father, whose life of service he emulated. He wrote his father's biography, and his soundness in the Protestant Faith is illustrated by his note that he uses "layman" as "a common and convenient term, but protesting against it as Popish in its origin, and as tending to maintain a distinction unscriptural in its nature, and injurious in its operation".

These two, together with others mentioned in the subscription list below, took the lead in the movement for the provision of a Congregational Library and Denominational Home. In 1830 a prospectus was issued referring to the fact that the Dr. Williams's Library was now under the control of Unitarian Trustees, and that there was no place where Independents could transact business on their own premises. They had no right to use the London Missionary Society's office, which they frequently did, while it was not fitting that the meetings should be held in taverns and coffee houses. The Baptists had a Library and Museum at Bristol, the Wesleyan Methodists premises adjoining City Road Chapel, while the Countess of Huntingdon's Connexion had also a house. Thomas Wilson offered £1,000 on condition that £10,000 was raised, and on that proving too ambitious, gave £500. Among others whose names[1] appear in the first list were, Joshua Wilson, W. Alers Hankey, Thomas Challis, J. Remington Mills, Thomas Piper, and George Hadfield (Manchester), who contributed £105 each, and Dr. Baldwin Brown, John Wilks, M.P., and Edward Dawson (Lancaster) £52 10s. each, while among the ministers who helped were Dr. Pye Smith, Dr. Raffles, J. A. Coombs, James Berry, and James Stratten, £52 10s. each; and John Blackburn and Arthur Tidman,

---

1 Most of these men were of the type of Samuel Favell, mentioned above. Many of them became M.P.'s as well as officers of denominational and religious societies. William Alers Hankey (1771—1859), who may be taken as a type of them all, was a deacon for 50 years at Stepney Meeting, a generous supporter of all Congregational enterprises (with an exception to be noted later), and incidentally the great-grandfather of Donald Hankey, "A Student in Arms". An excellent account of Hankey's life appears in John Kennedy's funeral sermon, *Your fathers, where are they?*

£26 5s. A building in Blomfield Street, Finsbury Circus, intended for use as a Concert Room, was secured and opened in May, 1831, immediately preceding the time of the first meetings of the Union. Steps were at once taken to obtain books for the Library, Joshua Wilson giving the major portion, a practice which did not cease with his life, for the collection which came to the Library after his death still forms its most valuable feature. The buildings were only small, but they provided a satisfactory meeting-place for the Union for several years. In Dr. Stoughton's words : "A local habitation was prepared for the Union before it was formed—a cradle was provided ere the child was born".

Meanwhile, after several private meetings attended by ministers and laymen from the country as well as from London, a circular was drawn up at the Poultry Chapel on the 28th June, 1830, widely circulated, and printed in the *Congregational Magazine* for October. It stated three principles on which the Union should be based :

I. That the Union consist of all the County Associations already in existence, or hereafter to be formed ; and that the London Churches be considered collectively as one Association.

II. That it shall not authoritatively interfere with the plans or proceedings of the respective Associations, or intermeddle with the management of the internal concerns of particular Churches.

III. That a General Assembly of Delegates and Representatives, consisting of Ministers and private Members of Churches, in equal numbers, from all County Associations, and from the London Churches, be held once in every year, for promoting the purposes of the Union, and that such Assembly be held only every third, fourth, or fifth year in London, and in the intermediate years at such of the large cities and towns in the country, as may be hereafter determined.

Further, it gave a list of five principal objects which Union would promote. The names of the Provisional Committee quoted, which differs slightly from those of a manuscript list dated 28th May, are :—

HENRY ALLON

JOSEPH FLETCHER

Rev. James Bennett, D.D.
    Thomas Binney.
    John Blackburn.
    H. F. Burder, M.A.
    John Clayton, Jun.
    J. Dean.
    J. P. Dobson.
    Joseph Fletcher, M.A.
    Caleb Morris.
    Andrew Reed.
    Arthur Tidman.
    R. Winter, D.D.

Messrs. J. B. Brown, LL.D.
    Thomas Challis.
    William Hale.
    Benjamin Hanbury.
    W. A. Hankey.
    J. R. Mills.
    Henry Parker.
    Apsley Pellatt.
    Thomas Piper.
    Joshua Wilson.
    Robert Winter.
    William Yockney.

Ministers and members of churches were asked to send their suggestions to the *Congregational Magazine* so that a definite plan could be laid before the County Associations in the spring of 1831. These were speedily forthcoming. John Angell James wrote for the ministers of his district, and Dr. Redford for Worcester. The Sussex, Salop, and Gloucester Associations, and the Congregational Union of Ireland, all expressed sympathy with the project. Everything seemed to be proceeding quite satisfactorily, and we can imagine John Blackburn and Joshua Wilson smiling to themselves and rubbing their hands as one commendatory resolution after another came to hand. They little thought what a bombshell was in store, and it is easy to imagine their surprise when they received a printed circular headed in large block capitals, GENERAL CONGREGATIONAL UNION, occupying three closely printed pages (much larger than foolscap) setting out the detailed plan of Union, and making the tiny London circular look modest indeed. There lie before me on the table the two huge circulars addressed to Thomas and Joshua Wilson, and one can picture the consternation with which they were opened. Robert Winter the younger had written to his father, Dr. Winter, in June, saying he could not attend the Provisional Committee on 28th June and suggesting that the circular to be prepared should state the objects and plan of the Union so as to prevent correspondents from sending impracticable schemes to which they were wedded. The father must have been struck by his son's prescience, for a day or two before he had re-

D

ceived from Mr. John Brown, of Wareham, a letter[1] giving his idea of a Union. Brown was vigorous and thorough; he had already urged the matter in the Dorset Association, and the outline he submits goes into such details as the time of the Assembly (November), the place ("the new building"), and the raising of a fund to meet expenses. The objects of the Union he states thus :—

> 1st.—Every Minister of a Dissenting Church in every County to send per County Representatives an Account of number of Church Members annually—Number of sittings in his Chapel—Number of sittings occupied or taken—Average of Morning, Afternoon, and Evening Worshippers —State of Sunday Schools—of general Education—moral state of surrounding Districts—Chapel Cases and wants and resources—To knock in[2] the head that *disgraceful System of Begging* equally loathsome to the Soliciter and the Solicited—To address an annual Epistle (Quaker-like) to the Churches—To petition, as a Body, Parliament on Slavery, Jewish Disabilities, Church Rates and *Tythes,* Register of Births and Baptisms—To demand a Right to marry by our own Ministers—To displace Clerical Magistrates from the Bench—To secure our places of Worship, without £30 or £40 Expence every 25 years for Trust Deeds—To abolish Sunday Baking and Sunday Travelling —To open Corporations of Towns on the principle of Election instead of close Representation.
>
> All its decisions (that is, of the House) to be conveyed as *Recommendations only* to every Church in the Kingdom —Its Deliberations to be duly reported—In one Word, to form a Representative Body, by which the Churches should be acted upon as by an electric Shock from Sunderland to the Land's End.

It was Mr. Brown, no doubt, who was most responsible for giving such a shock to Mr. Blackburn, the Wilsons, and the rest of the London Committee. In October the Dorset Association had considered and approved this huge circular, which, dated 26th November, 1830, was sent to 1,500 churches, "separate links, of good material undoubtedly, well wrought and highly polished", in the hope of making them into a "noble chain". Replies to the circular were

1 This letter and the one from Robert Winter are both in the Congregational Library.

2 As MS.

invited, five ministers and four laymen, including Mr. John
Brown, being appointed a committee, with the Rev. James
Brown, Secretary. The objects of the Dorset Plan may
thus be summarized :

1. To give churches effective union in national
   emergencies (as in the case of Lord Sidmouth's bill in
   1811).
2. To organize a complete system of itinerancy.
3. To establish new causes.
4. To diffuse the best principles of Church Government.
5. To provide a method to supersede "Begging Cases".
6. To protect meeting-houses from being perverted from
   their original design.
7. To strengthen weak causes.
8. To arbitrate in disputes where desired.
9. To procure impartial management and distribution of
   public charities.
10. To provide a general system of daily Christian educa-
    tion.
11. To introduce a better style of church building.
12. To get rid of the great expense of the renewal of
    Trust deeds.
13. To remedy defects of Baptismal Registers.
14. To procure a complete census of the Independent
    body.
15. To establish a Life and Annuity Insurance Office for
    ministers.
16. To send an Annual Letter to the churches.
17. To establish friendly relations and receive deputa-
    tions from Independents in Scotland, Ireland, America
    and the Continent.

Stating that these are but the most prominent of the
objects, the Plan then enters into details about the Assembly and representation (lay-delegates must be more than
25 years old !).

These specific aims are, without exception, admirable,
and as an ideal to be aimed at could scarcely be bettered,
but there would be a greater prospect of persuading a dear
old lady in 1931 to attempt a solo flight to America than of
persuading the Independent Churches, fearful of any external authority, and suspecting that *any* co-operative effort

would encroach on their rights, to accept a plan of this kind. As well invite them to join the Roman Church right away! And the London Committee, which had been moving so warily, trying to offend nobody, fearful of another failure, and knowing the tremendous difficulties to be overcome, was now suddenly confronted with this elaborate Dorset scheme. John Blackburn without doubt lost his temper. The *Congregational Magazine* for January, 1831, was just going through the press, and he added to it three pages of Postscript, in which he expressed his feelings about Dorset, with capital letters and italics galore. It really looked as if jealousy between London and the Provinces, together with the Dorset overloading, would capsize the frail vessel *Union* even before it could reach the harbour bar. But oil was poured on the troubled waters. Henry Rogers intervened with wise and calming words. The Dorset leaders made clear that their efforts were well-intentioned, and that they had no desire of making the centre of the Union at Wareham or Poole. Dr. Winter was clearly a peacemaker, and in a letter to John Brown[1] he said that the period since May had conclusively proved that the country brethren desired union, and that it was not being imposed on them by "any Metropolitan rulers". Joseph Fletcher wrote in the same strain, saying that though the Dorset circular was

> a precipitate and injudicious interference with the measures commenced at headquarters[2], still it is desirable for the *rural* jealousy of Metropolitan influence that *we* should bear our faculties very *meekly* on this point. On various accounts it is also desirable that as much as possible the Union should appear to emanate and should really emanate from the feelings and wishes of "the Country Churches", and therefore this very Dorsetshire affair may be overruled for good.

In February the *Congregational Magazine* announced that

---

1 This letter (in the Congregational Library) in asking Brown to delay action until the Provisional Committee has met, uses an epigram which may some day still be useful to a secretary of the Union: "Discussion will be destruction"!

2 The first use of this expression noted.

as a result of its "warm remonstrance" harmonious co-operation had been secured[1].

There were still rocks to be avoided, however, and skilful pilots were needed. The Dorset ministers had been ventilating their ideas for some time in *The World* newspaper, then in the hands of Stephen Bourne, who was evidently no friend of the *Congregational Magazine,* about whom even Henry Rogers uses very strong language, and whom Joseph Fletcher calls "that frothy and conceited meddler". Bourne violently attacked the Union project, and especially its association with a denominational building, saying :

> It is not buildings we want, but the Spirit of the Fathers. They have, it appears from the *Magazine,* actually laid out money in the purchase of a building, and it is affirmed that no authorized meeting on this subject can be held in London in any other place. Now we beg to ask, whither the authority to fix a place of meeting, not yet constituted, has been derived? Was it from the Pope of Rome? Or the Head of the English Church? or the Presbytery of the Church of Scotland, or some living Pope of the nineteenth century? The first teachers of Christianity required no splendid buildings to mature their plans in; the very chief of them worked with his own hands as a tent maker, rather than be chargeable to the Churches; they met in an upper room to transact the greatest business ever entrusted to the management of human beings.

This kind of talk was much more than cancelled by a fine, manly, Christian letter[2] from John Brown to Dr. Winter.

There were more serious challenges, however, for many who were wholehearted in their belief in Independency and zealous in the service of the churches found the Union project very disquieting, for it seemed to them to jeopardize Independency's distinctive witness. Throughout the year

---

1 It is interesting to note that in 1838 Dorset was still claiming to have begun the Union :
  "Recollecting, as we do, with much satisfaction that it was at a meeting of the Dorset Association held at Shaftesbury eight years ago, that the Congregational Union originated, . . ".

2 Original in Congregational Library, and one in a similar spirit from the Rev. Thomas Durant, of Poole, to Joshua Wilson, in which it appears that *The World's* reference to a nineteenth century Pope was aimed at Joshua's father, Thomas.

1831 the *Congregational Magazine* printed arguments for
and against, some of them very well reasoned. Unfortunately most of these contributions are anonymous. Did
we know who "Roffensis", "Dunelmensis" and
"Theologus" were, it might be very useful. The arguments of "Roffensis" dealt with first principles, and his
disquiet had some ground. He fears for the independency
of the churches, for the tendency of a system may be
dangerous, though the individuals conducting it may be
all honourable and holy men.

> It is for us to profit by the past. Episcopacy arose out
> of the presidency of the more influential men in the assem-
> blies of presbyters holding equal rank; and the churches
> lost their internal rights by appealing to the wisdom of
> such assemblies. Metropolitans next claimed priority of
> provincial bishops. Patriarchates were at length erected;
> and the pastoral chair of a single church became, in the
> end, a throne lifted high in supremacy over all the
> churches. Hierachies have sprung from the most incon-
> siderable beginnings.

To him, the union was "cumbrous and useless", the
various societies and the County Associations already
existing performing their different functions and uniting
the churches in them. Churches in immediate connexion
with Christ needed no other medium of incorporation.
There were certain to be non-concurring churches, and this
would tend to disunion, not union—there would be Independents on the one hand and Congregationalists on the
other. The greatest drawback of the proposal, however,
would be that it would make Independency into a sect.

> It is our glory that hitherto we have been no sect. We
> subscribe no creed. We submit to no synod or conference.
> We are not properly a body. We recognize but two defi-
> nitions of the term church. It designates the separate
> assembly of believers united together for the observance of
> religious ordinances; and it designates the whole number
> of the redeemed. We know no intermediate sense. By
> courtesy we may speak of the episcopal church, or the
> Lutheran church; but we could not arrogate to ourselves
> the name of the independent church; it would seem to us
> to savour of schism. But incorporation would go far to
> constitute us a sectarian church, whether we accept the
> designation or reject it.

The churches were united already, and a General Union would not add to the spirit of fellowship. It would, however, erect a barrier between the Independents and other Christians, and "Roffensis" prefers to dwell in "a land of unwalled villages".

To this, the reply was given that County Associations were often weak, and that a General Union would help them to extend the Gospel, as well as function in districts in which there was no Association. It would also help struggling churches in another way :

> They find themselves opposed by other denominations —treated with contempt by *Christians par excellence,* who are most *methodical* in attempting to injure them, as well as zealous in their own peculiar cause. But let these weak and despised churches be assisted by other larger and wealthier churches ; let it be seen that they constitute a part of the Congregational body, and this unworthy attempt to destroy them would cease.

The slogan of "Theologus", who replied to "Roffensis" in detail, was, "Let the world know that there is a Congregational denomination". He regrets that "esteemed brethren" should be "morbidly jealous of this close, and extended, and universal fellowship", and says that to oppose union is "most unnatural, impolitic, and presumptuous, and, it may be, displeasing and offensive to Him who prayed that His disciples might be one".

If Unions were good for districts and counties, why not for a country ? If Scotland for 18 years, and America for a century, had found Unions of service, with no hierarchies or other evils emerging, why should not England have a similar experience ? And then comes this enthusiastic peroration :

> No county association—no book society—no magazine can stand instead of a Congregational Union, embracing in its designs the diffusion of scriptural principles of the faith, order, and practice of the Church of Christ.—"The field" of its operation is "the world" ; and though no one Union can comprehend all Congregationalists, yet by system and order they may all be made to appear to the whole world "as one in Christ Jesus". And who can tell what may be the glorious effect of such an exhibition of "the unity of the spirit, and the bond of peace"?

Such an exhibition, however, it seems would have no charms in the eyes of some, who imagine that the Congregational Christians throughout the world would then appear to be one great *sect*. Well, let it be so. Suppose they should appear one great sect; Is not Christianity itself *a sect* in relation to other religions? It was originally *"a sect* everywhere spoken against". *It was its glory that it was a sect*—that all its members were so distinct from the world—so closely united to each other—so zealous for the propagation of its principles throughout the earth! This is all we ask on behalf of a Congregational Union. And let *our* sect be everywhere spoken against, "while we thus bear the marks of the Lord Jesus, let no man trouble us". *A sectarian is not necessarily a schismatic.* We do not hold the etymology of the word to be *seco,* but *sequor.* We are not of a *dividing* spirit, but of a *uniting* spirit. Our sectarianism is simply a *following* of the Lord Jesus in "all his ordinances and commandments blameless". Such *sectaries* He approves; why should we be ashamed of them? The Lord grant us more of a true sectarian spirit, in the proper sense of the term! Let not the "shadow of a shade" terrify us!

Walter Wilson, whose severe strictures on Independency as far back as 1814 have already been noted, attacked the proposals from another angle. His pamphlet, *Remarks upon the Present State of the Dissenting Interest, with Hints for its Improvement by means of A Consolidated Union,* published about this time, has already been mentioned. Wilson's acute mind and vigorous style had full play in this controversy. In some ways he was far ahead of most of his contemporaries, as, for example, in believing "that no form of ecclesiastical polity now in being has any legitimate claim to a divine right; neither are the institutions of the apostolical Church so clearly defined in every particular as to prevent the possibility of mistake". It has already been seen that he "had little use for" the Methodists, while he believed that there were so many drawbacks to Independency that he recommended a form of Presbyterianism. His great plea was for a union of all Protestant Dissenters (*i.e.,* Presbyterians, Baptists, and Independents) which would proclaim and extend their principles, safeguard and fight for their rights, and, at the same time, carry out many of the objects of the Congregational scheme. Among other things, Wilson's Consolidated Union aimed at the improvement of public worship, the institution of schools, more effective means for securing and maintaining a learned ministry and providing new churches, a central office and library with security for trust deeds, registers, *etc.* He denounced the Congregational project as having "no objects of a purely dissenting character", and thought that it would be as useless and hopeless as a previous attempt, in short, "a *nothing doing* business".

In two succeeding numbers of the *Eclectic Review* Josiah Conder replied to Wilson. He held that his case was overstated : he had altogether exaggerated the lack of connexion between the churches—they had their County Associations, they steadily and harmoniously supported the Missionary Societies, *etc.*, *etc.*, and, when the occasion arose, could act as unitedly as the Quakers or Wesleyans. After carefully examining Wilson's analysis, he concluded that his suggested Scheme would mean control, not union, would result in intermeddling with congregations, and in the secularization of churches, and he thus sums up :

> With the friends of a consolidated Union we wish to leave the parting admonition that no plans, no machinery, can produce union; the object ought rather to be to ascertain, recognize, and turn to the best account the degree of substantial union which exists. Union is an object which is more than half attained as soon as it is unaffectedly and mutually desired.

It is clear that there were wise heads leading the Union movement. Despite all criticisms, they continued to communicate with likely supporters in the country and to ponder how best the case for Union could be stated. There is in the Congregational Library a long document prepared at this time, either for the consideration of the Provisional Committee or as a draft of a circular to be sent out, as the pencilled notes on it indicate. I have not been able to identify the writing, and it does not appear to have been printed, but it puts the aims and ambitions of the Unionists much more fully than the circular sent out in January, 1831. A finer ecclesiastical document does not appear during the century of the Union's history. After a preamble it goes on : —

The following reasons—among many others which might have been named—may shew the propriety and necessity of such a Union being formed.

There exists at this moment among the Independent Denomination a unity of religious opinion and a uniformity of religious observances greater than can be found in any other Communion, though we have NO articles of faith of human devising. It appears most desirable therefore as we already possess the principal part of Union—the unity of the spirit—that any plan by which this can be rendered more operative and efficient should engage the attention and secure the best wishes of our Denomination.

1. To prove to the world that our principles lead to united co-operation in doing good, and not to anarchy and confusion.

2. To shew to our own people and especially to the rising portion of our community that they are not connected merely with an isolated church and congregation but united in the closest bonds with hundreds of churches holding the very same doctrines and exhibiting the same practice.

3. To defend our own Denomination against the attempts made to injure us—from whatever quarter such attempts may come.

4. To carry into fuller effect the great principles of civil and religious liberty which we cherish as our birthright and consider essential to the spread of true religion at home and abroad.

5. To bring into more complete operation the spirit of Christian love which united the Primitive Churches so closely in the bonds of a holy brotherhood.

The following considerations may shew that various circumstances combine in making an attempt to form a Congregational Union proper at this time.

1. The remarkable coincidence of feeling on the subject experienced and expressed by individuals in many of the Counties of England, though no public or private notice respecting it had been given.

2. The facilities of intercourse and communication possessed by us are greater than perhaps were ever possessed before by our Denomination.

3. The intercourse already so widely promoted by means of the London Missionary Society and other kindred institutions has produced a general acquaintance and mutual confidence between many of the churches and ministers of our Denomination, the circulation of the *Congregational*

Magazine and the valuable lists of ministers and churches furnished three several times have enlarged this acquaintance. The spirit of active exertion which now happily prevails in many Counties in aiding the general cause of Christ and in extending the boundaries of our own denomination—the strength which we *do* possess and *can* put forth though weakened by isolation—as evidenced in the cases of Lord Sidmouth's Bill and the repeal of the Test and Corporation Acts, may be viewed as encouraging signs of the times and induce us the more readily to occupy that high moral vantage ground which we have a right to take and which for the advantage of mankind we should be anxious to defend.

4. The Union of other Denominations and their success in extending the knowledge of their opinions and in promoting the increase of their number and efficiency render our union necessary.

Having thus stated a few reasons why such a Union is proper and desirable the following plan is presented to the Churches for the purpose of ascertaining their opinion and forming, from what appears the general sentiment, a code of rules which may be satisfactory to the Denomination :

1. That there be formed a voluntary Union of Independent Churches and Ministers throughout England and that it be called the Congregational Union of England, and that the Churches thus united shall contribute to one general fund by Annual Collections and by the Donations and Subscriptions of individuals.

2. That every County Association of Congregational Ministers and Churches now in existence and wishing to be connected with this Union be considered as a part of it. That the Ministers and delegates from the Churches in each County form the Committee, and that one of their number be appointed secretary in order to correspond regularly with the Committee in London in carrying into effect the objects of the Union.

3. That while the Committee or Association in each County be considered as having devolved upon it the duty of attending to its own locality yet that the advice of the Union be sought in cases of emergency.

4. That there be an Annual Statement or report from each County Association throughout England addressed to the Committee in London containing particulars respecting the state of religion in our own Denomination and that of others in the several Counties. That these reports be inserted in a record kept for that purpose and that from these

be compiled a general report which shall be published by itself or in the *Congregational Magazine.*

5. That the Congregational Board appoint a special Committee of twelve Ministers and twelve laymen whose business it will be to attend to the communications from the Country; that a treasurer and secretary be chosen to manage the funds and correspondence of the Union.

6. That there be an Annual Meeting of the Union consisting of Ministers deputed by the different Associations and of delegates from the different Churches or Associations. That the time of the Annual Meeting be in the month of May or at any other period deemed most suitable. That a chairman be appointed for the time of the Meeting that the business may be conducted with regularity. That no business come before the Meeting which would interfere with Church discipline or with the Independency of the Churches. That *advice* only be given if asked for by both parties in cases of difficulty and that even this be given with the greatest caution lest it should lead to the exercise of control over the ministers or churches.

7. That the following objects be kept in view by the Union and assistance rendered to the various objects according to the amount of funds placed at its disposal—or by recommending them to those institutions which already exist for specific purposes.

1. The Encouragement of infant and weak churches in their struggles for existence or in attempting to diffuse the Gospel around them.

2. The assistance of poor and labouring ministers.

3. The circulation of publications containing a statement of our principles and especially the support of the *Congregational Magazine.*

4. Assistance to the Congregational School[1].

5. To consider the best plan of modifying or altering the present practice of ministers begging for the debts of chapels.

6. The deeds of Chapels—in lessening their expense and increasing their security.

7. To use means to procure an alteration in the Marriage Ceremony as applicable to Dissenters.

8. To secure a more uniform and correct system of Baptismal registering.

These and other secular matters could be promoted as the various objects come from time to time before the Union.

[1] Lewisham,

8. That in order to give greater stability to the Union means be employed to obtain a building in London sufficiently spacious and convenient to be exclusively devoted to the interests of the Independent Denomination, that all meetings of the Union be held there; that various rooms be appropriated to those Institutions and objects connected with our Denominations—such as Committee Rooms for each of the Independent Theological Academies, place of Meeting for the Congregational Board—for Congregational School—Ecclesiastical Knowledge Society and any other Institution established for promoting either the secular or spiritual welfare of our Denomination. That this building form the centre of Union in London and the place of meeting for ministers and laymen properly introduced from the churches of the country. That it is most important to connect with the building as valuable a Library as possible, and especially to collect and arrange all the Documents, Printed and in MS., which can give information respecting our Denomination during past and present times. That for this purpose Dissenters throughout England be requested to contribute to this department of the object as being calculated to promote the consistency, harmony, and permanency of our Union.

It will be observed that the promoters of the Union, while too wise to frighten the churches by publishing this detailed scheme, were yet largely guided by it in the Plan finally formed. That Plan was considered at a meeting of delegates of Associations and ministers and officers of churches, which met in the Congregational Library (opened the previous day) on Tuesday, May 10th, 1831.

V. THE LAUNCHING, 1831.

IT may be well to look a little more closely at those who assembled in the Congregational Library on Tuesday morning, 10th May, 1831. There were 101 present (82 ministers and 19 laymen), of whom 34 (23 ministers and 11 laymen) were delegates from County Associations. Most of them were from London and the Home Counties; Yorkshire had no representatives, though there were ministers from Morpeth and Sunderland; Raffles was the only one from Lancashire; J. A. James and two laymen came from Birmingham. Among other places, Bristol, Worcester, Derby, Macclesfield, Cockermouth, and Holyhead may be mentioned.

The proceedings of this historic assembly deserve to be carefully noted. In the chair was the Rev. A. Douglas, of Reading, the Chairman at the adjourned session on the following Friday being Dr. Joseph Fletcher. After the minutes of the Provisional Committee had been read, favourable communications from various counties and districts were reported, 22 in all, namely:—Kent, Berkshire, Leicestershire, Surrey, East Devon, Durham, Sussex (Eastern), Sussex (Western), Somersetshire, Monmouthshire, Gloucestershire, Shropshire, Dorsetshire, Worcestershire, Cumberland, Staffordshire, Cornwall, the Board of Congregational Ministers in London, the Western Committee formed at Shaftesbury, and verbally from Derbyshire, Wiltshire, and Essex. The Associated Ministers of Cambridgeshire and of Lancashire wrote " expressing doubts as to the practicability of the measure, and the desire for further information."

That the programme had been carefully prepared may be gathered at once from the names of those entrusted with the resolutions, evidently chosen to represent the different districts and interests, ministerial and lay. John Angell James, perhaps the leading provincial minister in the country, moved, and Dr. J. Baldwin

Brown, a prominent London layman, seconded the motion :

> That it is highly desirable and important to establish a Union of Congregational Churches throughout England and Wales, founded on the broadest recognition of their own distinctive principle, namely, the scriptural right of every separate church to maintain perfect independence in the government and administration of its own particular affairs.

Dr. H. F. Burder, of Hackney, and the Rev. George Redford, of Worcester, moved—

> That such Union consist of County and District Associations.

Then, on the motion of the Rev. T. Stratten, of Sunderland, and the Rev. J. Gawthorne, of Derby, the matter was referred to a Committee of the delegates present, together with representatives of the Provisional Committee and the London Board. On Friday, the 13th, the following plan was agreed to *nem. con.* :

> I. That it is highly desirable and important to establish a Union of Congregational Churches and Ministers, throughout England and Wales, founded on a full recognition of their own distinctive principle, namely, the scriptural right of every separate church to maintain perfect independence in the government and administration of its own particular affairs ; and therefore, that the Union shall not in any case assume legislative authority, or become a court of appeal.
>
> II. That such Union consist of County and District Associations.
>
> III. That the following be the objects contemplated in its formation.
>> 1. To promote Evangelical Religion, in connection with the Congregational Denomination.
>> 2. To cultivate brotherly affection and sincere co-operation in everything relating to the interests of the Associated Churches.
>> 3. To establish fraternal correspondence with Congregational Churches, and other bodies of Christians throughout the world.
>> 4. To address an Annual Letter to the Associated Churches, accompanied with such information as may be deemed necessary.

5. To obtain accurate statistical information relative to the Congregational Churches throughout the Kingdom and the world at large.

6. To enquire into the present methods of collecting funds for the erection of places of worship, and to consider the practicability of introducing any improved plan.

7. To assist in maintaining and enlarging the civil rights of Protestant Dissenters.

IV. To promote the accomplishment of these objects and the general interests of the Union, That an Annual Meeting shall be held, consisting, if practicable, of an equal number of Ministers and Laymen, and that each Association may appoint such a number of representatives as it may deem necessary; that the Annual Meeting be held in London, or such other town or city as may from time to time be appointed; and that at the Annual Meetings of Delegates, every Minister and Officer connected with any Association united in the general body shall be eligible to attend and vote.

The Committee and officials were appointed as follows:

1. That a Provisional Committee be formed for the year ensuing, consisting of the following Ministers and Gentlemen in London and its vicinity:—Drs. Bennett, Burder, and Fletcher; Rev. Messrs. Blackburn, Clayton, and Reed; Dr. Brown; Messrs. Challis and Parker, and including, as Corresponding Members, the Secretaries of all County and District Associations, favourable to the formation of the Union.

2. That the Rev. Joseph Turnbull, B.A., be associated with the Rev. A. Tidman, and Joshua Wilson, Esq., as Provisional Secretaries; and that B. Hanbury, Esq., be Treasurer *pro tempore* of the proposed Union.

It was decided that the *Congregational Magazine* should be the official journal and means of communication, and a resolution was passed expressing thanks to the Congregational Library and to Joshua Wilson.

There was now a definite plan for the churches and Associations to discuss, and discussed it was, officially in the Associations and unofficially in the *Congregational Magazine* and elsewhere. How the minds of Independents were playing on the possibilities may be gathered from a correspondent in the *Congregational Magazine* for May, 1832, who said that the Congregational Union was

ARCHIBALD DOUGLAS

THOMAS WILSON

" deficient in its objects." He made two definite proposals : (1) That the June Sacramental collection in the
churches should be devoted to raising a fund for ministerial superannuation. It should bring in £1,500 a year.
(2) That a Hymn Book should be prepared and published,
the profits on the sale going to the fund just mentioned.
A supplement to Watts was very badly needed, for there
were many occasions for which Watts supplied no suitable
hymns. The Baptist example here ought to be followed.

On 11th May, 1832, the delegates to the Union again
met in the Congregational Library, the Rev. William
Chaplin, of Bishop's Stortford, being Chairman. There
were present 82 ministers, 26 " Lay Gentlemen", and 8
" Visiters ", three from America, three from Ireland, one
from Prussia, and Mr. R. M. Beverley, an Anglican who,
having denounced his Church in unmeasured terms, was
for a time a Congregationalist.[1]

The Committee reported that they had circulated the
Plan as instructed, asking for suggestions, etc., and for
any pertinent statistics. The Plan had been sent to the
Editors of the *Congregational* and *Evangelical Magazines,*
the London Board of Ministers, the Congregational
Unions of Scotland, Ireland, New England, and " the
Missionaries connected with our body at Calcutta, Madras,
South Africa, and the Windward and Leeward Islands in
the South Seas".

Of the 34 English counties having Associations 26 were
" most favourably disposed " to the Union, four had
" declined for the present ", and four had sent no answer.
It was resolved to communicate with all churches not in
the Union. An informing communication was submitted
from the Rev. Dr. Snell, Secretary of the Massachusetts
Association, welcoming and approving the Plan, making
one or two practical suggestions, and explaining American
practice. He volunteered the information that of 750
churches in Massachusetts, 350 were orthodox Congregational churches, 56 Unitarian, only 31 Episcopal, and 4

---

[1] At one time he was a wealthy man. He was a friend of Joshua
Wilson, to whom he gave many valuable books, some of which ultimately
found their way into the Congregational Library.

Roman Catholic. Of the 350 Congregational churches 276 were in the Association (the rest being in the main feeble churches without pastors), the Association representing 40,000 church members. The Committee used one of Snell's phrases in summoning all Congregationalists to avow their principles by joining the Union and thus exhibiting " a united and marshalled host against error, ungodliness, and vice ". After the Report had been adopted, resolutions were submitted, and in the choice of those who moved them once more tact and wisdom had been at work. Dr. J. B. Brown moved that in conformity with the resolutions of the previous May " THE UNION BE NOW FORMED ", and it was seconded by John Brown of Wareham ! ! This resolution incorporates the Plan of Union circulated, with few changes only, and but one of them significant. In II, to " That such Union consist of County and District Associations ", the words " together with any Ministers and Churches of the Congregational order recognized by an Association " were added. This addition not only brought the general Union into contact with individual churches, but it changed the character of the Assembly from a Council mainly of officials, to a public meeting of representatives.[1] Churches were asked to send an annual contribution on or before the 1st May to meet necessary expenses, and a Committee and officers were elected as follows :

> That the Committee for the following year consist of the Treasurers and Secretaries of all the united Associations (being members of churches), together with the following gentlemen, resident in London, with power to add to their number, *viz.,* the Rev. Dr. Bennett ; the Rev. Dr. H. F. Burder ; the Rev. Dr. Fletcher ; the Rev. John Clayton, M.A. ; the Rev. John Blackburn ; the Rev. John Burnet ; the Rev. W. S. Palmer ; Thomas Wilson, Esq. ; Dr. J. B. Brown ; Mr. Challis ; Mr. Coombs ; Mr. Morley ; Mr. Coles ; Mr. Jackson ; Mr. W. C. Wright ; and that the following gentlemen be the officers of the Union for the year ensuing,—Mr. Benjamin Hanbury, Treasurer ; the Rev. Arthur Tidman, the Rev. Joseph Turnbull, A.B., and Joshua Wilson, Esq., Secretaries.

[1] On this point Dale's *History of Congregationalism,* p. 695, is useful.

On the motion of the Rev. J. Burnet and John Brown it was decided that an attempt should be made to collect at least £10,000 for a denominational house, Dr. Fletcher and the Rev. G. Redford moving that the Committee confer with the Committee of the Library on this point.

A representative was welcomed from Ireland and a greeting received from the Congregational Union of Scotland.

It was decided that there should be a public religious service at each annual meeting.

Much of the time of this Assembly was given to the discussion of a Declaration of Faith and Order. John Angell James introduced the subject and said a draft had been prepared [by George Redford] at the request of several brethren. This was read, and, after a two-days' interval, was discussed, and it was agreed :

> That this meeting respectfully invite the opinion of Associated Ministers and Churches on the following questions :
>
> Whether, in accordance with the example of our Nonconformist ancestors, it be desirable *to present to the public* a Declaration of the leading articles of our faith and discipline; and whether, if it be deemed desirable, that Declaration should be made by such a statement as the following, which has been read, but not discussed in the meeting of the Union, subject to such modifications as may be suggested, and generally agreed on at the next annual meeting?
>
> That the Committee be instructed to prepare a letter to accompany the proposed Declaration, carefully stating its object to be the communicating of information to the public, on the doctrines generally held and maintained by the Congregational denomination, at a period when so much ignorance and misrepresentation prevail upon those subjects.

In sending the Declaration to the churches the Secretaries say :

> You will observe, in connexion with the DECLARATION appended to the Report, a Resolution, instructing us to explain more particularly its intent. We might satisfy ourselves with directing your attention to the Preliminary Notes prefixed to the document, as sufficient to guard it from misapprehension ; but we would in addition

fulfil the direction of the General Meeting, by assuring you of the great caution with which the document was received, lest it should be suspected that any portion of our body entertained the most distant wish to impose a Creed upon others. It was felt that such a document was but little required for our own information, and must necessarily be an imperfect statement of the sentiments held by us, in proportion as it may descend in its application to individuals. Still it was concluded that, for the information of others, not of our denomination, it was essentially requisite, at the present time, when such revolutions of opinion and extraordinary changes are occurring, and also while such misapprehension, and even gross misrepresentation, exist, respecting our real character. It was stated by several brethren, that they were persuaded a very large proportion of our countrymen take us to be either SOCINIANS or METHODISTS. We are not answerable for this strange alternative, and entire misapprehension—renouncing, as we do, with abhorrence, the tenets of the one, and differing so materially in some important respects from those of the other—except as we are wanting in some proper statement of our faith and order.

They also sent Dr. Snell's letter, referring to the value of his statistics, and asked to be furnished with similar information.

In 1833, the Rev. Joseph Gilbert, of Nottingham, presiding, 66 ministers (members and delegates) were present, 28 " Lay Delegates ", and 50 " Visiters ". Some of the visitors were from the United States, some were missionaries, but many were English Ministers and laymen who had evidently come to spy out the land—the names of Walter Wilson and of Josiah Conder are specially noteworthy. Twelve divinity students from Highbury and Homerton were also present. It was resolved to invite the Principals and Tutors of the Academies and Schools to become members of the Union. It was reported that 37 County and District Associations were now in the Union, but that eight still stood out—Hampshire, Norfolk, Suffolk, Northamptonshire, Cambridgeshire, Cheshire, Leicestershire, and Lancashire. The first balance-sheet was presented, showing a total expenditure of £27, the receipts being £9. Communications had been opened with other churches, and correspondence with some of them was read, notably with the General Presbyterians of the United States, in which special mention is made of a State establishment. The New York Congregational Association, in welcoming the formation of the Union, began its resolution with the preamble :

> That whereas the General Union formed in England makes no encroachment on the rights of individual churches to maintain their own government, and bids fair to advance the interest of a body of Christians whose unceasing aim has ever been to preserve the simplicity of a Gospel Church, and to promote the true evangelization of the world . . .

The rest of the business of this Assembly is retained for consideration in the next chapter. At present we must concentrate on that which took up most of the Assembly's time—the Declaration of Faith and Order.

DECLARATION

OF THE

FAITH, CHURCH ORDER, AND DISCIPLINE

OF THE

CONGREGATIONAL, OR INDEPENDENT DISSENTERS,

ADOPTED AT THE ANNUAL MEETING OF THE CONGREGATIONAL UNION, MAY, 1833.

THE CONGREGATIONAL Churches in England and Wales, frequently called INDEPENDENT, hold the following doctrines, as of Divine authority, and as the foundation of Christian faith and practice. They are also formed and governed according to the principles hereinafter stated.

PRELIMINARY NOTES.

1. It is not designed, in the following summary, to do more than to state the leading doctrines of faith and order maintained by Congregational Churches in general.

2. It is not proposed to offer any proofs, reasons, or arguments, in support of the doctrines herein stated, but simply to declare what the Denomination believes to be taught by the pen of inspiration.

3. It is not intended to present a scholastic or critical confession of faith, but merely such a statement as any intelligent member of the body might offer, as containing its leading principles.

4. It is not intended that the following statement should be put forth with any authority, or as a standard to which assent should be required.

5. Disallowing the utility of creeds and articles of religion as a bond of union, and protesting against subscription to any human formularies as a term of communion, Congregationalists are yet willing to declare, for general information, what is commonly believed among them, reserving to every one the most perfect liberty of conscience.

6. Upon some minor points of doctrine and practice, they, differing among themselves, allow to each other the right to form an unbiassed judgment of the Word of God.

7. They wish it to be observed, that, notwithstanding their jealousy of subscription to creeds and articles, and their disapproval of the imposition of any human standard, whether of faith or discipline, they are far more agreed in their doctrines and practices than any Church which enjoins subscription and enforces a human standard of orthodoxy; and they believe that there is no minister and no church among them that would deny the substance of any one of the following doctrines of religion, though each might prefer to state his sentiments in his own way.

Principles of Religion.

I. The Scriptures of the Old Testament, as received by the Jews, and the books of the New Testament, as received by the Primitive Christians from the Evangelists and Apostles, Congregational Churches believe to be Divinely inspired, and of supreme authority. These writings, in the languages in which they were originally composed, are to be consulted, with the aids of sound criticism, as a final appeal to all controversies, but the common version they consider to be adequate to the ordinary purposes of Christian instruction and edification.

II. They believe in one God, essentially wise, holy, just, and good; eternal, infinite, and immutable in all natural and moral perfections; the Creator, Supporter, and Governor of all beings, and of all things.

III. They believe that God is revealed in the Scriptures, as the Father, the Son, and the Holy Spirit, and that to each are attributable the same Divine properties and perfections. The doctrine of the Divine existence, as above stated, they cordially believe, without attempting fully to explain.

IV. They believe that man was created after the Divine image, sinless, and in his kind, perfect.

V. They believe that the first man disobeyed the Divine command, fell from his state of innocence and purity, and involved all his posterity in the consequences of that fall.

VI. They believe that, therefore, all mankind are born in sin, and that a fatal inclination to moral evil, utterly incurable by human means, is inherent in every descendant of Adam.

VII. They believe that God having, before the foundation of the world, designed to redeem fallen man, made disclosures of His mercy, which were the grounds of faith and hope from the earliest ages.

VIII. They believe that God revealed more fully to Abraham the covenant of His grace, and, having promised that from his descendants should arise the Deliverer and Redeemer of mankind, set that patriarch and his posterity apart, as a race specially favoured and separated to His service; a peculiar church, formed and carefully preserved, under the Divine sanction and government until the birth of the promised Messiah.

IX. They believe that, in the fulness of the time, the Son of God was manifested in the flesh, being born of the Virgin Mary, but conceived by the power of the Holy Spirit; and that our Lord Jesus Christ was both the Son of man and the Son of God; partaking fully and truly of human nature though without sin—equal with the Father and "the express image of His person".

X. They believe that Jesus Christ, the Son of God, revealed, either personally in His own ministry, or by the Holy Spirit in the ministry of His apostles, the whole mind of God, for our salvation; and that, by His obedience to the Divine law while He lived, and by His sufferings unto death, He meritoriously "obtained eternal redemption for us"; having thereby vindicated and illustrated Divine justice, "magnified the law", and "brought in everlasting righteousness".

XI. They believe that, after His death and resurrection, He ascended up into heaven, where, as the Mediator, He "ever liveth" to rule over all, and to "make intercession for them that come unto God by Him".

XII. They believe that the Holy Spirit is given, in consequence of Christ's mediation, to quicken and renew the hearts of men; and that His influence is indispensably necessary to bring a sinner to true repentance, to produce saving faith, to regenerate the heart, and to perfect our sanctification.

XIII. They believe that we are justified through faith in Christ, as "the Lord our righteousness", and not "by the works of the law".

XIV. They believe that all who will be saved were the objects of God's eternal and electing love, and were given by an act of Divine sovereignty to the Son of God; which in no way interferes with the system of means, nor with the grounds of human responsibility; being wholly unrevealed as to its objects, and not a rule of human duty.

XV. They believe that the Scriptures teach the final perseverance of all true believers to a state of eternal blessedness, which they are appointed to obtain through constant faith in Christ, and uniform obedience to His commands.

XVI. They believe that a holy life will be the necessary effect of a true faith and that good works are the certain fruits of a vital union to Christ.

XVII. They believe that the sanctification of true Christians, or their growth in the graces of the Spirit, and meetness for heaven, is gradually carried on through the whole period during which it pleases God to continue them in the present life, and that, at death, their souls, perfectly freed from all remains of evil, are immediately received into the presence of Christ.

XVIII. They believe in the perpetual obligation of Baptism and the Lord's Supper; the former to be administered to all converts to Christianity and their children, by the application of water to the subject, "in the name of the Father, and of the Son, and of the Holy Ghost"; and the latter to be celebrated by Christian churches as a token of faith in the Saviour, and of brotherly love.

XIX. They believe that Christ will finally come to judge the whole human race according to their works; that the bodies of the dead will be raised again; and that, as the Supreme Judge, He will divide the righteous from the wicked, will receive the righteous into "life everlasting", but send away the wicked into "everlasting punishment".

XX. They believe that Jesus Christ directed His followers to live together in Christian fellowship, and to maintain the communion of saints; and that, for this purpose, they are jointly to observe all Divine ordinances, and maintain that church order and discipline which is either expressly enjoined by inspired institution, or sanctioned by the undoubted example of the apostles and of apostolic churches.

PRINCIPLES OF CHURCH ORDER AND DISCIPLINE.

I. The Congregational Churches hold it to be the will of Christ that true believers should voluntarily assemble together to observe religious ordinances to promote mutual edification and holiness, to perpetuate and propagate the Gospel in the world, and to advance the glory and worship of God, through

Jesus Christ; and that each society of believers, having these objects in view in its formation, is properly a Christian church.

II. They believe that the New Testament contains, either in the form of express statute, or in the example and practice of apostles and apostolic churches, all the articles of faith necessary to be believed, and all the principles of order and discipline requisite for constituting and governing Christian societies; and that human traditions, fathers and councils, canons and creeds, possess no authority over the faith and practice of Christians.

III. They acknowledge Christ as the only Head of the Church, and the officers of each church under Him, as ordained to administer His laws impartially to all; and their only appeal, in all questions touching their religious faith and practice, is to the sacred Scriptures.

IV. They believe that the New Testament authorises every Christian church to elect its own officers, to manage all its own affairs, and to stand independent of, and irresponsible to, all authority, saving that only of the Supreme and Divine Head of the Church, the Lord Jesus Christ.

V. They believe that the only officers placed by the apostles over individual churches are the bishops or pastors and the deacons; the number of these being dependent upon the number of the church; and that to these, as the officers of the church, is committed respectively the administration of its spiritual and temporal concerns—subject, however, to the approbation of the church.

VI. They believe that no persons should be received as members of Christian churches, but such as make a credible profession of Christianity, are living according to its precepts, and attest a willingness to be subject to its discipline, and that none should be excluded from the fellowship of the church, but such as deny the faith of Christ, violate His laws, or refuse to submit themselves to the discipline which the Word of God enforces.

VII. The power of admission into any Christian church, and rejection from it, they believe to be vested in the church itself, and to be exercised only through the medium of its own officers.

VIII. They believe that Christian churches should statedly meet for the celebration of public worship, for the observance of the Lord's Supper, and for the sanctification of the first day of the week.

IX. They believe that the power of a Christian church is purely spiritual and should in no way be corrupted by union with temporal or civil power.

X. They believe that it is the duty of Christian churches to hold communion with each other, to entertain an enlarged affection for each other, as members of the same body, and to co-operate for the promotion of the Christian cause; but that no church, or union of churches, has any right or power to interfere with the faith or discipline of any other church further than to separate from such as, in faith or practice, depart from the Gospel of Christ.

XI. They believe that it is the privilege and duty of every church to call forth such of its members as may appear to be qualified by the Holy Spirit to sustain the office of the ministry; and that Christian churches unitedly ought to consider the maintenance of the Christian ministry in an adequate degree of learning as one of their especial cares, that the cause of the Gospel may be both honourably sustained and constantly promoted.

XII. They believe that church officers, whether bishops or deacons, should be chosen by the free voice of the church; but that their dedication to the duties of their office should take place with special prayer, and by solemn designation, to which most of the churches add the imposition of hands by those already in office.

XIII. They believe that the fellowship of every Christian church should be so liberal as to admit to communion in the Lord's Supper all whose faith and godliness are, on the whole, undoubted, though conscientiously differing in points of minor importance; and that this outward sign of fraternity in Christ should be co-extensive with the fraternity itself, though without involving any compliances which conscience would deem to be sinful.

It is very striking that the Declaration was accepted with comparatively little discussion, and no division of opinion. The Chairman, Dr. Ralph Wardlaw (who was attending from Scotland and had spoken of the advantages of the Scottish Congregational Union), and Redford were appointed a sub-committee for revision after it had been announced that that Draft had met with general approbation. On Friday morning (breakfast at 7.0, meeting at 8.0) they presented a revised Draft, which was agreed to. The changes that were made can be studied by comparing the Draft in *Documents connected with the Formation of the Union* (pp. 23-28) with the final form printed above, or by reading the excellent summary in Dale's *History of Congregationalism*.[1] It is specially interesting to note that the opening words were changed from "The Congrega-

[1] pp. 700-709.

tional Pædo-Baptists of England and Wales" to "The
Congregational Churches of England and Wales, frequently called Independents". Fortunately this is not the
place to analyse the theology implied in the Declaration.
It was that of a diluted Calvinism and found apt expression in a farewell exhortation of Algernon Wells to a
colonial missionary going to South Australia in 1837 :
"Adhere to your sound and moderate Calvinistic theology
and to the faithful, warm, evangelical preaching of Christ
crucified". This was also expressed in the words of the
Committee a year or two later, when it was said that

> the attachment of Congregationalists is firm and unshaken
> to evangelical doctrine understood agreeably with a
> moderate Calvinistic theology ; and to vital godliness as
> the life of faith in the soul and conduct of man.

Compared with the Savoy Declaration of 1658, which the
founders of the Union regarded as " though most orthodox, too wordy and too much extended for our purpose",
the Declaration of 1833 is popular rather than scholastic,
the product of preachers rather than of theologians. There
is a want of theological precision that would have shocked
the seventeenth century divines, but this accurately represented the mind of the churches at this period. Williston
Walker[1] says of the Declaration :

> The Declaration is a sweet-spirited statement of which
> the English churches have no cause to be ashamed. In
> doctrine it is Calvinistic and distinctly Evangelical. Its
> departures from the earlier creeds of Puritanism are not
> essential. In regard to church polity it asserts a *jure
> divino* Congregationalism with much positiveness. Dr.
> Stoughton, writing in 1884, affirmed it as his opinion that
> " no member of the denomination who has reached an
> advanced age can deny that these articles set forth the
> current belief of fifty years ago".

The churches and their ministers had, however, moved
away from the old Calvinistic doctrines, perhaps even
further away than the Declaration showed, for much of the
old phraseology still employed was interpreted in a
far looser way than would have satisfied Thomas Goodwin

1 *Creeds and Platforms of Congregationalism*, pp. 546, f.

or John Owen. Dale's view[1] of the 1833 attitude, based very largely upon John Stoughton's *Reminiscences,* cannot be improved upon. He points out that there was the same significant change in the attitude to the two Sacraments. The theory of an objective element in the Sacraments had more and more been discarded in favour of the subjective view, as can be plainly seen by putting the pertinent clauses in 1658 and 1833 side by side.

Of course, there were those who deplored the weakening of the old Calvinism, though they do not seem to, have been very vocal in the Assembly. R. W. Hamilton, of Leeds, was a vigorous thinker whose powerful advocacy of conservative theology was impeded by a florid and rhetorical style. Some of his words a year or two later aptly state his position : " The good old way, even to its ruts, will always be preferred by me to the road-making of the present day". He was specially severe on the " quest for novelty, the holders of crotchets, the pursuers after new lights ". About the Declaration he wrote thus to Algernon Wells :

> I do fear that there is creeping among us a refining method as to the great propoundings of the Gospel. The full-blooded dogma of the old school must be revived. Popery, Methodism, *etc.,* can speak of Divine sacrifice, " the blood of God "; our own hymns abound in the expressions, " God the mighty Maker died "; but there is a modern shrinkage from them. This is but a type of a class. Our Congregational Union symbol of faith is to me unsatisfactory and lamentable. Doctrinal and experimental purity ought to be everything to us, ends—Nonconformity but means to it. We are under close microscopic inspection. Many would come over to us, but they think there is a falling-off from our rigid patristic theology; not with me or you; but some departments are tainted.

It is probably true that the Declaration represented the average opinion in 1833, both in what it said and in not casting away familiar terms which no longer expressed living experience. It stood for the best part of a century as the outline of theology generally held by Congregationalists. It was printed separately in five editions

1 Dale, *History of Congregationalism,* p. 704.

(20,000 copies were sold in a year), an edition was prepared
for hanging in vestries, and another in Welsh. In 1835
another 5,000 copies were sold. In 1838 the first Colonial
missionaries were asking for copies, for they were finding
it very useful, and in 1840 the sale in the Colonies and at
home was still continuing. In 1858 the custom of printing
the Declaration in the *Congregational Year Book* began,
and there it remained long after it had possessed any
significance other than that of an historic document.

There were some, of course, whom it did not represent,
for there have always been those with a strong doctrinal
bent who have regretted the lack of virile theology in the
Congregational Churches. A boy of 18 in 1905 applied
for admission to the Theological College of which D. W.
Simon was Principal. The boy's school record, his
examination results, and what was hopefully and euphe-
mistically called a sermon, passed muster, but Simon
returned his answer to a question concerning his
theological beliefs, and asked that it should be amplified,
and enclosed the Declaration of 1833 for his guidance ! The
theological beliefs of the youth were of a very elementary
and amorphous kind. He believed that Christianity was
the most important thing in the world, and that he was
called to proclaim it, but he had neither the knowledge
nor the wish to commit himself to detailed theological
statements. He said so, and rather cheekily suggested
that it was to obtain such theological knowledge that he
was applying for admission to College, and he made very
little use of the Declaration of 1833. The youth was duly
admitted, and is now writing these words. Turning over
this experience in the light of Simon's attitude as revealed
in Dr. F. J. Powicke's biography,[1] it can be imagined how
the College Principal would feel this youthful ignorance
but another sign of Congregationalism's laxity and weak-
ness, for just about this time he is deploring " the proposed creedlessness of the new Constitution of the
Congregational Union ", and fearing that the day has
passed to get Congregationalism back to a strong doctrinal

1 p. 246; compare pp. 218 ff., 228.

position. Simon knew that he had few with him in this fight, and certain it is that there were no regrets when in 1918 motives of economy led to the omission of the Declaration from the *Year Book*.

Surveying the century, it is rather remarkable that theology plays so little part in the life of the Union. Apart from the *Rivulet* discussion in 1855-6, the "Religious Communion" debates in 1877-8, and the "New Theology" in the early years of the present century, organized Congregationalism has been but slightly concerned with theological speculation and development, despite the fact that during these years Fairbairn, Dale, and Forsyth have been among its most prominent figures.

VI. EARLY VOYAGES, 1833-1839.

ONCE the Union was formed it becomes difficult to classify its activities, this difficulty increasing as those activities swiftly multiply. In this chapter an attempt is made to summarize the development of the Union until its first Autumnal Meeting at Birmingham in October, 1839. Reading about the early Assemblies of the Union, it must continually be borne in mind that they are very unlike the Assemblies of to-day. During this first decade the Congregational Library, not a large building, was quite big enough to house those present, though in 1839 the numbers had increased to 183 Ministerial Delegates and Visitors, 54 Lay Delegates and Visitors, and 28 Theological Students (42 students, from seven different Colleges, had been present in the previous year). John Stoughton has described the quiet, homely gatherings, with the Chairman sitting beneath Thomas Wilson's portrait, the fathers talking in easy colloquial style, and the young students all eyes and ears as they gazed with becoming reverence. The day began early, and the Tuesday meeting was generally adjourned until Friday at 7 a.m., at which hour the delegates seem to have breakfasted together, the session beginning at 8 a.m. Lunch seems to have been served on the spot too, " On the cloth being withdrawn " being the usual introduction to the Minutes of the afternoon session. Thus, in 1839 : "about two o'clock (N.B., the meeting began at 8.0 !) a large number of ministers and gentlemen sat down in the Library to a cold dinner provided by the Committee of the Union. On the cloth being withdrawn . . . "

The Committee meetings, too, seem to have been of a very informal kind. By 1835 the Committee consisted of 17 ministers and 17 laymen, with power to add, but all ministers and delegates were invited to attend !

It was speedily decided that the Tuesday meeting should be preceded by a religious service on the Monday night, and on the Monday evening in 1834 the devotions were conducted by John Angell James, George Redford, and T. Stratten of Hull, Algernon Wells giving an address from *Zech*. 12^8. It was soon found, further, that deputations had better be received on Monday so as to leave Tuesday free for business.

The fullness of May Meeting week finds interesting illustration when Dr. Matheson suggests in the *Congregational Magazine* that during the week the old students of the various colleges should meet together. While approving the suggestion, the Editor thinks it impracticable, and gives a programme of the week's engagements :

Monday.	4.0 p.m.	Open Union Committee, to which all delegates invited.
Tuesday.	8.0 a.m.	Breakfast.
	9.0 a.m. to 3 p.m.	Annual Assembly.
	3.0 p.m.	Dinner.
	4.0 p.m.	Open meeting of Directors of L.M.S.
	6.0 p.m.	Irish Evangelical Society's Annual Meeting.
Wednesday.		L.M.S. The Annual Anniversary Services, with Social Meeting between.
Thursday.		Annual Meeting of L.M.S. (It is just possible a " plain dinner " could be wedged in here, before the L.M.S. "Church Service ".)
Friday.	9.0 a.m.	Union Assembly.
	11.0 a.m.	Colonial Missionary Society Anniversary.
	3.0 p.m.	Union Dinner in Library.
	6.0 p.m.	Various sacramental services.

The Editor goes on to give advice to the L.M.S. :

It is our deliberate conviction that the directors of the Missionary Society should make extensive changes in their anniversary arrangements. Forty years ago there were no anniversary services but those of the London Missionary Society, and good sermons were then far more rare than happily they are in the present day. The Lord's Day preceding, or that following the anniversary meeting, should be appropriated to collections in every chapel in London connected with the Society. This is done not only

by our Baptist and Wesleyan brethren in the Metropolis
for their Missions, but we believe also by all the great
auxiliaries to the London Missionary Society in the
country. One, or at the most two sermons would be
sufficient during the week. The directors and friends of
the London Missionary Society must learn that as its
support is now thrown almost entirely upon the Congregational churches, so they must allow their pastors and
more active members opportunity to deliberate on the best
means of promoting the prosperity of that denomination,
which, under God, will be the means of promoting the
welfare of the Missionary Society.

One of the first customs to be established was that of
addressing an Annual Pastoral Letter to the churches, the
first of these being sent out from the Assembly in 1834.
At the previous Assembly the task of preparing the Letter
was entrusted to a little group of ministers in the Essex
Union, and it was fitting that it should be presented on
their behalf by Algernon Wells of Coggeshall, who was to
be the first paid Secretary of the Union, and one who had
most to do with moulding its policy. The astute
diplomacy which marked these early years is once more
made evident in the selection of the group for the preparation of the second letter. Lancashire had just joined the
Union, and so to Raffles and other Liverpool ministers was
given the duty—and the privilege—of preparing the
Union's message. This system of delegation to a group
was followed for many years, the subject of the letters
being left to the writers. Naturally they touched on a
great variety of points, and they contain many valuable
indications of the state of the churches at the time. The
Lancashire address urges that

next to the full and plain exhibition of the great doctrines
of the Gospel, there is nothing of greater importance than
a close and prudent adherence to those Scriptural principles
by which our churches are professedly regulated.

It exhorts the churches to be zealous to preserve

a Scriptural purity of communion . . . they only who have
embraced the Saviour . . . are entitled to Christian
fellowship, or qualified for its duties and enjoyments.
The admission of those who are strangers to the power of
the Gospel is in every way injurious.

F

It stresses " the necessity of a faithful administration of Scriptural discipline ", which is " indispensable to the continued prosperity of the churches." This discipline should be the act of the whole church. The letter goes on to say, " We have no defence to offer for any details inconsistent with the imperative directions of the Sacred Volume ". It holds that the delegation of power to a few people is dangerous. If churches adhere to New Testament directions the feeblest societies will be preserved. The 1836 letter strongly presses the point that for the adequate working of the voluntary principle " great attainments in personal piety are absolutely necessary".

The sales of subsequent letters fell off very considerably, and it seems to have been felt that as the years went by the letters might become desultory, and so from 1839 onwards a definite subject was given to the group appointed, the one for that year being " The Choice of Pastors ".

In general, the period was one of wise and persuasive advocacy of the wisdom of union and of the benefits to be gained by it. Recognizing the timidity of many of the churches and the widespread prevalence of anxious fears that independence would be lost and the scriptural basis of the churches destroyed, the Committee took no step without reiterating its belief in the fundamental Congregational principle. It realized that the advantages of fellowship had to be shown to be not incompatible with the maintenance of freedom. Gradually success attended these patient efforts. Many ministers and churches anticipated the Associations to which they belonged by joining directly with the general Union. The Associations which had stood out came in year by year—North Devon in 1833, Derby, Lancashire, and Suffolk in 1834, Leicester and Rutland, and Monmouthshire in 1835, East Devon in 1837, Staffordshire in 1838, the East Riding of Yorkshire, and Hull and North Lincolnshire in 1839. In this latter year John Alexander[1] of Norwich announced that

---

1 Stoughton's *Reminiscences,* p. 9, is wrong in saying that Alexander was "if not one of the fathers, one of the founders of the Union".

his district had begun to look on the Union more favourably, and that he himself had been warmly opposed to it,
but had now changed his mind. As the Associations
came in their ministers were at once drawn into service for
the Union, and generally became enthusiastic supporters.

It was not until the end of this decade, however, that
the Union could be said to be safely launched. Many
times the Committee used words showing that they recognized the situation as precarious, though hopeful. In 1837
they say that if this attempt to form a general Union
should fail it would utterly discourage, if not absolutely
prevent, any future design for the same object : " it would
go far to prove a Congregational Union an impossibility".
Probably the turning point came when Wells was
appointed Secretary in 1837. He was a true statesman,
and he had realized that it was through efficient county
organizations that a general Union could best function.
One of his first tasks was to prepare an address to the
pastors and churches, from which words have been quoted
in the paragraph above. In the address he outlines the
ideal and policy of the Union, and it deserves extended
quotation.

He points out that

> there are great and most valuable religious objects to be
> attained (by union) which can in no other way be even
> attempted : and that if our churches continue isolated
> bodies, not uniting and co-operating for great objects
> common to them all, they will remain destitute of the most
> efficient of all means for promoting their own prosperity
> and increase, and for acting with happy effect on other
> religious communities, and on the opinions, the liberties,
> and the welfare of mankind at large. The moral force
> arising from the unconstrained union of great numbers of
> Christian ministers and churches all of one mind in their
> views of doctrine and discipline, and of enterprises for
> advancing the triumphs of the Gospel, is incalculably
> great. This power will be felt with solemn, elevating
> influence, when the united body assembles for devout
> fellowship, and calm discussion of great interests and plans.
> It will be felt in the declarations of opinions and purposes
> put forth by the assembled brotherhood with no assump-
> tion of authority, either over each other, or over other men.

It will be felt in the separate operations of each individual belonging to the great fraternity as an animating impulse and sustaining power.   It is thus that power is gained, while liberty is not infringed, for individual freedom and associated power are not incompatible . . . The Committee believe that Congregational churches are the only elements out of which it is possible to construct a union combining all the advantages of separate and united action. The distinct, indestructible independency of each separate church effectually guarantees liberty.   The happy oneness of opinion prevailing among them all on every important subject is the firm basis and the easy facility for their union. They may construct among themselves all the organization that is necessary without being injurious, and they *can* establish no more.   The mere attempt to carry association to the point at which the liberty of our churches would even seem to be endangered would be fatal to all union whatever.

The letter goes on to outline the objects of the Union in more detail.   The Committee recognize that some Congregationalists feel that the effort to spread their own distinctive views of truth and church order is sectarian. They do not agree, believing that to improve and to enlarge their own denomination

is a primary indisputable duty of Congregational Christians.   If those views of doctrine and church order, from attachment to which we have separated from other Christian churches, are not deemed by us of such importance and truth as to be worthy of strenuous efforts for their defence and spread, then our existence as a distinct body of Christians is needless and sectarian.

They point out that other denominations endeavour to propagate their views, and

every other large community of Christians has its distinct organization for its own denominational improvement; its own separate denominational mission to the heathen; its own distinct denominational efforts in England, Ireland, and the Colonies.   And the Committee feel it cannot be just that Congregational Churches, who, late and slow, are at length meditating for themselves movements in imitation of the efforts of other bodies of Christians each to build its own house, should for this suffer the reproach of especial sectarianism : and when that taunt proceeds from members of their own body, it is to be presumed it must originate in want of due consideration.

Looking back, the Committee speak of the " seven successive general assemblies " which have proved delightful seasons of holy fellowship " ; the sending and reception of delegates to and from the United States and other countries; the commencement of the Colonial Mission; and the publication of the *Hymn Book*. They are in a measure discouraged by the fact that a very considerable number of pastors and churches still hesitate to join the Union. The want of a more vigorous and general co-operation has caused them to suspend a big effort to discharge all chapel debts, while they are unable to commence the plans for Home Missionary operations which they believe to be of paramount importance. The work of the Union has also been handicapped by the sparing way in which even the churches in the Union have contributed funds. The great need is organization, which is " first, second, and third in importance and necessity ". This organization, however, is merely making effective the familiar and only organization desirable or requisite— the County and District Associations at present existing. It is of such Associations that the Union consists, and if they could become universal and efficient, then the machinery of the general body would be complete. The Union desires to conduct all the correspondence of its Home Missionary work through the County Associations. It does not " design to undervalue or supersede them ". They are to be " the instrumentality by which all its operations are to be conducted ". A " very large proportion " of the churches, however, were not united in any Association at all. Many Associations were very inefficient : some were formed of ministers only, others of ministers and churches : some undertake Home Missions and village preaching, others have no aims beyond friendly intercourse. That Associations should become universal is the desideratum. They should not be too big, and should include both pastors and churches : ministers could have their own meetings for fellowship, but these should be additional. Every Association should have Home Missions, forming new churches and increasing old ones by the labour of evangelists, and the Associations should be connected in fellowship in and through the general Union.

This letter from Wells brought into the open general criticism of the Union. In the *Patriot* " A Layman ", who was understood to be a member of the legal profession, wrote three letters, to which Wells replied. Mr. R. Peek intervened in the discussion on the side of the critic of the Union. This controversy was so important that the *Congregational Magazine* for 1837 printed the whole of it, though it took forty pages of its Supplement. " A Layman " complained that all the papers, the *Congregational Magazine,* the *Eclectic,* and the *Patriot,* were on the side of the Union, and that it was impossible to state the opposing case. The *Congregational Magazine,* although faithfully supported by the denomination generally, had become the reporter, the record, and the advocate of the Union; it was " not the publication of the Independent denomination ". The editor replied that he " has laboured now for twelve years to make it such ". The Magazine has provided the only list of churches and pastors that has been available, while its contributors have represented " the learning, intelligence, and piety of the denomination ". Nevertheless, no communication from those sections of the denomination which have not joined the Union has been excluded.

" A Layman " holds that the Union does not embody and represent the majority of the members of the churches *on any system of equal and adequate representation.* The Union, it is admitted, has not met with the success its founders expected. It should never be forgiven for using the term " Congregational " instead of " Independent ". Especially culpable has been the decision to make the Colonial Missionary Society a Committee of the Union, and to obtain £1,000 from the London Missionary Society, a non-sectarian Society, for a Society merely denominational.

Wells's first reply defended the *Congregational Magazine,* but said that neither it, nor the *Eclectic,* nor the *Patriot* was denominational in the sense that it was

controlled by the Union Committee. Their support of the
Union was entirely spontaneous, and the result of
conviction. The facts of the case were these :

> The whole body of the London ministers, with exceed-
> ingly few exceptions, have sanctioned and sustained it ;
> the great majority of names of country brethren, known
> as the most active and influential of our body in their
> respective localities, stand recorded as present at its annual
> assemblies, and bearing part in its important transactions ;
> it has received cordial recognition from the associated
> brotherhoods of the Congregational churches of America,
> Scotland, and Ireland ; it has maintained a public standing
> for seven years before the church and the world, as a
> recognized organization of our churches, without, as far as
> I know, a single protest from any quarter, or even a single
> paper calling in question its principles or proceedings,
> being ever sent for insertion to the known organ of the
> Union, and the professed organ of the body at large.

Wells had no difficulty in defending the reference to the
Colonial Society, nor did he hesitate to support the
employment of the term " Congregational ", which, he
points out, was used in almost all the standard documents
of the 17th century. He showed that dread of the growing
power of the Union was misplaced, while undue ministerial influence was avoided by the fact that for every
hundred ministers there would be two hundred and fifty to
three hundred lay representatives.

" A Layman " replied that most of Wells's defence
was irrelevant. The admission that very few churches had
sent money for the support of the Union was a confession
of its failure.

> Close pockets have not been the usual proof of recog-
> nizing adhesion furnished by the Independents.

He held that the votes of the Associations to affiliate with
the Union were not really representative of the churches,
and pointed out that there was no uniformity in the
constitution of these Associations.

> The Congregationalism of America, or even that of
> Scotland or Ireland, has existed and grown too near power-
> ful Presbyterian influences and habits for the professors of
> our principles in those countries to be cited as decisive
> examples for us.

At this point Mr. Peek contended that ecclesiastical power had been injurious to religious liberty, and that it would be so in the case of the Union. Already the Union was acquiring revenues from its publications, and

> It appears to me as by no means unlikely that the Union may be made a corporate body and a court of appeal to decide exclusively on ecclesiastical matters pertaining to Dissenters. One of Her Majesty's Ministers asked me the other day whether Dissenters would consent to form a Corporation in which all their chapels and trust property might be vested. This would never become extinct, and save the expense of trust deeds.

He believed in local Associations, but advised " all County Associations to pause before they sacrifice their privileges to a centralized convention in London ".

Wells retorted that the Union had been formed on lines suited to the free genius of the churches in being built upon existing Associations. No Association or church was required " to surrender, in order to fraternize with the Union, one single particle of right, power, or liberty ". Non-union and the break-up of the present federation of Associations and churches would be a great reproach.

" A Layman " pressed the point as to whether the Union was one " of Associations only, or of churches joined by authority of Associations and other churches joining separately in spite of that authority ". He reiterated the contention often urged by others :

> In the infancy or rise of ecclesiastical systems, the beginnings are small; the pretensions of the founders are fair; the motives pure; the objects to be accomplished good; but in time a great and commanding power, capable of being sadly diverted in its exercise, is almost imperceptibly established.

He was not opposed to the churches in a particular neighbourhood uniting " for the purpose of counsel and influence respecting both doctrine and discipline ", and he objected entirely to the common description of Independent Churches as " isolated ".

> What then are the Associations? What is our co-operation in missions? What the voluntary and unshackled interchange of services between the ministers

of every part of the country? What the kind of reception of the deputations of all our benevolent societies? What the unquestioning acknowledgment of the pastoral and Church recommendations of each independent Church by all others? An isolated Independent Church! Where does it exist? Where is there any proof of any material discrepancy of opinion or action in the Independent Churches?

Such of the objects contemplated by the Union as were unquestionably good could be better accomplished by " free unecclesiastically constituted societies. There is a Home Missionary Society already. Why may there not be a separate and independent Colonial Missionary Society ? "

The reply was that such union as " A Layman " described was not evident to those outside the churches, and it was necessary to present it in some visible form.

The correspondence must be read in full in order to realize the enthusiasm and skill with which Wells espoused the Union's cause. At once he began the work of stimulating the local Associations. In 1838 they presented reports to the Assembly, and these were warmly welcomed, especially that of Worcestershire, which reported that all the churches and preaching stations in the area had been visited. The Associations were asked to send up their rules to Headquarters, and in 1839 the Committee said that the more they knew of the denomination the more they were impressed with the importance of County Associations. Wells himself visited some of the counties in that year.

At this point it may be well to look at those who had been called to official positions. The Union began with three Secretaries, two ministers and a layman. The layman was Joshua Wilson, of whom we have seen a good deal already. He held office for a short time only, being replaced in 1836 by Joseph Wontner, who was "Cash Secretary". The ministers were Arthur Tidman and Joseph Turnbull, neither of whom served for long, Tidman resigning in 1833 and afterwards becoming the devoted Secretary of the London Missionary Society, and Turnbull, who had moved from Bromley to Brighton, being succeeded in 1834 by John Blackburn. Tidman's successor was William Stern Palmer of Harecourt. In 1836 the duties of the office were divided thus : Blackburn (Home Secretary), Palmer (Minute Secretary), Wontner (Cash Secretary), and it was announced that another Secretary was needed to attend to foreign correspondence. At this time several important matters of business had to be held over because the Secretaries had other and prior duties, and the need for a paid Secretary became clear. After much consideration Algernon Wells was in 1837 appointed to be Secretary both of the Union and of the newly-formed Colonial Missionary Society. It was intended that he should devote the whole of his time to these duties, but in 1839 he accepted the pastorate of a church at Clapton and thenceforward returned part of his salary to the Union.

Nobody reading through the Minutes of the Union's proceedings will be inclined to minimize the part played by Wells. Before becoming Secretary he had not only been a successful pastor and seen his chapel at Coggeshall twice enlarged, but he had also thrown himself heart and soul into the life of the missionary organizations in Essex. He had some hesitation about a Union of greater area than that of a county, and attended the first meeting of the general Union as a doubter. His skilful advocacy of the Union through the period of his Secretaryship, which lasted until his death in 1850, shows how completely his doubts, had been removed. Thomas Binney, his great friend and co-secretary with him of the Colonial Missionary Society, thus summed up his qualities when preaching his funeral sermon :

> In his combined offices of secretary to the Union and to the Colonial Missionary Society . . . it is hardly possible to award him excessive praise. His wise suggestions, his efficient plans, his judgment in counsel, his prudence in action, his full official preparations for business, whether of private committees or public meetings, his talent for correspondence, his tact in difficulties, his beautiful addresses, printed or spoken, his bearing and deportment, spirit and tone—everything belonging to him, without him, and about him, marked him out as one whom God had peculiarly

qualified for that kind of work which he did so well, and of which, therefore, he was called upon to do so much.

Stoughton was another of Wells's great friends. He tells us that, like Thomas Aquinas, he had "the gift of tears", and "was apt to weep on public occasions when his heart was touched, or his carefully finished plans were interrupted". What consternation there would be in an Assembly of the Union in 1931 were a Secretary thus to reveal his feelings!

The first Treasurer of the Union was Benjamin Hanbury, whose official duties in these years seem to have been little more than to hold the deficit, while the "Cash Secretary" attended to the details. Hanbury, we imagine, was more interested in early Puritan literature than in the details of the Union's finance; he easily surpassed all his contemporaries in knowledge of the history of the Independents. He had no gifts of style, either in speech or writing, and it was perhaps a mistake for the Union to take responsibility for the publication of his *Historical Memorials of the Independents* as one of its first literary ventures. A small History, to be attached to the *Declaration of Faith and Order,* had originally been planned, but Hanbury dug deeper and deeper, receiving annual congratulations for his laborious researches, which at last appeared in three volumes in 1839, 1842, and 1845. These volumes are of the utmost value to the student, but they are, in Stoughton's words,

> not of a sensational character, not such as would keep young ladies awake on a summer's afternoon or a winter's night, but full of good hard stuff, which young brethren of an historical turn might put to good account.

Repeated efforts were made to whip up subscribers, but the volumes were disposed of with difficulty. An interesting sequel to the story of this protracted publication is to be found in the action of the Union in 1864, when, in appreciation of the work of the local Secretaries at the autumnal meetings in Hull, they presented them with copies of Hanbury's *Historical Memorials*!

Nevertheless, Hanbury was an asset to the Union alike in his appearance, his erudition, and his character, and he remained its Treasurer until his death in 1864.

Finance.

It has already been suggested that there was not much
to treasure in the early years. Churches took very little
notice of requests to send subscriptions, and the first financial statement (1833) shows an income of £9, and a deficit
of £18. In 1834 the figures were swelled by items referring
to a deputation to America, but though some churches and
Associations sent contributions, the income from churches
and individual donations, even in 1839, was only £117, by
which time the deficit was £457. It would have been considerably larger had not money begun to come in from the
sale of publications, and especially from the profits of the
Hymn Book, which produced £134 in 1838 and £330 in
1839. The first legacy that came to the Union was in 1838,
when Dr. Fletcher gave £50 from a residuary legacy at
his disposal. In this year the Secretary's salary (£150)
began to figure, and the Report drew special attention to
finance. It said that if the churches would but furnish
£2 or £3 each, a sum would be available for publication
purposes, Home and Colonial Missions, chapel debts, and
the relief and superannuation of ministers. Every
Association ought to get a sum from each of its churches
annually, and remit it to the Union. The London churches
were bearing more than their share of the burden, having
contributed to date £549 as against £197 from the country.

Publications.

From finance, we turn naturally to Hymn Books, the
two things having a much closer relationship in the life of
the Congregational and other denominations than the
casual observer would suspect. In 1833 the suggestion of
a denominational Hymn Book, as a Supplement to Watts's
Psalms and Hymns, was approved "it being desirable to
produce a greater uniformity in public praise, and also to
supply a variety of hymns adapted to our ecclesiastical
polity, which are not found in ordinary collections". Joseph
Fletcher, John Blackburn, Henry Rogers, and Josiah
Conder were appointed a Committee to prepare such a
Book, the profits to go to the Union. Two of these de-

clined, and 8 others were added in the course of preparation, but most of the work fell upon the Editor, Conder, to
whom a tribute is paid in the Report of 1836. There was
some delay owing to the fact that many urged that the
best Psalms and Hymns of Watts should be incorporated
in the one volume, but finally it was agreed to proceed
with a volume supplementary to Watts. In 1835 the
publication of the volume was delayed for the Assembly's
comments, and it was published in the following year.
The book contained 620 hymns, 500 for public worship, the
rest for domestic and private use. In 1837 it was reported
that 25,000 copies had already been sold, and a special
message of appreciation was received from Carrs Lane,
Birmingham, saying that "an enlivening freshness has
been imparted to our psalmody, and a new impulse given
to our praise". By 1839 the numbers sold had risen to
40,000. Meanwhile, the revision of Watts's *Psalms and
Hymns* had been proposed. The revision proposals met
with general favour, a correspondent with the familiar
initials "J. W." writing in the *Congregational Magazine*
to urge that the Independents must not be as blindly
attached to Watts as the Anglicans were to the *Book of
Common Prayer*. But the Committee needed more assurance before they proceeded with the task, and it was only
when it appeared that the revision was extensively
approved that a sub-committee was appointed to go over
the first book of hymns and print a small experimental
edition to circulate among pastors. If the Union declined
to publish it, this edition was to be the property of those
who had done the revision. They hoped that

> a judicious and strictly limited revision may be effected,
> which shall on the one hand remove all that is seriously
> objectionable, without, on the other, giving occasion of
> complaint to the most scrupulous, or the most ardent
> admirers of our venerated psalmodist.

A Tune Book was a natural corollary and it was agreed
that the churches should

> adopt every lawful means to improve our method of public
> praise, so that persons of correct musical taste may not be
> repelled from our churches by our neglect of simple harmony
> in that delightful part of the service of God.

The other publications do not require much mention. The *Congregational Magazine,* 1s. monthly, was the accredited organ of the Union, although the Union had no financial responsibility for it.

The "Congregational Lectures" were begun in 1833, but had no official connexion with the Union, a few generous individuals associated with the Library providing a fee of a hundred guineas for the lecturer, and apparently arranging for publication. The first lecturer was Dr. Wardlaw, whose subject was "Christian Ethics". Series of lectures were given year by year, with some intermissions, until resources failed.

The sales of the *Declaration of Faith and Order* have already been noticed. The Annual Address started off in promising style, 10.856 copies of the Primary Address being sold in the year of publication. The Second Address went to two editions, but only 5,500 copies in all, and less than 3,000 were sold of the Fourth and Fifth. This gave rise to a cry—to be repeated often and often during the century to follow—that it was to the ministers the Committe must look for the success of all denominational efforts.

> Will our ministerial brethren allow the Committee kindly to hint that the success of this our Union in every respect, and particularly in the circulation and usefulness of its addresses, depends almost entirely on them? If our ministers cordially approve the Union, and zealously co-operate to promote its efficiency, it cannot fail, with the divine favour, to prosper, and become a great and lasting blessing to our whole denomination; but there is no other agency, except that of our pastors, through which it can be sustained, and effect its salutary purposes.

The only other publication of note, apart from the *Hymn Book,* was the narrative of the travels of Reed and Matheson in the United States and Canada[1]. Lack of means, as well as fear of encroaching on the rights of the individual church, delayed many projects. As early as 1834 it was resolved to prepare :

1. A series of cheap scriptural tracts, adapted to the circumstances and duties of Congregational Churches.

[1] See below, p. 97.

Subjects suggested were "The choice of pastors and deacons"; "The neglect of the Lord's Supper"; "Offences among brethren, with the scriptural means of their prevention and remedy".

2. One or two sets of Catechisms, containing the doctrinal sentiments and ecclesiastical polity of our churches.

3. A volume containing the history of our body, and the documents that belong to it.

These projects slumbered for a time, not even an offer of £25 towards £100 for prizes for Catechisms accelerating publication. The Committee were concerned about the books read by young people, who were turning to reading insidious attacks on religion which could only be counteracted by "furnishing a supply of literary aliment that shall be both alluring and helpful. We call on slumbering genius to awake, to unlock its treasures and pour out its wealth at the feet of the Saviour". Before this it had been pointed out (*Congregational Magazine*, 1833), that the Independents were failing to make adequate literary and scholastic contributions to the religious life of the times. The Anglicans supported literature munificently, and had a corps of writers ever ready, and *fas est et ab hoste doceri*.

Excessive caution is seen when an Association suggested the publication of an Order of Service for Marriages, the Committee replying that it would feel it presumptuous to undertake this unless directed by the Assembly.

Generally speaking, however, it is finance that holds back publication. After the first Autumnal Assembly in 1839, when a decided advance was made, it will be seen that publication proceeds more rapidly. Meanwhile, as property in the way of stock began to accumulate, Trustees had to be appointed on behalf of the Union, the four appointed in 1836 being Dr. James Baldwin Brown, John Remington Mills, Joshua Wilson, and Benjamin Hanbury.

Ministers' Assurance Society.

The small amount of money that found its way to the Union is in some measure to be explained by other heavy demands which were being made on Congregationalists in these years. A large part of the income of the London Missionary Society, which varied from £37,000 to £51,000 in the seven years before 1833, had come from them. That there were munificent supporters of chapel building has been seen, and these same men were largely responsible for the purchase and equipment of the Congregational Library. In 1833 it was reported that the proposal to raise £10,000 for a denominational building had not received the support expected, and it was suggested that the denomination should be satisfied for the present with the use of the Library. Instead, it was proposed that £5,000 be raised for a Ministers' Assurance Society. Thus early steps were taken to carry out the suggestion that one of the first objects of the Union should be provision for Ministerial Superannuation. In 1832 the Committee considered the possibility of forming a Fire and Life Assurance Society. The institution of a *Fire* Assurance Society was found too risky, and was immediately abandoned, but investigations were made at once on the other line. Three actuaries were called into consultation, and they drafted a scheme which was widely circulated. It offered a great variety of options : the minister could insure his own life or his wife's, could provide for an annuity for his widow or a deferred annuity for himself, could obtain endowments for his children when they reached the age of fourteen or twenty-one, or could provide for deferred temporary annuities to meet the cost of their education. Payments could be made annually or in a lump sum ; the insurances effected could be not less than £50 nor more than £1,000. No purpose would be served by printing the detailed tables, but Mr. Owen Kentish, the present actuary of the Union, who has examined them, states that they are based on sound actuarial principles, and embody almost all the tables found in a modern Life Office prospectus.

It was estimated that voluntary contributions amounting to £5,000 were needed for the establishment of this Society.

In 1833 this scheme was approved by the Assembly and it was suggested that should the number of ministers

THOMAS RAFFLES.

JOHN ANGELL JAMES

immediately joining be as many as 400 or 500, this £5,000 would probably be untouched. In the following year it was reported to the Assembly that the Society could not be established unless and until 300 assurances were ready to be effected. It was pointed out that the benefit of the Society was not confined to ministers : congregations would benefit, too, as the annual interest of the subscribed capital "and a portion of the anticipated profits of the publications of the Congregational Union" would constitute an Aid Fund from which grants would be made to assist poor churches in making suitable provision for the declining years of their pastors, and in rendering them financial assistance in providing for their dependent families also. Contingent promises were made totalling £360, including £100 each from John Angell James and H. F. Burder, and £50 from Joshua Wilson.

In 1835 it appeared that there were insuperable obstacles in the way of the scheme, and the experiment was abandoned as impracticable. It was found that the established Assurance Offices could offer better terms, while the small numbers in the Congregational Society would make administration expensive. In announcing the failure the Committee expressed the hope that a benevolent fund would be formed to assist ministers to insure in Offices already established.

Another demand made on Congregationalists at this time was that for Colonial Missions. The Union had speedily set to work to carry out the aim of getting into contact with Christians in other lands. Joseph Turnbull visited the Continent, and in 1835 gave a long report of the state of the Protestant Churches in France, Germany, and Switzerland. Interchange of correspondence and delegates with the Unions of Scotland and Ireland at once commenced. It was with the churches in the United States, Presbyterian and Congregational, however, that the most important channel of communication was opened. Americans were present at most of the Assemblies, and in 1834 Andrew Reed and James Matheson were appointed delegates to the United States. Their visit, which they describe in the two-

volume *Narrative* mentioned above, resulted in a large
American deputation to England in the next year, and a resolution (not put into effect) to interchange deputations
every six years. But neither this resolution nor the appreciation of the deputation's visit by the American churches
was its most important outcome. Reed and Matheson
crossed over into Canada and were greatly impressed with
the need for the Congregational witness there. Before they
returned the Union had been approached by the Rev. F.
Miller of Hobart Town, Tasmania, asking for help in
Australasia, while British missionaries in Cape Town had
also been in communication with the Union. These
appeals, together with the advocacy of Reed and Matheson
and the powerful support of Thomas Binney, brought the
whole colonial enterprise before the Union. It was agreed
that "some missionary object" was "necessary to give
completeness to the Union", but then the question arose:

1. Should the Union father Colonial Missions or ask
   the London Missionary Society to continue its
   help?
2. Had not the rural areas of England a prior claim,
   and should not a more vigorous attempt be made
   to co-ordinate and extend the work of the Home
   Missionary Society and the County Associations?

The London Missionary Society agreed to grant
£1,000 for Colonial work in 1835, to be administered by a
special Colonial Committee, but this grant was not renewed. It was therefore proposed to form a Colonial
Missionary Society, but in a resolution before the Union
welcoming the project emphasis was thrown on the need
for Home Missions. Wells and Redford urged that the
Colonial Society should be part of the Union, and after
long discussions and negotiations it was so agreed, and
when the Society was formed in May, 1836, it was as the
Colonial Committee of the Congregational Union—Blackburn, Wells, Redford, and J. A. James being among those
who took part in the inaugural meeting, others including
Edward Baines, M.P. and Binney. The Treasurer of the
Society was J. Remington Mills, and the Secretaries Reed,

Binney, and the Rev. George Gull, Wells being added (as a paid official) in the following year. The first meeting of the Union in 1837 was a valedictory service for T. Q. Stowe, about to depart to South Australia, Wells giving the farewell charge to him, but the Committee had to complain that the churches had not supported their adopted child, the Colonial, and had thus disappointed the expectations of the officials, who did not think that they would need to be *goaded into sending supplies*. They appealed to the churches for an annual collection for "their own Colonial Missions", which now had annual liabilities but no annual income. The first Colonial Report, 1837, shows that £1,102 had been received.

In the following year the Constitution of the Society was determined. It was called the "Colonial Missionary Society" in connexion with the "Congregational Union of England and Wales", its objects being described as

> to promote Evangelical Religion among British or other European Settlers, and their descendants, in the Colonies of Great Britain, in accordance with the doctrine and discipline of Independent or Congregational Churches.

The officers of the Colonial, chosen at its annual meeting, were to be *ex officio* members of the Union Committee, and vice versa, and an Annual Report of the work was to be presented to the Union Assembly. The income of the Society in 1838/9 was £2,409 (including subscriptions and donations £1,647, collections £709) and the deficit £760. It was estimated that the income required was £3,500 to £4,000 a year.

It has already been indicated that to some minds the claims of Home Missions were paramount. There were thousands of villages where Congregationalism was unrepresented, hundreds where the only ministerial representative of Christianity was an incumbent of the Established Church whose interests were in sports and pleasure and society rather than in his work. Many of the County Associations employed itinerant evangelists and maintained preaching stations, but there were large areas where nothing at all was done. Twenty of the counties spent in a year £5,549 for the diffusion of the Gospel, maintained

579 preaching stations, and taught over 53,000 scholars. The Assembly decided that sufficient was not being done, and asked the Committee to consider a general system of Home Missions. First, however, came the question of chapel debts. Where chapels had been built, often they had not been paid for, and it was generally felt that one of the first tasks of the Union must be to remove the scandal caused by pastoral begging in London and the larger cities. In 1833 a Committee of Dorset men was asked to report on the question, John Brown presenting the Report in 1834. It contained proposals the Assembly was not at once prepared to adopt, and it was referred to the Committee. In the following year it was suggested to the churches and Associations that collecting by the personal application of ministers was objectionable and ought to be superseded, and that the success of the Baptist Building Fund and of the recent efforts of the Welsh churches to liquidate their debts was encouraging. Practical proposals were that there should be co-operation between the churches and ministers of London and those of the country; that a number of County Associations should form Provincial Unions which should raise their own funds and deal with chapel cases in their own areas, and that these provinces should be Southern, Western, Central, North-Eastern, and North-Western. No case was to be eligible for a grant unless recommended by an Association, and every Association should form an Auxiliary Fund Society to deal with the matter. A province with funds in hand could make grants to needy cases in another province.

It was also decided to ascertain the total amount of the debts on chapels. By 1836 twenty-five counties, including those with the heaviest debts, had sent in returns. The total, estimated at two-thirds of the whole, was £57,024. A Metropolitan Chapel Fund Association was started, and similar steps taken in Manchester.

The general question of Home Missions, which had become even more urgent with the rise of the Tractarian movement in the Anglican Church, was then faced. In the words of the Committee:

The Congregational Churches of England must not look supinely on, and see the semi-papal doctrines of Apostolic succession and sacramental efficacy spread over this land, and added to the already too numerous causes that are operating fatally in the destruction of the soul of Englishmen, without vigorous efforts to diffuse their own more healthful theology, their own more scriptural ministry and polity.

The Committee was "impressed with the vast extent of ignorance and irreligion", and recognized that "arguments on church polity are but imperfectly understood by the multitude, but they will love the Church best which cares for them most". Much attention was given to the subject in 1838, but tact and delicate handling were required. How to secure that more should be done through the General Union without depreciating the services of the Home Missionary Society and the Associations was a problem that called for all the Committee's skill. While they were considering it, £100 was offered for a Prize Essay on condition that the Union would give a second prize of £25, the subject to be "Lay Preaching and Agency for the Spread of the Gospel in connexion with Congregational Churches around the localities in which they are placed" There were to be three judges, one of whom was to be a layman, and the Union selected James Bennett, Joseph Fletcher, and Joshua Wilson. Possibly the last-named was the "thoughtful and zealous Christian gentleman" who, having been "much impressed with the spiritual ignorance and wretchedness of great multitudes of our countrymen", had offered the prize. The prizes were won by an anonymous person (the adjudicators "attested his respectability"; as a matter of fact, he was Dr. John Campbell), and Dr. Matheson, the Secretary of the Home Missionary Society, and their Essays were duly published.

In 1839 it was reported that an attempt to connect the Home Missionary Society with the Union had failed. Although the Society was managed for the most part by Independents and got almost the whole of its support from Independents, it had been founded on an open basis, and that basis its management refused to forsake. It was strongly felt that the Union should take some action, however, so that the churches might be as one community, the strong caring for the weak, and the formation of a Congregational Home Missionary Society was urged. Eventually it was decided to have a Special Assembly of the Union in a provincial city in October, 1839, to discuss Home Missions. The Annual Letter touched on the subject, though its special topic was the "causes that limit or impair ministerial efficiency, arising from the people". It suggested that members ought to invite the multitudes who neglect the Sabbath to come to worship, for "a personal invitation to attend can scarcely be given by a minister consistently with feelings of delicacy and propriety"! There is a good deal in the Letter about the "humbler classes", and "extra free accommodation for the poor", which suggests that Congregationalism was not making a great deal of impression on the masses of the people. To the next chapter we leave the further consideration of this problem.

Some steps were taken during these years to carry out two more of the objects set forth in the Plan of Union.

1.   The Gathering of Statistics.

In 1834 the resources of the Union were insufficient to send out schedules of enquiry to every part of the country, but they were sent to six agricultural and six manufacturing districts. Appeals are constantly made to the County Associations for figures, but the response is far from general, this being attributed to the imperfection of their organization. In 1836 the returns from Bucks., S. Devon, Kent, Lancs., Sussex, and Warwick are commended as a pattern. In that year a list of 39 Associations was printed, with the names of their Secretaries, and the number of churches in each, 994 in all, with 579 Home Mission Stations. This is difficult to reconcile with the *Congregational Magazine's* total of 1,840 for the same year. A list of Academies is also given—9 in England (Airedale, Blackburn, Coward, Exeter, Hackney, Highbury, Homerton, Newport Pagnell, and Rotherham) with 146 students,

2 in Wales, (Newtown and Neuaddlwyd), 1 in Scotland, and
1 in Ireland. The Schools at Lewisham and Silcoates are
also mentioned. These lists are obviously incomplete, and
in 1838 the Committee begin to urge in much stronger
terms the need for complete information. Public men inquired in vain for statistics in regard to matters of legislation, and especially for comparison between the voluntary
and compulsory modes of supporting religion. The Committee confess with shame the deficiency and inferiority of
their records compared with the Annual Reports of the
Baptist Union. This stirs up many Association Secretaries by 1839, but "numbers have as yet failed to
respond", and in 1843 a speaker in the Assembly laments,
"We have no statistics".

A correspondent, W. H. H., writing in the *Congregational Magazine* for 1836 on "Hints for the Congregational
Union", showed what might be done. After urging the
need for a scheme for chapel debts and for sending lecturers
on Congregational principles to every town, he went on to
say :—

> Our body is most woefully negligent of ecclesiastical
> statistics, and we should not allow another year to pass
> without adopting some mode of ascertaining the amount
> *of accommodation provided* and *funds raised* by every
> church of our order in the country.

He then gave an example of what one church had done
—he calls it "the church of which I have the bishopric"—
"*without State assistance, and in spite of State oppression.
by a little love and zeal*", and quoted these figures, saying
that similar accounts, printed as an Appendix to the
Annual Address, would encourage and stimulate many
churches.

Abstract of the Deacons' Report, 1835.

	£	s.	d.
Chapel accommodation 900 sittings, 380 free.			
Seat Rents, etc.	81	1	7
Income of Trust Property ...	70	9	4
Chapel debt, £310.			
Minister's income, £116.			
For Benevolent Institutions	135	11	7¾
Sabbath school, 500 children.			
For the Debt on the Chapel	168	17	0
	£455	19	6¾

Public Questions.

What were the public questions for the discussion of which accurate statistical information was desired? In 1833 a statement of the public grievances under which Independents and other Protestant Dissenters suffered was drawn up. After referring to the Establishment, and protesting "with firmness and unanimity against this aberration from the purity of the gospel church", six specific complaints were made :

1. The contempt and persecution frequently experienced from Episcopal dignitaries.

2. The exclusion of Dissenters from the Universities of Oxford, Cambridge, and Durham, while they are prevented from obtaining degrees in the University of London owing to the Oxford and Cambridge opposition to a Charter.

3. Church Rates, Easter dues, *etc.*, which they have to pay equally with those who approve the Established Church. If they refuse to pay their property is distrained, and they are made to appear disaffected subjects.

4. Legal requirement of a certificate of baptism by clergy of the Established Church, instead of a certificate of birth only.

5. The refusal of the right of burial according to their own forms, though they have to contribute to the purchase, *etc.*, of graveyards.

6. The necessity of conforming to objectionable rites in the Marriage Service. The State's relation to marriage is civil only—all denominations should be at liberty to employ their own forms and ministers for the religious celebration.

A Petition to the House of Commons, embodying these grievances, was prepared, and it was agreed to co-operate with a specially appointed London Committee of Ministers and Lay Deputies to secure redress.

In 1836 resolutions were passed welcoming, though regretting the slow progress of, the Bill for Registration of Marriages, and the Government's proposal to establish a Metropolitan University.

Painful disappointment was expressed at the Government's hesitation to abolish Church Rates, and the House of Commons was informed that no Report of Parliamentary Commissions would reconcile the Dissenters to payment of the Rates, for the abolition of which the Assembly pledged itself to use every constitutional means.

In 1837 satisfaction was expressed that the Government was to introduce a Church Rate Bill, and at the passing of the Marriage and Registration Act, though it had "obvious, and indeed galling, defects". Letters were prepared for pastors and deacons, advising them of the terms of the Act and recommending them to license their buildings for marriages, but to "avoid the establishment of anything like fees, as the system of fees is alike unscriptural and injurious; Christianity knows nothing but free-will offerings". 7,500 copies of these suggestions were sold within a year.

In 1838 it was announced that so many were the ways in which religious liberty was being threatened, and so many were the questions that it touched—education, the Colonies, Poor Law administration, *etc., etc.*—that a general and effective organization of Dissenters was needed, especially in view of "the powerful opposition now organized against voluntary churches by all the friends of Establishments".

In 1839 the Colonial Churches were advised to decline grants from the legislatures and rely on voluntary support : "Expediency is not our guide, but the Word of God". Sympathy was expressed with those imprisoned and distrained upon for Church Rates.

Wider interests were occasionally touched. 1st August, 1834, was recognized as a day of Thanksgiving for the Abolition of Slavery. Two years later, Vaughan, Burder, and Reed were asked to prepare an "affectionate remonstrance with the American Churches on the continuation of slavery in the United States".

In 1839, on John Brown's initiative, it was resolved to petition the House of Commons for a uniform penny postage. There is no indication of any resolutions dealing with social questions that concerned the masses of the people. Children and women were working in mines and factories under revolting conditions. The Union said nothing. Mr. and Mrs. Hammond's *The Age of the Chartists*, which deals with the years 1832 to 1854, shows how the majority of English people were living without any of the amenities of life, and how appalling were the schools in which they were "educated". There is no reflection of this in the proceedings of the Union.

In 1830 a Beer Bill had been passed, which made it possible for anybody to sell beer on payment of a licence. Thousands of beerhouses sprang up in no time, and a few days after the passage of the Act Sydney Smith said : "Everybody is drunk. Those who are not singing are sprawling. The sovereign people is in a beastly state".

The Total Abstinence Movement had started in 1832, no doubt instigated in large measure by the indulgence that resulted from the passage of the Beer Bill. With this question, too, the Union did not meddle. Two of the American visitors to the Union in 1835 criticized the Independents for taking so small a part in Temperance propaganda, and especially for being so little in evidence at a meeting of the British and Foreign Temperance Society they had attended. The Established Church and the Quakers were said to be the principal supporters of the Society, and the apathy of the Independents was deplored. Two practices also pained the Americans, "the free use of stimulating liquors," at public meetings, decanters of wine being on the platform for the use of speakers, and the universal custom of offering wine to the preacher on his descent from the pulpit. In reply it was urged that more Independents were allied to the Temperance Society than was generally supposed, and that others were only held back in reaction from the extravagance of "*Tee-totalism*".

To banish "the fruit of the vine" from the table of the Lord, and to forbid "such as be faint" to drink of it, appears to many so contrary to reason and scripture, that they stand aloof from operations which terminate in such conclusions.

The use of wine as a stimulant, preparatory to any

sacred service, is, in our judgment, like kindling strange
fire for the altars of God; but we must own that we do
not see the moral evil of a man relieving the
exhaustion which public speaking has occasioned
by the use of wine. On physical grounds it may be,
however, expedient to employ a less exciting beverage,
but we are not prepared to submit to censure for the tem-
perate use of that which we regard to be one of the choice
blessings of a beneficent Creator.

A pledge of abstinence is "unscriptural, and likely to
ensnare its subjects, and to lead, if fully carried out, to
monkish austerities". A Temperance advocate writing to
explain the objects of the Society and the advantages of
abstinence, the Editor of the *Congregational Magazine*
(1836) thus brings down the heavy editorial hammer:

> "We believe that *'total abstinence'*—for it seems
> that its friends are now ashamed of *their own ' bar-
> barous term, Tee-totalism'*,—has appeared to many
> fanatical and absurd".

With such divisions of opinion patent, it is easy to see
why total abstinence was not mentioned in the Union
Assemblies. Indeed, as yet the only trace of a social conscience to be observed in the Union's proceedings is in
reference to slavery. First, the preaching of the Gospel,
second, the securing of religious freedom—on these the
aims of the Independents were concentrated, and they had
not yet felt the call to the struggle for the remedying of
social ills.

VII. THE FIRST AUTUMN TRIP :—
BIRMINGHAM, 1839.

THE First Autumn Assembly must have special mention,
though it is impossible to do more than give a brief summary.   A very full report appears in the *Congregational
Magazine*.

There was general anxiety about the response of the
churches to a summons for an Assembly in the provinces,
but John Angell James expressed himself gratified at the
number who came to Birmingham.   Long afterwards
James Spicer used to tell how he and two friends "engaged
the Hen and Chickens Hotel, which at that time afforded
sufficient accommodation for all its [the Union's] visitors".
There were 138 present, representing the following counties (the figures in brackets stating the number from the
most largely represented counties) :

Berks.	Northampton.
Bucks.	Nottingham.
Cheshire.	Northumberland.
Derby.	Oxfordshire.
Devon.	Salop.
Dorset.	Somerset.
Essex.	Stafford (13).
Gloucester.	Suffolk.
Hants.	Surrey.
Kent.	Sussex.
Leicester.	Wilts.
Lancaster (15).	Warwick (22).
Middlesex (24).	Worcester.
Monmouth.	Yorks. (4).

Dr. Raffles presided, and Dr. Leifchild and Dr. Halley
preached.   The Northamptonshire Association was received into the Union.   A Hampshire minister, in
proposing a brother minister, regretted that he could

> bring no more favourable tidings than on a former occasion
> as to the prospect of adhesion on the part of the Hampshire
> Association, but he felt persuaded that if anything could
> remove the objection of his dear and honoured brethren
> to such a measure, it would be to see the intended plan
> for evangelizing the whole country brought into effective

operation. Meanwhile, they must be content with declarations of adhesions from individual ministers and churches. He desired to correct the false impressions caused by a statement made by him at the May Assembly, for there was nothing but the most fraternal feeling in Hampshire for the Congregational Union.

It was to this plan for evangelizing the whole country that most of the time of the Assembly was given. The Committee had very carefully prepared a "draft of a plan for Home Missions, in connection with the Union". In brief outline it was as follows :

I. "The Object. Home Missions at this time an Urgent Duty of Congregational Churches." Three resolutions on this were submitted :

1. That in the judgment of this Assembly it is an especial duty at the present time of the Independent churches of this country to unite in vigorous home missionary efforts conducted in entire harmony with their distinctive views of the truth, ministry, and ordinances of the gospel, and of the constitution, discipline, and liberty of Christian churches.

2. Why Home Missions are now specially needed.
   That this Assembly, while gratefully acknowledging the efforts already made by individual churches, by County Associations, and by other institutions, for the spread of the Gospel in destitute localities, yet recognizes a pressing necessity for greatly increased exertions, and a loud call of Divine Providence to the Independent churches to engage in them, in the following circumstances :
   (i) The awful extent of ignorance and irreligion which prevails in both town and country ;
   (ii) the active efforts now revived for the spread of Popery, and the extensive and alarming diffusion, by divines professing to be reformed but not Protestant, of semi-papal doctrines concerning the Christian ministry, sacraments, and way of salvation ;
   (iii) the absolute necessity of revived and extended religion, and of multiplied Christian churches in our own country, in order to sustain the increased efforts so loudly called for in all enterprises for the conversion of the world.

3. Why to be conducted on Congregational principles.
   That in the opinion of this Assembly it is the course of

wisdom and duty for the Congregational churches to unite, and conduct their Home Missionary efforts in harmony with the entire range of their distinctive views of Christian doctrine and church polity; so as

(i) to render the very doing of this great work beneficial to the churches themselves, by promoting among them union and brotherly love, concerted efforts and mutual helpfulness;

(ii) to multiply churches professing a pure faith, and maintaining a scriptural polity.

(iii) To show the practical adaptation and tendency of Congregational principles and institutions, both to preserve and to spread, in its purity, the knowledge of the great salvation.

II. "Principles to be adopted in prosecution of Home Missions."

Home Missions the Work of Churches Especially, but not of Churches Exclusively;

Pecuniary Resources;

Towns as well as Rural Districts to be embraced;

Parts to be borne by Central Committee and by Churches or Associations locally;

Education of Ministerial Missionaries Indispensable;

Evangelists to be employed;

Best Gifts and Great devotedness Required;

Prosperity and Usefulness of Congregational Churches will be greatly advanced in Home Missionary Labours;

General Education an Important Auxiliary to Home Missions;

A Sectarian Spirit and Object Disavowed.

III. "The Congregational Union to undertake Home Missionary work."

1. The Congregational Union to undertake a Home Mission under the designation of the Home Mission of the Congregational Union of England and Wales.

2. [This Home Mission to have a distinct Annual Meeting to which every subscribing church may send two delegates, Monday, 11th May, to be the first of such meetings.]

It is clear from this outline that discussion would range about the relation of the Union to Home Missionary enterprise, especially as the situation was complicated by the existence of the Home Missionary Society. The delegates were unanimous in thinking that there must be much greater activity in this field. They disagreed on the question whether the effort should be distinctly Congregational. The strong supporters of the Union urged that the reply to the frequent question "What is your Union doing?" should be "Evangelizing the towns and country districts". Others thought that the Union should leave the control to the undenominational Society. A long discussion took place, the term "Catholic" in the sense of "undenominational" being the bone of contention. Dr. Redford refused to see any distinction between "catholic" and "denominational". He said :

> My denomination is the catholic denomination. I am a Congregationalist because Congregationalism is the catholic principle, because we can admit Christians of all denominations to our communion. I, as a Congregationalist, discard all human legislation, set aside, as of any authority in the church, in its government, the opinions, or decisions of men, lay, ecclesiastical, political, and what not. Well, then, I say I am as catholic as any man. No man ought to wish me to be more catholic than my Bible, that contains the universal gospel, reveals the universal Saviour, and the universal plan for the salvation of the world, and that is the plan which I adopt as a Congregationalist. I enforce nothing of what I consider to be the proper management of church affairs upon any person who wishes to join our fellowship.

Redford felt that the Home Missionary Society was not catholic enough : it preached the Gospel, but did not set up churches, and it was very confined and restricted in its operations.

Dr. Joseph Fletcher, while not depreciating those operations, held that if Congregational principles were worth maintaining and defending, they must be maintained and defended :

> I value any attempt to diffuse the knowledge of Christ at home, but I am quite sure that our churches have never yet risen justly and properly to the dignity, or the sanctity, or the efficiency of their own principles. We have not been sufficiently concerned in this matter; we have been doing everybody's work but our own, the common fags of the whole Christian workshop. We have worked for schools, missions, and Bible societies, and for every other good or general object, but, Sir, we have not, in my own judgment,

taken care of ourselves, and we shall be far better prepared even to take care of others if we can more effectually
serve ourselves.

John Angell James said that this was not a time to sit
lightly to the principles of Congregationalism. Just as
Carrs Lane raised £200 in small subscriptions for the town
mission in Birmingham, so the churches generally could
take Home Missions upon their hearts, and their members
could contribute a penny a week for them. He preferred a
denominational scheme, for the "catholic" plan for raising
money was not successful.

> What does the London Missionary Society get by its
> catholicity? What has the Home Missionary Society got
> by being catholic? Where are the resources to be found?
> Whence does the money come? Talk as long as you will,
> gentlemen, about catholicity, depend upon it the money
> comes, after all, from yourselves. You divide the honour,
> as regards the designation of the Society, with others, but
> you pay for the honour yourselves. And after all we say,
> as far as our observation extends, those whom you wish to
> conciliate care nothing for the catholic principle. They
> don't want to be catholic. You must be aware that this is
> the case, and that, in fact, all the catholicity is on one side.
> Here is a fallacy, as I have already shown you, in this term
> catholic. In what are your operations catholic but in
> name? What are your agents? Dissenters. What kind
> of ordination do your evangelists receive? Congregational
> ordination. Everything is denominational, gentlemen, al-
> ready. Why, then, should we shrink from our own desig-
> nation, when, in fact, we already act upon the principles of
> our denomination? Again, upon what principles do your
> Associations act? Are these catholic? What your County
> Associations? No. Do you shrink from the denomina-
> tional designation in them? I trow not. You never pro-
> fess catholicity there. I believe you are strictly
> denominational. What is your Congregational Union? A
> union of unions. And, therefore, why be denominational
> in your County and in your smaller Associations, and talk
> of catholicity in your larger one—the general Congrega-
> tional Union. On these grounds I am certainly and
> entirely for the establishment of a denominational home
> mission.

George Smith, of Plymouth, a subsequent Secretary of
the Union, said it must be recognized that if a new denomi-

THE

CHRISTIAN WITNESS,

AND

Church Member's Magazine:

UNDER THE SANCTION OF

THE CONGREGATIONAL UNION OF ENGLAND AND WALES.

1844.

"The influence of literature is perpetually increasing. Reading, once the privilege of a few, is now the occupation of multitudes, and is to become one of the chief gratifications of all. Writing is now the mightiest instrument on earth. Through this the mind has acquired a kind of omnipresence. To superior minds, which may act through this, we look for the impulses by which their country is to be carried forward. We would teach them that they are the depositaries of the highest power on earth, and that on them the best hopes of society rest."

"We love our country much, but mankind more. As men and Christians, our first desire is, to see the improvement of human nature. We desire to see the soul of man wiser, firmer, nobler, more conscious of its imperishable treasures, more beneficent and powerful, more alive to its connection with God, more able to use pleasure and prosperity aright, and more victorious over poverty, adversity, and pain."

"I want to get up a real 'Poor Man's Magazine,' which should not bolster up abuses, and veil iniquities, nor *prose* to the poor as to children ; but should address them in the style of Cobbett—plainly, boldly, and in sincerity—excusing nothing, concealing nothing, and misrepresenting nothing ; but speaking the *very whole truth in love*—Cobbett-like in *style*, but Christian in spirit."

THE PROFITS OF THIS WORK

ARE

DEVOTED TO THE BENEFIT OF AGED MINISTERS.

VOLUME I.

LONDON:

PUBLISHED BY JOHN SNOW,

PATERNOSTER ROW.

FACSIMILE OF FIRST NUMBER OF "CHRISTIAN WITNESS"

national Society were set up the Home Missionary Society would go down.

> Nine-tenths of its support, after all that might be said of catholicity, came from Congregational churches.   If that support, then, were withdrawn, or turned into a new channel, it must come to an end; it must be altogether swamped, or else retained in being by a connection with the Congregational Union.

Smith said that village stations were started by the Society year after year, town opportunities being refused for fear of offending some denomination therein. The money that had been spent could have started many churches which would speedily have become self-supporting.

Dr. Matheson admitted that plans to work together with the Anglicans in Home Missions had failed, and went on to say :

> No denomination of Christians can be more Catholic than ourselves, or more ready to hold out the right hand of fellowship to others ; but we cannot, if we are true to ourselves, suffer our missionaries to be withdrawn, in order to conciliate those who are enemies to our polity.   We are driven by the very movements of the day to establish and support a mission of our own.

After John Blackburn had announced that the Home Missionary Society had declined an invitation to stand on the same terms as the Colonial Mission in regard to the Union, the first Resolution (above) was passed.

The crux of the problem emerged the next day.   The great fight raged on the responsibility of the Union for the new Home Missionary enterprise.   The Rev. R. Burls said that the Essex Union, of which he was Secretary, "was not at all connected with" the General Union, and many of its supporters were opposed to a national Union ; difficulties would thus arise if the new "British Mission" were connected with the Union.   He therefore recommended that the Society that should be formed should be a "Congregational Union for British Missions", but not identical with the present Union.   This would enable churches and Associations not yet in the General Union to support the new Society. When John Angell James said he was inclined to support this view, Algernon Wells was

H

speedily on his feet.   If a Congregational Union could
not work a Home Mission, he said, it would lead to its final
and speedy dissolution.   As he saw his plans being undermined he was deeply affected, and said he felt as if his
child were being taken and strangled before his eyes, and
that he "might as well be this day the pastor of my poor
people at Coggeshall".   Algernon's tears, won "very cordial cheers which lasted for some time", and, of course, they
gained the day.   Who could resist a Secretary who felt
so keenly as this?

Burls, James, and others put their heads together, and
everybody seemed satisfied with the decision that "a Home
Mission should be undertaken by the Union with the title
the Home Mission of the Congregational Union of England and Wales", and should have a separate annual
meeting for the transaction of its business.

The Assembly had begun by passing this Resolution :

> That the statement now laid before this meeting, by
> the Rev. Algernon Wells, of the constitution, design and
> operations of the Congregational Union of England and
> Wales, is eminently satisfactory, as proving that, while
> that body represents a noble instance of voluntary and com-
> prehensive association, it violates neither the rights of
> private judgment, nor infringes upon the independence of
> individual churches ; and, at the same time, demonstrates
> the vast importance of the institution, as tending, by the
> blessing of God, to increase the harmony, the strength,
> and the efficiency of the denomination which it represents
> —an object at all times important, but especially so in the
> present age, when the strife of parties is so fierce ; and, on
> the other hand, when such efforts are made for the more
> entire evangelization of our country, our colonies, and the
> the world.

After it a letter was sent to the Pastors and Churches
describing what had been done, and saying :

> That the work should be undertaken and managed by
> churches and their pastors, severally or in Associations.
> That the Congregational Union, as consisting of con-
> federated churches and Associations, shall undertake the
> proposed Home Missionary operations.   That the entire
> work should be conducted on Congregational principles.
> That appeals for pecuniary aid should be first addressed to
> churches on the ground of their peculiar obligations and

responsibilities. That lay agency be employed under the superintendence of churches and pastors, but that ministerial missionaries be invariably educated. That energetic evangelists be sought out and employed. That stronger churches or districts be brought to aid those that are weaker by a general fund, first obtained and then distributed by a central agency. That the benefits of centralization on the one hand, and of independent action in every district on the other, may be obtained and combined without incurring the mischief and risk of either when excessive. Lastly, that by the diffused information of a general Report, each district acquainted with the proceedings of all the rest, may obtain the advantage of useful suggestions, cheering intelligence, enlarged sympathy, and perceived mutual co-operation.

This first Provincial Assembly had been a pronounced success. Fairly representative, it had discussed a difficult problem and had come to an agreement which meant united and aggressive missionary work at home. From this time every autumn saw a Union Assembly in some provincial town, the only exceptions being on a few occasions when the Assembly met in London, and in one or two of the war years (1914, 1918; the 1917 May meetings were postponed, and held in London in October).

Whether by good fortune or design these autumn Assemblies proved to be excellent propaganda for the Union. There were few of them before 1850 in which Algernon Wells did not expound the principles, objects, and policy of the Union, and meet possible objections, with the result in most cases that there were immediate accessions of ministers, churches, and Associations in the neighbourhood.

VIII. OVERLOADING THE SHIP, 1840-1845.

These were six of the most important years in the history of the Union, for in them the foundations on which the Union was to build in the succeeding century were laid. Almost every problem of future days emerged during this period, while most of the possible lines of advance were indicated, and some *culs-de-sac* discovered. It is necessary, therefore, that this chapter should deal in some detail with the various demands made on the young and almost untried organization.

Growth.

During these years the Union gradually increased in influence as the Associations that had stood out affiliated one by one. In 1841 Wilts and East Somerset, and Oxford and West Berks came in, while the delegates representing the Congregational churches connected with the Surrey Mission were welcomed. In 1842 the " Welsh Connection of Independents in the County of Monmouthshire " were received. In the following year, when Glamorgan and the Channel Islands joined up, the Committee made special mention of Norfolk because of John Alexander's previous attitude, saying :

> The brethren of that County have resolved to seek an entry into your Union as a result of a resolution adopted by the church at Princes Street, Norwich, and transmitted to every church in the city and county, recommending for consideration a proposal for union with this body. On no occasion has an Association been received into this Union on grounds more satisfactory and encouraging.

In the autumn of that year Wells remarked that since 1832 no church or Association engaged in forming the Union had withdrawn from it, and that now the Union had " very generally the sanction and confidence of the denomination." Thomas Adkins of Southampton had remarked ere this (1840) that opinion in his neighbourhood was growing so strong that if the Hampshire Association did not join as a body, scarcely a church but would do so in its individual capacity.

The Autumn Assembly in 1843 was held in Leeds, and many of the Leeds ministers joined the Union. Not without amusement, and suggestive of the free-and-easy way in which things were still done, was the fact that, the Chairman having had to leave, the Rev. John Ely, of East Parade Church, Leeds, was asked to take his place, though he was not yet in the Union. He declared that now, at all events, he could hold out no longer, and ere long he became one of the Union's most useful leaders. In the following year his church was admitted, the care with which the question was considered being shown in the resolution dated 29th November, 1843, and passed *nem. con.* :

> That this church having carefully examined the principles, and observed the operations of the Congregational Union of England and Wales, approves of the Union, as adapted to promote brotherly love, and enabling the representatives of the churches to take counsel together on all questions of common interest; is well pleased with the determination to appropriate to a specific purpose any fund that may arise from the sale of its publications, and so to throw itself on the voluntary support of the churches; and will ever rejoice to co-operate in the great practical objects which it pursues in the department of British missions[1].
>
> And that the church proposes, therefore, to connect itself with the Union, and authorizes the deacons to appropriate such annual sum as may seem fit to the fund which is requisite for conducting its affairs.
>
> N.B.—The sum annually appropriated to this object will probably be five pounds, which will be, I apprehend, a fair and full proportion for our church.

Side by side with this may be put the resolution of Salem Church, York, a month later :

> That this church, while recognizing the strict and essential Independency of Christian communities as the law of the New Testament, also feels the importance of advancing the general efficiency of the Congregational body; and trusting that the Congregational Union, formed in the year 1831, will, without infringing on the rights of individual churches, be found conducive to such a result, this church is ready, and desires, to become associated with that institution, both in order to testify affection toward the

1 See below, p. 150.

brethren, and in order to co-operate, as far as practicable, in the furtherance of the objects, in which the interests of evangelical piety at home and abroad are so deeply involved.

It was natural growth of this kind that enabled the statement to be made in 1843 that the position and prospects of the Union were encouraging—" your cause is good and true, strong and rising ". Nevertheless in a paper read in 1846 John Blackburn had to say that there were probably at least 600 churches in no Association whatever.

The Autumnal Meetings generally produced a number of entries from the neighbourhood in which they were held, witness Leeds and York, above, and the Cornwall Association after the Plymouth Meetings in 1846. Being less crowded with business, they were generally more effective for propaganda purposes than those in London. The numbers attending were as follows :

		From a distance.	Resi- dents.	Total present.
1839.	Birmingham	124	14	138
1840.	Bristol	110	36	146
1841.	Nottingham	109	13	122
1842.	Liverpool	157	40	197
1843.	Leeds	182	32	214
1844.	Norwich	103	34	137
1845.	Manchester	444	81	525
1846.	Plymouth and Devonport	121	52	173

The *Christian Witness,* which gives these figures, pointed out that the Plymouth meetings meant, even for London delegates, 500 miles of travel, including 70 by coach, an expense of at least £5 or £6, and a week's absence from business.

Finance.

It was now becoming increasingly necessary to tackle the financial situation. In 1843 the Committee estimated that the annual cost of working the Union was from £300 to £500, while the annual income from contributions had never reached £100. From the annual accounts it appears that the situation was saved year by year by the profits the *Hymn Book,* £380, £335, and £517, for example, being drawn from that source in 1840, 1841, and 1843 respectively. The deficit was growing, until in 1841 it was over £600. Two years later a timely legacy of £300 from Mrs. John Angell James gave some relief.

All kinds of suggestions for coping with the problem were made, including the ingenious idea that every church should contribute a minimum 10s. annually, for which it should receive back 5s. worth of " tracts " !   In 1843 at Leeds the Assembly adopted the Committee's Memorial on the financial position, which stated that the Union had been financed by the profits of its publications, and emphasized that this principle was unsound, while the practice might be found injurious were the profits to become large.   It was therefore decided—

1.   That an appeal be made to the churches for contributions of £2, £5, or £10 to meet the deficit, and for personal subscriptions to meet the annual charges.

2.   Should these appeals prove successful, that future profits from publications should be devoted to a fund for the assistance of aged ministers.

These resolutions were excellent on paper, but other urgent demands, such as the Education appeal,[1] prevented them from being put into practice.   In 1844 it had to be admitted that the contributions to the Union in the past three years had averaged only £67.   It was decided to have separate accounts for the Union and Publication Departments, so that the amount drawn from the latter for Union purposes could be plainly seen.   It was definitely resolved to apply publication profits to the fund for aged ministers, and the delegates undertook to use their influence both to secure the Union an adequate income and to increase the circulation of its publications.

In 1845 the judgment that it was " objectionable in principle that the management of a public society should be sustained by trade profits in any form " was reiterated, but £224 was taken from the profits, the churches having contributed less than £100, an opportune legacy *per* Dr. Burder

1 See below, p. 178.

alone preventing the deficit from being larger. An appeal was made to friends to contribute £5 each to put the Union in a satisfactory position, and the 1846 account shows that £230 was received in response. That account reveals how small still were the contributions made by churches and Associations. One Association alone, Worcester, contributed, and the number of contributions from churches and individuals together was only 21, these including Carrs Lane, £5; George Hadfield, £10; and Mrs. Blyth, £5 ("as a testimony to the feeling entertained by her late father, the Rev. William Kemp, respecting Congregational Principles"). Finally, when the Constitution was revised in October, 1846, it was decided that the Union should " no longer be constituted of Associations entire, but of churches severally ", each of which should pay 10s. a year.

Publications.

From finance we naturally turn again to publications.

I. First, there were some publications which made a loss rather than a profit :

1. *Tracts*—or, as they would be called to-day, "pamphlets". The aim of these was to emphasize Congregational principles, against sacerdotalism on the one hand and anti-pædobaptism on the other. The series opened with the *Declaration of Faith and Order,* and consisted, in the main, of several of the Annual Letters and of papers read by Wells and others at the Assemblies. It had a considerable but only a temporary sale. All kinds of suggestions were made for publications of this sort, including one from the London Board of Ministers for a series to combat "the errors and dangers of these remarkable times".

2. *The Congregational Calendar.* The need for a denominational handbook was soon felt, and the first attempt to meet it was in the shape of a *Congregational Calendar.* This was issued for the 9 years 1840—1848, its size varying from 144 pages (1846) to 76 pages (1847). A summary of the contents of the first issue will indicate its scope :

pp.   1— 37 : General Information, such as is contained in a modern diary;

  38— 66 : National Affairs (including some
general ecclesiastical statistics);

  67—109 : Denominational Intelligence. Here
we have the History and Plan of the
Union, the Declaration of Faith,
the Sixth Annual Address, particulars about various Associations,
Societies, Missions, Colleges,
Schools, and other organizations.
Sketches and accounts of new
chapels are given, and also some
obituary notices of ministers.

110—120 : Miscellaneous Information, including the Population of the World,
the text of the Marriage Acts, an
account of some Dissenting
Societies, and Devotional Readings.

Here we see in embryo the *Congregational Year Book*
of to-day. The *Calendar* met a need, and the 5,000
printed were sold. So much extraneous matter had been
introduced, however, that there was a loss on the publication, and double the circulation was asked for. A larger
number was printed in 1841, but there was no extra
demand, and in subsequent years the sale began to fall.
In 1843 this was attributed to the hard times, but in 1844
the Committee were talking about the regret that the
dropping of so convenient a reference book would cause.
The *coup de grâce* was given by the decision to publish a
Year Book. The practice of holding two Assemblies a
year meant two sets of Minutes; and this, and the general
development of the organization, made the issue of a
Year Book both necessary and inevitable. The first one,
that for 1846, was published in the spring of 1847, in which
year and in the following year the *Calendar* was issued
reduced both in size and price. The two publications
obviously were in each other's way, and the separate publication of the *Calendar* then ceased, the 1848 *Year Book*

(published in 1849) incorporating the *Calendar* for 1849.

3. The prize essays on Home Evangelization, of which every church was urged to possess copies, had a disappointing sale.

4. These, however, were by no means so great a fiasco as the publications of the Wycliffe Society. Congregationalism, for some strange reason, has never given its history a proper place. With a story of which any denomination might be proud it has never encouraged, except in words, any attempt to deal with that history in an adequate way. John Blackburn was not without grounds when he said in 1846 :

> We are a people who have a history, but we neglect our documents. Let us awake to a consciousness of our own history as doing much to teach statisticians and legislators that, after all, the Kingdom of Christ is best governed by its own laws, and sustained by its own resources—resources not wrung from a reluctant contributor by the force of law, but cheerfully given by the force of love.

The Parker Society's remarkable collection of volumes naturally suggested the formation of similar Nonconformist Societies. In 1842 Blackburn put before the Assembly a proposal of this kind. Quoting the Library of Anglo-Catholic Theology, the Parker Society, and the Camden Society, he suggested that a Nonconformist Society was a desideratum, and maintained that for an annual subscription of £1 it should be possible to issue to subscribers three volumes each year. The proposal to publish a series of reprints of valuable tracts and treatises illustrative of the theology and polity of the British Nonconformist churches, commencing with the works and times of Wycliffe and proceeding regularly to the present period, was cordially approved. Two years later, however, only 750 subscribers had been obtained, and the most strenuous efforts produced little further result, the list of subscribers never numbering more than 950, of whom only 850 paid, a very meagre result when it is remembered that 37,500 prospectuses were printed, 13,300 circulars issued, £70 spent in postages and £80 in advertising. The Society had cost £267 to bring to birth, and it was clearly doomed to be short-lived unless somebody came to its rescue. In 1846 Blackburn appealed to the Assembly and to individuals for support, saying that if the Duke of Manchester and the Bishop of Georgia thought it worth while to subscribe, surely Nonconformists should do so. He pointed out that collections of " the scattered tracts and treatises of those noble confessors who fought the battle of Scriptural Protestantism and of religious liberty in this country, and to whom the Nonconformist communities are under lasting obligations ", did not exist,[1] and could not be found in the British Museum, the Bodleian, or Dr. William's Library, while 17th century folios of the writings of the Nonconformist divines, published by the munificence of their contemporaries, were rapidly becoming extinct.

The Assembly regretted the report, said the design was excellent, patted its promoters on the back, and suggested that they looked into the matter further ! The end of the discreditable story may soon be told. The Society published *Tracts and Treatises of John de Wycliffe,* edited by Robert Vaughan, and *Select Works of David Clarkson,* edited by Basil H. Cooper and John Blackburn, and then ceased its activities. A bundle of papers in the Congregational Library will give the details to any student who desires them.

Preparations made for reprinting John Robinson's works had to be suspended. The Union in 1850 approved this reprint, but it was not until Dr. John Campbell came to the assistance of the editor, the Rev. Robert Ashton, and undertook responsibility for the publication, that the way was clear, and *The Works of John Robinson* appeared in three volumes in 1851. The difference made by enterprise, drive, and a right approach to the public may be gauged from the fact that in May, 1851, Campbell was able to tell the Assembly that he had secured 2,400 subscribers to the work immediately on the announcement of the

---

1 The reproach still remains.

prospectus, and had also disposed of an American edition of 500 copies.

5. A project for the publication of a series of catechisms also hung fire, though John Angell James offered to contribute £25 towards the cost. The design was for a " well-arranged and interesting series of catechisms" for the use of families and schools, especially

> three catechisms of Christian doctrines and duties; the first, elementary, for children from their sixth to their eighth year; a second more advanced for those from 8 to 12 years of age, and a third with scripture proofs and illustrations for the higher classes. In these, the Committee would wish to see the excellence of Watts's and the Assembly's catechisms combined—the interest of Watts's infused into the accurate and sound theology of the Assembly's.

The Committee hoped that these two products would be amply used in " the arduous work of training children of English Nonconformists in the paths of piety and virtue." It is not surprising to read that in 1842 the " object was found too difficult of attainment " and the project seems to have been dropped.

6. Another plan already made which did not reach fruition in these years was the revision of Watts's hymns. In 1843 it was reported to be far advanced, but still incomplete, those in charge being overworked men.

In the autumn of 1851 Conder, maybe tired of waiting for his colleagues, himself published a revised edition of the *Psalms and Hymns of Dr. Watts*. His son and biographer says[1] :

> The work had been in hand at intervals for many years, and cost him a vast amount of labour. His hope was, by casting aside all those compositions which have become obsolete, discarding superfluous verses, correcting objectionable phrases, and arranging all the hymns in one methodical series, to aid in preventing these noble strains from falling into disuse (through the adoption of hymn-books containing but a small number of Watts's hymns), and to furnish an edition suited, in every way, for congregational use.

7. The Tune Book proposal remained also in a state

---

[1] Conder, *Josiah Conder*, p. 311.

of suspense, though Algernon Wells wrote in 1840 to the *Congregational Magazine* saying that it was known

> that several gentlemen of acknowledged taste and skill have, of late, employed their leisure hours in the pleasant and elegant pursuit of the composition of sacred music,

and stating that

> the truth thus designed to be displayed and promoted [was] the just adaptation of the music to the poetry, and of both to the worship of God; avoiding equally the extremes of a noisy strident vulgarity and a heavy dullness on the one hand, and of an excessive affected refinement on the other.

II. Turning, now, to the publications from which profits were made, we come first to the

1. *The Hymn Book.*

The sales continued to be satisfactory, having reached a total of 90,000 copies by 1834. It had been objected that too extensive alterations had been made in some hymns " justly dear to pious minds ", that familiar hymns had been omitted, and that the arrangement was faulty. To meet these objections as far as possible, and also to satisfy the demand for a cheap edition for Sunday Schools, a revised edition was issued in 1844.

2. *Periodicals.*

The need for periodical literature became more and more manifest. There were already several magazines and papers edited by Congregationalists, but, apart from the *Congregational Magazine,* a monthly which, of necessity, had but a small circulation, there was no direct means of communication between the Union and the man in the pew. There was a *Home Missionary Magazine,* which was enlarged and improved in 1842, and made to include both Colonial and Irish news, but Wells, as usual, was not far from being right when he said in that year :

> The Press among the Independents presents the same only want, the want of more energetic action. Never was there a time in which periodical and tract literature was so influential as now. There is no want among the Independents of vigorous minds and pens. Why are they not employed and encouraged? Where are the pithy and

pointed tracts? Where is the constant supply of weekly and monthly papers exhibiting or defending Congregational principles with every advantage of variety, repetition, and spirit? Other bodies are so sustained through the Press—this also must be so, or must suffer consequences most mischievous, if not fatal.

The suggestion for a cheap denominational magazine aroused some difference of opinion, while the Committee's attempts to gauge what kind of welcome such a journal would receive proved discouraging. It was agreed that a cheap magazine, which would not injure other magazines, was desirable, but the Union had no capital and could not risk a loss. It was decided, however, that the Committee should endeavour to get funds and make a start, but in the autumn of 1843 it was announced that they had failed to obtain an editor, and so had not proceeded with the preparation of a specimen. It had been found that Dr. John Campbell, of Moorfields, who was already a contributor to the *Patriot* and the *Eclectic Review,* was prepared to become editor provided that the price should be threepence and the form octavo. This offer was gladly accepted, and in 1844 the *Christian Witness* saw the light. To everybody's amazement, the monthly sale exceeded 30,000. But Campbell was far from satisfied : he felt that if the churches in general supported the paper a circulation of 100,000 might be expected. Although he emphasized that with such a cheap magazine large profits could not be expected, in 1845 he had to be congratulated on having a settled circulation of 31,000, and a profit of £708. A confidential Committee, consisting of the Secretaries and Dr. Matheson, of the Home Missionary Society, conferred each month with the Editor on the conduct of the magazine, while a Finance Committee, consisting of Palmer and Messrs. East, Peachey, and Spicer, managed the trade department. In the following year, at Campbell's instigation, a more popular magazine (32 pages), to be sold at a penny a month under the title of the *Christian's Penny Magazine and Friend of the People* was started.The profits of these publications went to the "*Christian Witness* Fund in Aid of Aged Ministers".

The "Christian Witness" Fund.

To be eligible for grants ministers must be 60 years of age, and have been in the ministry 25 years, without following any trade or profession other than that of schoolmaster; they must produce a certificate testifying to these facts and to character from the officers of the Association to which they belonged. Appropriations from the Fund to assist younger ministers to purchase deferred annuities on reaching 60 years were not ruled out, but this departure from rules must first be sanctioned by the Assembly. The Committee of the Union, the officers of all Associations affiliated, and the Editor were to be distributors. The first distribution, in May, 1845, gave £261 of the £708 profit in sums of £5 to £20 to 28 applicants, the balance being invested. The Wilts. & East Somerset Association pressed for the Deferred Annuities, the Rev. J. Harris setting forth a scheme for the formation of an Annuitant Society. He said that ministers did not subscribe to the Dissenters' Assurance Office for an annuity because they could not afford its premiums. A sum of £20,000 would provide sufficient interest to supply half the premiums in a Congregational Society, and a denomination that could raise £70,000 a year for the London Missionary Society, and the children of whose Sunday Schools could raise £6,000 for a missionary ship, could easily obtain £20,000 for this purpose. The Wesleyans had raised £200,000 as a Centenary Fund, and the Free Church of Scotland had shown what could be done. Wealthier ministers would give a lead, and one of them had already offered to be one of twenty to subscribe £200 each. Harris suggested that an actuary should be asked to work out the cost, and that after the first two years no minister over 40 should be allowed to subscribe. The matter was referred to the Aged Ministers' Fund Committee.

Mutual Provident Societies.

Here a paragraph must be interpolated to show that the needs of the people of the churches were not overlooked. In October, 1845, James Sherman, of Surrey Chapel, read a paper on the " Origin, Principles and Advantages of Benefit Societies ", showing how useful Friendly Societies could be in time of sickness and bereavement. Under the leadership of the Churches they could be soundly, efficiently, and economically managed, and their meetings held elsewhere than in public-houses. A Special Committee was appointed to investigate the proposal. Subsequently suggested rules were discussed in the *Christian Witness,* and, the tables having been completely revised, a scheme was recommended to the immediate attention of the churches. Only one fact of the regulations for these Christian Mutual Provident Societies need be mentioned :

> The clause in the rule which states that a member shall be excluded "if he ceased to be a member of a Christian church or regularly to attend Divine worship", has been omitted, because your Committee thought it unadvisable and unjust to inflict a temporal punishment for an ecclesiastical offence.

It may be well to anticipate here and say that these Societies proved of great service. They were combined in the " Mutual Provident Alliance ", and in 1859 it was reported that they had in all 16,000 members, and had received £75,000, their present funds standing at £47,000.

The Denomination and Its Literature.

This may be the appropriate place to introduce some reference to other developments in the way of denominational literature. Dissatisfied with the theology and the politics of the *Eclectic Review,* Dr. Robert Vaughan started the *British Quarterly Review* in 1845, and it soon made a place for itself, and not merely among Independents and Dissenters, though the starting of it was much criticised and caused sharp division of opinion in the denomination generally, and also among the Committee of Lancashire College, where Vaughan was Principal. Nobody, however, seems to have foreseen that the establishment of the *Christian Witness* and the *Christian's Penny Magazine* by the denomination, and the beginning of the *British Quarterly Review* under Congregational editorship, would adversely affect the *Con-*

JOHN STOUGHTON

JAMES BALDWIN BROWN

ROBERT VAUGHAN

THOMAS BINNEY

gregational Magazine, which from 1818 had served the denomination extremely well.   That journal received another blow when in the autumn of 1845 John Blackburn announced his approaching retirement from the editorship.   The Assembly passed a tepid resolution of thanks, which was far less than Blackburn deserved : its nature may perhaps be explained by the fact that he was already entangled in the financial troubles which clouded his later years.   The fatal mistake was made of putting the editorship of the magazine in commission, and a commission, too, of theological professors !   The title was changed into the *Biblical Review and Congregational Magazine,* afterwards the *Biblical Review* only, but despite the fact that the editors were called " five of the most efficient men of our own or of any denomination for the work assigned to them ", the journal decreased in interest, its circulation dwindled, and in 1850 it met the common fate of Congregational periodicals.

John Blackburn was one of the outstanding men of the early years of the Union, to which he rendered sterling service, especially in the endeavour to secure full and accurate statistics as editor of the *Congregational Magazine* and of the *Year Book.*   It is a pity that his career ended in shadow.   He died in 1855.

An even more remarkable man was John Campbell, the editor of the first periodicals definitely published by the Union.   He was truly a " Son of Thunder ", and storms naturally gathered round him.   Called from Kilmarnock to succeed Matthew Wilks as pastor of the Tabernacle and Tottenham Court Chapels in 1829, he was soon engaged in a strenuous fight with their managers with the purpose of discovering whether these chapels of Whitefield's were Independent churches, controlled by their members, or proprietary chapels controlled by Trustees.   Finally victorious, he next turned his attention to the Bible Printing monopoly, in intervals of leisure writing the " Jethro " prize essay.   A vigorous campaign was once more successful, the price of Bibles being reduced by two-thirds, and by the forties Campbell's name was as well known in the country as that of any Independent. Josiah Conder tells how, when the Union met in York in 1847, he and about one hundred delegates attended service in the Minster, where the precentor, immediately after announcing the anthem, was heard to whisper, " Is Dr. Campbell among them ? "

Already writing frequently in the *Patriot* and the *Eclectic Review,* Campbell was a strong advocate of cheap denominational periodical literature, and we have seen how it was to him that the Union turned in 1843 when the *Christian Witness* was being planned.   The prospectus he drew up shows how he endeavoured to make the journal

> so comprehensive that, without violating the great principle on which the work itself is founded, it can hardly admit of expansion. It comprises the whole empire of morals and religion . . . Properly worked out, it will be found in its operations to touch Christian Society at all points, from the heart to the extremities.

The prospectus holds up a mirror to the religious life of the times.   It is far too long to print, but its main points must be given :

I. THEOLOGY AND BIBLICAL ILLUSTRATION.   " The paramount object of our Journal will be, by every means, to promote the work of God in the hearts of his children ".   Each number is to contain discourses for instruction, comfort, *etc.,* but " no profound and perplexing theological controversy will be admitted ".

II. BIOGRAPHY AND OBITUARY.   " Grace reigning in life ; grace triumphing in death ! "

III. ESSAYS, EXTRACTS, AND CORRESPONDENCE.

IV. CHURCH AND STATE.   " The separation of Church and State is the grand—the paramount—question of our times . . . The human mind cannot even approximate the formation of a true estimate of the calamity and evil which flow from this most unscriptural and most baneful union ! To fire the mind, we must illumine the judgment, and awaken the conscience."

V. ANALYTICAL REVIEWS AND SHORT CRITICISMS. This admirable section ends : " Of one class of books, the substance, the scope, and the aim, will be care- fully set forth, and a judgment pronounced on their merits and claims. Of another class, only the subject and object will be stated, and the character critically described. By this process, notwithstanding its brevity, great things may still be achieved for literature, as much, indeed, as by reviews of greater length. All that is really *judicial is generally contained in a few sentences.*"

VI. SABBATH AND BRITISH SCHOOLS.

VII. RELIGIOUS AND PHILANTHROPIC INTELLIGENCE.

VIII. POETRY. " The choicest productions of our Christian Poets will be summoned to aid in refining the taste, regaling the fancy, and purifying the heart of our readers ".

IX. BRITISH MISSIONS. " As Missionary Institutions are the glory of the Churches, so every Denominational Periodical ought to endeavour, to the utmost of its power, to further their interests. With a view to this, a digest of the operations of these Missions will form a part of every number ".

R. W. Dale, whose father and mother were members of Campbell's church, long afterwards described the " immense success " of the magazine, with its unprecedented circulation for a periodical of its kind :

> Those of us who belonged to Dr. Campbell's congregation thought that the success of the *Christian Witness* was the greatest ecclesiastical event of the century ; and we had some encouragement in thinking so from Dr. Campbell himself.

Dale's acquaintance with the *Christian Witness* led him to send an article signed " Gaius "—" a common signature for old men to use in religious magazines in those days "— and Campbell accepted the contribution, little dreaming it was from a boy of thirteen or fourteen. Had he known it he would probably have given more encouragement to the youth a little later when he wanted to enter the ministry.

Campbell's next step was a more popular paper, and the Assembly in the autumn of 1845 decided to publish *The Christian's Penny Magazine and Friend of the People,*

> one sheet in 32 mo. . . . the contents to be for the most part of a directly religious character, but not exclusive of elementary articles on denominational principles and benevolent objects.

The profits were to be treated like those of the *Christian*

Witness, and the paper was to be an experiment for a year, the Editor taking no pay in case of failure. This second venture " caught on ", too, its circulation, more than 100,000, never being equalled by any periodical with the Congregational name before the establishment of the *Congregational Church Monthly* in 1924. Until 1864 Campbell edited both journals, which he called " the pride and joy of my life ". By that time he reckoned their total circulation had been over 14,000,000, while the profits for aged ministers amounted to many thousands of pounds.[1] Waddington thus sums up their merits :

> This unprecedented success arose from no meretricious attractions. The magazine contained neither pictorial illustrations nor sensational tales, but clear and consistent theology, practical counsels and the fullest intelligence respecting the principles, the order and the work and the influence of the denomination. Every number issued was accepted with eagerness and read with avidity, from the notes of the Editor to his correspondents to the last word in the text. The goodly volumes remain as a treasury of information on all points connected with the movements of the time and the interests of the denomination.

Would that that were the whole story ! But with the best intentions in the world—for he considered editors " God's ploughmen "—Campbell was not satisfied by merely editing monthlies for the Union. He had tremendous energy, and was afflicted with the *cacoethes scribendi.* His biographers have described him working away against time in Bolt Court, inaccessible to everybody, with four amanuenses receiving 15 minutes' dictation in turn. The two monthlies by no means exhausted his energies. He believed that the Dissenters needed both a daily and a weekly as well, and when Alderman Challis—chairman of the *Patriot's* managers, and afterwards Lord Mayor of London—wrote to him to say a new weekly would be established if he would edit it, and offered to supply his pulpit for twelve months if he agreed, he finally closed with the offer, though he would accept no salary. The *British*

---

1 Stated as £12,000 by Campbell's biographers, Ferguson and Brown, and £7,000 by Waddington (*Congregational History,* IV, 588).

Banner thus saw the light in 1848, its editor asking for a circulation of 100,000 as a counterblast to the Sunday Press —he said that one London Sunday paper had a circulation of 60,000. By this time he was so well-known that he could quote the *Evangelical Magazine's* words :

> Dr. Campbell is assuredly one of the boldest men of his age. But for his unexampled success, in reference to the *Christian Witness* and *Christian's Penny Magazine,* we should tremble for his present position. His prospectus of the *British Banner* is now before us, and who would *dare* it but Dr. Campbell? With his other literary labours, how strong must be his confidence in his own powers, and in the favour of that public which has so nobly responded to his past efforts ! He has a *right* to be *meekly* confident : for God has made him the instrument of a great achievement for the Religious Periodical Press of our country. We cheerfully acknowledge *our* debt of obligation ; and we are confident that posterity will gratefully own the claim. Nor are we less sensible of the immense value of Dr. Campbell's labours because we have not always been able to sympathize with his modes of dealing with particular questions. Such a man must have large scope, generous freedom of action, kindly interpretations of his motives, and, withal, candid allowance for the difficulties which beset his path. He has a more benevolent heart than many who write blandly and simperingly, while bitter malice lurks within and their lives are spent in " scattering firebrands, arrows, and death ". If we are to have an antagonist, let him be honest, straight-forward, and undisguised ; and, with truth on our side, we have nothing to fear. We dread nothing in controversy but cant, hypocrisy, secret conspiracy, and mischievous one-sidedness. Of these Dr. Campbell will never be guilty ; he has too much manliness of character ever to resort to them ; and he will never tolerate them in the contemporary press.

In return he could refer to the *Christian Witness* and the *Evangelical* as complementary :

> Those of milder mood will repose in the refreshing shade of the *Evangelical,* and those of sterner mould may gather animation in the more fervent atmosphere of the *Witness.* The elder journal will more particularly administer the Peace, the younger the War department of the Church of Christ.

Imagine a man of strong opinions on all subjects, editing two periodicals under Union auspices, and one for which the Union was not responsible, and it is easy to see that trouble was certain to rise. Remember that Campbell was essentially a controversialist who believed that, in his biographer's words :

> he was set for the defence of the Gospel. He was jealous of God's truth and of God's glory. Any attempt to disturb our repose in the Bible as a divine revelation he met with unsparing severity. Whenever and wherever he could discover any effort to depreciate or abandon the cardinal doctrines of our holy faith, his soul became fired with a holy indignation ; and in tones of thunder, he uttered not only his protest, but his most solemn denunciation.

Remember, too, that not only was theological opinion among the Independents by no means fixed, and that controversy was easily aroused, but that also there was manifest division among them about the part they should play in political propaganda, especially in regard to the separation of Church and State. Here were all the materials for a fire, if the match should be applied, and we shall see the Union in frequent turmoil about its periodicals.

Campbell was, however, even more uneasy in the editorial chair of the *British Banner* than of the Union journals. It was not difficult to arouse opposition among the proprietors to one who thus looked on his office :

> But a man of decided views, of public spirit, of ardent zeal, and resolute purpose, with vigour of mind, and amplitude of knowledge sufficient to deal with great questions, and courage to proclaim his honest convictions, and to defend what he believes to be the vital truth, and setting his face as a flint against deadly error, may lay his account, sooner or later, with opposition. Such a man must bid a long farewell to unbroken tranquillity, and from time to time, prepare for conflict, oft-times fierce and ruthless, on every side.

We shall see how, in 1856, in order to secure his freedom he resigned the *Banner,* which, no mean tribute to his editorship, speedily languished and died. He immediately started *The British Standard,* where he enjoyed independence and which was self-supporting until his retirement in 1866. During the period in which he edited the Union periodicals he was mixed up in several libel actions, while sometimes the *Banner* or the *Standard* would be vigorously advocating a course objectionable to many Independents. The Union, therefore, had a hard riddle to solve. It needed periodicals, and there seemed to be only one man able to make them succeed. He had the editorial *flair,* and people wanted to know what he had to say. He never spared himself of time or of money, and by means of the periodicals he was gradually building up a fund for which aged ministers had constant reason to give thanks; but nobody knew where he would break out next, and he could neither be curbed nor cured.

When the *Christian Witness* died in 1871, R. W. Dale, who became the editor of its successor, *The Congregationalist,* wrote a paragraph which aptly describes the man and his methods :

> I am old enough to remember the original Prospectus of the Magazine, and still retain a vivid impression of one sweeping sentence, in which the Editor, with his characteristic vehemence and largeness of manner, gave his readers to understand that there was hardly any function to which human genius and energy could be called, so worthy of a noble ambition, or so calculated to kindle enthusiasm and stimulate industry, as the editorship of a popular religious Magazine. To him the Editor's chair was a royal throne. I remember, too, the half-humorous, half-serious declaration which he made in his preface to one of the early volumes, to the effect that the creed of the readers of a Magazine, in reference to the Editor, should contain only one article—Infallibility. The strongly-marked individuality of Dr. Campbell was impressed upon every number that appeared. His " Answers to Correspondents ", which generally filled the page of the cover on the back of the title, were unique. In the Magazine itself he constituted himself the general judge and arbiter of the fate of Christendom. His literary idol was Samuel Johnson, and with something of Johnson's manner, but with very much more impetuosity, he inflicted summary chastisement upon all offenders. Sometimes he denounced Romanists. Sometimes he raised the war-cry against heresy. Sometimes he was very " faithful " to the Methodists. Whatever other charge was brought against the *Christian Witness,* no one could say that it was dull.
>
> For several years it had a splendid circulation. There was nothing to compete with it . . . Dr. Campbell had the

field very much to himself. The *Evangelical Magazine* was his only powerful rival, and the quiet, subdued tone of the *Evangelical* in those days had little chance against the vehemence of the *Christian Witness*. Nor was the vigour of the new Magazine the only secret of its popularity. It contained many articles of real and substantial value, and the Editor laid his hands on everything which he thought would interest his readers. A fortnight or three weeks after the appearance of Mr. James's *Earnest Church*, I happened to meet him accidentally at his Birmingham publishers. It was the first of the month, and he took up the *Christian Witness*, which was lying on the counter. I very well remember the look with which he turned to me, and said, " Why, Dr. Campbell has taken nearly the whole of my new book and put it into the *Christian Witness* ; who will give three shillings for my book when they can get it in a Magazine for threepence? " The enterprising Editor was anxious, he told Mr. James afterwards, to make the book as useful as possible, and did not seem to have considered that by transferring a great part of it to the double columns of the *Christian Witness,* he might perhaps make the publication a dead loss to the author.

Had there been a little relief to Campbell's intense seriousness much trouble might have been avoided. Two of the " Answers to Correspondents " Dale mentions are sufficient in themselves to indicate Campbell's lack of humour, and his failure to use light and shade :

Juvenis.
" Chess playing " *is* undoubtedly *a waste of time* which might be a thousand times better employed. To encourage our ingenuous young correspondent we frankly tell him we never spent one minute in any sort of game or play whatever. A book, *Juvenis,* a book ! A book ! Nothing like a good book !

Eliza.
Will she write again?

The story has been considerably anticipated in order to show what manner of man John Campbell was. Without a correct picture of the editor and his methods it is impossible to see why the Union periodicals were such a cause of trouble. Turning back to 1844, these troubles must now be described. Right away Campbell showed his mettle, announcing, at the beginning of the *Christian Witness,* that he was trying the experiment for a year : "The Public, not the Editor, are now on their probation ".   At the end of the year he prefixed to the bound volume a grandiloquent and bombastic Dedication " To the Congregational Churches of England and Wales, with their Pastors and Deacons", in which he thus outlined his task, his policy, and his achievement :

> Instead of the catholicity of our excellent contemporary, the *Evangelical Magazine,* which, merging all sectional distinctions, launched out on the boundless Pacific of Evangelical Protestantism, the motto of the *Christian Witness,* as if written in letters of fire, was, " *Dissent from all Ecclesiastical Establishments* ". Instead of the mitigated, but still large catholicity of the *Eclectic Review,* of happy memory and distinguished merit, which, merging all peculiarities of ritual, polity, and doctrine among Evangelical Dissenters, stood forth on the broad Atlantic of Nonconformity, the *Christian Witness* unfurled its sail on the bounding billows of the stormy Baltic of Pædobaptist Independency—the system of a people whose indifference to their denominational interests, and whose neglect of their own peculiar literature, have hitherto been their real reproach, their imaginary glory—the system of a people who had, for a quarter of a century, left their own, their only Magazine—in some respects the best of its age, to languish, and, at times, almost to die !

Of 15,000 prospectuses of the *Christian Witness* sent out only 200 were returned, of which only two or three were from pastors of large congregations, and only three or four from London.   Despite this, the journal had succeeded, and its twelve numbers had given readers as much matter for three shillings as four octavo volumes at half a guinea each.   To those who were now praising the magazine Campbell not unnaturally quoted Johnson's famous letter to Chesterfield.   He then proceeded, just at the time, be it remembered, when Robert Vaughan was starting the *British Quarterly Review,* to deprecate quarterly journals and to attack those who believed that " no religious community was ever respectable and strong without a high-priced and large-typed Quarterly Periodical ".   His outlook and style are well seen in this quotation :

> What Nobles have done for nations may be ascertained from history ; but what Quarterlies have done for religious

bodies we have yet to learn. A good Nobility, if it can be created, may, for aught we know, be a good institution; and a good Quarterly, if it can be established, in its own little sphere, may be a useful organ : but for the advancement of a nation's real good we would not give 10,000 well-disciplined British-School Teachers for all the Nobles in the world; and for training, purifying, elevating, animating, and impelling on to virtuous deeds the souls of the Christian portion of the British people, we would not give a well-conducted Weekly Religious Paper, with a circulation of 100,000 copies, and so cheap as to bring it within the reach of the poorest, for all the Quarterlies that British talent could produce, and British wealth support. We say, therefore, whatever else you do, attend to the organs of the Millions ! Would that the minds of our gifted ministers, and of our opulent, liberal, and public-spirited laymen, were fully alive to this subject, and that they would direct their energies into this channel ! Neglect what you may, remember the Millions ! Let your first object and your last be to advance, in all possible ways, your own cheap periodical literature. This is your life ! Even the opulent, instead of overlooking, should most prize the excellence which is cheapest. The cheaper it is, the more it approximates to all God's chief blessings. That which only few can purchase, only few can read. The numbers circulated of half-crown Monthlies, and six-shilling Quarterlies, whatever their respective merits, must always be limited to comparatively a few hands, and therefore utterly and in every way impotent for popular objects. But fact in this matter is better than argument. The present Number of the *Christian Witness,* for example, publishes 33,000 copies of the important Documents of the Union in one day, thus diffusing them among myriads of minds, of every order, in all the coasts and districts of the British Empire, and through most parts of the civilized world, and this at such a price as a child pays for the most insignificant plaything ! This is a boon that could not be conferred on the Church of Christ by all our expensive Monthly and Quarterly Reviews and Magazines, both religious and secular, united. Six-shilling Quarterlies belong to the reign which gloried in castled waggons, drawn by twelve horses, and moving at the dignified pace of twelve miles a day; half-crown Monthlies are of a species with the handsome English stage coach, driving at twelve miles an hour —good things, *inside,* for people possessing wealth and leisure; but Cheap Periodicals belong to the age of the Railway ! Every man, then, to his taste; Gothic things for Gothic men; but light postage, quick transit, cheap Bibles, and cheap Periodicals, for the Millions of England!

Ending with a plea for a circulation of 50,000, to be effected by the " *unanimous, simultaneous, and resolute exertion of our entire community* ", he thus concludes :

> Now for action, in the prospect of 1845. Whose bosom glows with warm desires for the good of his country and of mankind? Who bears an ardent love to the Congregational community, and fervently longs to see their churches improved, elevated, animated, and multiplied? Who prays with all prayer and supplication for the spread of the gospel, the triumphs of truth, at home and in our distant Colonies? Whose sympathizing heart bleeds over the benighted heathen, and burns to behold the whole earth filled with the glory of Emmanuel? Let all such diffuse the *Christian Witness*! Pastors, Deacons, Communicants, Auditors, Door-keepers, Collectors, Visitors, Home Missionaries, Travelling Agents, we urge, we conjure you to devise all practicable methods, and watch for every opportunity, to diffuse the *Christian Witness*!

And while he was sounding this call to action, he was laying about him on all and sundry, freely criticizing Union speakers, arrangements, and policy. " Ceasing then to drivel, let us act as men ", he cried, as he urged the establishment of a Congregational Central Fund, especially for church building, and the appointment of an agent to collect the Education Fund. He made scathing remarks about the proceedings at public meetings where speakers did not know they were to be called upon until they were handed resolutions on the platform. The meeting in support of "British Missions" at Norwich (1844) was " highly exciting rather than effective ", and followed " a method the most successful that could have been devised for defeating the object of the friends of these Institutions ". The Autumnal Meetings, he agreed, were much more valuable than those in May, but the rational plan would be to have Monday evening, Tuesday, Wednesday, and Thursday mornings and afternoons for Union business, and the three evenings, Tuesday to Thursday, for the three Societies[1] in turn.

---

[1] Home, Colonial, and Irish Evangelical. See below, p. 150.

He criticized the Congregational Library, making the
sensible proposal that a cheap edition of the Congregational Lectures should be published, but doing it in as
offensive a way as possible. The 12s. asked for the
Lectures would buy the *Christian Witness* for four years,
which would make 16 volumes the size of the Lecture,
matter which would cost £9. 12s. 0d. instead of 12s. for the
four years' *Christian Witness* !

> Utility is everything. With Eternity before us we
> would rather produce a single number of the threepenny
> *Christian Witness* than one of these sumptuous 12s.
> volumes. The readers of the one are probably little more
> than 200,000, the readers of the other are, perhaps, little
> more than 2,000.

All this will make it easy to understand why there were
those who had a strong dislike to John Campbell. This
found expression at the Manchester Assembly in 1845,
when Campbell, thinking of his millions of readers, set out
the proposal for the *Christian's Penny Magazine and
Friend of the People.* The official Minutes of the Union
discreetly skate over the discussion in a few sentences, but
Campbell gives a full report in the *Christian Witness,*
with a long defence of himself. Dr. Halley bluntly said
that if the question was whether " Dr. Campbell is a fit
and proper person to manage [a new magazine] there
will be a difference of opinion in the Assembly", and there
was much doubt and hesitation about the wisdom of starting another paper before the first was firmly established.
Campbell's force and fervour swept away all opposition :
he produced specimens of similar papers, and showed what
could be done. He urged the Union to start the journal
whoever might be the editor, and he told them that if they
did not, the paper would be started without them !

Campbell did not mince matters at all. He spoke of the
sacrifices he had both made and was prepared to make,[1]

---

[1] Compare his proclamation when the *British Banner* was started.
After saying that the proprietors will receive only five per cent on their
capital—*i.e.,* as they did from the *Patriot,* he goes on :
   May we now ask a word for ourselves? OUR PERSONAL SERVICE IN
CONDUCTING THIS GREAT EXPERIMENT IS WHOLLY GRATUITOUS. The Committee undertake the expenses of our Pulpit Supplies, an arrangement
with which our flock has very reluctantly complied; and mainly, we

and of his attitude to editorial work :

> It is truly impossible for the holder of the office to discharge his varied functions with vigour, fidelity, impartiality, and efficiency without giving frequent and oft-times great offence both to individuals and to parties. This is the unalterable condition of real utility and eminent success. *He who makes no enemies will have few friends. He who excites no hostility to himself will do very little for you as a Denomination.*

John Angell James did not vote for or against the proposal, saying that some dreaded that the paper would be " too liberally charged with the *democratic element,* and prove the instrument for over-stimulating the lower classes of our people ". Campbell pointed out that it was to be "entirely elementary in its principles and theological in its character ", and suggested that an editor of more conservative and aristocratic principles should be appointed. Speaking of James, he said :

> Why should not our much-honoured friend and brother himself step forward and tender his personal services? Why not give to this project for the good of the millions the full benefit of his practised and powerful pen—of his well-earned and widespread reputation?

He was proud of these democratic tendencies, and confident in what he could do with the magazine, crying,

> The myriads ! leave us to them, and them to us. We are safe in each other's hands. Our confidence is mutual, and our reciprocal regards improve with time. We do not deem ourselves chargeable with either arrogance or presumption when we prophesy that under our management thousands of the *Friend of the People* will be sold for

---

regret to say, on account of much diminished physical strength for some time past, which has gone far to unfit for efficient pulpit labour, in the kind hope that a respite may be the means of its recovery. They have also placed at our disposal the sum required to meet the salaries of those gentlemen who are regularly engaged on the Journal as our Assistants ; *but to ourselves for personal service,* NO EMOLUMENTS, IN ANY SHAPE WHATEVER, ACCRUE. We could accept the arduous task on no other condition. Of the labours physical and intellectual, which, especially at the outset, that task imposes, we have nothing to say. Men of sense will estimate them. Be they what they may, in the hope of advancing our country's good, and the glory of that " kingdom which cannot be moved," we cheerfully throw ourselves into the enterprise, in the confidence that our endeavours will be seconded in a spirit, and on a scale, worthy of the object, and honourable to the English Nation.

hundreds that would be disposed of were it under the management of those who most disrelish our "democratic" views and are most opposed to our outward policy.

Such was John Campbell,[1] and he proceeded to report the very meetings where he was such a centre of controversy, describing an evening session addressed by such worthies as Alderman Kershaw, Dr. Matheson, Dr. Halley, Dr. Morison, Messrs. Ely, Aveling, Sherman, Parsons, and Wells (who " poured out at once, from the head and the heart, a blended flood of intellect and emotion ") :

> One half at least of the speaking was not worthy of the occasion . . . There must be an end to that loose, rambling, pithless, pointless small talk and twaddle which has so long prevailed on platforms. *There must be preparation!* Self-respect, respect for the Church of God, the honour of religion, the interests of truth all unite in demanding on such occasions the most thorough preparation.

It will be realized that the Union, launched on the sea of periodical literature, was in for a stormy time.

In other ways 1845 was a year in which literature was much to the fore. As has been mentioned, it was then the *British Quarterly* began its useful career. In the same year Dr. Redford read an important paper on "The Literature of our Denomination", which is really a survey of the attitude of Independent Churches to learning. He pointed out that

> we have not yet produced a historian of our Church principles, though we have invaluable memorials, yet no succinct and standard history of Independency—that we greatly need a purely scriptural exposition of our Church system—that we have not yet a catechism for the young or a *Vade Mecum* for the youth who leave our schools, and who after being instructed generally in the Gospel are left without any tie of preference for our denomination, and who in consequence are in vast numbers lost to us.

He ended by suggesting :

1. The preparation of a superior and cheap supply of reading, in which distinctive principles should not be for-

---

[1] Skeats & Miall, *History of the Free Churches,* p. 611, is very good on Campbell, though critical.

gotten, but should be subservient to "the promotion of our views on religion".

2. The "zealous encouragement of the higher class of our literature . . . Is it not a fact that many educated persons, professional men and rich men firmly attached to our principles, scarcely ever look into our best periodicals, or know the amount of literary talent which their own denomination possesses?"

3. The formation of a Literature or Book Committee. This third suggestion was immediately adopted, and Drs. Bennett, Harris, W. Smith, the Revs. J. Blackburn and A. Wells, and Messrs. B. Hanbury and W. A. Hankey were appointed as the Committee, with power to add to their number.

The Assembly's Activities.

With the growth of the Union all kinds of developments were seen. The Library was no longer big enough for the May meetings, and in 1843 a move was made to Crosby Hall, Bishopsgate, the Library being used for refreshments. There was pressure on time as well as space, and it became clear not only that the Assembly must have more time for its business, but also that two types of meeting would have to be arranged: (a) confidential, and limited to delegates, as previously; (b) more public, but still ticket meetings open only to members of churches.

It is well to remember that the meetings were still of an informal kind; often the reports read more like conversations than set speeches. Thus, at the Bristol Meetings in 1840, the Rev. D. E. Ford, of Lymington, said:

> I hope, Sir, you will not think me very far gone in Methodism, if I allude, for one moment to female prayer-meetings. In the church where I labour we have adopted the practice of holding such meetings, and we find them attended with unmixed benefit. Again, we have prayer-meetings for the little children, which are held once a week in private houses, and conducted by the teachers. On these occasions mere babes are permitted to pray.

The same account continues:

> Rev. R. Gill, of Charmouth, said he wished to put ministers on their guard against an insidious practice of some socialists, who have actually sent their books as presents for Congregational libraries, which, for want of examina-

tion, have actually got into circulation before their character was detected.

The Rev. G. Stevens, of Totton—And for want of the same examination, a publication was circulated containing five-and-twenty reasons why I ought not to be a dissenter.

Attempts were made to get into direct touch with the churches, pastors being asked to supply the addresses of their deacons. It was hoped that in this way and by closer organization churches might be enlivened and invigorated. Josiah Conder, who was always wishing that the churches "would not mistake selfish supineness for spirituality, and worldliness for catholic liberality", urged that

> what we want, next to more of the vital spirit from the Head, is organization, ecclesiastical and political. I look to the Union to promote the former, and *The Patriot* and the Church-Rate abolition agitation to create the latter.

In 1845 the Union met for the first time in Manchester, and it is not surprising to learn either that Manchester suggested the subject for consideration—"The State of Religion in our Denomination"—or that the Minutes have a prefatory note to say that attempts to get correct lists of those present were made but "as many gentlemen, especially of those resident in Manchester, entered while the proceedings were in progress, their names are unavoidably omitted". These meetings were the high-water mark to date—265 ministers, 51 students, and 209 lay delegates and visitors being present—and they were the most lively.

In innumerable ways, large and small, the Union was trying to extend its usefulness. In 1842, for example, a model Trust Deed was in course of preparation, while two years later Blackburn and Henry Richard went as a deputation to the churches of South Wales. The Annual Letter was still sent out, and about it Thomas Binney, great man of the denomination though he was, was rapped over the knuckles in 1844. One of a group of London ministers appointed to prepare a Letter on "Worship", he reported that there had been a discussion on the subject in the *Congregational Magazine,* so that he thought an official Letter superfluous, while indisposition had prevented him from writing on private devotion in its place, as he had

JOHN CAMPBELL

JOHN BLACKBURN

planned. The Assembly repeated its request, refusing to
recognize that a *Congregational Magazine* discussion
superseded the annual epistle, but though they asked
"Binney & Co." to prepare the Letter for October, it was
not until the following May that it was presented.

Cognizance was taken of important public events,
conferences, *etc*. The leaders of the fight against the Bible
monopoly were congratulated; a deputation was sent to an
International Conference for the Abolition of Slavery, and
it was made clear to the American Churches that no delegate who was in favour of slavery would be *persona grata;*
a resolution was passed in 1845 rejoicing in the Jubilee of
the London Missionary Society.

In the main, however, activity in regard to public
questions was limited to the parallel lines of education and
resistance to measures which infringed civil and religious
liberty. There were different grades of opinion about the
best way of fighting the Establishment, and several com-
petitive Societies were formed, but the British Anti-State
Church Association (afterwards the "Liberation Society"),
founded by Edward Miall in 1841, and supported with the
utmost vigour in his weekly paper, the *Nonconformist,*
established in the same year, prevented most of the
Independents from being indifferent to this and kindred
questions : in the fourth issue of the journal he roundly
charged Dissenting ministers with "unfaithfulness to
sacred principles and evasion of a noble mission".

The Union, which had, in the previous year, petitioned
the House of Commons against any grant of public money
for Church Extension, in 1841 renewed its protest against
Church Rates, saying that

> In the presence of a powerful and now aggressive
> hierarchy, the utmost constancy and activity are demanded
> of all to whom civil, and still more, religious liberty
> is dearer than life.

In 1841 "A Declaration of Views and Principles on various
Deeply Interesting Questions agitated during the Present
Crisis, as they affect the Duty and Reputation of the In-
dependent Churches" was passed after much discussion,

K

and sent to members of both Houses of Parliament, the Heads of Colleges in Oxford and Cambridge, and all Baptist, Independent, and Methodist ministers. Protests were made against infringements of religious liberty by Continental Governments under Popish influence, while long resolutions were passed against the Dissenters' Chapels' Trusts Bill in 1844. This, and the Maynooth proposals in 1845, caused a great outcry, and resolutions against the Maynooth Grant were carried, a circular letter and form of petition being sent to every pastor and the call sent from the Committee : "Let Nonconformist electors prepare for the next general election. Let them register, consult, and prepare".

At this time a petition to the House of Commons was agreed on, asking them to discontinue the grant of the *Regium Donum*. There was little to be said in favour of the acceptance of this grant, and it was strange that Dr. Pye Smith, one of the most enlightened of men, far ahead of his fellow Independents in theological and political outlook, and a member of the Anti-State Church Association, should have been the distributor to the Independents and have contrived to find reasons for accepting the grant. It was as unusual then as now for a Chancellor of the Exchequer to find anybody who did not wish to receive money from the State, and in 1851 the grant was discontinued.

Throughout these years Independents felt strongly that the fight was between Popery and Voluntaryism, and there was no hesitation at all about the lead the Union gave.

Nevertheless, there was evident all over the country

a growing desire for union and mutual helpfulness—an increasing conviction of the value and vital importance of those principles both of theology and church polity which are distinctive of our body.

Ministers were meeting together and expressing the desire for "Catholic fellowship with Evangelical brethren in other communions"; the growth of Tractarianism was naturally causing Evangelicals of different denominations to draw together. Now an attempt was made to form them into an organized Union. Even with the Baptists the Independents had had little to do, though a Baptist gave £50—the largest donation—to the cost of the American Deputation in 1834. A deputation from the Baptist Union attended the Assembly in 1838 and the Baptist Union Reports were often held up as an example. In 1843 a resolution was passed protesting against the persecution of Baptists in Denmark.

In 1842, however, the project for an Evangelical Union between all Protestants began to take shape. The Assembly passed resolutions in support, and deplored the spread of Popery in the Established Church. In the following year the Chairman of the Union called a meeting of ministers of various denominations, and afterwards the Secretaries summoned a public meeting. John Angell James took the lead in the development of the Scheme, the Union duly appointed delegates, and in 1845 the Evangelical Alliance was formed.

Sometimes attempts to co-operate with other Protestants caused difficulties. In 1843 a congratulatory message was sent to the Scottish Presbyterians at the bicentenary of the Westminster Assembly, and on the Disruption sympathy and practical support were forthcoming for the Free Church of Scotland. This evidently aroused a protest from the Scottish Congregationalists, and their outcry was not lessened when they were told it was inopportune for them to come South to collect for their Home Missions because great efforts had been recently made for education and for the Free Church of Scotland.

In the same way there were those who had no confidence at all in the Evangelical Alliance movement, which to a man like Campbell seemed to be a glossing over of vital differences, and a weakening of the Nonconformist witness. He had lively altercations about it both with pen and tongue, and poured scorn on those who were always talking of "crisis", "splitting the denomination" and "breaking up the Union". It will be seen that one of the main counts against Campbell's management of the magazines was his treatment of the Alliance.

At this time, too, there was renewed insistence on the New Testament character of the Independent Church.

While, in 1838, the Rev. Alexander Stewart of Barnet (father of Mr. Halley Stewart), to take one example, at an ordination at Bushey "gave a very lucid statement of the nature of a Gospel Church", five years later, at the height of the Oxford Movement, the Union itself circulated "an Appeal to the Independent Churches . . . and to their Bishops and Deacons, on the importance of a decided testimony to Evangelical Truth at the present crisis".

It is scarcely possible, to-day, to realize the fierceness of the conflict between the Established Church of the time and the Dissenters. Constructively the Independents embodied their view in such statements as that of John Angell James :

> Whenever Christian fellowship is substantially exercised, there is a Church : nor does that congregation, however duly organized, deserve the name in which that object is not realized.

In general, however, both sides attacked each other with great bitterness, especially in their periodicals, as we saw above. Among the weapons employed by the Independents was one frequently used later. They pointed out that 887 prisoners in the County Gaol of Middlesex in 1838 were divided among the following denominations : 1 Independent, 2 Baptists, 6 Jews, 11 Methodists, 11 Presbyterians, 137 Roman Catholics, 719 Church of England. And John Campbell was not the man to miss noting that in four prisons the figures for Episcopalians and Independents were 479 to 10, 266 to 12, 540 to 3, 719 to 1, at the time that the State grants in three years to 1,167 National Schools amounted to £149,211, and to 53 British Schools £8,961.

Chapel Building.

It is interesting to see how important aspects of the life of the Congregationalists of the time were intertwined. It was because of education and kindred questions that full and accurate statistics were so urgently demanded. It was because of the new aggressiveness of Anglo-Catholicism that renewed demands were made for increased efforts in the way of chapel building. Thus, John Angell James sounded the clarion cry in 1839 :

LET US BUILD MORE PLACES OF WORSHIP. It seems to be the present policy of the Church of England to build us *down* and to build us *out*. Its members suppose that our congregations continue with us, only because there are no Episcopalian places to receive them; and acting upon this mistake, they are multiplying chapels and churches, many of which are erected in the immediate vicinity of ours, for the purpose of drawing into them the people *we* have gathered. To prevent this we must keep pace with them in this blessed spirit of building. Enlargements, re-erections, and new erections must go on amongst us, according to our ability, and with an energy in some measure resembling the Church of England. Town Missions, *etc.,* are all well in their place; but there wants something in addition, to gather up, consolidate and retain to ourselves, the effects which these means produce : and that something is the erection of places of worship. We must catch the building spirit of the age. We must *build, build, build.* . . . . We cannot multiply our persons, unless we multiply our places. We must not wait for congregations to be gathered before we build : we must build to gather. . . . For, this, money, much money, far *more* money will be wanted : we must give it. The time is come when Nonconformists must prove their love for their principles by the sacrifice of poverty : and it is the only sacrifice they are called to make for maintaining and extending them. There must be a liberality far above any thing we have yet witnessed. Nor must we allow our own denomination to be lost in the splendour and magnitude of foreign missions. I would not have a single shilling withdrawn from these to support Dissent and multiply Dissenting places of worship, but I would have Dissenting places and congregations multiplied to increase the support of foreign missions. . . . We *must* bestir ourselves, and build more places; this I repeat, and urge again and again. And to occupy them we must send off, as a nucleus for the new congregations, colonies from such as are already large and overflowing. There must be no grudging of our members for this purpose. Congregationalism tends, if it be not watched, to Congregational selfishness. Ministers must be willing to part from their people, and the people from their ministers for this purpose. We must seek to *increase* : we have the means : there is room for us; and I believe God will bless the attempt.

With a policy of this kind it is easy to see how chapel debts arose. It is worth while noting how the policy was carried out, and how the resulting debts were liquidated. In 1805 North Wales had only 17 chapels. By 1835, 15 of these had been enlarged, and 157 new chapels built. The Welsh churches in the early years of the Union made a great effort to clear their debts; in the two years before 1834 they raised £18,404, and then sent raiders to England, not for the first time—or the last. John Angell James gave them £20, and Thomas Wilson £50, and English congregations contributed £3,000 in collections in a few weeks. Between 1827 and 1839, 20 chapels were built in Warwickshire, between 1818 and 1838, 25 (costing £22,000) in Sussex. With buildings springing up like this all over the country debts naturally piled up too. Some churches managed to clear off a considerable portion at their opening services. Thus in 1838, when Queen Street, Chester, was enlarged, Raffles, McAll, and Sherman preached, and the collections were £211, £112, and £81. And this did not exhaust the generosity of the people, for when their pastor, Samuel Luke, conducted the services on the following Sunday, the offerings were £101.

In the *Christian Witness* for June, 1844, two paragraphs side by side show the working of the system.

> NEW CHAPELS :—April 5. A new chapel was opened at Kipping Thornton, near Bradford, capable of seating 1,200 persons, and—*free from debt!*
>
> April 16. A new chapel was opened at Broadway, Worcestershire. A debt remains of £193, to raise which the pastor proposes to visit the Metropolis.

"British Missions".

After the Birmingham Assembly in 1839, steps were taken to discuss the future with the Officers of the Home Missionary Society, with the result that it was possible to put before the May Meeting in 1840 far different proposals. Not merely the Home Missionary Society, but also the Irish Evangelical Society was willing to become associated with the Union on the same terms as the Colonial Society, their officers being *ex officio* members of the Union Committee, and vice versa, an account of their work to be presented to the Assembly each year in May. An Autumnal Meeting was to be arranged by the Home Missionary Society in connexion with the Autumn Assembly of the Union. The three Societies were to make a united appeal to the churches under the name of "British Missions", a simultaneous collection on an October Sunday being asked for, and they were to be regarded as Congregationalism's evangelizing front among fifteen million people at home, in the Colonies, and in Ireland. To quote the Committee's letter to the churches :

> Amidst the dark shades of papal superstition—taught to depend for salvation on sacramental efficacy, and priestly ministrations—crowding the scenes of Sabbath desecration —filling the lecture halls of socialism or of chartist agitation—spread over your fair rural districts in hopeless ignorance and apathy—or filling with squalor and vice the busy scenes of your commercial and manufacturing activity— they are the victims of intemperance and infidelity—of scanty wages and neglected education—they fill your jails, man your ships, found your colonies.

Look at the three Societies in turn :

(a) The Home Missionary Society.

The Scheme for "British Missions" was approved at Bristol[1] in October, and an anonymous donor gave Wells £1,000. Full consideration was given to the work of the Home Missionary Society, for which Matheson reported progress. The Society now had 120 missionaries and agents, proclaiming the Gospel to over 60,000 people in a population of over 700,000, and 130 Sunday Schools, with 8,500 children and 580 "gratuitous teachers". There was urgent need of help, for the annual increase of population in the country was 300,000, and of church accommodation 60,000, at most. The number of students from the Colleges was insufficient, and many of them preferred pastorates to Home Missionary work as "more respectable and comfortable", and the supply of suitable men was thus insufficient, eight of twelve new stations being unsupplied. The Society ought to have from 20 to 30 men in training regularly. The

---

[1] H. O. Wills gave the Union £20 as a thank-offering at the end of these Meetings.

need for the preaching of the Gospel was all the greater because so many of the clergy were becoming Puseyites :

> In many country districts there is a new cry raised against the efforts of our churches. It comes from the Oxford divines, and breathes the very element and spirit of the Vatican. Our ministers are declared to be *no* ministers of Christ's holy Gospel; our home missionaries are denounced as breaking into Christ's fold. Our religious services are pronounced null and void; and even the Gospel, which depends on the Spirit's influence for success in saving men, is declared to be worthless, when preached by others than apostolically ordained men.

The plan of the re-constituted Society was to work with both National and County Unions, to spread information of the need for Home Missions all over the country, and to transfer help from more prosperous districts to more needy. "At present Cornwall and Cumberland have no more mutual knowledge, sympathy and help than Otaheite and Jamaica". In 1845 only 6 of the 40 Counties were doing Home Missionary work without appealing to the Society for help, and urgent requests were made continually to the wealthier areas. In 1843 at Leeds, Matheson bearded the lion in its den when, praising the West Riding Home Missionary Society for its local work, he pointed out that the West Riding gave only £9 to the National Society, which had to spend £450 (nearly all raised in London) in the North and East Ridings, where it maintained 12 missionaries and made grants to 6 pastors. Wells had also reminded Lancashire that when they raised £2,000 for Home Missionary operations in their County, and £5,000 for sending the Gospel to the heathen, they could certainly afford to send something to those parts of England where the denomination was poor and where there were millions of people who did not hear the Gospel.

The Society both maintained whole-time agents (from 60 to 70 during these years) and made grants to pastors. Many of the agents were trained under John Frost at Cotton End, and under ministers who were willing to receive students into their Manses. The *Home Missionary Magazine*, enlarged in 1842, contains reports of the work of the three Societies, and these were also a regular feature of the *Christian Witness* from 1844, there being plentiful accounts of Puseyite persecution, petty and otherwise; conversions; death beds; and providential interpositions of various kinds, including "the awful death of a Socialist".

The aim was to "render England a land of churches"— not an easy thing to do by a Society with an income of less than £8,000, with a constantly recurring deficit, and only saved from insolvency by using a legacy as income.

(b) The Irish Evangelical Society (formed 1814).

The Association of this Society with the Union speedily brought trouble, for the Irish Congregational Union felt itself slighted, and the interests of the two Irish Societies were in conflict.   After long arguments five arbitrators— Wardlaw, James, Raffles, Kelly and Fletcher—met representatives of the two organizations in Liverpool, and an agreement was reached, the Society agreeing to co-operate with the Irish Union and to contribute to it double the amount of the sum raised by the Union in Ireland. The work in Ireland was carried on against great odds. The Society acknowledged that Congregationalism in Ireland was exotic and that no speedy results could be expected.   In 1845 there were only 26 Congregational Churches in the country, 4 of them unattached, 14 belonging to the Irish Evangelical Society, and the remaining 8 forming the Irish Union.   The Committee call Ireland a Mission Field "as much as Tahiti or Hindostan", and it was only by support from England that the work could be carried on, and yet all the Protestant denominations in England supplied less than £7,000 a year for Irish work. Of this, the Irish Evangelical Society's income was about £3,000, which supported about 130 stations.   They suggest that 2,000 English churches might contribute £2 each !

(c) The Colonial Society.

During these years the work of the Colonial Society was developing in both Canada and Australia, though the income was only about £3,000, and in 1841 it was said that only 250 of the churches were supporting it. Its advocacy being in the hands of Binney and Wells there was little fear of its interests being overlooked by the churches.

Year by year the three Societies presented a Report to the Assembly. In 1844 an attempt was made to substitute spoken addresses for the Reports, but it was made clear that the "practice of presenting written documents should not be again deviated from".

Gradually the churches took up the October collection for "British Missions", though by no means with regularity. Apparently they exercised the right of ear-marking their contributions, and occasionally a church even remembered the Union itself. The results for these years were (£'s only) :

Year	No. of Churches.	Home.	Irish.	Colonial.	Union.	Total.
1840	125	1,812	601	747	28	3,190*
1841	213	1,281	608	881	11	2,783
1842	231	1,273	728	926	9	2,937
1843	256	1,451	907	1,062	36	3,457
1844	311	1,640	1,076	1,605	22	4,345
1845	342	Particulars not given				5,617

Year by year the Union Committee urged the collection and asked the churches to support "British Missions", not only in this way but by local "British Missionary Auxiliaries", which would collect weekly, monthly, and annual subscriptions, and by juvenile and ladies' societies, *etc.* The three Societies needed £3,000 more a year to meet their expenses, £5,000 more to make advance possible. This could easily be obtained if all the churches would adopt the collection, and especially if each church member would contribute a penny a week in addition, for this would produce £52,000.

County Associations.

Time and again Wells said that the key to the success of the Union and of the denomination's work generally was to be found in the Associations. In 1840 two important

---

* This includes the anonymous £1,000 (divided £500, £200, £300 for the three Societies).

complementary papers were read to the Assembly. Blackburn spoke of the varied duties of the churches—Bible
Classes for the Young, Meetings for Prayer and Fellowship, Vestry and School Libraries, and the Loan of Tracts,
Sunday Schools, Visitation, Lay Agency, Care for the
Poor, Joining an Association, Multiplying Churches, and
Preducing Ministers. Wells's subject was "The Improvement of Associations". These were ancient and voluntary
institutions for Christian and Scriptural objects, but their
unification was desirable. They should all aim at obtaining the benefit of extending Christian fellowship in these
particulars among others :

1. Recognition of the Churches and Pastors admitted.
2. Intercourse between Pastors.
3. Combined efforts to spread the Gospel.
4. United proceedings concerning the general interests of
   the Independents, sacred or civil.

The means for accomplishing these objects were the
efforts of each church and pastor to support the Association,
the contributions of the combined churches for their own
local efforts and then for the general Union; general
Annual Meetings[1] of the Association, which should include
meetings of pastors only for fellowship; meetings of pastors
and delegates for business; devotional meetings, including
Communion; and public meetings.

The Ministry.

It was some time before the Union felt strong enough
to tackle the difficult question of the ministry. In 1834 it
had decided to appoint a Committee to consider what
measures could be most safely taken to raise the qualifica-

---

1 Wells outlines the following programme for an Annual Meeting of
an Association :—
  I. A Meeting of Pastors for ministerial fellowship, to commence at
     4 p.m., and continue through the evening.
 II. On the following morning, an early public devotional Meeting, to
     begin at 7 a.m.
III. A morning Meeting of Pastors and Delegates, to commence at
     9 a.m., and to be continued in the afternoon.
 IV. A Sermon in the evening, followed by a Communion Service.
  V. On the following day, the early devotional meeting, and the meet-
     ing of pastors and delegates to be repeated.
 VI. In the evening, the whole to be closed by a public meeting.

tions of candidates for the ministry, but there is no sign of any report or action. In 1840 and 1841 John Blackburn read papers on "The State of the Ministry" and "The Validity of the Ministry as Exercised in Congregational Churches". The first, which estimated that Congregationalism needed not less than 2,000 educated ministers, was welcomed, but it was felt that a document like the second should not be put forth by the Union without mature deliberation. It was referred to a Committee for consideration and report.

In 1842 a Resolution was passed approving the views of the Declaration of Faith and Order on the "Validity and Scriptural Character of the Ministry of Congregational Churches". All Associations were recommended at the same time to follow the example of Dorset in giving testimonies to ministers leaving the Association. Ministers recommending others to vacant churches were advised not to do so without such testimonies from Associations or without communicating with the tutors of students. In the same year the colleges were said to be "increasing in number and respectability", and resolutions were passed welcoming the formation of Spring Hill and the opening of Lancashire College.

In 1844, in a paper on "The History, Position, and Prosperity of the Independent Colleges", Blackburn gave a history of the Colleges, and then went on to make an estimate of the number of students required. Of the 2,557 churches in England and Wales, 2,000 needed pastors, which meant that between 50 and 60 new men were needed each year. The 12 Colleges had, at that time, 235 students, and Blackburn estimated that if seven new churches were built each year, there would be a yearly deficiency of ten men. The 12 Colleges, with 25 tutors, were useful but expensive—three of them could not teach Independent principles because of their constitutions, and in others the tutors seemed indifferent. He felt that it was right that the courses should not be uniform, but that the Colleges should train different types of men. It was important, however, that a Committee in each Association should examine any candidates for admission to the colleges.

Blackburn's paper went into a great many details.   It suggested, among other things, that churches should have collections for the Colleges in their vicinities every five years; that there should be a College Corresponding Committee in London consisting of representatives of the colleges; that students should make some payment for their training; and that Associations should give testimonials to students entering the ministry.   A vital matter to him was that students seemed either unaware of, or unwilling to seize, Home Missionary opportunities, but rather dreamed

> of occupying pleasant pastoral spheres . . . instead of having "to endure hardness", and to exercise rigid self-denial, until they shall have gathered around them, by the blessing of God upon their labours, a people who will so appreciate their services as gladly to contribute to their support.

It was finally resolved that the Union should take the initiative in summoning a conference of representatives of all the Colleges.   This was done in January, 1845, Algernon Wells being very apologetic about the part the Union had played, and disclaiming any desire to interfere in any way with the Colleges and their administration.   Papers were read[1] on almost every aspect of College life by principals, tutors, and well-known ministers, and many resolutions were passed.   These resolutions in general followed the titles of the papers, but it was suggested that instead of a preparatory seminary for men little qualified "this subordinate education will be more appropriately given in the homes of competent ministers receiving small numbers under their care".

John Blackburn's suggestion of a Central Committee in London appointed by the College Committees to promote their interests was deemed well worthy of attention and, as may be imagined, a resolution was passed in favour of an annual collection in each church for the Colleges.

Nobody perhaps had his finger on the denominational

---

1 They are printed in the *Minutes of the Proceedings*, separately published.

pulse more often than the minister of Carrs Lane, Birmingham. He spoke at Norwich in 1844 on the choice of a pastor, and subsequently published an article in the *Christian Witness* on "Aiding the Church in the choice of a Pastor". Here he wrote with his usual foresight and insight, claiming that the principles of Independency were sound, but they sometimes had failed in practice, especially in vacancies. Independent ministers were well educated, but the Home Missionary Society had brought many uneducated but earnest men into its service. When a church was vacant, to whom could the deacons apply for advice? There used to be Thomas Wilson, who did yeoman service of this kind, even though he had a great partiality for students of Highbury. Help should be given in a way that would neither interfere with the autonomy of a church nor establish a system of patronage. He suggested that County Associations should be made more efficient, and should have sub-committees which vacant churches could consult. These committees should be in touch with a central committee in London, to be appointed by the Union. Perhaps the College Committee Blackburn had suggested might serve this purpose also, and it could have under its notice a list of ministers anxious for a change of pastorate. There were difficulties and dangers attached to the proposal, for the Committee would need a paid agent.

Campbell fully supported these suggestions, saying :

> The committees having before them the age, talents, education, temper, history, and habits of ministers, with their family circumstances—as also the locality, tastes, numbers, wealth, wants, and condition of a congregation—would be enabled to give vacant churches a list of ministers suitable as candidates for their service in the gospel. The province of the committees would be wholly confined to this labour of prudence and of love. There would be no interference whatever with their choice ; and, if they thought good, they might still look beyond the nomination of the committee. Such an arrangement would, therefore, be an affair of unmixed good to the churches. It would in all cases be a security for character ; and, in addition to this most important point, it would most materially expedite the progress of proper settlements, by bringing the churches at once into contact with suitable subjects, and saving much

time in the fruitless hearing of individuals not likely to suit the particular sphere.

The Results of Wells's Leadership.

All through these and subsequent years Wells had seized every opportunity to urge the cause of the Union. An Assembly was rare in which he did not present a memorial, showing the principles of the Union, the safeguards of Independent churches, the advantages to be gained, the achievements to date. Sometimes, as at Norwich in 1844, his address "delivered with tears, deeply moved the entire Assembly"; at other times his intellectual gifts were more conspicuous, as at York in 1847, of which Assembly Josiah Conder wrote in a private letter :

> In all respects it was one of the best sustained series of meetings I ever attended. Wells exceeded himself in the unaffected eloquence and good sense of his speeches; and his rebuke of one of Mr. J——'s[1] croaking lamentations was one of the most effective and admirable I ever heard— its perfect good humour and respectful tone preventing its being in the slightest degree offensive. These truly fraternal meetings must be productive of the happiest effect.

Sometimes he stressed the "necessity and paramount duty of a steadfast adherence to evangelical truth" :

> To priests we must oppose preachers. Instead of sacraments, we must exhibit truth as the great instrument of salvation. In place of a blind confidence in rites, we must teach men salvation by faith in Christ. We must contend for the life of religion in the soul, produced by the power of the Spirit, as opposed to a mere routine of forms, with whatever solemnity administered, with whatever scrupulosity observed, with whatever pretensions recommended.

At others he set forth the theory of the Union in attractive words :

> Liberty is the first great element of human power—the liberty that consists in security of rights, and freedom of action. Union is the second great principle of power among mankind, in which many combine, and act together with concert, with counsel, and with order. Together, liberty and union in due combination and balance, form the perfectness of social force. Liberty without union enfeebles

1 Probably John Angell James.

by scattering and dividing. Union without liberty only employs the force of those already enslaved, for enslaving others; but when men are free, though united, and united, though free, they are strong for good, and only for good. This is the theory of the Congregational Union of England and Wales. It would combine liberty and union. It would constitute a free union—a union of churches severally free, and no less free when united. It would make those churches strong in liberty, union, and love; but strong only for truth and charity; a union that could do nothing against the truth, but for the truth; a union whose first act of usurpation would dissolve and terminate its existence.

In its Secretary the Union had one of the most powerful and persuasive advocates. So successful was he that, writing in the early days of 1846, a sound, well-informed, and discriminating critic can thus sum up the history of the last 15 years and the outlook for the future[1]:

The Congregational Union of England and Wales struggled into existence in the year 1831, amidst some contentions for its paternity, and attended by numerous and varied prognostications as to its future history. Many of its warmest friends doubted whether it possessed the elements of perpetuity, and trembled for its welfare and success, as they contemplated the possible and probable opposition it would be called to encounter. Some of the persons who, from principle or prejudice, were unfavourable to its formation, were not slow to predict its speedy dissolution, and to attempt their best to fulfil their own prophecies; while others—fearing that it might eventually assume such legislative authority, or so constitute itself a court of appeal, as to interfere with the independency of churches and pastors, and lay the foundation of Presbyterian rule, or Episcopal domination, by which our Congregationalism would be gradually undermined, and eventually destroyed—looked upon it with doubt and suspicion. A few of the wiser and farther-seeing of our fathers and brethren were alone confident in the belief, that not only such a union was feasible, and that it could do no disservice to our denomination, but that it would, on the contrary, impart incalculable benefit to our churches and to the cause of Christian truth at large.

The career of the Union has been in all outward

[1] These paragraphs are selected from an article in the *Congregational Magazine*.

EDWARD BAINES

SAMUEL MORLEY

HENRY RICHARD

J. R. MILLS

appearances as prosperous from that day onwards as its most sanguine friends could have anticipated.

Nothing like rashness or undue excitement marked the procedure of the persons more immediately concerned in its formation. Their aims were from the first intelligible and feasible, and they addressed themselves to their great undertaking as men who understood the responsibilities of their position, and the nature of the difficulties with which they had to contend. They laid the foundations of the institution deep and broad, and they with others have continued to build upon it a superstructure much in harmony with the original design. Their prudence was the footstep of wisdom, in which their successors have safely walked. There has never been, in our judgment, any actual or virtual departure from the fundamental principles adopted at the beginning. The Union has gradually silenced all objections, by attending to its own appropriate work; it has carefully abstained from any and from every act which, by the most ingenious construction, could be regarded as an infringement of the independency of our churches; and it has unquestionably done good service to our denomination.

Our only astonishment is that, with such limited pecuniary means as it has had at its disposal, it should have been able to set so many valuable agencies at work, and to have actually accomplished so large an amount of good.

To that prince of secretaries, the Rev. Algernon Wells, all our institutions are deeply indebted. His soundness of judgment, moderation, and forbearance, have done much to harmonize discordant opinions and to secure a unity of judgment and feeling. But for his plodding industry and untiring zeal, the Union itself would more than once have been perilled, and one of its Missions has at times leaned almost entirely on him for support.

Perhaps, at times, an undue anxiety has been manifested on the part of the principal friends of the Union to avoid any apparent division of opinion on a vote embracing some question of principle or policy of action; and thus, to some quiet spectators, it has seemed as if the complete canvassing of opinions were sacrificed to a timid anxiety for uniformity of expression. Now, as we believe that uniformity is not, in and of itself, a good; so do we strongly feel that, if the endeavour to preserve it does the slightest violence to any conscientious scruple, it becomes an actual evil.

Great care, we think, should be taken in all the publications of the society, so as not to commit the whole body, even by implication, to an approval of what may be nothing more than individual opinion, or that of a portion of the whole denomination.

Care, we think, should be taken by the committee, not to bring forward great questions at the autumnal meetings without due notice; nor to take votes upon them without previous opportunity afforded the brethren of deliberately pondering the details of the measures about to be submitted for adoption. The excitement of a large assembly is by no means favourable to the exercise of all that calmness of mind and comprehensiveness of view which should be predominant in the acceptance of measures, the influence of which may be great, for good or for evil, on the history of unborn generations.

Hitherto it has wisely abstained from using the power it might have claimed. The British Missions, while associated with the Union, are not under its direction, but under the management of separate committees. The Board of Education is controlled by a committee distinct from the committee of the Union, and responsible to its own constituents. This is just as it should be, and any departure from this line of procedure would be injurious. To place our colleges, for instance, under the management of the Union; or to make it, or any similar board in London, the medium of communication between vacant churches and unemployed or moveable ministers, would be to throw an amount of patronage into the hands of a few which would be incompatible with the welfare of the many. The centralization of power may be good in a perfect state of society, but is not well adapted to the present imperfect condition of mankind.

IX. STRUGGLING WITH THE LOAD, 1845-1848.

THE last chapter has failed in its purpose if it does not show that the Union had developed so rapidly that it already possessed most of the features that marked its maturer days. By 1845 there was a General Committee, a Literature Committee, an Education Committee, a Superannuation Committee (the *Christian Witness* distributors), and a Publication Department, and proposals for something very much like a Moderators' Committee, as well as an embryo March Council. The foundation had thus been laid on which the Union was to build through the century. Not only so, but the plan covered so wide an area as to include the Home Missionary, the Irish Evangelical, and the Colonial Societies. It was soon to become clear that this attempt at so large an organization was mistaken; the company, so to speak, had been floated with insufficient capital. The Union was like a kneeling camel, loaded with an unwieldly, badly-balanced load altogether too heavy for it, and it was unable to rise. The burden had to be unpacked and a new start made. The years from 1845 to 1858 are years that see this unpacking process going on. This chapter describes efforts to cope with the situation in the earlier years of this period.

1. *Finance and Constitution.*—It was manifest that something had to be done speedily to put the Union on a sound footing, both financially and as a representative body. Churches and Associations sent subscriptions or not as they liked, generally not. Pastors and deacons attended very much as they pleased. A more rigidly defined membership and a sufficient income were essentials. It was therefore proposed that the Union should be of churches, not of Associations, a church's eligibility being determined by its membership of an Association and its willingness to pay at least 10s. annually. The pastor and two members of such churches were delegates, another delegate being allowed for every 100 members after the

first 100. Ministers out of charge, tutors, *etc.*, could become members on a minimum annual payment of 5s. Discussed at several Assemblies, this revised Constitution was finally adopted in May, 1847, so that Clauses 2 and 4 of the original Constitution came to read :

> That this Union shall consist of Associations of Congregational churches, and of individual churches severally adhering to the Union. The qualification of a church for membership in this Union shall be connexion with an Association; or where no Association is accessible, recommendation by the three ministers already in the Union residing nearest to the applicant church. Every church connected with this Union shall make an annual contribution to its funds, neglect of which for two successive years shall forfeit membership. The Tutors of the Theological Colleges of the Independents, and the officers of their general public societies, being members of Congregational churches; also ministers and deacons in fellowship with churches eligible for connexion with the Union, may become personal members of the Union by payment of an annual subscription of not less than five shillings.
>
> To promote the accomplishment of these objects, and the general interests of the Union, an Annual Meeting shall be held, and such adjournments of the same as may from time to time be deemed expedient, in London or some other principal city or town; and these Assemblies of the Union shall consist of the pastors of churches connected therewith, of delegates deputed by those churches, of whom each church may depute two, and each church consisting of more than one hundred members, three; or one additional delegate for every additional hundred of members; and of personal members of the Union. No persons not belonging to one of these three classes have right to vote in the Assemblies of this Union.

In the year this was passed, the Treasurer had to report that the appeal for donations to reduce the deficit had only brought in £306, the ordinary subscriptions being but £70, and £188 having to be drawn from the Publication Department, though it was remarked that so far the hymn books and the magazines were the only publications that had paid. The following year things began to look up; 218 churches and 163 personal members contributed £300, though as 18 months' expenses were brought in, £310 had to be drawn from publications to make the accounts balance.

Churches were urged to affiliate and pay their subscriptions, and deacons to become personal members. Salaries at this time were £150 for Wells and £50 for Palmer.

2. *The Assembly.*—It was agreed that the Monday night meeting should be of members of the Union only, and should be informed of all business to come up during the week. It should further nominate a committee (5 of the Union Committee and 7 from the country) to recommend to the Assembly the officers and the place of the Autumnal Meeting, all of which should be determined by the Assembly's vote. The week was thus as follows:

Monday, 7th of May.—At Two o'Clock, Meeting of Distributors of Fund in aid of Aged Ministers, in the Congregational Library. At Four o'clock Preliminary Meeting of the Members of the Annual Assembly, in the same place. At Seven o'clock, Sermon for British Missions, in the Poultry Chapel.

Tuesday, 8th of May.—At Half past Nine o'clock, First Session of the Eighteenth Assembly of the Union, in Crosby Hall, Bishopsgate Street; the Rev. James Parsons, of York, will take the Chair. At Six o'clock, the United Annual Meeting for British Missions, in Exeter Hall.

Friday, 11th of May.—At Half past Nine o'clock, First Adjourned Session of the Assembly of the Union, in Crosby Hall. At Six o'clock, Public Meeting for General Education.

Saturday, 12th of May.—At Half past Nine o'clock, Second Adjourned Session of the Assembly of the Union, in the Congregational Library.

LONDON MISSIONARY SOCIETY.

May 7.—Meeting of Delegates, at the Mission House, Blomfield Street, at Three, p.m.

7.—Sermon at Church, at Seven, p.m.

9.—Sermon at Surrey Chapel, at Half past Ten, a.m.; and at the Tabernacle, at Six, p.m.

10.—General Meeting at Exeter Hall. Chair taken at Ten, a.m.; and Adjourned Meeting at Finsbury Chapel. Chair taken at Six, p.m.

13.—Sermons on behalf of the Society in different Chapels in the Metropolis.

14.—Communion Service in twelve districts in and around London, at Six, p.m.

In the Autumn of 1848 a Committee was appointed to nominate a Chairman. Up to this time the officials had in the main sought a Chairman and had not always found it easy to persuade men to accept the post.

3.   The unsatisfactory character of the " British Missions " organization had also to be faced. Pleas for "rationalization", if a term may be anticipated, had already been heard in the Assembly, while the response to the October collection, and to the penny a week a church member appeal, did not produce sufficient income for aggressive work. In October, 1845, John Ely, in one of the most statesmanlike papers ever read to the Assembly, outlined the whole "vast and varied" field of the world's challenge to Independency, not overlooking the Jews, Seamen, and the Continent[1].

Ely's address so impressed the Assembly that a special Committee was appointed to discuss these "Congregational Economics" and also Chapel Building at Birmingham in March of the following year. Ely said that the primary difficulty was, the lack of statistics. The number of churches was not known, nor whether the average membership was 100 or 200. He quoted the Wesleyans and the Free Church of Scotland to show what might be done for denominational objects. 500 of the 627 congregations of the Free Church of Scotland collected for all five of their denominational schemes (only 25 of them failed to collect for one or other of them), but only 311 Independent Churches collected for "British Missions". The Home Missionary Society was having to curtail expense and reduce stations.

Our Foreign Missionary Society is constrained to contemplate curtailment among its fields of promise, for though its friends vapoured about raising the income to £100,000

1 Not much is heard about the Continent in these days; one of the few references is of the kind that might have been more happily expressed (the *italics* are the present writer's) :
The brethren then retired into the adjoining schoolroom for refreshment, and *as soon as attention could be given to a Public Address,* the Rev. Mark Wilks, from Paris, gave a full statement of the position of the Evangelical Protestant cause on the continent of Europe, and presented strong claims on the Congregationalists of England for aid on behalf of the funds of the Evangelical Society of Paris, which are at present greatly depressed.

it did not "stand", they have suffered it to dwindle to some £65,000. Our colleges are for the most part inadequately supported. It is to be feared that our educational scheme is languishing. In the meanwhile our congregations are crushed with the burden of chapel debts, and usually expend not less perhaps than twenty-five per cent in mendicant efforts for their liquidation. Interest has, moreover, to be paid on the unliquidated principal. It would be an instructive, and no doubt an appalling, aggregate that would appear, if the amount of interest paid yearly on the debts on our chapels and school-houses could be ascertained.

The administration of these Societies should be such as to command confidence. There were far too many separate bodies, and it had always been a matter of regret to him that our one great missionary society had not been made to comprise, under so many different departments, with the heathen, Ireland, the European continent, the colonies, and the Jews. Simplicity and unity would have been secured; distinct sub-committees might have managed the distinct departments; and the diverse claims would no doubt have won proportionate liberality from the churches.

General and County Home Missions should be worked together, and there should be a paid agent for collecting for "British Missions", while a Loan Fund for Chapel debts (free of interest and to be repaid in 10 yearly instalments), and a Sustentation Fund to raise stipends to a minimum £100 a year and Manse should be established, and provision made for Ministerial Superannuation and the education of ministers' children.

The Committee met at Birmingham in due course, having to pay its own expenses, greatly to Campbell's disgust, and it recommended :

1. The securing of statistics, giving a list of the details desired, and suggesting the appointment of an agent for this purpose. Full and accurate statistics, said the Committee, must precede both right appreciation of the situation and the obtaining of contributions.

2. Sufficient data not being available for deciding for or against a union of the three Societies, it was merely suggested that their accounts should be regularly investigated and their fields of labour reviewed.

3. County Associations were urged to tackle chapel debts, inadequate stipends, and chapel extension.

Some action on the lines of these recommendations followed immediately.   Steps were taken to bring the three Societies into closer co-operation and to re-arrange the Assembly programme, and also to compose the quarrel between the Irish Evangelical Society and the Irish Union, which had broken out afresh.   Blackburn was appointed to collect statistics, and the result of his efforts are seen in the first two *Year Books*[1], admirable,   if imperfect, productions.

Blackburn plodded away getting reliable information, providing model record and registration books, *etc.,* but the objection to numbering and to supplying a central authority with information died hard.   After laying the foundations, and editing the *Year Book* for two years, he handed over the editorship to Palmer and Algernon Wells.   The book, started with less than 200 pages for the first two years, increased to over 300 in the third year.   The early volumes do Blackburn great credit.   In the first issue, pp. 1—80 contain the proceedings of the two Assemblies, the Annual Letter, and the Accounts.   It is interesting thus early to find among the Committee printed in this first *Year Book* names so familiar as Morley, Shepheard, and Spicer.   Then follows a section on Congregational Associations, a historical summary preceding the list of Associations, which furnish the names of the churches and ministers.   Next is a list of colleges and seminaries, and an account of the University of London. Blackburn was proudest of his "List of Independent Ministers throughout England".   He acknowledged that it was incomplete, especially in regard to place of training, but pointed out that it was but the second attempt at a complete list, no other having been made since he included one in the *Congregational Magazine* in 1831.   The number of ministers appearing is 1,480, the place of training being

---

[1] A word of warning must be given to all students of the early *Year Books*. The first *Year Book,* that for 1846, was published at the beginning of 1847, and so on, the *Year Book* for 1851 being issued in 1852.   Then the practice of post-dating ceased and the present method was adopted; there is thus no *Year Book* dated 1852; the 1851 Book contains the business for 1851, the 1853 Book the business for 1852.   This change in the method of dating has often led students astray.

attached to 948 names. 11 pages are devoted to obituaries, the most noteworthy name being that of Dr. Matheson, Secretary of the Home Missionary Society, and Reed's companion on the First Deputation to America.

Three pages contain accounts of the formation of churches and the openings of chapels : then follow lists of chapels erected (26), or enlarged (13), ordinations (61) and removals and settlements. The last six pages are extremely valuable, containing as they do a list of publications by Congregationalists during the year, and ending with a list of monthly journals edited by Congregationalists :

It will be seen that here is a full framework of the modern *Year Book,* which, while it contains more new features and much more detailed statistics, yet lacks some useful items which appeared in 1846. In the *Year Book* for 1848 we have also lists of Religious and Benevolent Societies and of the Dissenting Deputies, *etc.* . . 1,024 independent chapels are stated to be licensed for marriages[1]. There are five pages of informing "Notes", and, hidden away, where it has no business to be, this summary :

Number of associations in Great Britain and Ireland ...	60
Number of Congregational ministers in Great Britain and Ireland (exclusive of those not belonging to, or, recognized by many associations)	1,979
Number of Congregational churches in Great Britain and Ireland (exclusive of branch churches)	2,173
Number of ordinations and new charges	82
Number of removals and exchanges	119
Number of chapels built and enlarged	31
Number of colleges	13
Number of students	186
Number of poor, aged, and infirm ministers assisted ...	530
Number of widows relieved	131
Number of ministers deceased	41
Amount of money contributed to poor aged and infirm ministers	£3,527
Amount contributed to widows	£1,150

1 The number of marriages in England, during the year ending 31st December, 1846, is stated by the Registrar, in his Ninth Report, to be as follows :—

Marriages according to the rites of the Church of England		130,509
,, in Chapels of Protestant Dissenters ...	7,669	
,, of Roman Catholics	3,027	
,, in Superintendent Registrars' Offices ...	4,167	
,, in Jewish Synagogues, *etc.*	224	
,, in Quakers' Meeting-houses	68	
	——	15,155

Superannuation.

The question of Deferred Annuities, previously raised, was fully considered. The aim was to create a legal right to an annuity, and as the number of members would be too few for a separate Society, the insurances were to be effected through Government annuities. It would obviously be unwise to base a scheme on the uncertain and fluctuating profits of the magazines, though the success of the journals at the moment seemed to make it probable that a portion of the profits might be available for investment annually. Annuities should be not less than £50, and should not be available for those whose total income was more than £200. £6 a year might be available for each pastor's premiums, those whose premiums were larger making up the balance themselves. In 1846 the Committee said that they were not recommending the creation of a capital sum at once, as there was a strong desire to further a cognate scheme—the raising of inadequate stipends. No donations were forthcoming towards the capital sum for Deferred Annuities, but in May, 1848, a scheme was established. The annuities were to be of £50, on completion of the 60th year. After grants to "aged brethren" not exceeding half the profits of the two papers, the remainder was to go to the Deferred Annuities Fund. The whole payment from the Fund in each case was to be £150, divided into annual contributions, and all insurances had to be effected before the age of 50. Applicants must be recommended by Associations, and their income must not exceed £200.

Other major problems of the Union emerged in these years. They were in the main connected with :

(*a*) Responsibility for and relationship to the affiliated Societies. This has already been mentioned.

(*b*) Responsibility for the magazines.

(*c*) The difficulty of reconciling the growing influence of the Union with the independence of the individual church.

(*b*) *Responsibility for the Magazines.*—The problem of the magazines was not made easier by their success, which did not tend to moderate Campbell's exuberance. His strictures on the Evangelical Alliance movement brought several protests, especially from Birmingham and Liverpool, while the Evangelical periodicals demanded his head on a charger. Thus the Anglican *Record* wrote:

> We therefore implore the Congregational Union to separate themselves, OFFICIALLY, from Dr. Campbell and his magazine, to which, we may hope, they have inadvertently given their sanction. If they have not Christian vigour to do this—if they allow Dr. Campbell to drag them at his heels through the mire of his political Radicalism and Anti-State and Church Ultraism, they will be failing egregiously in their duty, and allowing, by their supineness, a cloud of darkness, confusion, and weakness, to settle down with increasing gloom over the church of Christ".

The Wesleyan *Watchman*, concurring in the prayer, said:

> We think the *Record* fully warranted in *demanding* that the Congregational Union should separate themselves, OFFICIALLY, from such mischievous *attacks on another church*. The movement for Evangelical Alliance is too precious a thing to be in any degree perilled through deference to the waywardness of a headstrong individual.

To all which Campbell replied, in capitals, and in Knox's words:

> I AM IN THE PLACE WHERE I AM DEMANDED OF CONSCIENCE TO SPEAK THE TRUTH, AND THEREFORE THE TRUTH I SPEAK, IMPUGN IT WHOSO LIST.

The Committee's report in 1846 had to refer to the general uneasiness about the periodicals. It said that the Union was "more than its magazines. Were we shut up to the alternative, 'No Union or no Magazines published by the Union', there would be no hesitation". With Campbell's concurrence the Committee submitted a resolution to the Assembly to the effect that the Union was to be considered as bound only by papers that emanated from the Committee; the sole responsibility was with the Editor, and a note to this effect was to be affixed the following year. After a full discussion this resolution was withdrawn, but Campbell nevertheless printed a full report of the debate, and announced that he would "for ever set the question at rest by the voluntary publication of a standing *Notice,* avowing for himself the sole and undivided responsibility for the contents and conduct of the magazines". Apparently his main critics had been John Angell James and George Redford. In the discussion Campbell offered the editorial chair of the *Christian Witness* to James for six months, to "infuse into it as much of a meek and loving spirit as he wished", and the chair of the *Penny Magazine* to Redford, to "illustrate his own ideas of benevolence and beauty". He went on to say that many people were "afraid lest henceforth the spirit of the *Witness* should be reduced to the temperature of the Alliance". Criticism did not make much difference to John Campbell. If he had anything to say he said it, no matter whom it might touch, a leading minister or layman, another denomination, or even a Congregational Union Secretary. When, as he triumphantly announced, the *British Banner* had obtained a greater circulation than all other religious weeklies, he was not disposed to moderate his tone. So if Methodism savoured of despotism he must tell Methodism so; if its Mission House were palatial he must cry, "Spirit of Wesley! Liveried porters! Red cuffs! Red collars! Was it for these your poor subscribed their hard-earned pence"? And if Wells's eloquence carried him away, Campbell would comment thus, with a dig at "the Angel" by the way:

> It so happens, that while "the Prince of Secretaries" is the ablest of reasoners, as well as, when he chooses, the most philosophic of thinkers, he is also a most persuasive orator, and in oratory there is always peril, as in its higher flights and impetuous bursts it generally skirts the realms of fancy and exaggeration. Of this a splendid example is supplied by the Rev. John Angell James, many of whose unsuspecting and well-intentioned utterances have been ungenerously, unjustly, and maliciously turned against himself, his brethren, and the community he so eminently adorns: that which, in his brilliant effusions, was only rhetoric garnishing truth, for the purpose of practical impression, has been taken as logic, and converted into pointed missiles, dipped in poison, and hurled against the Nonconformist body; and our fear is, lest the language of the Secretary should be turned to the same purposes.

(c) *The difficulty of reconciling the freedom and independence of the individual Church with the increasing power and efficiency of the central body.* This difficulty was thus expressed by Wells in 1846 :

> The great problem for all Societies is to adjust in due proportions individual and combined action—to mingle freedom and union skilfully—to sacrifice enough, but not too much—to secure at once the energy of separate, and the strength of united, effort. This problem the Congregational Union . . . would assist to solve for the churches it confederates. Its command is "Whatsoever pertains to the internal and separate affairs of any church, let that church alone transact and determine; whatsoever any one church can do for the common cause of religion by its own independent unassisted efforts, that let it do, without help and without interference. Whatsoever can be effected by the united churches of a set district or county without external aid or wider combination, that let this limited and local organization undertake as its proper department; but if there still remain energies to be developed, objects to be accomplished, and mutual help to be given and received by a confederation at once more extended and more central, yet free and unobtrusive on freedom; then let the sacred cause of truth abroad and salvation as served by the Congregational denomination have—as indeed it needs—whatsoever resources can be thus secured on its behalf.

The Union officials might make an excellent proposal to which a church might not agree. What was to happen then? It was in connexion with the ministry perhaps that this problem was most likely to emerge. The Congregational ideal and tradition were for a learned ministry. If a church decided to invite an untrained man, perhaps even a man whose character was, shady—"vagabonds" as they were sometimes called—what was to happen then, especially if the church were receiving aid from a County Association or from the Home Missionary Society? Here we see the situation which was to lead in time to the demand for a list of recognized ministers. The whole question is extremely well put by "M" to the *Congregational Magazine* of 1841 in a paper which forecasts so many future developments that this chapter may well end with it :

> We must touch upon tender ground, but shall try to do it tenderly. The efficiency of County Unions is often pre-

vented by too great a respect being had to unsound notions of what is due to churches. It would be ridiculous, were it not a serious subject, to hear the strange sayings of some Congregationalists respecting the rights and claims of every thing in the shape of a church. Churches take their stand upon certain conceptions they have got of Independency, and woe be to the man or the Union that whispers the thought of interference, in any way, with their fancied prerogatives. They ask for pecuniary help but resent every attempt or proposal to join in procuring the proper agency. They will invite their own pastor, though they cannot support him; they will give him a "call", though they have nothing else to give. Now we are as strict Congregationalists as may be, but some churches may be ill-qualified to select the fittest pastor for themselves, and fittest missionary for their neighbourhood. They may lack the faith, or judgment, or intellect to do it. What then? Would we deprive such churches of the right to choose their own spiritual officers? By no means. They have that right from Christ. We draw a wide distinction between *right* and *ability*. Individuals have authority to do many things, and it is their duty to do them, who are nevertheless unqualified to do them. Parental authority does not depend on parental godliness, or judgment, or temper; the political franchise is not invariably attended with the power or will to use it aright. And ecclesiastical functions, in whatever light they may be viewed, and whatever notions may be entertained of their nature or number are often discharged by persons who discharge them ill. A churchman maintains the authority of a bishop to ordain ministers, though he may, through ignorance, or carelessness, or sin, ordain improper men; and a Congregationalist may maintain the right of a church to choose its ministers, though it may choose improper men. Let the church have its right, and exercise it; but it does not follow that the Union should employ its funds in fulfilment of that choice. It is the right of the Union to expend its income according to its conscience, as it is the right of the church to choose its minister according to its conscience. The Union is responsible for the employment of appropriate and efficient agents, and if the pastor in any particular district is not what it would like, let it not adopt him as its agent. There is no necessity for identifying the missionary station with a previously existing church and chapel; in some places it would be most desirable not to identify it; there may be so much prejudice and ill moral odour in consequence of past folly, or immorality, or strife as to render it every way expedient for the church to die, and the chapel to be abandoned. Where it is so, and the church does not choose to allow any voice to the Union in the selection of the minister, if an agent were sent into the neighbourhood, with permission to serve that church, should it desire his services, and contribute toward his support, the result would generally be found, in our opinion, beneficial to the cause of truth and godliness.

It is to be wished that a more regular and general system of oversight and superintendence were adopted by County Unions, of their several stations. We are no advocates of a paid agency for this purpose. It has not been found to work well where tried, nor do we think it ever likely to do so. Something less formal and more fraternal might produce good results. If the county were divided into several districts, and one or two of the leading pastors in each district visited all the stations within it once or twice a year, inquired into the state of things on the spot, suggested points, gave advice, administered consolation, *etc.*, as the case might require, we are convinced it might be useful. It might prevent the need of questioning and cross-questioning at the meetings of the Union, which is often most painful to every generous and noble nature; afford a healthful stimulant to the minds of the agents; and promote a good feeling of brotherhood and sympathy among the ministers.

X. EDUCATION, 1831-1872.

IT will perhaps serve for convenience if one aspect of the Union's activity—that of education—is detached from the rest of the story, though it cannot be treated in any detail.

Resolutions were passed regularly about the exclusion of Dissenters from the Universities, and the advisability of forming colleges for Dissenters was suggested. The Annual Letter in 1846 asked whether Congregationalism's provision of education for poor and rich was "worthy of a body which pretends to have received the love of learning as an heirloom from the Nonconformists of the seventeenth century".

It is with elementary education, however, that most of the story deals, and it can only be touched upon as it concerns the Union, readers being referred to the full accounts in Dale's *History of Congregationalism,* and A. W. W. Dale's *Life of R. W. Dale.* In the main, the Independents had no day schools, making use, where possible, of British Schools. By 1840, however, the feeling began to be expressed that they would be wise to have their own schools. In that year Dr. Matheson said that it was now essential, if not to their existence yet to their progress and to their respectability, that wherever it was practicable there should be a week-day school in connexion with their churches. They could not but be aware that numerous and powerful attempts were being made to impede what they all considered to be the progress of true Christian liberty, and he was afraid that such attempts would succeed unless some means were adopted to counteract them, and that even their Sunday Schools might suffer. One minister spoke of a town of 50,000 people without an unsectarian school, and another showed how it was practicable for a church to maintain a denominational school. When the question was raised as to whether Government assistance for school buildings should be accepted, Henry Wills said that

> if they allowed themselves to take money for the purpose
> of scriptural education, they must allow the Catholic, the

R. W. DALE

JAMES GUINNESS ROGERS

> Socinian, and all other denominations to have the same assistance in disseminating their sentiments,

and he hoped that no such recommendation would be made. A division of opinion which has never disappeared was at once manifest. Sir James Graham met with united opposition, however, when in 1843 he introduced his Bill for the Education of Factory children. Utterly unfair in its proposals in that it gave further power and privilege to the Established Church, the Bill roused the Dissenters to such an extent as to surprise the politicians. Charles Hindley, M.P., addressed the May Assembly, and the strongest resolutions were passed, recommending "calm but strenuous, universal and uncompromising opposition", every church being urged to petition the House of Commons. In the autumn of that year the whole question of education was considered, and it was resolved :

> That without pronouncing a decided opinion on the propriety of Government interference in the education of the people, this Meeting entertains the gravest doubts whether any compulsory interference can take place without establishing principles and precedents dangerous to civil and religious liberty, inconsistent with the rights of industry, and superseding the duties of parents and of churches; while all the plans of national education by the agency of Government, suggested of late years, have been very objectionable either to the friends of the Established Church, or to the Dissenting bodies. This Meeting, therefore, concludes, without despondency or regret, that both the general and the religious education of the people of England must be chiefly provided and conducted by the voluntary efforts of the various denominations of Christians.

A representative Conference in the same year categorically stated the position that it was not the State's province to educate its people. Instigated by Edward Baines, the Conference, on the motion of Wells, passed a resolution, re-affirmed in 1845 :

> That this meeting, utterly repudiating, on the strongest grounds of Scripture and conscience, the receipt of money raised by taxation and granted by Government, for sustaining the Christian religion, feels bound to apply this principle no less to the work of religious education; and

M

considering that the education given by the Congregational churches must be religious education, advises most respectfully, but most earnestly, that no Government aid be received by them for schools established in their own connexion; and that all funds confided to the disposal of the Central Committee, in aid of schools, be granted only to schools sustained entirely by voluntary contributions.

This emphasis on the voluntary principle meant an attempt to provide schools. It was resolved that, wherever possible, every Independent church should have a boys' and girls' school, ministers giving what aid they could. At the same time it was agreed that more effective assistance should be given to the British and Foreign Schools Society. A Central Fund was opened for the provision of school buildings, with Samuel Morley as Treasurer, and a Committee of General Education appointed. This Committee was a very strong one, twenty-five from London and twenty-nine from the provinces, and it was ultimately agreed to appoint a paid Secretary. Its first report in 1844 said that £47,000 had already been received and arrangements made for closer co-operation with the British Society. By October Robert Ainslie, the newly appointed Secretary, could say that forty schools were built or building, and £70,000 had been received, though the application to 1,000 churches for collections had so far been disappointing, only seven having responded. Thirty counties had yet to contribute to the Fund, and it was hoped to erect 500 schools in five years. Steps were being taken to discover how far it was practicable for every church to have a school attached.

In the following May it was reported that the London Missionary Society Jubilee and other causes had diverted money from education, while the appeal for information disclosed much discouragement and torpor, but great need. For example, in 90 towns and villages where there should be 52,649 day scholars, there were only 27,182, 16,756 being in Church of England Schools, 6,152 in Independent, and 4,274 in all others. Co-operation with other Dissenters was taking place, some teachers were being trained, and a model school had been established. The position was very complicated, however, for the British Society was accepting State Aid for its Normal School and the Wesleyans were willing to do the same, the Baptists and the Congregationalists alone standing out. The Union determined to rouse the churches even more effectively than in the past two years. A strong Board of Education, 42 members all resident in London, was formed. Essex was systematically visited, and £8,000 raised in the county for school buildings. A Normal School for women was established in London and support given to one in Wales. Everywhere, however, there was need for good teachers and good School Committees.

By 1846 the £100,000 aimed at in five years had been raised, 100 schools had been built, and 47 adapted. In 1847 the voluntary position was again re-affirmed in a long resolution, part of which reads :

> Whereas, on no solid ground of principle can State support of religion in churches be resisted by those who acquiesce in its introduction into schools—and whereas it is believed that Congregationalists are unanimous and resolved in conscientious opposition to State support of religion in any and every form—and whereas their testimony on this great principle is felt to rest on sacred allegiance to Christ, and to be of the utmost moment to the purity and advancement of His heavenly kingdom among men—and whereas, finally, the moral power of the Congregational body is believed to consist chiefly in consistent, unwavering maintenance of principle ; and that this power is very great, and will ever grow while so maintained, but will at once be destroyed by abandonment of principle, or feebleness or hesitation in adhering to principle : therefore, this assembly most earnestly conjures Congregationalists universally and with one consent to preserve themselves clear of the least sanction of the grant thus offered by Government in support of schools, by refusing to receive the smallest sum for any school which is entirely their own, and by distinct protest against any participation therein in schools in the maintenance of which they are associated with Christians of other denominations.

A special session of the Union for the consideration of Education was held at Derby in December, 1847, 37 ministers and 24 laymen being present. The proceedings of this session must be carefully examined by all who would understand the Congregational attitude to education. Its resolutions may thus be summarized[1] :

1. Education, "to be efficient and safe for the people, must be free from Government interference, control, and support".
2. £120,000 having been raised, and the five years' campaign being nearly over, a more vigorous campaign still was needed.
3. The Congregational Board of Education was to "continue to be the recognized central organization of the Congregational Union for the advancement of popular education".

Agreed so far, some difference of opinion was manifested before (4) was passed.

4. "That the constituency electing this Board and its officers shall consist of the members of the Congregational Union ; of donors of £5 and upwards, of subscribers of 10s. *per annum* and upwards, to the Central Board ; and of delegates from School Committees, in the proportion of one delegate for every £1 *per annum* contributed : all such schools to have the preference in selecting educated teachers from the Normal Schools of the Board ; and, further, the treasurer and secretaries of the Congregational Union shall be members of the Board, and the treasurer and secretaries of the Board, in like manner, members of the Committee of the Union ; and the Board shall report its proceedings, as heretofore, at the spring and autumnal meetings of the Union ; and, if deemed desirable, shall hold a public meeting in London in the spring, and an autumnal meeting in the provinces."
5. In no circumstances was public money to be received from the Government.
6. Congregational School Committees were not prevented from having members of other denominations as supporters or managers of the Schools.
7. Schools that were evangelical though not entirely Congregational were allowed to associate with the Board, but their entire government and management was to be in the hands of the Local Committee.
8. The objects of the Board were to be the provision of Normal Schools for men and women, the inspection of Congregational Schools, the gatherings of statistics concerning such Schools, the provision of Schools for

---

[1] See also Rules of the Board of Education in *Year Book*, 1849, pp. 40-41.

working class and neglected children, the making of grants of apparatus, the selection of books, and the advancement of popular education by public meetings, deputations, and the press, *etc.*

9. Candidates in the Normal Schools must be in communion with a Christian Church.

10. Friendly relations were to be maintained with other believers in religious and voluntary education.

The objects and organization of the Board may be best summed up in its own words :

a. *General Object.*—To promote the extension of primary education imbued with evangelical truth, conducted by teachers of religious character, and sustained by the combined efforts of parents and the liberal aid of Christian benevolence.

b. *Organization.*—The Board of Education is in connexion with the Congregational Union of England and Wales, and reports its proceedings at the General Meetings of that body. Its constituency consists of the money contributors—namely, donors of five pounds and upwards, and subscribers of ten shillings *per annum* and upwards, and also of delegates from school committees, in the proportion of one delegate for every pound *per annum* contributed. This constituency holds an annual meeting in London, in the month of May, at which time a report of the proceedings of the Board and a financial statement of the past year are presented, and the Members of the Board, Corresponding Members, and Officers are elected.

This constitution has been adopted as best calculated to develop the resources of the Congregational body, which it is believed could not be so well accomplished by a general organization. The Board trains teachers belonging to the various evangelical sections of the church, and has no denominational teaching in its Training Institution. It prescribes, that neither the learning of any denominational formulary, nor attendance on any particular place of worship, shall be a condition of admission into schools connected with the Board. It supplies schools under the superintendence of mixed committees as well as Congregational schools with teachers ; and it will be prepared to assist schools requiring aid, irrespectively of the constitution of their committees. Stipulating that the religious teaching be conducted on evangelical views of religion, it leaves all arrangements, as to the substance and manner of teaching, with the entire internal government of the school, in the hands of the local committee.

A Normal School for men was established in Liverpool Street, London, with the Rev. W. J. Unwin as Principal, a depository for the sale of books was opened, and a series of pamphlets and a quarterly journal, the *Educator,* published. In 1849 Homerton College was coming into the market owing to its amalgamation with Coward and Highbury, and Samuel Morley led a movement for securing it for the two Normal Schools. The Union approved, and sufficient sums were obtained to meet the cost, £12,000 in all.

The denomination was not united, however, and this fact both hindered the flow of money to the Board and raised difficulties in regard to its connexion with the Union. In 1852, at the instance of some members of the Union who did not agree with the Board's policy and felt themselves compromised by it, the whole matter was re-considered. A statement was issued by the Union Committee, in which they placed on record the fact that the Board originated with the Union, which had several times approved the connexion :

> The Committee, aware that there never has existed in our denomination perfect unanimity of opinion on the subject of popular education, has always understood that the connexion existing between the Union and the Board of Education does not compromise any member of the Union ; since it has always been understood that individual members of the Union are not, by this connexion, committed to all the views embodied in the constitution of the Congregational Board of Education.

It is difficult to state exactly the extent of the movement for the provision of schools. Congregational schools were said to absorb 40 to 50 teachers annually. In 1853 Baines claimed that in ten years the Board had established 453 schools with 50,000 scholars, and compared this with the 514 schools with 80,000 scholars established by the British Society in nearly 50 years. Of the Congregational schools 117 were new buildings. In the autumn of 1853 Baines read to the Assembly what John Campbell called "one of the best papers ever delivered—and an irresistible argument for the voluntary system". It thus summarized the work of practical education which had been carried on :

> Funds have been raised—schools established and assisted—training institutions for male and female teachers formed—more than a hundred teachers actually sent out to the work—Homerton College purchased, and model schools built for the use of the training institutions—school books published, and apparatus of a superior kind provided—an educational periodical sustained—and a centre formed, to which our schools, all over the country, may look for counsel, as well as for a supply of teachers and school books.

It was already evident that the State schools had great advantages over voluntary schools in teachers, resources, books, *etc.*, and also that money could not flow in indefinitely at the rate in which it had done in the years immediately after 1843. The two Normal Schools, together with the model schools, could, however, be maintained even though money could no longer be provided for buildings. It was estimated that once the building campaign had ceased £3,000 a year was needed to maintain the other work in hand. The total amount raised for buildings through the Board, exclusive of that raised locally, seems to have been £173,677. The Board of Education, like the other Societies, ceased its definite connexion with the Union in 1857-8.

Education, 1858—1872.

The Board of Education was fighting a losing battle though doing good work within its limited sphere. By 1867 it was evident that the march of events had been too strong—"friends were falling away and none arising". The old guard were prepared to die fighting, though it became more and more evident that, receiving no State grants, they could not compete with the wealthy Church of England, which accepted grants both to build and to maintain its schools. A meeting was called in the Autumn Assembly, and Baines wrote a paper in which he described "the history and comparative failure" of the Board. He thus summarized the fight :

When all schools were alike supported purely on the voluntary system, that system proved equal to the sustaining, extending, and improving of education. But when public grants were introduced, they gave advantages so great to the schools which received them as to defy competition on the part of schools which had no help from the public purse. These did not possess the inestimable advantage of periodical visits and examinations by inspectors of learning, experience, and authority. The school committees and teachers became disheartened; the subscriptions declined; in short, the purely voluntary system, which had done such immense service in former years, was obviously overmatched and undermined. A well-principled and gallant struggle was carried on under all these disadvantages for twenty years. It is for you to say whether it shall still be continued, or whether you feel that adherence to the same system will defeat your own object by diminishing your power to aid in the education of the people.

He believed that the struggle "should not longer be continued", but that "they must change their tactics and seek the aid of the Government for the secular teaching in their schools". Against those who still urged no surrender, Samuel Morley agreed with Baines, with the result that at their invitation two hundred ministers and laymen met in November[1]. The view of this conference may be expressed in the words :

Presuming that an entirely new system of national education, and that purely secular, cannot be at present established, the conclusion appears to be generally reached that all public schools for the poorer classes, secular as well as denominational, ought to be assisted by Government grants; but that no grant should be made to any school, professedly denominational, without a conscience clause, allowing the withdrawing of children from all religious teaching which the parents or guardians may disapprove.

In the same year in the *English Independent* Dale had definitely advocated a national system of education enforced by compulsion and paid for by the public funds : so many people, he said, interpreted voluntaryism as "free-

[1] For the details of this meeting see the *Christian Witness,* 1868, p. 45.

dom to give nothing". In May, 1868, Allon addressed the
Assembly in a speech which endeavoured to get to first
principles, and then to discuss methods, stating that it
could be understood that "possibly, with some individual
exceptions, all parties among us agree to accept as the
basis of future educational action the principle of legislative recognition and aid".

Of course, all the efforts of the Congregational Board
of Education had not been a failure. It was with no small
pleasure that in 1870 Samuel Morley was able to quote both
in the Assembly of the Union and in the House of Commons the verdict of one by no means disposed to look with
gentle appreciation on anything connected with the Dissenters. The Union resolved :

> That this Assembly learns with satisfaction from the
> Report of Mr. Matthew Arnold, Her Majesty's Inspector
> of Schools, that that experienced public officer, after a
> careful examination of Homerton College and its practis-
> ing schools, has expressed a high opinion of the training
> in the College, the ability and influence of the Principal,
> and the unsurpassed excellence of the schools; and that he
> also considers the liberal principle on which the College
> is based, of admitting students from all denominations of
> Evangelical Nonconformists, as eminently calculated to
> meet the wants and wishes of the country. They receive
> the impartial verdict of the Inspector of Schools as a reward
> for many years of labour and sacrifice; and they feel
> warranted in recommending, with additional confidence,
> Homerton College and the operations of the Congregational
> Board of Education to the generous support and co-opera-
> tion of the Congregational body.
>
> And further,—That this Assembly, participating in the
> interest which the subject of popular education is exciting
> in the country, would earnestly recommend the more
> vigorous support of existing Schools, and the establishment
> of new Schools where the means of instruction are in-
> adequate.

Allon's joy at agreement among Congregationalists on
education was premature. Confronted with the demand of
the National Education League, founded in Birmingham
in 1869 for "the establishment of a system which shall
secure the education of every child in the country", with its

implication that local authorities, and not merely the clergy, were able to manage education, the majority of Congregationalists at once fell into line, but quite a number of the older men, notably Baines, joined the National Education Union, which stood for denominational education and was made up in the main of Conservatives and Churchmen. It is not the province of this volume to examine the Bill of 1870 with its acceptance of the League's chief contentions, but with its large concessions to denominationalism where the religious question was concerned. Neither have we to describe the intensity of the conflict which raged both in Parliament and in the country. In May, 1870, the following resolution, moved by Rogers, was carried in the Assembly with two or three dissentients :

> That the Assembly, cherishing a strong confidence in the attachment of Her Majesty's Government to the principles of religious equality, recognizes in their measure for the advancement of primary education, an anxious desire to respect the conscientious convictions of all classes of the people, as shown especially in the proposal to abolish denominational inspection; in the application of a conscience clause to all schools to which religious instruction is given, and to admit undenominational schools to the enjoyment of Government grants,—but, at the same time, is compelled to express a decided conviction that the Conscience Clause, as at present framed, will prove inadequate, that the liberty given to inspectors in certain specified circumstances to enquire into the religious teaching in Government schools is inconsistent with the principles of the measure, and that the power entrusted to local boards to determine the religious character of the schools they establish, and to aid denominational schools at present existing out of the rates, is open to very serious objection. The Assembly has learned with great satisfaction that the Government are willing to reconsider the provisions of the Bill, and hope they will adopt and carry out such amendments as will secure a satisfactory settlement of the question.

Some slight amendments were secured, but they did not meet the Nonconformist objections. 1,390 Congregational ministers joined in a Memorial to Gladstone, and in October the Union passed this resolution :

> That this Assembly records its solemn protest against the application by the Government of the resources of the

State to the religious teaching of the people, whether in the schools or in the churches of the land; that it regards with deep dissatisfaction the legislation of the past Session, in so far as increased facilities were provided by it for conducting sectarian education at the public expense; and that, while heartily approving of any action which may be needful in order to give the Elementary Education Act practical effect as a means of promoting the education of the people, it warmly deprecates sectarian rivalry in extending the present denominational system.

The Assembly, further believing that the existence of Churches in this country aided and controlled by the State not only contravenes the principle on which this protest is founded, but is the chief barrier in the way of the just settlement of many other questions, besides that of National Education, which affect the civil and religious interests of the people, counsels that energetic help be given to any wise movement which may be originated for the disestablishment and disendowment of those Churches.

The Bill, though it was called by John Bright " the worst Act passed by a Liberal Government since 1832", went through Parliament, and there was great resentment among Nonconformists, especially when many of the clergy secured building grants before the last day, December 31st, 1870, although they were not in a position to build. The Union's Report in 1871 admitted that the Bill was "an undeniable triumph for those who contend that provision should be made by the State for the religious education of the people". The resentment increased when many School Boards began to use the powers given them in Clause 25[1] to pay the fees of poor children in denominational schools. A resolution protesting against this in May, 1871, divided the Assembly, but it was carried "with almost entire unanimity", while in October Dale carried unanimously a motion :

I.

That this Assembly, while acknowledging the distinguished service which has been rendered to religious liberty

---

[1] It was of this clause, concerning which there was furious controversy in the country, that Disraeli said : "Ah ! the 25th Clause ; we all go down to our constituents and say that the Constitution depends upon it : and we none of us know what it means".

by the present Government in its measures for the disestablishment and disendowment of the Irish Church, and the abolition of university tests, desires to express the deepest dissatisfaction with those parts of its educational policy which tend to perpetuate and extend sectarian religious teaching in schools aided by national funds, and specially to protest :—

First. Against the persistent efforts of the Education Department to force upon School Boards the payment out of the rates of fees for indigent children attending denominational schools ; and

Secondly. Against the sanction given by the Education Department to the provision contained in the schemes of the Endowed Schools Commissioners for the government of Endowed Schools, by which, contrary to the spirit of the Endowed Schools Act, a clergyman of the Established Church is, in nearly every case, made an *ex officio* member of the governing body of the School.

II.

That this Assembly earnestly calls upon Congregationalists throughout the kingdom to resist by all legitimate means the appropriation of the rates to the maintenance of sectarian schools ; to use their political influence to obtain such amendments of the Elementary Education Act as shall prevent sectarian schools from receiving aid from local rates and to press upon the Government the necessity of so embodying the spirit of the Endowed Schools Act, 1869, in the several schemes for the government of Endowed Schools, and, if necessary, so altering that Act, as more fully than at present to secure the interests of religious liberty.

Dale led the campaign in the country and was largely instrumental in gathering 1,885 representatives of Nonconformist churches in Manchester in January, 1872. This Conference, in the words of the editor of the *Year Book,*

with almost entire unanimity, passed strong resolutions respecting the distinction between secular and religious education, and the State restricting itself to the former, and religious parties promoting the latter. The determination was formed to seek the repeal of the 25th Clause of the Elementary Education Act, whereby State aid to denominational schools is rendered possible, if not absolute, and in other respects so to improve the Bill as to make the State education purely secular and national.

There was much dispute about the representative nature of this conference, especially as such respected leaders as Binney, Stoughton, and Conder were opposed to its proceedings. Conder was the nominee of the Committee for the Chair of the Union in May, and had it not been for Dale a division on his name might have followed the lines of the cleavage on education. The Report contained the Committee's resolution, stating its objections to the Scottish Education Bill, and urging the friends of religious equality to prevent its provisions from becoming law, "and in general to bring the educational policy of the legislature into full harmony with Liberal principles". On the motion for the adoption of the Report, Binney and Stoughton said they could not accept the references to education. Immediately Dale moved a rider to the Report, thanking the Committee for its action and expressing concurrence with the principle affirmed at the Manchester Conference that in any system of national education secular instruction alone should be provided by the State, the care of religious instruction being the province of parents and churches. This gave rise to a lively debate, but the rider was carried by a large majority, and the nomination of Conder could then be supported without it being assumed that his views on education were being confirmed.

Dale, who fought the education battle month by month in the *Congregationalist,* to the Editorial chair of which he was called when it superseded the *Christian Witness* at the beginning of 1872, said that not one-tenth, perhaps not one-twentieth, of the Assembly voted against the rider. He analysed the list of 500 or 600 signatures of "Nonconformist Advocates of Religious Education by the State" who had recorded that "as strenuous efforts are being made to exclude the Bible by law from public elementary schools we . . . believing such exclusion would be a great national evil . . . publicly record our disapproval". He found the list contained only 42 Congregational ministers and 45 laymen, though he had to admit it included men like Morley and Charles Reed.

XI. ALMOST WRECKED, 1848-1858.

A NEW Constitution, flourishing Magazines, some provision for superannuation, a new spirit in the denomination —so Wells might have said to himself as 1848 dawned. Wider problems came before the Autumn Assembly in that year, Sunday Schools and work amongst children being discussed, and also the relation of the Church to the working classes.

On every side there were signs of life, though some of them were decidedly disconcerting to those in authority. At the end of 1844, for example, the students of two of the Colleges resolved to boycott the *Congregational Magazine* and to do all that they could to discredit it.   The Editor replied with heavy sarcasm, saying that the Magazine was " not overwhelmed with the apprehension of immediate extinction ", but he took care to print in justification of himself letters which called the behaviour of the students outrageous.

In 1848 " A Protestant Dissenter Indeed " was moved to write to the *Christian Witness* by the sight of an advertisement which referred to "a pile of bricks and mortar as a Congregational Church ".   He suggested the following epitaph :

Here lies
Independency.
Born in the Apostles' Days,
In a trance during the Dark Ages,
but alive again when they were past ;
Immortal
(though " in deaths oft ")
Till killed by his own children.
" They have corrupted themselves, their spot is not the
spot of his children".

A reply came from one whom the Editor called " one of our ablest ministers ", couched in language which Campbell, of all people, described as " needlessly strong " !

> Which is most likely to injure Nonconformity, the calling our places of worship by a proper title, or the employment of weak and ignorant arguments, the indul-

gence of an unchristian temper, the adherence to absurd customs, and the imputation of bad motives?

During these years the great figures of the early days of the Union disappeared from the stage. At the end of 1850 Algernon Wells died after a long illness. This narrative has altogether failed in its intention if it has not conveyed the idea that to his skilful guidance the Union owed its very existence. When his leadership was missing conflicts at once arose, as was seen during the 1850 Assemblies.

As the Chairman, Dr. Morison, said in May, when Wells was absent from the Assembly for the first time, his absence taught the Union " the real value of his inestimable labours ". He went on :

> The name of Algernon Wells will always be associated with the truest and best interests of " The Congregational Union of England and Wales ". His masculine sense, his power of adjusting the most complicated portions of our business, his loving heart and eloquent tongue, have been a tower of strength to the Union. With his ready pen, and his truth-telling and pathetic appeals, he has done us incalculable service ; and, whenever this happy fellowship is thought of, our good and wise Secretary will be remembered, and remembered only to be loved.

A glutton for work, combining a pastorate with the Secretaryships of the Union, the Colonial Missionary Society, and Mill Hill School, he gave all his talents to the service of the Independent churches. Sixteen months after his death his co-Secretary, W. S. Palmer, followed him. Minute Secretary at the beginning, the growth of the Union's publications soon demanded his attention, and he became the officer in charge of that side of the work. He, too, combined a pastorate, that of Harecourt, with his official duties, while he was also a Director of the L.M.S. and frequently visited Ireland for the Evangelical Society.

Of John Blackburn, whose brilliant and useful career ended under a cloud in 1855, mention has already been made. The same year saw the death of Josiah Conder, perhaps Independency's most famous layman at the time. Poet and hymn-writer, editor and scholar, lay preacher and theologian, Conder was held in high regard by men who by no means shared his religious and political opinions.

He was a type the churches could ill afford to lose. The close of John Angell James's long life came at the conclusion of this period, and his great friend, George Redford, the author of the Declaration of Faith and Order, did not long survive him. As these faces that have become familiar vanish, new faces, to become equally familiar, arrive on the scene. Wells's successor was George Smith, first a Methodist tent missioner, then Independent minister in Liverpool and Plymouth, whence he came to Poplar in 1841 to minister in the chapel built by George Green, the shipowner. Appointed in 1851, he had a thankless task : to follow a man like Wells was difficult enough in itself, and Smith was called to the bridge when the weather was distinctly threatening. His way was made easier when Robert Ashton was appointed co-secretary, a satisfactory division of labour being made, Ashton taking finance and publications, and Smith the general work. Their partnership lasted until Smith's death in 1870. Ashton had been minister at Dedham, Warminster, and Putney, and secretary of various denominational societies, and was now Secretary of the London Board of Ministers. He resigned his pastorate at Putney on becoming Secretary, but Smith continued to minister at Poplar.

Before the end of this decade the leaders of the next age of Independency are actively associated with the Union's proceedings. Allon, Dale, Newman Hall, Guinness Rogers, and Samuel Morley are stepping into the front rank. No longer is John Morison's name on the *Evangelical Magazine*, but John Stoughton's; J. B. Paton has taken the place Conder filled so long and honourably on the *Eclectic*, while one Joseph Parker appears as Editor of one periodical and another. And 1859 shows these figures :

Churches—England	1600
Wales	636
Scotland and Channel Islands	147
Colonies	208
Ministers and Missionaries throughout the British Empire, so far as they can be ascertained	2734
Colleges and Theological Academies	10

GEORGE SMITH

T. T. LYNCH

Students in the same   206
Works published by Congregationalists in 1859   ...   90
Periodicals conducted by Congregationalists   ...   24
Associations of Churches in Great Britain and
    Ireland, besides numerous private Ministerial
    Associations in almost every County   68

These were difficult years in which war and pestilence
and mutiny all found a place. Cholera was rife in many
parts of the country. Newcastle could not entertain the
Union in 1853 because of its prevalence, while in three
months of the following year 10,000 people died from it in
London. And the difficulties without but reflected those
within, for it was in this period that the Union became
acutely conscious that it had assumed much heavier responsibilities than it could well carry. Now that it was a Union
of churches rather than of Associations, it is not possible to
see its growth as Associations affiliate, though Hampshire
joined in 1848. Measured by the financial support of the
churches, it does not seem to have grown at all. In 1848
381 contributors, *i.e.* 218 churches and 163 individuals,
gave £300 in subscriptions and donations, but in 1858 the
income from these sources was only £144, the number of
churches contributing being but 71, while the majority of
personal members were ministers (the numbers are given
in 1853 as 180 ministers and 50 deacons). Many were the
appeals made to the churches to join the Union and to send
subscriptions; and sometimes complaints were made that
even those who attended the Assembly did not join the
Union, and that, with 2,000 churches and as many ministers, there were not 300 subscribers. On the other hand, it
was claimed that most of the larger churches and the more
influential ministers took an active part in the work of the
Union, whose strength was said to be " in inverse ratio
to its numbers ". It had to be remembered, also, that
distance and expense made it impossible for many pastors
to attend the Assembly, the smaller churches being quite
unable to meet their expenses.

Nor did the attempts to attract the churches by tinkering
with the Constitution help, though it was said that the
changes made in 1847 were universally approved. Later

N

it was suggested that the *fixed* subscription was a deterrent, and so in 1852 Rule II was made to read :

> II.—That this Union shall consist of Congregational churches, and of personal members, as hereinafter described, severally adhering to this Union. The qualification of churches for membership shall be in connexion with an Association; or, where no Association is accessible, recommendation by three ministers already in the Union, residing near the applicant church. Every church connected with this Union shall be expected to make an annual contribution to its funds, neglect of which, for two successive years, shall disqualify for the privileges of membership. The amount of contribution from churches is, in every case, left to their own judgment, having respect to their numbers and capabilities. Tutors of colleges, and officers of public societies, being members of Congregational churches; also, ministers and deacons in fellowship with churches which are eligible for connexion with the Union, may become personal members by payment of an annual subscription of not less than five shillings.

At the same time the provision under Rule III for sending an " annual or occasional letter to the churches " was altered to " address, as occasion may require, a letter to the churches ", while, in place of the Regulations " for the Annual Assembly " a new Rule (V) was added :

> V.—A preliminary meeting of the Annual Assembly, convened by public notice, to consist of members of the Union exclusively, shall be held on the Monday afternoon of the Missionary week, to which meeting shall be submitted a statement of all the business to be brought under the consideration of the ensuing sessions, whether by the Committee of the Union, or by any other party; and the meeting shall thereupon nominate, as it may deem necessary, a Committee on each matter of business, to consider and report thereon to the Assembly; and, in particular, this preliminary meeting shall advise the Assembly in the choice of Officers and Committee for the year, and of Chairman, and place of Autumnal Meeting for the next following year, all which matters shall be decided by vote of the Assembly.

It is not to be wondered at that Wells lamented " how slowly our churches move towards concert and co-operation ". This is not surprising when it is seen how strongly even some of those called to the Chair suspected centralization and the development of organization. In

1855, for example, Robert Halley, in saying that the Assembly was truly representative, though not elected by the churches, went on :

> By such direct representation may our Assembly never be constituted ! Delegates so elected would soon become invested with authority, and whatever precaution was taken, would soon overrule the free and independent action of our own people.

The representation as at present was to him " the only fair and convenient executive for the expression of opinion in harmony with the principles of Independency ", and he hoped these would not be betrayed " in the delusive hope of gaining closer union, better order, or more effective government ". He hoped, too, that the Union would never have a monopoly of the denomination's periodical literature.

In the same year, when a deacon wrote to the *Christian Witness* suggesting that it would be a good thing if the Union would arrange the supply of the pulpits on the Sunday when the simultaneous collection for " British Missions " was made, Campbell told him that he misapprehended the province of the Union altogether, and that his proposal " assumed Central Power and a full-orbed Despotism which could only exist through the utter destruction of the churches as Independent communities ".

On the other hand, when Morison, the Editor of the *Evangelical Magazine,* was in the Chair in 1850, he referred to a paper he had read 29 years before " On the Best Methods of Promoting an Evangelical Union among Congregational Churches, without infringing their Independence ". While rejoicing that nothing could come before the Assembly to infringe the liberty of the churches in the way of appeals or questions of discipline, censure, or authority, he said that " the experience of twenty years has shown the compatibility of effective union with the maintenance of strict and scriptural Independence ". Two years later the Chairman, Dr. Harris, of New College, went further, holding that " it was the Congregational Churches only that had true union, because theirs was a union of free communities ", and he spoke of

" the perfect compatibility of the independence of the separate church with the confederation of many churches ". He said that closer union still was possible, but it must be real and not forced union.

More than once, too, it was claimed that the freedom of Independency enabled the denomination to unite in beneficent enterprises in a way and to an extent other denominations found impossible. This was never expressed better than in the *Christian Witness* two years after this period ended :

> and it is an indisputable fact, that the Independents, as a body, have generally taken the lead in all the associated movements of the time. They *alone* have been ever ready to unite with any other, and every other section of the Church of God, in efforts to advance the Kingdom of Christ, or mitigate the sufferings of mankind. So catholic is the spirit of the system, that they have, somewhat unwisely, perhaps oft-times been more ready to unite with other bodies for general, than among themselves for denominational objects ; although in this they have been exemplary. Is evidence sought? We have it in that great and noble organization, the London Missionary Society, which, notwithstanding its true catholicity, is, to all intents, their Institution. We have it in the Home, the Irish, and the Colonial Missionary Societies ; and last, not least, in the Societies for erecting chapels in London and the provinces, respectively.

While the income from the churches remained so low, expenditure on salaries and on annual meetings and deputations was increasing. Sometimes there was a welcome gift from the towns which entertained the Autumn Assembly as they found themselves with a surplus on their Entertainment Fund. In 1849 Sheffield sent £50, in 1853 Manchester £36, and in 1858 Halifax £20. In the main, however, the Treasurer had to look to *Hymn Book* profits to clear his deficit. From this source he received £368 in 1858. For some years the accounts were presented in the autumn, and from October, 1854, to May, 1858, £1,311 in all was taken from the profits of the *Hymn Book*.

If the churches did little in the way of direct financial support, they showed distinct appreciation of some of the services the Union rendered. The *Year Book* was skilfully edited from the beginning, for two years by Blackburn, for two by Palmer and Wells, for two by Palmer and Ashton, and then for 26 years by Ashton alone.   Often the churches testified to its usefulness by buying every obtainable copy.   At first, when the price was only 1s., the loss was over £100 a year, so in 1858 the price was raised to 1s. 6d.   It is not surprising that the *Year Books* were snapped up quickly.   They provided a mass of information for ministers, churches, and the officials of denominational and benevolent organizations, and so were found increasingly useful.   But they also contained all kinds of historical matter of great interest.   Thus, the 1851 Book contained, for the first time, the names of missionaries of the London Missionary Society, as well as a valuable list of extinct Independent Colleges and Academies, with their Tutors.   Without adopting the extravagant language John Campbell used in regard to the Book, yet it is interesting to read his opinion in 1859 :

> This book is a peculiar achievement in English Ecclesiastical Literature.   It presents the most thorough analysis of the greatest, the most enlightened, and the most influential Dissenting community in the land, that can be imagined.   Fully to describe it would be almost to repeat it. It is a full and complete development of the ecclesiastical economy of the entire community, and everything appertaining to it.   To the Ministers and members of the Independent Body it is a strong and happy necessity ; to the members and Ministers of all other bodies an instructive and interesting curiosity.   We commend it most heartily to both, Churchmen as well as all Dissenters, who will find it to be the largest and the best eighteenpennyworth of Ecclesiastical knowledge ever presented to the public.   It is the most magnificent lecture on the power of the Voluntary Principle ever delivered.

Two years later he wrote :

> It is to the honour of the Independents that they possess the best Hymn Book in England, and the best Year Book in the world.

Those connected with the Union to-day will find nothing more surprising in its past history than the fact that in a year when fewer than 100 churches were contributing to the Union Funds 4,400 copies of the *Year Book* were sold : in the following decade the number sold reached 6,750.

Another bright spot was the *Hymn Book,* on the profits of which, as we have seen, the work of the Union was run. Fortunate, indeed, it was that the book continued to sell well, so well that in 1858 its sales were higher than in any previous year. This makes the publication of a new *Hymn Book* a rather strange proceeding. Discussion on psalmody was, however, incessant, and new churches especially found it irritating to have to purchase two books, Watts's *Psalms and Hymns* and the *Hymn Book.* A circular elicited the fact that 413 out of 502 correspondents would prefer a single book, and in 1855 a well-selected Committee of sixteen members was appointed to compile a new Book, with the assistance of fifty corresponding members. In October, 1855, the report of this Committee was presented by the Rev. Henry Allon, who thus began a career of service which was to transform the worship of the Congregational Churches. The Committee met for three hours every week, and in May, 1858, the *New Congregational Hymn Book* was submitted to the Assembly for criticism, and published the following year.

The churches seemed content to allow the *Hymn Book* to provide funds for the work of the Union. They did not seem to realize at all the need for the Union to have anything in the way of capital in its Publication Department. While that Department could be " milked ", they seemed unwilling to supply funds. Probably, too, there was the feeling that they were already contributing a good deal to denominational enterprises. They were supporting the London Missionary Society, and many of them had given generously to the Education Appeal. There was also the October collection for " British Missions ", and new Societies were beginning to make claims. It was, of course, only a comparative few of the churches that took up the " British Missions " collection, but they were, no doubt, the churches who contributed to all denominational efforts. Three hundred and eighty-five churches in 1848 gave £5,200 in the " British Missions " collection, 318 in

1851 gave £5,305 (nearly one-half of this was from London ; in 14 counties there were only 25 collections) ; the amount fell to below £5,000 in the years of the Crimean War, with their increased taxation and high prices. In 1850 it was stated that while 741 churches had taken up this collection in one year or another, only 28 had consistently supported it every year. For the three Societies, too, there were all kinds of special demands. The churches helped very liberally during the Irish Famine, while the Colonial Society had to grapple with the rush of emigrants to Australia in 1853, when 116,000 people left England in three months. Many able missionaries were sent after them, including Richard Fletcher and J. L. Poore, whose valedictory meetings were held in Manchester during the Meetings of 1853. By that time the Colonial Society had 100 ministers at work.

It has to be remembered, too, that many of the Independents took a very active part in the Anti-Corn Law Agitation, which was also a strain on their resources.

The Assembly had grown considerably. The May Meetings were held first in New Broad Street and then in the Poultry Chapel. Throughout, the outlook of the churches making up the Union must be remembered and all their activities seen against the background of the secular history of the time. Theatre-going and novel-reading were still taboo and most amusements discountenanced. A Yorkshire church which re-opened its organ by a " Grand Performance " of Sacred Music on Easter Monday afternoon was mercilessly pilloried in the *Christian Witness*. *Soirées* seem to have afforded the main relief, and Binney successfully pressed for their inclusion in the Union programme. It was also the age of lectures. At Northampton in 1851 the public was admitted to a lecture on Doddridge by Stoughton. Though he " passed over large portions of his MS." he lectured for two hours, to what the Minutes called " a very large, delighted and deeply affected auditory ", and the next Report says, " It would be impossible to convey any adequate impression of the deep, thrilling, subduing emotion which attended the deliverance " of the lecture. Halley, some years later, spent two hours discoursing on Oliver Heywood.

Not yet had the Chairmanship of the Union, still the nomination of the Committee and, in practice, of the Secretary, become a post of honour. Waddington says that it was difficult to find ministers or laymen to accept the Chair in the early days, for it was " at that time attended with inconvenience and rather doubtful credit ". It was only afterwards, " having risen in estimation, that the distinction was coveted". James Gawthorne, of Derby, declined the Chair on the score of age, Campbell lest he should lose his freedom of criticism. In 1854 Halley, who was to be Chairman, went on a Continental tour, and the Rev. A. Morton Brown, of Cheltenham, who took his place, was " thanked for his kindness in accepting the office of Chairman ".

The custom of two Chairman's Addresses began with Hamilton in 1847. A Sermon also began to be a regular feature, and before the end of this decade it was often followed by a Communion Service. The Autumnal Sessions were well attended, and in 1852 thanks were expressed to two Railway Companies for allowing delegates to make the double journey at single fare. Some years later, when the Union Meetings were at Liverpool and the Church Congress at Manchester, the L.N.W. and L. & Y. Railways made a similar concession for the Congress and *not* for the Union. Samuel Morley at once enquired the meaning of this discrimination and obtained equal treatment.

Visitors came regularly to the Assembly from Scotland, and delegates were sent yearly to Scotland and Ireland. There were also numerous visitors from the Continent and the United States, including Finney, the evangelist, and Harriet Beecher Stowe. Mrs. Stowe was given a great reception when she entered with Binney in 1853, but of course she was not allowed to speak, her husband being called upon to reply for her. As yet no woman had appeared in the Assembly even as a delegate. In 1848, however, Samuel Martin remarked that " many youth of the female sex are ensnared by the imposing drama of Popish and Puseyite worship ".   " No Popery ", Ritualism, and kindred subjects were constantly in the minds and on the lips of the Union speakers, while the grievances of the Dissenters in regard to the marriage laws, education, University tests, and church rates were continually emphasized.

In 1849 a Memorial for the closing of Post-Offices on Sundays was despatched, in 1852 a protest made against opening the Crystal Palace on Sundays, and in 1856 Palmerston was thanked for stopping the playing of military bands in the parks on Sundays.   Vigorous resolutions were passed on slavery in the United States and against Roman Catholic persecution on the Continent.   There was considerable intercourse with the Evangelical Protestants of France, no doubt reflecting the political and military alliance of the two nations.   In 1851, before the Peace Society's " General Congress . . . to bring about the abolition of War ", the Assembly expressed its interest and prayed for its success :

> . . . entertaining, as they do, the firm conviction, that the predicted time is approaching, when, as the result of the reign of justice and freedom, nations shall learn war no more.   That, without pronouncing on the principle of the unlawfulness of military defence, or of the military service when employed in the repression of crime, disorder, or hostile irruption, this Assembly avow their utter abhorrence of international war for purposes of territorial conquest, or on the pretext of effecting the settlement of differences, as condemned alike by religion, reason, justice, humanity, and the interest of peoples.

No resolution seems to have been passed about the Crimean War, though the Congregational journals seem to have supported it, Campbell in the *British Banner* violently attacking Cobden.   The denomination's attitude to problems where the nation's interests were concerned is perhaps accurately suggested in a *Year Book* comment on the Indian Mutiny, written at the end of 1859 :

> The extinction of the INDIAN MUTINY calls for the gratitude of the nation.   A few rebels linger and skulk among the distant jungles, but their day is nearly at an end, and

complete tranquillity will soon, by God's blessing, be restored. The rebellion has caused an immense sacrifice of life, brought unspeakable wretchedness on multitudes, and entailed a debt of thirty-four millions sterling on the Indian exchequer, but may prove eventually a blessing to India. It has shown the natives the power of the British arms, and crushed thereby the hopes they have ever entertained of destroying the British and restoring the native rule. It has awakened attention and solicitude among British patriots respecting the future administration of India, and has led to measures which will ameliorate the social condition of the Hindoos; and, still more than all, has roused the entire church of God to prayer and effort for the salvation of the idolatrous millions that people those distant presidencies of our Empire.

Yet even while we shudder to-day on reading that the Chairman of the Union in October, 1857, could speak of

those whose office it is, are employed in adopting all suitable measures for repressing the mutiny—for restoring peace, and diffusing confidence among the natives, so that our beloved Queen's crown may not be robbed of what has been said to be its brightest gem,

we notice that he goes on to deplore that so little has been done for the moral and spiritual welfare of the vast Hindoo population. And this same Chairman, the Rev. A. Jack of North Shields, had the courage to denounce the get-rich-quick individualism of his time, saying the

high pressure of competition has in some quarters risen to such a height that honest men, we are told, can with difficulty carry on business and maintain a conscience void of offence. This is one of the crying evils of the day.

In other respects Jack's address is strikingly modern, as when he speaks about cheap trips on Sundays, highly-seasoned fare in newspapers, and " the world in the Church ".

Similarly, though our view of child psychology makes us horrified at the thought of a " Children's Sermon " as a recognized part of the Autumn Programme, especially when the subject is " The Soul ", yet the increased attention to the work of Sunday Schools is noteworthy. The protagonist of Sunday Schools on the Union platform was Charles Reed, afterwards Sir Charles Reed, M.P., Chair-

man of the London School Board. Many were the papers
he read on the subject, that in 1855 stating that there were
2590 Congregational Sunday Schools, with good buildings,
but with deficient provision for infants, seniors, and
teacher-training.

The Census of 1851 and Its Results.

The census of 1851 included a religious census, with
the aim of discovering the number of places of worship,
their seating accommodation, and the number of persons
who attended them on a set Sunday. It was some years
before Mr. Horace Mann, who was in charge of this part
of the census, issued the resultant returns, but very reveal-
ing they were. This volume is not concerned with the
violent controversy between the Established Church and
other Christians which the returns evoked, but merely with
their effect on organized Congregationalism. In the first
place, they gave considerable impetus to the demand for
full and correct statistics. Then they made the Independents realize their numbers, their growth, and their power,
and strengthened the demand for Disestablishment. But
mainly they made the denomination realize, too, the need
for increased efforts in regard both to chapel building and
to evangelization at home. The *Year Book* for 1854
published an Appendix on the census, and in the same
year the Rev. John Kennedy dealt with the subject in the
May Assembly. The figures were :

	Places of Worship.	Sittings.
Church of England	14,077	5,317,915
Wesleyan Methodists of all kinds ...	11,007	2,194,298
Independents	[1]3,244	1,067,760

All denominations other than the Church of England had
20,399 places of worship with 4,894,648 sittings, the
Wesleyans and Independents being the most numerous.
Of the 3,244 Independent places of worship, 2,960 were
separate buildings, though some of these were of a tem-

---

1 This figure was 110 too high, as Independent Methodists had been
included.

porary nature only. The rate of increase of the Independent chapels may be gathered from this table :

1801	... ...	914
1811	... ...	1,140
1821	... ...	1,478
1831	... ...	1,999
1841	... ...	2,606
1851	... ...	3,244

For every 1,000 persons in 1801 the Independents provided 34 sittings, in 1851, 59 sittings; the corresponding figures for the Wesleyans were 18 and 123, and for the Baptists 20 and 42.

An analysis of the figures drove home the fact that there was a lamentable deficiency in the accommodation for worship, especially in some parts of the country. More important, however, was the revelation that the attendance fell far short of the accommodation. Mann's figures were based on the assumption that 58 per cent of the population were able to attend public worship at one time, that is, 10,398,013, throughout the country. There were present in the

Morning	...	4,647,482 ⎫	of ⎧	524,612 ⎫	were
Afternoon	...	3,184,135 ⎬	whom ⎨	232,285 ⎬	Congregationalists
Evening	...	3,064,449 ⎭	⎩	457,162 ⎭	

With these facts before them the challenge could not be escaped. Already in 1848 Wells had called the attention of the Union to the failure of all the churches to grip the working classes, who were

> quite unconcerned spectators of our struggles for religious liberty . . . not converted by Romish zeal, or any longer gathered by Wesleyan energy, or drawn by the more intellectual discourses of Independent and Baptist preachers.

He asked why the Independent churches attracted tradespeople but not artizans, and spoke of their "essentially middle-class character", saying that they were more exclusively middle-class than a century before. He thought that possibly the Independent conception of the Church had much to do with the neglect of the masses, for their churches were born to strife and separation, having to witness against error in doctrine, worship, and polity, and to attack powerful vested interests. Thus they had become unpopular and greatly disliked—there was nothing about them to attract the timid, the careless, and the self-interested.

Wells was followed by Edward Swaine, a thoughtful layman of the type Independency has always been able, and proud, to produce, and by Dr. Massie, the new Secretary of the Home Missionary Society, who was either helped or handicapped by the fact that not long before his appointment he had urged that the three Societies for " British Missions " should be united in administration. After these papers it was resolved to urge the Committee to establish lectures for the working classes, and also to correspond with representative men throughout the country on the best way of approaching them. The resulting communications contained a few home-truths. Some said it was vain to hope for a hearing unless the churches " manifested greatly increased sympathy with the working classes in their strong desire to possess the elective franchise ". Others recommended " a more consistent and thorough carrying out of democratic principles . . . a freer mingling of classes in church office, in arrangements for worship ", etc., etc. Good stuff, this, and showing the right spirit throughout the country! Experimental lectures were held in London in 1849 with good results, but it was felt that this was not quite the Union's province. During the Autumn Meetings at Bradford in 1852, however, the Union asked the Revs. A. Reed and Brewin Grant to lecture to working men, and these were so successful that, at the instance of the Union, private individuals supplied the means for Grant to spend three years in this kind of work.

More lasting, however, was the result of the census in the stimulus it gave to chapel building. It has been seen how James and others were constantly urging the need of new places of worship. The disclosure of the shortage drove home the fact that there was still much to be done, and even before the returns were tabulated there was renewed activity. In the autumn of 1851 the Rev. J. C. Gallaway read an admirable paper on Chapel Extension, first asking how it could be carried out consistently with Independent principles : it was in accordance with those principles " to gather to build " ; could it be right sometimes " to build to gather " ? Having justified this procedure he urged that a Chapel Extension Society should be formed for the whole Kingdom, the London and Manchester Societies, both of which were setting themselves to build fifty new chapels, continuing work in their respective areas. The Assembly urged full consideration of the project, James at once offering a prize for the best essay on the subject if the Union thought it desirable. After the Associations had expressed approval, and consideration by a special committee, a draft Constitution was presented in October, 1852, generally approved, and referred to another special committee, which met at Birmingham in December, and called a meeting of all interested at Derby in March. Then the " English Congregational Chapel Building Society " was formed, with Gallaway as Secretary and Joshua Wilson and Arthur Morley as Treasurers. By May £7,000 had been promised, and the erection and completion of 50 chapels in five years was planned. The Union Report said :

> Your Committee cheerfully undertook to meet the expenses involved in originating this Society, in the hope of repayment at an early day. At the same time, they deliberately declined to be responsible in future for its movements, or in any way to stand connected with its operations, beyond that of friendly, affectionate concern, believing, as they do, that while the Union should aid, according to its ability, in forming Societies intended for our denominational advantage, it is every way desirable that your organization should not exert any controlling power over their operations, but leave them at perfect liberty to pursue their own plans, without the influence of any centralizing power.

The Chapel Building Committee consisted of 42 members, of whom 8 only were resident in London, the majority being laymen. Its meetings were held quarterly, two of them during the Union Assemblies, the other two in different districts.　Donors could earmark their gifts for a district or for a specific building.　The Society was prepared to take the initiative if needful, but it conceived its main business as the guiding and stimulating of local effort.　An income of £10,000 a year would enable not 50 but 100 chapels to be built.　The benefits anticipated were :

> increased economy and much practical improvement in our ecclesiastical architecture; the entire removal of the vicious system of perambulating the country with separate chapel cases ; a deeper interest awakened throughout the denomination in our general progress; a strong conviction of the great practical utility of the Congregational Union, in which this Society had its origin, which cheerfully bore the expenses incurred in the preliminary arrangements, and which continues to extend to it its parental counsel and good-will ; a reflex benefit conferred upon our churches, by leading them to engage in works of Christian aggression ; the raising up of valuable auxiliaries to our colleges, and various religious societies ; the most telling of all arguments in proof of the efficiency of the voluntary principle, and in favour of the separation of the Church from the State ; and a wide extension, among classes not hitherto touched by our ministry, of the knowledge of that Gospel which is the power of God unto salvation to every one that believeth.

Soon the Society was actively at work, not only making grants, but trying to raise the aesthetic standard of buildings and circulating a *Manual of Practical Hints* for the use of architects and chapel-building committees.　Soon, too, they were suggesting a simultaneous collection in the churches, the last Sunday in February being their choice. It was " the princely liberality of some nine or ten gentlemen ", however, which enabled the Committee to report in 1856 that 39 chapels were built or building, for the number of collections during the previous year had been 15 only, producing £117.　A paper by the Rev. Thomas Aveling in October, 1857, gave an excellent summary of the history of chapel building and an account of the work recently accomplished.

The Ministry.

It is now necessary to turn to the question of the ministry.　Notice must be taken first of attempts to assist ministers in old age, in making provision for widows and children, and in the way of raising stipends.

1. *The "Christian Witness" Fund.*—Throughout the decade the two Magazines continued to make profits, though their very success brought a host of competitors. The influence of the Crimean War, too, tended to reduce the circulation, while the fact that Campbell made an honest endeavour to keep controversial topics out of their pages did not serve to make them more readable. The *Banner*, spiced with personalities, and with divines thwacking each other lustily week by week, was certain to make a greater appeal than a conventional and stodgy *Witness*. Nevertheless the profits were sufficient

(*a*) To make grants to aged ministers, and also to those suffering from illness or incapacity;

(*b*) To provide £150 to meet the yearly premiums for the purchase of deferred annuities for each of fifteen ministers. These annuities were not popular, and though missionaries of the Home Missionary Society were made eligible, fifteen was the total number purchased. The invested profits provided sufficient income to meet these premiums, and this method of help ceased as these cases matured.

2. In 1853 the *Pastors' Insurance Aid Society* was formed. Its aim was to assist ministers to make provision for their widows and children by aiding them to pay insurance premiums, as a rule in the Protestant Union. Subscriptions, donations, and legacies were invited; only two-thirds of the income was to be spent until a capital fund of £5,000 had been raised. Ministers with over £200 a year were ineligible, and those with over £150 could receive half their premiums only. The annuities were to be not less than £25 and not more than £50. J. R. Mills offered £250, with the promise of another £250, if this £5,000 were obtained within five years. By 1856 twenty-three ministers had been helped through this Society.

3. *The Maintenance of the Ministry.*—In 1848 an attempt to discover the views of the churches on a Sustentation Fund for this purpose produced this summary:

Nearly all respondents appear to concur in thinking that to render safe, or even possible, any plan resembling a Sustentation Fund, by which a minimum income should be guaranteed to every recognized minister, a stringency of control as to the ministers to be recognized would be necessary quite incompatible with the principles, practices, and genius of our denomination.   There appears a like unanimity of opinion that we have of late years so unduly multiplied small chapels in poor districts, and by almost necessary consequence, feeble churches and ill-supported ministers in these chapels, that the number of brethren needing and deserving external aid has become too great for our means to provide it; that we have extended our line beyond our power to give it due support.

In 1849, at Sheffield, Wells read two important papers "On the Aid to be given to Feeble Churches for adequate Support of their Pastors", and "An Appeal to Congregational Churches for the suitable support of their Pastors, specially addressed to those Churches needing assistance for this purpose". It was not until 1852, however, that any definite steps were taken. Then Edward Swaine spoke on the inadequacy of pastoral incomes, going into the matter very thoroughly, moved by his intense regard for the ministry—"a more intelligent and estimable body of men does not exist". He argued for a Sustentation or Supplementary Fund to lift salaries to £120 or £130. No church ought to have a pastor unless it could raise £50.

> The fund should be under the control of a wisely-constituted committee or board (separate from the Union), never entertaining or acting in a case except with the concurrence of the County Association or other trustworthy referees, or without the previous formal application of the people of the pastor's charge, through their deacons.

Other denominations should be communicated with in order to obtain information with regard to Funds of this kind. Swaine's paper went into all manner of details, and the subject was referred to a Committee of 13 laymen, 7 of whom were M.P.'s. George Smith said it was difficult to obtain information, but

> whatever diversity of opinion may obtain amongst us as to the propriety of forming a Sustentation or Supplementary

Fund, there can be no variety or sentiment on the importance of augmenting, in some way consistent with our principles, the incomes of many of our zealous and devoted pastors, who are labouring in agricultural and thinly populated districts, among a poor people, without liberal, and in some cases adequate means of support.

The country was circularized, with the exception of Wales, where it was said that many ministers had incomes from farms and from other employment. 33 of 44 Associations sent returns, which showed that the average stipend varied from £188 (higher in London) to £60. 217 ministers had less than £70 a year, 93 less than £50. The multiplication of small pastorates was partly responsible for low stipends, but one Secretary reported :

In judging of the support which Congregational ministers receive, it is necessary to exercise a cautious and wise discrimination. The most prominent cases are not always the most deserving. Our smaller places are often occupied by men not long stationary anywhere, because not well qualified for their work ; yet they will persevere in preaching. They are frequently seeking an introduction to some vacant congregation, which they find low, but do not raise ; they are applicants for a share of every exhibition : hence their poverty is continually forced on public attention. A good deal of this sort of privation must be set aside, if we would form a correct judgment of the claims of our poorer brethren.

The minds of ministers and churches continued to play around the idea of a Sustentation Fund, and in 1856 the Committee, while "regretting their inability to make any specific recommendations respecting it", arranged for the Rev. J. Ashby, Secretary of the North Bucks. Association, to speak on the subject. Ashby outlined a scheme for bringing salaries up to £100 where the churches raised £50, the ministers eligible being

such as have been ordained, and have presided over a Congregational Church not less than one year, and who are either in union with a County Association, or have the confidence of their neighbouring brethren.

He estimated that a capital sum of £44,800 would be required, but if existing County and other Benevolent Funds were merged and used there should be no difficulty in rais-

ing the balance, especially if John Campbell would give
his powerful advocacy. The feeling in regard to such a
scheme he thus stated :

> Many of the Associations now possess funds, which they
> appropriate to necessitous churches without creating the
> feeling of their independence being infringed. Is that in-
> dependency, then, likely to be affected by a plan which
> would simply enlarge the means already existing?
>
> It is vain to expect the general concurrence of the
> churches in any plan, on account of the widely-spread fear
> of Independency being endangered. All that may be prac-
> ticable, at first, may be to make an experiment on a limited
> scale, with a view to its gradual comprehension of the whole
> body of necessitous churches, in the event of success re-
> commending it.

What was needed was correct statistics, getting the subject to the notice of the churches, and a definite judgment
on these points :

> Is such a fund needed?
> Are the means of such a fund existent in the churches?
> Could such a fund comport with Independency?
> How should such a fund be administered to preserve In-
> dependency intact?
> Is there a probability of a majority of the churches rising
> to a proper status without such aid?
> Has a sufficient effort for correct statistics yet been made?
> Ought not such effort to be made without delay?

This scheme was examined by George Smith in a paper
(1857) in which the whole question of sustentation was summarized. He pointed out that the income of £22,000 a
year from the various Funds was held under trusts, and
probably could not be secured for a general Sustentation
Fund. Sometimes there were too many churches in one
town ; sometimes two churches could be united under one
pastor. Generally the standard of conscientious giving
should be raised, but the Committee, while "prepared to
advise and aid any judicious scheme which can benefit
pastors without hindering churches", felt it was "beyond
their province and power to originate any large plan
adequately to meet the actual wants of the case". The
subject was referred to the County Associations, and it was

resolved to call a special conference of ministers and lay-men. This was held in January, 1858, and again during the May Assembly. It recognized the need, which it urged upon churches and Associations. The Associations were recommended to ask to be allowed to send deputations to churches, and not to make grants when the ministerial income was below a certain figure. The principle of the weekly offering was commended, and two papers prepared, one for deacons and one for church members. The managers of Funds, asked to consider whether their administration could be improved, declared against amalgamation but for increased co-operation. At this point the movement seems to have fizzled out for the moment, attention probably being diverted to the Pastors' Retiring Fund, in advocacy of which Dr. Ferguson was proclaiming at this time that half the ministers had less than £80 a year, that many people did not give at all, and that the principle and practice of the weekly offering were essential.

4. *The Pastors' Retiring Fund.*

IF the plan for a Sustentation Fund seemed to be too ambitious and beyond the reach of the Union, perhaps some more adequate means of superannuation could be found. A lead was given by John Angell James in 1858, when he offered the £500 presented to him by Carrs Lane on his jubilee, plus £200 of his own, for this purpose, on condition that a fund of £5,000 was raised in two years. James's offer was subsequently increased to £1,000, and in October, 1858, Dr. Ferguson was asked to present a superannuation scheme. He expressed disappointment that it was impossible to form a Mutual Benefit Society, from which ministers would obtain pensions as a right, and went on to outline a Pastors' Retiring Fund with a capital of £5,000, subscribing pastors to have the first claim, those to be eligible who had subscribed for five years, a letter backed by the Treasurer and Secretary of the County Association being sufficient application "without going through the humiliating process of answering a long sheet of printed questions". To maintain the Fund he estimated:

500 ministers would make contributions averaging £3 a year	£1,500
Collections, donations, and legacies	1,500
Interest on the capital	200
	£3,200
Allow 60 pensions at £20 to £70, say ...	2,750
Surplus	£450

A Committee was appointed to examine this scheme, and by Samuel Morley's generosity a leading actuary was set to work. He at once reverted to the idea of a Pastors' Retiring Annuity Association based on equity, not charity. He presented tables as follows:

Pastors	Annuity of £50 to begin at age of	Premium	Premium in general Insurance office
Under 30	60	£4 12 0	£7 18 0
40	65	£5 6 0	£8 4 6
Under 50	70	£5 17 0	£8 8 0

Fifteen hundred ministers were asked if such a scheme were practicable and would be supported by their churches. To the series of questions sent to them, 546 replied, the replies being divided into nine classes:

1. The object important, the practical difficulties too great.
2. In favour, but cannot promise support.
3. In favour, but premiums too high.
4. In favour, but recommend a separate fund for widows and children.
5. In favour of the principle, but had already made provision by insurance or county funds.
6. Prefer the raising of a fund from which grants could be made according to amounts subscribed by a minister and his church.
7. Sure to fail; folly to attempt.
8. Form a fund by merging existing funds.
9. Circulars returned without place, date, or name.

From these answers the Committee concluded with regret that it would not be wise or expedient to form the Association, and they must fall back on a charitable fund. They recommended immediate acceptance of James's challenge as a basis for a much larger fund. James was dying, but he was cheered by the news that the £4,000 to qualify for his gift had been raised during the Assembly. By the end of the year 1859 £9,000 had been received.

The Union and The Societies.

Before the Pastors' Retiring Fund was definitely established, however, the relationship between the denominational Societies and the Union had undergone a drastic change. The Union in its early days insisted that the three Societies known as "British Missions" should present a written report to the Assembly. To these three had been added the Board of Education, the Chapel Building Society, and the Insurance Aid Society. The Secretaries of these Societies naturally desired to make the most of the opportunity presented by their Annual Report to the Assembly, with the result that the Reports became a weariness to the flesh, and in 1856 the Committee had to make the humiliating appeal :

> Complaints having frequently been made of the length of Reports read in your Assemblies from the Affiliated Societies of the Union, and an unmistakable disposition having been evinced not to hear them, your Committee have arranged with the officers of these Institutions that in future each paper shall be so short as to occupy only five minutes in reading. They do, therefore, earnestly entreat that the brethren will give their kind attention to these documents, and show their interest in the valuable Institutions thus presented to them, by remaining in the Assembly to listen to the speeches which may be made in their support.

This was a contributory, but not the main, cause of the decision to sever the connexion between the Societies and the Union. The fact was that in respect of some of the Societies, especially the Board of Education, the Union might be committed to courses which not all its members would approve, just as it might in the case of the Magazines, with which the question of the Affiliated Societies was at this time interwoven. In May, 1857, an attempt was made to re-affirm the view of " not authoritative, but friendly ; not involving responsibility and control . . . " but it was clear that this did not meet the feeling of the Assembly, which had come round to Baldwin Brown's opinion that such a position was intolerable. In a letter addressed to members of the Union in January, 1857, he said :

The present state of affairs can no longer be endured. It is an old history. The Union "has nourished and adopted children, and they have rebelled against her". Societies, popularly supposed to be connected very nearly with the Union, have each a list of subscribers, a committee and an official apparatus; and each carries on its work in an independent way. So long as all goes well, nothing can be pleasanter; but if the Union should happen to be dissatisfied with the management of a Society and should seek to mend it, the committee of that Society can say, and have said, "We are responsible to our own subscribers alone, we will hear your advice thankfully and act upon it if we like it". Thus the Union is powerless to control, but most powerful to aid and prosper their work. It is just Independency run mad.

A special committee was appointed, representing the different views, and including Dale, Hall, and Rogers. In October this committee submitted a long report, accepted on the motion of Morley and Dale, in which they recognized the diversity of opinion and recommended that "the formal connexion of the Societies with the Union be altered" so that the Secretaries be not mutually *ex officio* members of the committees, and the obligation to present annual reports, no longer hold. Meetings of the Societies were still to be held in Assembly week, and, in general, arrangements made to give friendly support.

In the last year of the Societies' association with the Union it may be well to summarize the reports they presented to the Assembly.

1. *Colonial.*—140 ministers at work. Need for more ministers in Australia, South Africa, Nova Scotia, and Newfoundland. Prospects of the Society good. Debt of £1,500 cleared by special gifts. Income £5,959; Expenditure £5,864.

2. *Home Missionary Society.*—Fifty missionaries, 57 ministers receiving grants, 118 stations in 36 English counties, 365 chapels and rooms, adult hearers 30,000, scholars 13,492; 430 received into church fellowship during the year, making 4,400 members; 180 lay helpers. Income £7,500; Expenditure £6,313.

3. *Irish Evangelical Society.*—Nine Scripture readers,

3 teachers, 17 missionaries.   Income £2,300 ; Expenditure
£2,092.

4. *Board of Education.*—36 students just leaving
college ; 43 students in college ; total sent out altogether,
266 ; 800 children in practising schools ; 13,000 children in
schools connected with the Board.   Income £2,801 ; Expenditure £1,785.

5. *Chapel Building.*—Total receipts, £14,000.   Grants
made to 62 chapels costing £118,000.   Trying to raise a
permanent Loan Fund of £20,000.

6. *Insurance Aid Society.*—Capital £8,000.   Income
£250.

The Union and the Magazines.

It was in regard to the Magazines, however, that there
was most trouble.   Already it has been seen how the Editor
roused the ire of many members of the Union.   He had
announced that the Union journals would not discuss
matters on which there was difference of opinion among
Congregationalists, but sometimes they crept in, while it
was difficult to separate the Editor of the Union periodicals
from the opinions he was expressing so vigorously in the
British Banner.   Even in the *Christian Witness* Campbell
was still no respecter of persons.   Though he might call the
Lancashire Union the "pattern Union of England" or
praise the *Year Book* one day, there was no knowing on
whom he might fall the next.   In Sheffield, in 1849, he rejoiced in the welcome given to the public at the meetings,
for he held that the "closed doors" policy had prevented
them from learning about the Union.   But James Parsons,
who preached, was put on a low platform instead of in the
pulpit, and he tried to read his sermon.   Campbell did not
hear a word, but he knew Parsons would talk sense, so he
held up both his hands for the publication of the sermon !
He went on to say of the organizers of the meeting :

> They well knew that, even when speaking, it is no part
> of the contract that Mr. Parsons shall be generally heard
> for the first five or even ten minutes, since he could not,
> if he would, render himself audible to a whole assembly.

But it is distinctly understood—and never was an audience disappointed—that, when fairly out at sea, and with all sails set, he shall move and melt all hearts—thundering and lightning, and shaking the spheres! But to bury him in a pit, and chain him to a manuscript, on a desk so low that it required him to stoop, was to sheathe in lead the wings of the eagle, and then expect him to soar to the sun! Under the circumstances, it was, we believe, the first time the Man of York ever read, and we trust it will be the last. He was born and is fitted for a very different order of service. Any dull Dutchman with a good voice, can read; but the number of those is not great to whom it appertains to electrify masses of living men, and of that number, and a chief in it, is Mr. Parsons.

In 1850 the guiding hand of Wells was missing in the Assembly, with the result that Campbell's editorial conduct was openly discussed. Recently he had censured the *Eclectic,* and another episode had drawn from T. T. Lynch, a minister of extremely independent outlook, the judgment —very significant in view of later happenings—

> Most serious is my conviction that Dr. Campbell's publications, if not amended, must be extinguished. Amended I fear they will not be. Is he, or is he not, a voice from the heart of the Independents of England? We must disown him as we distrust him.

It was an outspoken attack on the Anti-State Church Association in the *Christian Witness* which made Miall in the *Nonconformist* refer to its editor as "Bombastes Furioso, Brag, & Co.", and demand his removal from the editorial chair of the Union. It was no light matter to tackle in the Assembly one who had Campbell's position and who, in the previous year, had said that there had been no single complaint about the Magazines, remarking at the same time that "John Foster said it was surprising to see how the space cleared around the man of decision". Perhaps only young men would have done it, especially when they had to circumvent the rule which said that notice must be given at the Monday night's private gathering of all matters to come before the Assembly. But younger men like Andrew Reed, Joseph Fletcher, and Baldwin Brown, all of them sons of highly esteemed Congregational fathers, had been greatly stirred, and, on the motion for the adoption of the Report, the two first named moved an addendum instructing the Committee to consider the best arrangements whereby the Magazines should no longer be regarded as the organs of the Union. The Union Minutes are unsatisfactory here, as generally in times of controversy, but Campbell printed a verbatim report of the discussion in the *Christian Witness*. Reed and Fletcher both spoke of the Union having been compromised by its Editor, who, in reply, said that the real attack was not on the Union papers, but on another which they could not touch. He knew he was supported by the mass of Nonconformists. He had no objection to the words "The Official Organ of the Congregational Union" being struck off the cover of the papers : he had never pretended to represent the opinions of a body of whom no two were agreed.

> It were perfectly preposterous ! You take widely different views from each other, on the subjects of inspiration, doctrine, ordinances, polity, education, and much besides,—such a piece of mosaic, I am sure, you seldom cast your eye upon.

The Report and addendum were unanimously adopted. Then George Smith, in moving the vote of thanks to Campbell (which was supported by Kennedy and James) probably attempting to be humorous, said that the resolution had gone begging round the platform before it could find a mover—and the fat was in the fire again ! After the Session it was felt that matters could not be left as they were, and Samuel Morley, after consulting with others, the next day, in order to prevent public misapprehension, moved a resolution which declared that the Union,

> So far from intending the slightest imputation on the integrity and right-mindedness, or general qualifications of their laborious Editor, cherishes a high estimate of the value of his past services, and cordially desires for him a long career of usefulness in promoting the cause of Christian truth; believing that the arrangement proposed, while it will relieve the Congregational Union from an undesirable responsibility, will leave to the Editor a more unfettered right to the expression of his own personal views on many of the great subjects which now prominently occupy the public mind.

Tidman, Reed, Burder, James, Massie, and Smith, who apologized for his *faux pas,* all spoke in support of the resolution. Campbell's reply was not conciliatory. He complained of being hissed the previous day by a little knot of young men who would not have been present had he not advocated opening the galleries. He said he would enjoy being unofficial because he would be able to say freely what he thought about the Union's proceedings! As reference had been made to the "property" in the periodicals, he pointed out that if he went out from the Union the past and future profits of the Magazines would go, too.

> What is the market value of your title-page? You contributed nothing towards establishing it. Not a farthing. The property is a pure self-creation.

In the autumn the Committee recommended the transfer of the Magazines to 48 Trustees, four of whom should hold the vested property and any future additions to it, while "The Chronicle of the Union and of the British Missions", which had been a regular feature of the *Christian Witness,* should appear as before. In the course of a long discussion Campbell admitted that his attack on the Anti-State Church Association was a breach of his own regulations, and that by it he had offended the younger men. In attacking the Evangelical Alliance previously he had grieved the older men, but he believed at the time that the Alliance was a waste of time and money, and had not altered his view. He accepted the Editorial Chair of the *Witness* without prospect of pay when they could find nobody else, and if the *Witness* was not his idea, the *Penny Magazine,* which made over £500 in profit in its first year, was entirely his own, and its profits might have been his instead of the Union's. He further complained that a young man, who had never been seen at the Union, had gone to the Secretary a few days before the Assembly and paid his five shillings, saying he was joining the Union in order that he might move the Editor's dismissal! The discussion ended with an agreement that the Magazines should go on as before, though Samuel Morley said he still thought it would be better to separate them from the Union. The words "An Official Organ of the Congregational Union" disappeared from the title-page, and were placed upon the pages devoted to the Union Chronicle only. Campbell received a vote of thanks yearly, being called "a man of iron—whose powers seemed incapable of being overtaxed". He was often rallied on his violence, as when Sherman expressed thanks in 1853, although he had "occasionally had a few gentle strokes from his loving pen".

On another occasion James remarked :

> True it is that, perhaps, there has been a little more moderation in the tone of some of the doctor's remarks than there was once. We were then rather familiar with the idea of the club of Hercules than of the loving pen. There was a time when each of us looked askance at that club, not knowing but that it might descend on his own head very soon. However, the club is very much liked, after all. Dr. Campbell is a very loving man. There is under that exterior a heart of tender and deep affection; he loves his cause, and loves the friends of his cause; and even when he has been severe it has been the severity of love.

The *Banner*, meanwhile, was going from strength to strength, Campbell saying at the *Patriot* and *Banner* banquet (Lord Mayor Challis presiding) in 1853, that it had a greater circulation than any daily paper, with but two exceptions. It was the *Banner* that was to cause all the mischief, and the biggest storm that organized Congregationalism has ever known. Campbell's views on politics and education might not be those of many Independents, but these questions did not cut as deep as religion and theology. In 1849, replying to the annual vote of thanks, Campbell made a statement which, though it was applauded, was ominously significant :

> One thing he wished distinctly to intimate—while the Magazines were under his care they need fear nothing from Germany. He discarded all such speculations. He had burned, he might say, reams of a speculative nature. He had dropped his anchor in Westminster, where he found matter in abundance, in the Confession of Faith, in the Shorter and Larger Catechisms—shutting out chapter xiii., on the province of the civil magistrate.

Theological opinion was still very conservative, and everything German was taboo. In the *British Quarterly Review* Vaughan had spoken of

> . . . Rugby men, who take the free principles of their master in Biblical interpretation to an extent which allies them much more with German Rationalism than with English orthodoxy.

and there was suspicion on every side. Ashton, in his Preface to the 1856 *Year Book,* spoke of the number of Wesleyans and of Town and City missionaries becoming Independents and of the "danger from an uncalvinistic and uneducated ministry". There was a good deal of aggressive infidelity among working men, only six per cent of whom in the country and two per cent in London were said to attend worship, while there were general fears of the rationalism and scepticism which were associated with German thought. Something of this unrest naturally found its way into the Magazines. Campbell was always on the look-out for any falling from grace, any declension from the full-blooded orthodoxy, and in 1856 his moment came. T. T. Lynch, who had gathered round him an esoteric little congregation in Grafton Street, Fitzroy Square, published in November, 1855, *Hymns for Heart and Voice* : *The Rivulet.* Nobody reading the *Rivulet* to-day will find occasion for extravagance of either praise or blame, but of course they will not go to it with the set purpose of discovering orthodoxy, or the lack of it. Some hymns, like "Gracious Spirit, dwell with me", "Dismiss me not Thy service, Lord", and "O where is He that trod the sea", have taken their place in the worship of the Church; others, like "Our heart is like a little pool", laid themselves open to criticism. The volume was welcomed by the *Eclectic* and by the *Nonconformist,* which said respectively :

> We shall be surprised if it does not become a favourite in hundreds of musical families, its hymns gradually taking their places among those which have been long consecrated by dear and hallowed associations.
>
> We fully believe that they will live and express the joys and aspirations of the devout Christian, as long as divine praises are sung in the English tongue.

James Grant, the Editor of the *Morning Advertiser*, a paper connected with the licensed trade, had other views, and he violently denounced the *Eclectic* for praising a volume which "might have been written by a Deist, and a very large portion might be sung by a congregation of Freethinkers", which had "not one particle of vital religion or evangelical piety", which made no mention of Christ's divinity, atoning sacrifice, and mediatorial office" and was "pervaded throughout by the Rationalist Theology of Germany". As this violence continued, fifteen of the best known ministers in London—Allon, Binney, Baldwin Brown, Fleming, Newman Hall, Harrison, Jukes, Kent, Martin, Newth, Nunn, Watson Smith, Spence, Vaughan, and White—wrote to the *Eclectic*, protesting against the treatment of Lynch. Enter Campbell. In Lynch's words:

> Sound the trumpets, beat the drums,
> Clash the gongs, great Magog comes;
> Shout according to your manner,
> Ye who bear his dusky banner.
> Black it is, with gory stains,
> Praise him in your harshest strains:
> He is King of wrath and clamour,
> And his sign—The brazen hammer.

In the Union publications Campbell said not a word about the *Rivulet*, but in the *British Banner* he called the volume "crude, disjointed, unmeaning, un-Christian, ill-rhymed rubbish", and "incomparably the most unspiritual publication of the kind in the English tongue". Campbell said he had waited until people had begun to ask the reason for his silence, as every other Nonconformist journal had joined in the fray. Thursday after Thursday for seven weeks Campbell analysed the *Rivulet* until the denomination was in a ferment, in the midst of which the Congregational Union met in the Poultry Chapel. The *Nonconformist* was demanding that Campbell's "rude and uncouth despotism" should end, and saying that "the intelligence of the Congregational Union is against its continuance". Could the matter be kept off the agenda? It scarcely seemed so. The previous Autumn, Dr. Halley, in his Chairman's Address, said:

I thank Dr. Campbell especially for great service, far greater than our thanks can express; and I thank, also, those who watch him jealously, attack him boldly, and tell him plainly when and why they think him wrong. About all our Magazines, Reviews, and Newspapers, whether under the superintendence of our Union, or conducted by members of our denomination, I hear a feeble, low sort of murmuring, which hardly, as yet, has come to an articulate voice.

This articulate voice it found in May in the person of Baldwin Brown, though the Union's Minutes will be searched in vain for any account of the discussion. Brown's ideal of religious literature was that it should have "the salt of spiritual earnestness and truth", and he asked, "Has our Religious Literature, under the conduct of Dr. Campbell, fulfilled even moderately the conditions which should be regarded as essential by all Christian men"? On the Tuesday morning, on the annual vote of thanks being moved to Campbell, Brown, who said he knew he was, regarded as a "troubler in Israel", urged that something must be done about "our literature", which had been lowering its tone; Lynch had been "shamefully and cruelly treated". He announced he would move a resolution on the subject in the autumn.

Binney, perhaps the most respected and the most widely known minister in Congregationalism at the time, asked what was "our literature"—the denomination's or the Union's? It was "a bit of humbug" to prevent a subject being touched upon in discussion because it was concerned with a denominational paper not controlled by the Union.

Campbell held that matters extraneous to the Union were being dragged in. He was willing to abide by the judgment of the laymen of Churches. Young people loved tumult and contention—"twenty or thirty heels will make a tremendous noise under a roof like this"—but it was not seemly or decent. He was willing to retire in favour of those who thought they could do the job "immensely better", but they might make a "tremendous, mull" of it. He was much concerned for the state of the churches when he saw "so much of the vague, the empty, the arrogant, the forward, and the self-sufficient in many quarters".

On the following Saturday morning a critical private session was held at Milton Club, Lynch saying of it : "This meeting may possibly prove its [the Union's] last, or the last as it now is". Binney apologized for expressions he had used on the Tuesday, said he was the eldest of the Fifteen, and that he sympathized with his younger brethren in their enthusiasm for a truly spiritual man whom they thought wronged. There had been faults on both sides : "Mr. Lynch's friends interpret the book by the man; outside observers interpret the man by the book[1]". Binney appealed to Campbell not to re-publish his *Banner* articles. Enoch Mellor made a strong speech against the "negative theology". James also spoke, and James Spicer followed, even defending Grant, and strongly urging orthodoxy. Campbell, who held that he had not brought charges of theological unsoundness against the Fifteen and the Independent ministry generally, responded to Binney's overture, and agreed not to reprint the articles.

A fortnight later, however, the reprint appeared, and Campbell was accused of breach of faith, though he said he was not responsible, the publication being beyond his control. Binney sent a long explanatory letter to the members of the Union, especially those present at the confidential meeting, in which he made a most important pronouncement in regard to the Union :

> Another object I have in view is this. I always disapproved the change of the Union Meetings from those of a private Conference to those of a public Assembly. I have often tried to get, in the course of the meetings, some opportunity for serious, confidential interchange of thought, and also for friendly social intercourse. It has always been with difficulty that I have succeeded. The late meetings have perfected a long-growing suspicion into a deep and ineradicable conviction, that all the *business*-proceedings of the Union ought to be given up, and that it should become a purely religious and fraternal Confederation. From becoming more of a Public Body than it is fitted to be, it has been tempted to appear to *do* something. There is no interest felt in much that is talked about, and several regularly re-

---

[1] Lynch thought Binney had "let him down" in this speech. See White, *Memoir of T. T. Lynch*, p. 180.

"THE CONTROVERSY."

I.

Price Sixpence, post-free, TENTH Edition, with numerous important Additions,

THE CONTROVERSY ON IMPORTANT THEOLOGICAL QUESTIONS;

Between the "Eclectic Review," and the Rev. Messrs.

Allon,	Fleming,	Jukes,	Newth,	Spence,
Binney,	Newman Hall,	Kent,	Nunn,	Vaughan,
Brown,	Harrison,	Martin,	Smith,	White,

On the one side, and Mr. JAMES GRANT, Editor of the "Morning Advertiser," on the other.

"Mr. Grant has struck more terror into the soul of the Congregational body than any antagonist that has ever appeared against it. He has truth on his side, and he has wielded his weapons most triumphantly. Both Churchmen and Dissenters will do well to study this pamphlet. We wish it much success. It has already attained to nine large editions."—*Church Warder.*

"The pamphlet should be read extensively, as it gives an insight into a state of things of which many men have little or no notion * * * well worthy of perusal * * * it is curious and instructive."—*Christian Annotator.*

II.

7th Edition, 6d., post free, with Correspondence between Dr. Campbell and Mr. Binney

NONCONFORMIST THEOLOGY;

Or, Serious Considerations for Churches, Pastors, and Deacons; being SEVEN LETTERS to the Principals and Professors of the Independent and Baptist Colleges of England, on the Pernicious Errors of Mr. Lynch's *Rivulet*. By JOHN CAMPBELL, D.D.

"Every friend of vital religion, be he Independent, Baptist, Presbyterian, or Episcopalian, should further the circulation of this pamphlet."—*Glasgow Examiner.*

III.

SEVENTH Edition, price Sixpence,

NEGATIVE THEOLOGY:

Analysis of the Letter of the Rev. THOMAS BINNEY, addressed to the Congregational Union of England and Wales. Being an Exposure of its Fallacies, Perversions, and Misrepresentations; and further Developments of the Nature, Operations, and Dangers of the Negative Theology. By JOHN CAMPBELL, D.D.

"No one can be *read up* in the important subjects that now agitate the Dissenting Churches, without possessing this pamphlet."—*Local Preachers' Magazine.*

IV.

SIXTH Edition, price Sixpence,

"WHAT'S IT ALL ABOUT?"

Or, Both Sides of the "Rivulet" Controversy: with a Fourth Appendix for Mr. Binney's Letter to the Congregational Union. By the Rev. BREWIN GRANT, B.A.

"In every page displays surpassing cleverness. * * * We have rarely read anything of a controversial kind which could oe compared to it."—*Morning Advertiser.*

"Racy and vigorous, yet a calm and candid review of *both sides* of this Controversy."—*Gospel Herald.*

V.

Price Sixpence,

THE "PROTESTERS" AND PEACE-MAKERS;

Or, Letters addressed to Mr. NEWMAN HALL (Minister of Surrey Chapel), in answer to Letters received from him relating to the "Protest" and the conduct of the "Protesters." Also Letters addressed to JOHN MIDDLETON HARE, Esq. (Editor of the "Patriot:") being Animadversions on certain Articles which appeared in that Paper. By W. PALMER (Minister of Homerton Row Chapel, Homerton).

Price Fourpence,

THE WATCHMAN'S WARNING TO THE CHURCHES.

A Fearful View of those rapid Ministerial Declensions from the Truth, and the wide spread of Arminian, Pelagian, and Socinian Heresies. By VERITAS.

"This is a true but lamentable picture of the state of religion among us as a nation. * * * Let them that think there is little danger, purchase the book, and judge for themselves."—*Diadem.*

LONDON: W. H. COLLINGRIDGE, CITY PRESS, 1, LONG LANE.

curring resolutions might be dispensed with. Many things reported to us, or taken up by us, are things which can be done, and which *are* done, by other and more appropriate agencies : while the impossibility, from our constitution and principles, of effectually carrying out anything that may be resolved upon, makes the passing of resolutions very much of an empty form.

The connexion of the British Missions Societies with the Union, has done nothing for any of them *that might not have been secured by each acting on the churches by its own power*. The Educational Society excites little attention now, and never had universal sympathy. It was really melancholy to see Mr. Viney addressing the listless and restless audience at the Poultry the other day. In its proper place the Society has a right to be heard, and can make itself heard ; but it would be far better if it stood on its own merits, distinct from the Union altogether. The time of the Union is frittered away by business which we can really do better in other capacities ; while we have no time at all, or very little, for what was the primary and proper object of its institution—godly, loving intercourse, as ministers and members of Christ's church—men meeting together to confer, to pray, to speak, and hear, so that the life of God might be nourished in them, faith strengthened and love promoted, and that thus they might go away better able to do the special duties to which each might feel himself called, or those which God in common had given to all.

A Union like ours cannot be the Synod or General Assembly of a Church ; it is not capable of doing business ; it may utter sentiment, but it cannot execute ; and it would be better, in my opinion, if we gave up all attempts at action, and confined ourselves to such intercourse, as, by making us better, holier, more loving, more united, should send us back to our several spheres better fitted to work there. If the Union is to be preserved, it must come to this. Things have been getting wrong for some time. The interest of the meetings, prospectively, has often depended on the name of the Chairman—it has ended at the conclusion of his address. *There,* reality has ceased, and routine begun. Sometimes interest has revived under the address of some visitor or delegate ; but I appeal to *all* whether the most of what is done, consisting of the reading of customary reports, and the passing of formal resolutions, has not been a weariness to both the spirit and the flesh? Time is spent, feeling exhausted ; hope disappointed ; and numbers find, whether they say it or not, that they have got nothing worth the trouble and expense of their journey. I know of my own

certain knowledge, that the Union has often closed, leaving
in many hearts, dissatisfaction and hostility, instead of their
having been refreshed by cordial, loving, profitable contact
with others.

. . . I feel it incumbent upon me, however, further to
state, that I see no difficulty whatever in your Magazines
being separated from the Union.   They could be conducted,
all the same, by the present Editor, and managed by a Committee, like the *Evangelical Magazine,* the profits going
to the benefit of ministers, as the profits of the *Evangelical*
go to widows.   There is no difficulty in this :—no severance
of Dr. Campbell from the press; and no peril to the poorer
of the brethren ;—and there are reasons, strong and manifold, why it should be done.

For my own part, my mind is made up.   I will not go
on countenancing a system of things, which for some years,
has been getting far worse than simply unprofitable.   I shall
willingly wait awhile, to see what is done, or to try what can
be done.   If the Union can be brought to acquiesce in its
original design,—if it again become simply a brotherly confederation ; if its meetings can be relieved of much that
oppresses, and of some things that distract them, so that
they may be anticipated as means of grace and seasons of
love,—well.   If not, no one can be bound to continue either
to support or to attend what neither carries with it his
judgment or his affections.   I shall quietly retire.   The
Congregational Union is not the Congregational Body.   Nor
is that Body the Christian Church.

It certainly looked as if Lynch's prognostications would
be fulfilled.   When August came round, and the *Banner*
needed something to keep up its circulation, Campbell
opened a full-dress attack on Binney.   Week after week he
continued, keeping up the interest with consummate
journalistic skill : "I have now reached the climax, and
shall complete and settle it in my next", he ended one
week, but the four columns the following week ended : "In
my next I shall invite the attention of my friend Mr. Binney
to a point far more serious than any yet brought forward".
In the next issue he said, "I shall bring this matter to a
close", but the following week he introduced correspondence on the subject, and the week after announced, " If
Mr. Binney will send a flag of truce, not another shot shall
be fired".   If not, a summary of the "personal part of the
business" would appear.   Finally, a short time afterwards,

the series ends, after asking : "Is the Rev. Thomas Binney
the Nonconformist body ?" :

> Such is the crime of the Editor of the *British Banner,*
> which you are called upon to visit with the severest penalties
> you have the power to inflict ! If Mr. Binney can carry the
> majority along with him, the sun of January 1st, 1857, will
> rise on the ashes of the Union Magazines; and the man
> whose hand created, and for 13 years conducted them, will
> drop the pen, to take it up no more in the service of the
> Congregational Union of England and Wales.
>
> Such is the Reward proposed for my poor, imperfect ser-
> vices in the cause of Eternal Truth, and in opposition to a
> System which ignores alike the law and the Gospel, which
> dishonours God and destroys man, . . .

Now, however, he turned to the theology of the *Eclectic,*
and so kept the battle going. So furious was the strife that
Cheltenham, the Union's hosts for the autumn, asked that
the meetings should be postponed unless the resolution on
the Magazines were withdrawn and an assurance given that
the proceedings would be amicable. Commenting on this
and on an article in the *British Quarterly Review,* the
Watchman spoke of "the eclipse of the Congregational
Union". Campbell replied that there was no eclipse—that
all the Committee of the Union were agreed about the old
and new theology—there was "not even a jar", though,
discussing the *British Quarterly Review* article, he said
that there was somewhat too much indulgence shown to
negative theologians.

In September the Committee called a special Conference
at the Milton Club, London, to endeavour to secure a solution of the controversy. John Kelly of Liverpool was chairman, and for twelve hours the situation was thoroughly discussed. Smith said that at the Committee's request those
urging the separation of the Magazines from the Union
had agreed to the appointment of a committee, to report on
the subject in May. He emphasized that the Union was
not a Court of Appeal, and it had been dragged into the
controversy. A resolution recording unabated attachment
to Evangelical principles was adopted, and another urging
the cessation of the quarrel and the resort to arbitration.
The problem was not made easier by the continuation of

press warfare, and the October Assembly was not held.
Thomas Thompson, the highly respected founder of the
Home Missionary Society, not merely wrote to the *British
Banner* justifying Campbell, and urging the Fifteen to with-
draw the protest and say, "Our friendship for Mr. Lynch
exceeded its legitimate bounds", but even warned Binney
that he and his friends would not be received if they went to
the West of England as a deputation for Home Missions.

Nor was Lynch entirely silent. The idea that exists in
some quarters to-day that Lynch was a kind of mystical
pacifist who believed in non-resistance is absolutely foreign
to the facts. In October, under the *nom de plume* "Silent
Long", he published *Songs Controversial,* in which he
printed fifteen new poems, all of them full of fight. Not
one of them is better than that in which he pokes fun at
those who are demanding a complete theology in every
poem and every sermon.

A NEGATIVE AFFAIR.

When sugar in the lump I see,
  I know that it is there,
Melt it, and then I soon suspect
  A negative affair :
Where is the sugar, Sir? I say,
  Let me both touch and see ;
Sweetness instead of sugar, Sir,
  You'll not palm off on me.

Don't tell me that the sugar lumps,
  When dropt in water clear,
That they may make the water sweet,
  Themselves must disappear ;
For common sense, Sir, such as mine
  The lumps themselves must see ;
Sweetness instead of sugar, Sir,
  You'll not palm off on me.

For instance, Sir, in every hymn
  Sound doctrine you should state
As clearly as a dead man's name
  Is on his coffin plate ;
Religion, Sir, is only fudge,
  Let's have theology ;
Sweetness instead of sugar, Sir,
  You'll not palm off on me.

Shortly afterwards he published the *Ethics of Quotation*, with a preliminary letter to the Secretaries of the Congregational Union. On the title page he prints these lines:

Quote him to death! Quote him to death!
  Hit him, and hear not a word that he saith;
Shout and cry out, for this is the man
  Out of whose Spirit the *Rivulet* ran.
What is his soul but a cauldron that brims
  Over and over with poisonous hymns?
Then quench his fire, the vessel upset,
  Who knows what mischief he'll do us yet?
Tear up his verses, and mangle his prose,
  Quote at him still, wherever he goes.
Cut him up! Cut him up! Send the pieces afar
  To gather our Israel for strife and war;
Black waves our Banner against the sky,
  Death! is our watchword: the man must die,
That with him may perish *Liberty*!

The forthrightness of Lynch's contentions are well represented in the following passages:

You are the Secretaries of a Union which is understood to represent—though it does not really represent—the Congregations of the Independents throughout the United Kingdom. I sincerely believe that Union to be an obstruction to real brotherhood, and to the advancement of spiritual religion . . .

Gentlemen, I appeal to you, and to that Union of so-called Independents in which you bear office—and, as you see, I can respectfully appeal to you—against the Editor of your Magazines, who is also the Editor of what has ever appeared to me a vain and vaunting journal, the *British Banner*. It is in this journal that offences, with which I shall charge and convict him, have been committed. The *British Banner* is not subject to your control, but it has had your moral support; and its Editor would not assume, as he does, to represent British Nonconformity but for the editorial position he holds among you . . . I believe, firmly, that your Editor is a *person* whom no Christian society can retain as their representative, without incurring the reproach of being utterly careless about the Christian principles that should govern the use of pen and tongue. I believe, that, in the fanatic attacks by which Mr. Lynch has been *personally* injured, the very ground principles of the moral treatment man should receive from his fellow men have been violated . . .

Gentlemen, is the maintenance of periodical literature your proper province? What have you corporately to do with literature? But, surely, for you to have, as an irresponsible and yet a representative Editor, one who disgraces you and us all in the public eye by the meagreness of his matter and the virulence of his manner—this is folly indeed. Oh, how do I wish that the Union itself would dissolve, as clouds sometimes do, leaving the sky clear and giving the light free course . . . and I have liberty to say that, though Mr. Lynch calls no man master, and abhors ecclesiastical coterieship, and hopes that the " Union " will soon perish, that its elements may, in new forms, live a new and nobler life, he would be most happy to meet any assembly of his brother clergymen, to give them such satisfaction about his views of truth as they might wish to obtain and he be able to afford.

Meanwhile John Angell James had printed the sermon he had been invited to preach at the Cheltenham Meetings, under the title, *A Tract for the Times, On Speaking the Truth in Love.* James had been called upon in order that the respect and affection in which he was generally held might prove to be a soothing influence, but the sermon had the reverse effect. It even roused Binney, who, before any invitation had been given to James, had promised Dr. Morton Brown, the minister at Cheltenham, to preach the special sermon there, and was intending to preach it. Binney therefore wrote a long letter to the Committee of the Congregational Union, dated 15th December, in which he held that throughout the Committee's position had been prejudiced and untenable. He pointed out that Campbell had been at all the Union Committees where the controversy had been discussed, but he himself had never been invited to any one of them. He concluded, "The Congregational Union of England and Wales will do what it thinks becomes it, in its present prostrate and humiliated condition".

Baldwin Brown, who had been laid aside by illness for some six months, also re-entered the discussion with a letter to the members of the Congregational Union, dated 10th January, 1857, which he called "The Way of Peace for the Congregational Union : with Remarks on the Morale of its Religious Literature, the so-called Young

School, and Negative Theology". He emphasized the
fact that the *Rivulet* was the occasion and not the cause of
the controversy, and re-affirmed his conviction that

> our Religious Literature is quite unworthy of us; and that
> Dr. Campbell, able as he undoubtedly is, is just the last
> man whom we should put forward as our literary organ
> and representative before the world.

He still believed that the right way was to put before
the Union the simple question, "Is it desirable that
religious periodicals under the editorship of Dr. Campbell
should be in any way related to the Congregational
Union?". The Union should not "set up a column of
figures and an assertion of popularity as a test of truth".
It could not continue "to have Dr. Campbell and to have
peace", and therefore the Magazines must be separated
from the Union, just as the Affiliated Societies must be
separated too.

> But nothing has shaken, rather everything has con-
> firmed, my conviction, that the Union has arrived at that
> crisis in its history, in which the alternative is plainly
> presented of Reformation or Death. I believe that if the
> present policy be pursued, nothing can hold the Union
> together—already some of our best men have expressed, to
> my sorrow, their determination never to enter its assemblies
> again; while on the other hand, if we can rid ourselves of
> all connexion with our, so-called, Literature, and the diffi-
> culties it entails, and can infuse into our meetings more of
> that element which binds brethren together in unity, and
> strengthens, purifies, and animates spirits for their work,
> I believe that we shall enter on the most prosperous era of
> our history.

In the north the storm was raging round the person of
Samuel Davidson, whom Mellor and Rogers, with the help
of Campbell and others, hounded out of Lancashire College. How deeply the controversy went may be seen in a
letter of James to Kelly, in which, having applauded those
who were trying to get rid of Davidson, he said:

> I am convinced that in ten or twenty years' time there
> will be another lapse in our body, on the side of heterodoxy,
> and the Baptists are as bad as we are—or perhaps worse.
> How deeply do I deplore Campbell's rashness and reckless-
> ness. He might have been a rallying-point round which

our sound men might have gathered. Oh, that he had been as calm as he is powerful! He has driven off from him many of his best friends, and is sustained, I am afraid, by others who hound him on in vehemence. This first number of the *Standard*,[1] however, is moderate. I do not think the *Banner* can live. Its readers are Campbell's friends, and they will all rally around the *Standard*. I cannot go to London on the 21st, but I mean to submit to the Committee a proposal to separate the magazines, the British Missions, and Education Board, and confine the Union to its original object, as a meeting for fraternal conference and devotion.

A special Assembly of the Union was held in London in January (1857), Stoughton presiding. The September resolution expressing devotion to Evangelical principles was confirmed, and Smith outlined the course of the discussions, saying :

A great crisis has arrived in the affairs of the Union. The compatibility of the independency of our churches with their intercommunity with each other is again to be tried. The eyes of the world, and of other denominations are upon you.

A Special Committee was appointed to consider the relationship of the Magazines and the Affiliated Societies to the Union, and a letter from Campbell was read in which he declared himself perfectly indifferent whether the Magazines were controlled by the Union or by Trustees, so long as the Union flourished, the denomination prospered, and the Gospel advanced.

Nevertheless, he pointed out that controversy of every kind had been kept out of the *Christian Witness*, and that the Editor of that paper was being arraigned for the sins of the *British Banner*. Such a course was discreditable to his attackers :

The expulsion of the Editor of the *Christian Witness* is the reward it is proposed to make to the Editor of the *British Banner* for the stand which he has made in that journal against the increase of German error.

James thus describes the proceedings in writing to Kelly :

---

[1] The *British Standard,* Campbell's own paper, started by him when he ceased his connexion with the *British Banner*.

Upon the whole there was as little, perhaps less, temper displayed than could have been expected; the most disorderly man there was Mr. Binney. He appeared to me to little advantage, and seemed to want to get up a discussion on the events of the case. Baines acquitted himself nobly, and so did Stoughton. Certainly Campbell had no great cause to be dissatisfied; there were things said by some of the members which were a little offensive to hear, but there was no condemnation of him by the meeting— which was what his opponents in their hearts were anxious to obtain . . . My mind is all but made up already on the subject. There will be little or no difficulty as regards the British Missions and Congregational Board of Education. These organizations do not stand so integrally connected with the Union as the magazines; *they* are our own property and we can do what we will with them; we can, if we please, discharge the present Editor and appoint another. This, I hope, the Committee will not do, but recommend the appointment of a body of trustees, to whom the property and management shall be assigned over, leaving it to them, as in the case of the *Evangelical,* to retain or dismiss Dr. Campbell. He has managed the magazines well, and, notwithstanding what Baldwin Brown may say, they are not despicable productions for threepence and a penny, and their theology is a great deal sounder than what some who despise them would bring into their pages.

This advice was adopted, and in May, 1857, it was resolved that the papers, and also the management of the Fund created by them, should be detached from the Union, being vested in not less than four Trustees, the management being transferred to a body of 48 Trustees, one-half being laymen, one third of the whole resident in London, vacancies being filled up at the first meeting after being created, the number never to be allowed to fall below 36. The profits of the Magazines were to be used as before, recipients and administrators being restricted to those whose general views were in accord with the Declaration of Faith and Order, the interest of the Fund and of any future accumulations alone to be available for annual distribution, being employed first to meet the Deferred Annuity premiums already arranged for, and then for grants to aged or afflicted ministers. In no case was the principal to be touched, and the Fund was not to be used to meet any losses on the Magazines if these should fail to pay, but to be deemed sacred to the purposes of charity.

There seemed to be the blundering usual when the Magazines were concerned, for, either deliberately or inadvertently, the Editor's name was omitted from the list of Trustees, and it had to be added the next day.

It having occurred to someone subsequently that a loss on the Magazines might be incurred before the Trustees were aware of it, it was decided that they should create a Reserve Fund, not exceeding £300, from the *future profits* of the Magazines as an indemnity against liability.

All was peace and calm at Cheltenham in October, 1857, and in the following spring the Committee report, with evident relief, that the transfer has been made, and

> Henceforth the magazines are completely detached from all connexion with the Congregational Union, and no allusion can, therefore, be made to their management in our meetings, as the Trustees, and not your Committee, will in future be responsible for their conduct.

Great had been the power of a rivulet!

The severance of the affiliated Societies and the Magazines from the Union is a good occasion for taking stock. In that year the aged John Angell James thus expressed his judgment in his Autobiography :

> Whatever importance attaches to the Congregational Union, I was one of its original projectors. When some of my seniors felt grave objections to this confederation, as containing a germ of mischief in the way of an organized controlling body, I thought their fears groundless, and went into the Association with my whole heart . . . The Union, if it has not accomplished all the good its friends predicted and expected, has not produced any of the evils which its opponents foretold. It is a question, however, which ought to be seriously considered, whether it is doing all for the denomination which it is capable of doing. Considering how large a portion of the missionary week is occupied by the meetings of the Union in London, and nearly a *whole* week at the autumnal meeting in the provinces, the work done hardly pays for the time spent in doing it. Much gratification, I know, is furnished by the meetings to the brethren who attend them; but ten days or a fortnight in

these busy times forms a long period to be so employed. Had it done nothing more than call forth the Lectures[1] which have been delivered and published under its auspices, it would have achieved a good work. The *Christian Witness* and the *Church Member's Penny Magazine*[2] are also among its fruits, which have not only given out much useful religious knowledge and edification, but have raised a fund for the relief of our aged ministers. I claim to have been the proposer of these works, or rather of one of them, for it was intended originally to have been but one. I shall ever consider it an honour to have done what I did in common with others, for thus gathering together into a body the *disjecta membra* of our denomination.

1 James is wrong in giving the Union credit for the Lectures, which were arranged by the Congregational Library. Year by year it was made plain in the *Year Book* that the Library and the Union were not one and the same institution. The *next* series of Lectures was arranged by the Union. See below, p. 246.

2 *The Christian's Penny Magazine* is obviously what James meant, but he was never very precise about titles.

XII. CRUISING ROUND THE BICENTENARY LIGHTSHIP, 1858-1870.

THROUGHOUT its history the Union had been sustained by the devoted service of laymen as well as ministers, though not yet was it thought fitting that they should be elected to the Chair : even as late as 1864 the suggestion that a layman might occasionally be Chairman was negatived by the Committee. In that year the death was reported of Benjamin Hanbury, the Treasurer of the Union from its foundation. He was succeeded by one as keenly interested as himself in the history of Nonconformity, but perhaps even more retiring. Joshua Wilson was for many years an invalid, but his mind was ever busy on the concerns of the Union with the beginning of which he and his father had had so much to do. In private letters and in printed articles he was always making suggestions in regard to possible ways of progress and constantly stimulating individuals to action and to generosity, and men like Samuel Morley, who took a very active part in public life, gladly worked in co-operation with him, and recognized their indebtedness to him.

In 1858 Morley had been appointed Treasurer of the Home Missionary Society, and Massie's successor in the Secretaryship of that Society, J. H. Wilson, of Aberdeen, was appointed largely on his nomination. Morley had been greatly impressed by the revelations of the 1851 Census, and it was borne in upon him that " We must go to the people ". He realized, in the words of the Union Report of 1859, " that the increase of evangelical religion had not been commensurate with the increase of population ". He assumed the Treasurership just at the time the Society was severed from the Union, and at once sent out a call for aggressive home evangelization. He did not believe in separating Home and Foreign Missions, but he said :

> I am convinced that if, during the last five and twenty years, we had been spending more in wise and well-directed

efforts in England, the London Missionary Society's income would be double what it is. I speak in the interests of India and Africa and China when I appeal to you on behalf of our great English interests in this matter.

Joshua Wilson thereupon published an open letter to Morley, which rejoiced in his challenge and insisted that the secret of Home Missionary enterprise was to be found in County Associations, which had to be made much more active and useful. Even Lancashire, " whose County Union is the most effective in the Kingdom ", had to admit that " the work is but begun "; while of the other Associations he said :

> At present, most of them are in a languishing and feeble state, raising naturally a very small amount of funds, and expending those funds chiefly in augmenting the salaries of pastors [of small churches].

The denomination's strength, he said, " unquestionably lies in the *cities and large towns* of the Kingdom ", and care would have to be taken to give proportionate attention to urban and rural areas. In September, 1859, the Assembly, on the motion of J. H. Wilson and Morley, recorded its judgment

> That many of the Congregational County Associations of England are capable of great improvement, and require a careful revision of their plans and modes of operation to enable them to put forth appropriate efforts adequately to support the existing ministry, and to extend the Gospel more effectually within their own bounds; that the proposals of the Home Missionary Society for future labours with the counties in an affiliated capacity appear to be judicious, and suited to the contemplated end; and that the pastors and other brethren here assembled entreat the hearty co-operation of the officers and committees of the County Associations with the Home Missionary Society in the revived and extended efforts it now wishes to put forth for the evangelization of the towns and villages of the country.

Morley gave much time to the work of the Home Missionary Society, visiting all parts of the country, encouraging the employment of lay evangelists and colporteurs, and personally soliciting subscriptions, so that the income rose from £10,000 in 1860 to £18,000 in 1870 and £25,000 in 1878. At Liverpool, in 1863, H. O.

Wills offered £300 for British Missions if 9 others would join him, and £3,800 was speedily raised.[1] In 1861 the Union Report said that the re-organization of the Society was " telling most beneficially on the County Associations, to whom properly its work belongs ".

Along with the development of Home Mission work came a renewed outburst of chapel building. Joshua Wilson had been asked to outline for the Assembly the best way of celebrating the Bicentenary of the Ejectment of 1662—the sort of task in which he revelled. First, he said, there must be new chapels; he pointed out that no chapels were built in London and its suburbs from 1790 to 1840 except those built by his father, and that everywhere there was leeway to be made up. In spite of the work of the Chapel Building Societies, building was not yet keeping pace with the population, and the aim should be to open 50 chapels before 24th August, 1862, and to lay the foundation stones of 50 more on that day, at least half of them to be in large towns. He then went into details about sites, size, and architecture. Then there should be propagation of principles by books, pamphlets, and lectures; a reprint of Calamy, Neal, and Brook; a monument in Bunhill Fields; and a Congregational Hall and Library, the present building being now quite inadequate.

The story of these years is very largely an account of the attempt to carry out Joshua's plans. Chapel building proceeded rapidly, it being reported in 1867 that the three Societies—English, London, and Lancashire—had been directly instrumental in erecting 365 chapels. Morley, feeling that too much was spent on ornament, urged a cheaper type of building, backing his opinion by offering £500 for each new chapel costing less than £5,000 if the rest of the cost could be raised. Twenty-four such chapels were built in this way, Morley giving £14,400 for the pur-

---

[1] The *Year Book* of 1865, pp. 351-2, gives the " Scheme of Union and Co-operation " between the Associations and the Society, and also the conditions on which evangelists were employed by the Society. The following page gives the expenditure by each Association and by the Society in every Association's area in the previous year; the Associations spent £11,553, the Society, directly, £5,686.

pose between 1864 and 1870. When the meetings were held in Sheffield George Hadfield, M.P., whose generosity in the north matched that of Morley in the south, offered £500 towards each of five new chapels in Sheffield, and, in response, the city set to work to raise £30,000. Large sums were lent free of interest by the three Societies from the Loan Funds which they raised. Before the end of the period, the active mind of J. C. Gallaway, whose paper had brought about the foundation of the English Chapel Building Society, introduced to the Assembly a proposal for a Mutual Chapel Insurance Society, and an attempt was being made to raise a guarantee fund, and to ascertain how many churches would insure their buildings in such a Society. Nothing seems to have come of this proposal, but it was brought forward again some years later by the Rev. S. R. Antliff, who secured commendation of the idea in a very small Assembly (20 votes to 12) in 1891, in which year the Congregational Insurance Company was formed. It is still active and, during 40 years, has made grants amounting to £21,400 to various Congregational institutions.

Apparently the donors to the Bicentenary Commemoration Fund were allowed to earmark their contributions for any denominational object. Morley summarizes the effort in a letter to Wilson :

> I am very anxious that such measures should be adopted as will leave us, as a denomination, stronger for our great work at the end of the year or two during which we shall be specially engaged, not only in spreading information, but in wisely expending money which will, I trust, be raised as an expression of gratitude for the service rendered by the heroes of 1662 to the cause of freedom of thought. I therefore rejoice that each is to be at liberty to direct the appropriation of his own money. One district will feel that new chapels are their great want, another that some largely increased agency in connection with their churches is their special need. I anticipate great results from the effort. Dr. Vaughan is preparing an address to be sent by the Bi-centenary Committee to the churches of our faith and order throughout the land.

Lancashire was in the throes of the Cotton Famine,

and some of the collections taken on 24th August, 1862, were sent to relieve distress in that county; in 1863 it was reported that £4,000 had been collected for this purpose.

The Memorial Hall project, while approved by the Assembly, was partly motived by the fact that the Congregational Library was too small and its lease soon to expire[1]. There were those who had no enthusiasm for a denominational building; William Alers Hankey, one of the most earnest and generous of London Independents, who had taken an active part in all denominational and missionary activities for many years, said as early as 1850 that the desire for a building was merely denominational pride. The building of chapels naturally made a greater local appeal, too, while it proved difficult to find a suitable site, and, when one at last was found, it had to be sold again. Finally the site of the old Fleet Prison in Farringdon Street was secured, and the foundation stone laid on 10th May, 1872.

The Bicentenary celebration had many varied results. The first was a great outburst of controversy. There were books and pamphlets of all sizes written both for the Nonconformists and for the Conformists. The official Memorial Volume, under the title of *English Nonconformity,* was written by Robert Vaughan, and the literature of the controversy fills many a shelf. There was co-operation with the Baptists, demonstrations were held both in London and in provincial towns and cities, and 24th August, 1862, was generally observed throughout the country. During the Autumn Assembly, held in London, there was a Congregational Commemoration in St. James's Hall, the speeches being published under the title of *St. James's Hall Addresses* : J. Remington Mills was in the Chair, and the speakers were George Hadfield, M.P., the Rev. R. W. Dale, Handel Cossham of Bristol, the Rev. H. W. Parkinson of Rochdale, the Rev. Andrew Reed, and Dr. Robert Vaughan.

With the principle of earmarking at work, it is rather

1 For some years (1867-1875) before the opening of the Memorial Hall the offices of the Union were at 18, South Street, Finsbury.

difficult to see how much money was contributed. At the
end of the year Vaughan spoke of £150,000; when the
Memorial Hall was opened in 1875 it was said that a
quarter of a million had been raised. A full report of the
Commemoration was presented by the Rev. J. Corbin in
the Autumn Assembly of the Union in 1862, but the effort
continued long after the end of that year. Corbin's
summary of the results is thus given :

> As far as the appropriation of contributions has yet been
> reported, the Pastors' Retiring Fund, among the general
> societies, has received the greatest number of favours;
> while, in the list of local objects that have been promoted,
> are many new chapels opened or in course of erection—
> school-rooms enlarged or new ones built—county efforts
> made for the evangelization of destitute districts—chapel
> debts that have been crippling the energies of churches for
> years completely removed, and others considerably reduced
> —ministers' houses purchased or erected—leaseholds made
> freeholds—and many valuable properties secured to the
> body.

He went on to look forward to 1962, saying :

> And when the Congregationalists of 1962 hold their
> Union meetings in London, it may be that, in *their own
> Memorial Hall,* some Vaughan or Stoughton of that age
> will recount the successive steps of a century of progress;
> and raise to God a praise for what *their* fathers of this age
> were enabled to accomplish.

General Progress.

During these years the custom of printing the names
of those present at the Assemblies ceased, a practice which
is to be regretted in that it deprives us of valuable information. It was hoped that this list would disclose when
the first woman delegate appeared at the Union. As long
as it lasts there is no mention of one. The names of
W. D. and H. O. Wills are often seen side by side. They
are for many years together as delegates at the Union
meetings, but during the May Week in 1865 W. D. was
knocked down by an omnibus, and did not recover from
his injuries.

The Committee was surprised in 1858 to receive an
invitation from Aberdare, and the Secretary visited the

town to see if hospitality could really be provided. He relates :

> The town is situated in a beautiful valley, accessible by rail from Cardiff, which is readily reached from the west, and north, and midland counties, and contains a rapidly increasing population, already amounting to nearly thirty thousand persons. They are distinguished by great activity and energy, a large portion of them speak the English language, and the principles of Nonconformity have taken deep root among them. Our churches in the neighbourhood are numerous : they have devoted pastors and liberal deacons; and they are making ample preparations for the advent of the Union on the soil of the Principality. All classes of the people are looking anxiously for the event.

There was a very representative gathering, which meant much to the cause of Independency in South Wales. The Right Hon. the Lord Mayor of London, Alderman Wire, presided at the " British Missions " meeting, and Baines at the meeting for the exposition of Congregational principles, now a regular feature in the autumn. The dinners were served to 400 people in the market-place, and on the last afternoon 15,000 people assembled on the mountain side to hear two Welsh sermons, the shops and works closing down for the occasion. The Minutes call this

> certainly the most remarkable of all the Autumnal Meetings, for the number of attendants, the largeness of the assemblies, and the unity, love and energy of the brotherhood.

At Blackburn in the following year there was special thanksgiving for improvement in the weather, which had saved the harvest from destruction, heart-felt gratitude being expressed

> Inasmuch as in this peculiar season God has so manifestly disappointed the fears of the people, and has proved Himself, as in all ages, the Hearer and Answerer of prayer; and would suggest to the pastors of our churches to make special reference to this great mercy, in the thanksgivings and teachings of the sanctuary.

Thanks for a good harvest were also expressed in Hull in 1864. In 1862 both Assemblies were held in London, the newly-formed London Congregational Union being responsible for the arrangements in the autumn. Occasionally, when one of the London ministers was Chairman, his church would entertain the delegates to an " elegant " (Union Chapel, Islington, in 1864) or a " sumptuous " breakfast (Harecourt in 1868). 1862 perhaps deserves special mention, for in addition to dinner in the London Tavern each day, there was a tea at Stepney Meeting, and a breakfast in a room, " tastefully decorated, as well as bountifully supplied with provisions ", at Westminster Chapel (Samuel Martin was Chairman that year). In 1867 Manchester broke all records with an attendance of 780. Such attendances resulted in limiting the Autumn Assembly to the big towns, and also in resolutions that only one free dinner be provided and that, if necessary, a grant in aid of a quarter of the local expenses, up to £100, be paid, while if need be lay delegates were to provide their own hospitality.

In 1869 it was decided that the Chairman should be appointed by a ballot of the Committee. Up to that time not infrequently the office was declined by the minister nominated, Tidman declining in 1863, Harrison in 1864 (because of ill-health, but accepting office later), and Spence in 1866.

Some of the Chairman's Addresses now became pronouncements that affected Union policy and gave a new direction to the work and worship of the churches. Allon's in 1864, Hall's in 1866, and Dale's in 1869 were all masterly in their own way. Allon's May Address caused a considerable stir, though at the present day there are few places where his statements would cause alarm. He said :

> Some of the most damaging assaults upon the Divine authorship of the Bible, have really been assaults upon only untenable theories of inspiration, which a more justifiable position utterly disables,

and

> It is only by fully and fearlessly recognizing the human element in the authorship of Scripture, that we can understand it, and find reality in it.

Then such ideas seemed dangerous, and brought immediate

protests from a leading minister, Enoch Mellor, while Samuel Morley said:

> I confess that my own mind is entirely out of harmony with the subject of the paper, and I should be wanting in fidelity to my own deep convictions if I did not feel that some slight injury has. been done to God's Word by what we have heard to-day. I feel myself utterly incapable of offering argument, but still I feel that some slight injury has been done to a book which I have been taught from my earliest youth to regard with the intensest reverence. I do not feel that it stands where it stood three hours ago.

By 1870 the Assembly was constituted on more business-like lines. In 1859 the income from subscriptions, donations, *etc.*, was only £193. In 1864 a collector, Mr. T. H. Collins, was appointed, and from then on, though not uniformly, there was an upward trend, the amount in 1870 being £412. Membership was thrown open to members of churches in 1864, but it was made clear that the affiliation of churches and pastors was to be preferred to personal membership. In 1869 the number of subscribing churches was 226, of personal members 733, of whom only 160 were laymen. When Hannay took the helm, the Union was in a sound financial condition: £3,000 was on deposit in the bank, and there was a credit balance of £1,246. The receipts for the sale of hymn books in the previous year had been £4,978, and only £110 had been drawn from the publication profits to meet the loss on the Union Account proper.

Various attempts were made to reform the Constitution during these years. In 1861 it was made plain that members of the Committee must be ministers or members of churches eligible for connexion with the Union and subscribers to its funds, either personally or through their churches; three years later men from the provinces were allowed on the Committee, which afterwards was sometimes referred to as the " Town and Country Committee " In 1864, as we have seen, all church members were made eligible for membership of the Union. In 1865 a Committee was appointed to enquire into the Constitution, and its findings were discussed and accepted in 1867

and 1868. They made comparatively little difference in
the rules, though the subscription for churches was again
made a minimum of 10s. It was in regard to the Committee that most difference was made. It was to consist
of 72 members, equally ministers and laymen, half resident in London and half in the country. One-third was
to retire each year, and the Committee was to be nominated
by the preliminary meeting and chosen by the Assembly
at its Annual Meeting. The question of the acceptance
of " Union Churches " divided the Committee, but it was
decided that the officers were " not to regard Clause 18
of the Declaration on Faith and Order as excluding from
the fellowship of the Union, churches in which the
privileges of membership and eligibility to office are not
dependent on the opinions held regarding the subjects or
mode of baptism". A new Constitution having been
accepted in 1869, the Committee set to work to codify the
by-laws. As the whole of the Constitution and Standing
Orders came under revision again immediately after
Hannay's acceptance of the Secretaryship in 1870, it is not
necessary to examine the details of this temporary
arrangement.

As the Assembly grew in numbers naturally some
changes had to be made in the arrangement of the meetings. A Reference Committee first makes its appearance
in 1866, and Sectional Meetings in 1869, the latter soon
giving rise to the question how far a resolution passed at a
Sectional Meeting committed the whole Assembly.
Complaints were made that speeches were far too long,
and in 1867 papers were limited to twenty minutes, and subsequent speakers to ten minutes. Courtesies were
exchanged between the Union on the one hand and the
Baptist Union and the Presbyterian Synod on the other,
deputations visiting each others' Assemblies.

In the main, both in regard to domestic and external
affairs, the Union seems to have been in the position of a
watchful observer commenting on the trend of events and
taking action where necessary. It saw the need for
increased attention to " midde-class education ", and

called a Conference to consider the provision of more Secondary Schools for Nonconformist children. It blessed the work of the School for the Sons of Ministers at Lewisham, and approved the proposal to build a similar school for girls at Milton Mount, Gravesend. It tried to prepare a " Model Trust Deed " for Independent Chapels, and found the task was far from easy, and it emphasized the need for the safe custody of deeds. It continually stressed the principle of the weekly offering, and urged the support of the October collection for the three Societies combined in " British Missions ". It listened to John Stoughton speaking on Congregational Reform, emphasizing the primitive rule of one church in the same town or the same city, and asking, " Is not a plurality of congregations perfectly compatible with one comprehensive church ? " It watched with some anxiety the experiments of County Associations with the American "Councils of Reference ", which were not permanent institutions but special meetings summoned by churches or ministers to consult with pastors and delegates of other churches on the appointment, ordination, and removal of pastors, and on disputes between ministers and their churches. It revived the Congregational Lectures, now becoming responsible for their maintenance, the first lecturers appointed for the new series being Henry Rogers and H. R. Reynolds, though these two lectures were not delivered, and were not published until after this period.

Looking beyond its own borders, it discussed revivals of religion, and watched with concern the spread of rationalism and ritualism and every sign of Roman Catholicism's increased activity. It strongly and successfully opposed Palmerston's attempt in the Census of 1861 to make every individual state his religious profession, while regretting that the 1851 return of church attendance was not again included. Its *Year Book* deplored the extent of marital unhappiness as seen in the fact that in the sixteen months January, 1858, to May, 1859, there were 302 applications for divorce, and 108 for judicial separation in the country, and commented " What a fearful amount

of infelicity do these applications indicate !"   Joy was
expressed at the success of Sir Charles Reed's fight to save
Bunhill Fields from a " contemplated desecration ", and
to secure that it would be open to the public.   Support
was given to the project for a revised version of the trans-
lation of the *Old Testament*.   Great interest was taken in
the Continental Protestant Churches, especially those in
France.   In Paris there were several Independent
Churches with pastors and missionaries, and in 1863 the
Union became financially responsible for a chapel that
had been secured.   Five years later, while approving the
work, it was decided that this church should be independent.   When the Colonial Missionary Society undertook
responsibility for work among Protestants on the Continent the Union made grants in support.

These were the years when the Nonconformists took a
pronounced interest in politics, though, in 1860, in passing one of its many resolutions on Church Rates, the
Assembly spoke of " leaving all political activities very
much to other organizations ".   The Education controversy attracted a great deal of attention.   Many
resolutions were passed on Irish Disestablishment, which,
at the Assembly of 1869, was called the "all-engrossing
topic ".   When Europe was in turmoil in 1859 neutrality
was urged upon the Government.

Relationships with American Congregationalists were
not entirely happy during this period.   Previously, on
several occasions, steps had been taken to keep the
churches friendly when there were national disputes, but
the outbreak of the Civil War brought with it difficult
problems.   Frequently the Union had passed strong
resolutions against slavery, and urged the American
Churches to take action, but about the Civil War there
was " doubt, hesitation, and pain ", and it was some time
before the " glad, confident morning " dawned again.
The Assembly was divided, and Dr. Sturtevant, a delegate from the American Churches to the 1863 Assembly,
was asked not to mention the conflict in his address.
Remembering the Union's remonstrances against slavery,

he felt that this was cowardice, and, in a pamphlet published on his return home, describes his feelings:

> I call to mind the oft-repeated and just remonstrances which come to us from our brethren in Great Britain against this iniquitous system, remonstrances which I doubt not have exerted no small influence in bringing on the very conflict in which we are now engaged with the rebel propagandists of slavery. And yet the Congregational Union of England and Wales is now divided in sentiment, and does not know which side to take, and suppresses all utterance on one of the gravest moral issues of the nineteenth century so she may shield herself from unpleasant agitation. This seemed to me marvellous and almost incredible: I know not what to think of British Christianity. I wondered whither the spirit of Wilberforce and Clarkson had fled. I felt that the present conduct of these men cast a painful suspicion over the sincerity of their past professions and was fitted to raise a serious doubt as to the position they may be expected to occupy in the future.

In the *British Quarterly Review* Dr. Vaughan strongly criticized both North and South, and there were parallel comments by other Congregationalists. When peace came, the Union passed a resolution of thanksgiving for the abolition of slavery and abhorrence was expressed at Lincoln's assassination. The resolution was warmed up by impromptu speeches from Dale and Halley, the latter bringing the meeting to its feet with tremendous applause as he complained of the cold and formal references to Lincoln's death and cried:

> Now, sirs, do not let us throw a crown of thorns upon the dead body of the martyred President; let us crown him with roses; let there be some fragrance in our eulogium, some feeling in our sympathy.

It was straightway resolved, uninvited, to send a deputation to the Congregational Churches of America. On their arrival the delegates, Drs. Vaughan, Raleigh, and Smith, found themselves confronted by Sturtevant's pamphlet, and by a collection of the Congregational criticisms of the North. Their welcome was frigid, and it was some time before there was a thaw. No doubt the gift of over £3,000 for the help of the freedmen made in response to an appeal by H. M. Storrs in the May Assembly helped to improve relationships.

The Publication Department.

The New Congregational Hymn Book was published in May, 1859. It contained a thousand hymns, of which 251 were metrical psalms. The number of Watts's hymns included was 381. 30,000 copies were sold in the first year, and 90,000 in the next year, in which 15,500 copies of the old book were sold. By 1870 the sale of the old book had almost ceased, but the new book was selling at the rate of 90,000 a year.

In 1865 it was decided to issue two abridged editions, one for cottage meetings and the other for Sunday Schools. The *Smaller Congregational Hymn Book,* often called the " Cottage Hymn Book ", published in 1866 at 2d., 3d. and 4d. according to binding, contained 150 hymns, and 15,000 copies were sold in the first year. On examination it was found that a Sunday School book ought to include hymns not in the *Congregational Hymn Book* and be considerably larger than was at first suggested. This book, issued in 1867, contained 302 hymns, of which Nos. 234—241 were on Death and Judgment, and 242—256 on Heaven. The Report in 1868 said that 16,000 copies had been sold already.

By 1861 the Committee felt able not only to pay off the annual deficit on the Union accounts from hymn book profits, but to begin to make grants to denominational funds. In 1861 £400 was granted to the *Christian Witness* fund, £200 to the Pastors' Retiring Fund, and £100 to the Pastors' Insurance Aid Society, while in 1864 £2,150 was distributed in the following grants :

To the *Christian Witness* Fund	£700
To the English Congregational Chapel Building Society	£500
To the Pastors' Retiring Fund	£200
To " British Missions "	£300
To the London Congregational Association ...	£200
To the Pastors' Insurance Aid Society	£100
To the Paris Chapel Mission	£100
To Poor Ministers	£50

In that year it was announced that the Finance Committee intended to publish a full balance sheet, including

the details of the Publication Department.   This did not
appear until 1867.   Meanwhile the profits were distributed
as follows :

In 1865

To the *Christian Witness* Fund	£100
To the Pastors' Retiring Fund	£500
To the London Chapel Building Society ...	£300
To the French Evangelical Union	£100

In 1866

To the *Christian Witness* Fund	£500
Memorial Hall Fund	£2,000
Vaughan Testimonial Fund[1]	£100
Evangelical Continental Society, for use in France	£100

In 1867 the promised balance sheet appears, the cash
received from sale of *Hymn Books* being £5,706, and from
Year Books, of which 6,750 copies were sold, and other
publications, £489.   The next account shows an encouraging £1,000 on deposit and £1,720 in hand, while grants
in 1869 and 1870 were as follows :

In 1869

To the French Canadian Mission	£100
To the Colonial Society for Bush Missions ...	£200
To the Jubilee Fund of the Home Missionary Society	£200
To the Irish Evangelical Society	£200
To Brecon College	£200

Grants to the *Christian Witness* Fund and the
Pastors' Retiring Fund were deferred in order to discover
whether co-operation between the two Funds was possible.

In 1870

To the French Canadian Mission	£100
To the Colonial Missionary Society	£200
To the Irish Evangelical Society	£200
Pastors' Retiring Fund	£550
French Evangelical Union	£200
Pastors' Insurance Aid Society	£100
Christian Witness Fund	£650

By the end of this period we have a full annual
financial statement, while in 1869 the duties of the Finance

---

1 Dr. Vaughan was presented with a testimonial of £3,000 on
retiring from the editorship of the *British Quarterly Review.*

Committee, really a Finance and Publications Committee, were defined. In that year, too, the provision of a book room was first suggested.

By this time the palmy days of the Union periodicals were over. Campbell was becoming older and feebler, and what life he had left he put into the *British Standard*. No longer do the Union proceedings furnish information about circulation and profits, but it is clear that the *Christian Witness* and the *Penny Magazine* were having a hard struggle to pay their way. In 1862 Campbell said that the disadvantages of the two magazines were great and peculiar. Other magazines, such as those belonging to the Baptists and the three Methodist bodies, had the earnest support of their denominations, but is was otherwise with the two Congregational journals.

> Since the severance . . . from the Union, to please a small party, they have stood alone. They are burdened with all the disadvantages of Denominationalism while utterly bereft of its benefits.

In 1864 he announced to the Managers of the *Christian Witness* that he would be resigning from the editorial chair of the two papers at the end of the year. He spoke of the loyal support of Wells and Smith, and then surveyed the change that had come over the religious press since the papers were founded. He expressed his conviction that

> we have now reached a period in the history of periodical literature in this country, by which Denominational Magazines are placed in a new and a peculiar position, which requires an appropriate adaptation. The love of illustration has so become a passion, that it is demanded in everything. There is also, I regret to say, a strong and growing distaste for everything denominational. That passion and that distaste have been prodigally provided for in divers ways.

He then pointed out that the Religious Tract Society now printed six magazines, largely illustrated; the Sunday School Union six more; and still another six were printed in Scotland, " heavily laden with illustrations and abounding in fiction ", while the religious papers and the " cheap press in its multiplied and manifold productions " made the way of denominational journals extremely difficult. He then sums up the history of the two he had edited :

> The Magazines are now about to enter their twenty-first year—a large portion of the mature life of man. Through that long period they have had to maintain a ceaseless and vigorous war with the disadvantages of denominationalism, novelty, death, emigration, and other obstructive elements; but the unparalleled position they achieved at the outset supplied a margin so ample as to admit of gradual and large reductions, and yet at the end of twenty years still to exhibit a mighty power for good. Had the *Witness* and the *Penny,* in their first year, started with simply their present circulation, it would have been deemed, and justly deemed, an immense success,

In accepting Campbell's resignation, the Managers expressed their appreciation, and sent him a present of £500[1], while shortly afterwards a public testimonial, amounting to £3,000, was presented to him at a breakfast over which Lord Shaftesbury presided, Thomas Thompson being the Treasurer, Dr. Ferguson the Convener, and Dr. Morton Brown reading the address[2].

Before Campbell finally laid down the magazines, there was just one spark of the old fire. At the Union Committee in the autumn of 1864 it was suggested that the magazines might again be brought under the patronage or control of the Union. He wrote to Smith to say that this would be an offence against decency and justice, a personal indignity which would be resented by many as a flagrant wrong :

> Might they not say with truth that, after all was done that could be done, both publicly and privately, to damage the Magazines, and after thrusting them out of the Union, nothing can be more incongruous than once more to bring them on the platform with a view to lift them up in public estimation and float them into popularity? After that, they might go on and say, the Union never so much as once cast a smile upon the publications, but left them, with their Editor, to sink or swim, apparently quite indifferent to their fate, and disposed to ignore their very existence;

---

1 See *Life,* pp. 509 f.

2 The last two were to be Campbell's biographers.

but the moment the Editor resigned, and even before he closed his engagement, the Union hastened to embrace the new men, and to restore the Serials to the platform.

The new Editors of the journals were the Rev. John Kennedy for the *Witness*, and the Rev. F. S. Williams for the *Penny*, and they found that Campbell's words about the hard times in store for denominational journals were amply justified. Kennedy did by no means badly with the *Witness*, introducing a more popular type of article, and some lighter features, and at the end of two years he was pressed to continue, and agreed to do so. Williams endeavoured to persuade the churches to localize the *Penny*. But the struggle was too fierce, and both magazines went down, the *Witness* at the end of 1871, the *Penny* in 1881. In the last number of the *Witness* Dr. Kennedy, the Editor, said :

> The *Christian Witness* (and the remark applies to other periodicals of its class) has had to contend for a long time with two difficulties. First : in its more general object as a medium of religious instruction, it has had rivals which came into existence long after itself, but which have been able to create and command attractions altogether beyond its reach. At this moment the streets of London, and we presume of other places, are placarded with immense bills announcing a single tale in a religious magazine, at a cost, it must be of many hundreds if not thousands of pounds. Competition with enterprise and speculation of this sort is impossible on the part of such a magazine as ours has been. Secondly : in its denominational aspect the *Christian Witness* has had to contend with a singular and unaccountable want of anything like an *esprit de corps* on the part of Congregationalists. We cannot dignify this absence of the Denominational feeling with the title of Catholicity. We regard it as much to be blamed and much to be lamented.

In the same issue Dale, who had been called to edit *The Congregationalist*, the *Witness's* successor, wrote :

> The history of Denominational Magazines contains very little to encourage the heart of an Editor ; for the Congregationalists of England and Wales have less of the denominational spirit than characterizes the adherents of any other great system of theological faith and ecclesiastical polity.

Dale was very severe on Congregationalists who disparaged their own literature. In his first volume of *The Congregationalist* he wrote :

> This frank and open policy not only lost them the support of many excellent persons, who regard Congregationalism with hostility and distrust; it offended and repelled many Congregationalists; for it is the habit of some of the ministers and members of our churches to disparage " denominational literature ". I do not find that ministers who indulge this cynical temper have more sense, more learning, or more taste than their brethren; or that the laymen who are betrayed into the same folly are conspicuous for the energy of their character, their liberality, or their zeal. It is quite time that this foolish and ignoble spirit disappeared. Silly women and sillier men may think that a bracelet, which is vulgar and worthless if it is known to come from a Birmingham workshop, is the perfection of good taste if shown to them by a London jeweller as a recent importation from Paris; but sensible people ought to show more discrimination. Congregationalists are among the very ablest contributors to the " non-denominational " periodicals; what they write is just as vigorous and just as valuable when it appears within the covers of the *British Quarterly,* or of *The Congregationalist,* as when it appears elsewhere.

The Ministry.

Sustentation. From time to time the matter was discussed from various points of view. Mr. Henry Lee, of Manchester (1867), spoke of " The Improvement of Ministerial Incomes ", but there was great fear of a central fund, and the Committee urged that " Stipend Augmentation Fund" rather than " Sustentation Fund" should be the expression used. By October, 1870, the Assembly had committed itself to the principle of a general fund to enable stipends to be raised to £150, such fund to be controlled by representatives of the Associations and of such non-Associated churches as desired to join.

The Pastors' Retiring Fund. In May, 1860, the Committee, in reporting that £10,844 had been subscribed, and commending the Fund to all churches and pastors, " whether belonging to the Union or not ", made clear that it would " be entirely independent of all control or influence from the Union ".   By October £15,000 was in sight, a generous benefactor in Cheltenham having given some thousands in various challenge grants. The Rules governing the administration of the Fund were passed at a subscribers' meeting on 22nd February, 1860, and are printed in the *Year Book,* 1861, pp. 325f.   Annuities were to be of £50, for ministers aged 60, who had been 25 years in the ministry, whose views were in accordance with the Declaration of Faith and Order, and whose incomes were not more than £100.   The Fund gradually increased, sums voted from publication profits and given in the Bicentenary year helping considerably; by 1864 the total was £35,000, and by 1869 £60,000.

Ministerial Training.

A great deal of attention was paid, but only in an intermittent way, to the colleges, and to entrance into the ministry.   There was a great variety in the status and curricula of the colleges.   In 1858 the ten colleges were Western, Rotherham, Brecon, Cheshunt, Airedale, Hackney, Edinburgh, Lancashire, Spring Hill, and New College, together with the Presbyterian College at Carmarthen.   " Private Theological Seminaries " were at Bala, Bedford, Bethesda, Cotton End (specially for Home Missionary students), and Huntington (Hereford), while certain ministers also took students into their houses— both the seminaries and the ministers sending men directly into pastorates as well as preparing them for the other colleges.   Other institutions, aiming specially at training Home Missionaries, sprang up, notably at Bristol and Nottingham, the former in time to be amalgamated with Western College.

In 1864 Allon devoted some time to the ministry in his Autumn Address.   He said that 450 of the 1,738 ministers in England had had no ministerial training; that during the last ten years, for every 28 students entering the pastorate from the colleges there were 25 others; and that, in the previous year, 30 college students entered and 47 others. This suggested a situation so serious that he felt a College Conference similar to that which met in 1845 was advisable. Such a Conference, at which 12 colleges were represented, met in the Congregational Library in January, 1865. Binney presided, and valuable papers were read, but there seems to have been no immediate practical result.

In 1871 Allon, as ever keenly interested in ministerial training, returned to the charge in a paper read at Swansea. He said that the 16 collegiate institutions had 38 professors, 368 students, and an income of £25,000. Of 2,468 ministers in Great Britain and Ireland, 645 had no ascertained college training. Of 104 men who entered the ministry in the previous year only 63 were from the colleges. The courses ranged from two to six years, and some tutors had to teach many subjects. The denomination made no systematic attempt to discover the number of ministers needed annually. For the first time in his life he proposed the creation of a society—an educational society for aiding students for the ministry, enabling them to go to an academy or public school, then to a university, and then, after graduation, to a theological college. He suggested the organization of the colleges into two groups—one in the north, one in the south—to act as a Nonconformist Oxford and Cambridge, each college specializing, one preparing for matriculation, another for graduation, and another for theology. Notwithstanding the disheartening results of previous Conferences, Allon suggested another. This met in the Library in June, 1872, the Union again convening, and Baines presiding. Allon produced more figures, and said that the number of imperfectly educated men entering the ministry was increasing. Dr. Falding admitted that the resolutions of the 1845 and 1865 Conferences had been buried in reports and had been entirely inoperative.

JAMES SPICER   WILLIAM CROSFIELD

SIR MURRAY HYSLOP   WILLIAM HOLBORN

Again there was little immediate result, though some seed was sown which was afterwards to bear fruit. Of course the references to men without college training brought the usual sheaf of protests. Paxton Hood replied at length in the *Eclectic,* of which he was then Editor, while in a paper addressed to the Union in 1876 Parker made great scorn of the limitation of the idea of " education " to a particular kind of training :

> A man is not necessarily educated because he can grind *gerunds*—or even because he can mumble elementary metaphysics in a voice inaudible beyond two yards of the pulpit . . . Was Dr. Robert Vaughan an uneducated man? Was John Burnet of Camberwell a man to be sneered at? Or Thomas Lynch? Or Alfred Morris of Holloway? Does this Union owe nothing to George Smith of Poplar? And yet not one of these men had the training that is by some accounted orthodox and sufficient. And if we pass the line and go into other churches, we shall see that the Most High has not allowed Himself to be limited by human notions of propriety and fitness, for time would fail me to tell of Richard Baxter, Thomas Scott, Andrew Fuller, Richard Jabez Bunting, Morley Punshon, Charles Spurgeon, who, through faith, wrought righteousness, expounded the holy mysteries, arrested men in their wickedness, and made strong men stronger.

The lists of ministers in the *Year Book* was at first quite unofficial, but in 1858 the words were prefixed :

> The following lists, compiled by the Editor with much care, are presumed to be correct, but the COMMITTEE OF THE UNION do not hold themselves responsible for their accuracy.

In 1859, the following addition was made :

> Additions are made to this list from time to time, only as parties are recommended by the Tutors of Colleges, the Secretaries of Associations, or three accredited Ministers of the denomination.

It was felt to be unsatisfactory that the Editor should have the responsibility for the insertion of names, and in 1866 the Committee was asked to consider whether alterations should not be made in the terms on which the names were inserted. In 1868 the County Associations were

R

made responsible for the provision of names, this heading being substituted :

> Alphabetical List of Independent Ministers in England, whose names have been furnished by the Secretaries of County Associations or Unions, or by the Secretaries of the Congregational Board, or who are members of the Congregational Union.

This proved to be unsatisfactory, and on the recommendation of a special Sub-Committee, a new heading was agreed upon :

> The Alphabetical Lists of Ministers in Great Britain and Ireland, published in the *Year Book,* shall contain only the names of Independent Ministers of Great Britain and Ireland whose names have been furnished by the Secretaries of County Associations or Unions; or by the Secretaries of the Congregational Board; or by five Ministers already on the list, and residing in their neighbourhoods; or who are members of the Congregational Union.
>
> N.B.—In every case where a Minister's name is not returned according to the foregoing Regulation, the Editor shall inform the said Minister of such omission in sufficient time to secure the re-introduction of the name, if eligible, according to the rule above.

It is not without significance that the proposer of the acceptance of this recommendation was Alexander Hannay.

In 1870 the Union lost its Secretary, Dr. George Smith, who died suddenly on 13th February, having held the office for 18 years. Smith had perhaps counted his work for the Union as second to the work of his pastorate, but he had rendered to it devoted and conscientious service, though he does not impress the student as a statesman of the type of Algernon Wells. Indeed, he seems to have been carried along by the stream of denominational development rather than to have directed its course. Ashton, his co-secretary, made things easier for the Committee, first by filling the gap until an appointment was made, and then by resigning his office. It was agreed that there should be a single Secretary, but that Ashton should continue to edit the *Year Book* at the salary he was already receiving. Where should a new Secretary be

found ?   In 1859 the delegate from Scotland had been the
Rev. Alexander Hannay, of Dundee, who made a good
impression on the Assembly.   In 1862 he became pastor
of City Road Church, London, and four years later of
the West Croydon Church, becoming about the same time
Secretary of the Colonial Missionary Society.   Hannay
addressed the Assembly in 1867 on " The Present
Ecclesiastical Condition of England ", and in 1868 his
address on Temperance "greatly commended itself to the
heart and judgment of the Assembly" : as one who often
said that his first public signature was at the age of 15 in
a temperance pledge book, Hannay always gave total
abstinence a foremost place in his message. He was
unanimously appointed Secretary in May, 1870, and held
the office for 20 years.

XIII. HANNAY AT THE HELM, 1870-1890.

HANNAY ranks with Algernon Wells as the greatest of the Union Secretaries. He assumed office at an opportune time, when the tide had begun to turn again towards centralization. While perhaps it may be argued that he did not deliberately pursue a centralization policy[1], there is no doubt that his powerful personality inevitably influenced this trend. He had the gift of leadership, and as a "master of Assemblies" was without peer in his day : even Joseph Parker had to acknowledge that he met more than his match in him. He was dignified and stately, clear-sighted and indefatigable, and his influence was felt in every part of the denomination's life. On the one side, he had been Secretary of the Colonial Missionary Society, and so was familiar with the work of Congregationalism overseas : on the other he was interested in the Schools, and when there was trouble at Milton Mount which caused great discussion throughout the country, arising out of disputes between the "Lady Principal", Miss Hadland, and the Secretary, the Rev. William Guest, his controlling hand was felt. And his love for the churches sent him through the length and breadth of the land in order to make the Church Aid and Home Missionary Society a strong and vital part of the denominational life. It was perhaps natural that one with all these gifts should come to be a denominational Louis XIV, with a *"L'Union, c'est moi"* attitude : Hannay had his weaknesses—he could not suffer fools gladly, and he brooked no rival near his throne, Rogers being the only man allowed to share his dominion in any measure. The inner circle in those days consisted of Rogers, R. T. Verrall (the Secretary of the Pastors' Retiring Fund) with, perhaps, Albert Spicer and Andrew Mearns at the end of the period. The counsel of these men, with their varied gifts, helped to make Hannay's position as leader of the denomination almost impregnable.

1 See Baldwin Brown's Chairman's Address, quoted below, p. 265,

It was all to his advantage that his time, and the time of the Assembly, had not to be devoted to the Constitution, the revision accomplished in 1872 lasting for the rest of his days. The twenty years of his secretariat covered the Jubilee Year, 1881, and saw a large increase of the Union's influence and activity.   Subscriptions from the churches grew from £381 to £759, salaries from £446 to £1,823, and sales in the Publication Department from £5,175 to £10,722. Perhaps a hundred years hence a date that will stand out as of supreme importance in the history of the Union will be 1872, when the Union made its first reported investment, £1,000 stock Great Indian Peninsular Railway; the investments grew to £5,010 by 1890.   The number of ministers increased in the period from 1,958 to 2,732, and the churches from 2,923 to 4,423[1].

Along the line of every one of the Union's declared objects there was considerable progress during these years.

This is not to say that Hannay was not confronted with difficulties of a serious kind. These may be described before proceeding to examine his opportunity and relate his achievements.

I. General Suspicion of Centralization.

Most pronounced of all was the inertia of many of the churches, and their deep-seated suspicion of a central organization.   Even Hannay could not extract statistics from them. His Report in 1872 pathetically stated

> that the full information he had asked from the churches had not been supplied, not being complete enough for publication in any case except the Welsh. Some churches had a conscientious objection to furnishing information; the independence of others led them to think the request for it impertinent, and there was general apathy on the subject.

In the Preface to the *Year Book* he repeatedly refers to the difficulty of getting statistics.   In 1884 he attempted

---

[1] It is characteristic of the denomination's attitude to statistics that, in the *Year Book* for 1871 we are told that, in addition to these 2,923 churches, the number of Home Mission Stations and Evangelistic Stations could "only be given approximately as 3,000, and that this number does not include various school rooms, cottages, *etc.,* in which Divine Service is held in connexion with the churches in their several localities".

to discover the number of churches and their seating accommodation, and reported that he had had more success than

> my knowledge of the indifference with which statistics are regarded in some quarters, and the positive hostility with which efforts to collect material for them are met in others, had led me to expect.

In 1885 he referred to the fact that it was impossible to speak of the progress of the denomination when there were no reliable statistics. Churches declined to supply the necessary materials, "and in this respect Congregationalism is at a disadvantage compared with every other denomination". Information in regard to membership could be given for aided churches only. The number of churches, branch churches, and mission stations in England and Wales in that year he stated as 4,347, with sittings 1,568,357, an increase of half a million since 1851. On another occasion he pointed out that the failure to state the number of members, scholars, and teachers, produced criticism of the *Year Book* and of the denomination, because opponents were able to say that the failure to produce figures was hiding a decline. In 1887 the Committee decided to make one more effort to discover school statistics. Previously, after a paper by the Rev. C. E. B. Reed in 1874, an attempt had brought in only 683 out of 2,100 returns. On the basis of these returns Hannay presented a long digest which contains a large amount of miscellaneous information about Sunday Schools of the time[1]. In 1887 there was greater success, and the Preface to the *Year Book* for 1889 shows that returns had come to hand from 2,921 schools with 619,371 scholars and 60,170 teachers. These statistics were completed in the following year, when 703,611 scholars and 68,270 teachers were reported.

This hesitation about statistics but reflected the ingrained suspicion of the churches about the Union, which will be evident again when Hannay's constructive proposals come to be considered. The critical attitude to the

1 *Year Book,* 1875, pp. 100-108.

Union is well represented in Parker's speech on "Organized Congregationalism" in the Assembly of 1876, which has already been quoted. Fear lest the ministry and the churches, their preaching and worship, should all be forced into one mould, and all individuality repressed, was still widespread, and it found natural expression in the minister of the City Temple.

In his address in 1876, Parker criticized organized Congregationalism in thorough and characteristic fashion. His main contentions were :

1.—That the public looked at the Assembly vote as the opinion of English Congregationalists. In this they were mistaken because the churches had not discussed the subjects brought before the Assembly, and the vote was not in any sense representative. He therefore urged that ministers and delegates should be allowed to record their names. One Union resolution[1] had been opposed by Binney, Halley, Stoughton, Thomas, Harrison, Conder, White, Baines, Morley, and Reed, and yet it was represented as the opinion of English Congregationalism. The previous year, on the subject of open pulpits, a resolution was passed against which six ex-Chairmen of the Union expressed distinct opposition.

2.—The insistence on a uniform method of training, coupled with financial assistance during training and the provision for superannuation at the end of a ministry, put a premium on mediocrity. Instead of getting men of individuality it was "suggested that certain men shall burn the denominational candle at both ends, having all the advantage of a gratuitous education, and all the solace of a retiring pension".

3.—Especially was Parker severe on the tendency of some men to assume leadership in the denomination.

> There are no hereditary or prescriptive leaderships in Congregationalism. We have leaderships, but they are natural, not mechanical. They are the proper honours of superior sagacity, spiritual insight, and commanding eloquence. Of other leaderships Congregationalism knows nothing.

---

[1] No doubt the Education Resolution referred to on p. 189.

He hoped that the day was far distant when the advertisements of the Union could be shortened into "The usual speeches will be delivered by the usual speakers". He would like an Assembly in which no man took part whose income was above £150 a year.

> It would do us good, and make some of us more intelligent and ardent Liberationists, if we could hear Congregationalism expounded by missionaries who are scorned by the vicar, damned by the squire, and half starved by the people, whose own poverty is extreme. I do not always want at our meetings to hear papers by doctors of divinity and masters of arts; I do not ask to hear at every meeting specimens of the acutest reasoning and the highest eloquence. Some of us have good memories, and have heard a good deal of that before. I rejoice in the glittering speech of Mr. Dale, the valiant energy of Mr. Rogers, and the delightfully-ingenious reasoning by which the secretary persuades himself that he is always right; but now and again I wish to hear such facts as our home missionaries alone can give us, and the pleadings of men whose daily life is a course of opposition and difficulty.

Further, Parker protested that organization was turning the Union into a politico-religious debating club.

> What an amazing amount of so-called "business" we have to do! We have to disestablish the Church, modernize the Universities, rectify the policy of School Boards, clear the way to burial-grounds, subsidize magazines, sell hymn-books, play the hose upon Convocation, and generally give everybody to understand that if we have not yet assailed or defended them, it is not for want of will, but merely for want of time.

These things were important, but they ought not to be the staple of discussion.

> I want to know what we ourselves are doing for the spiritual enlightenment and progress of the world. What are we doing in foreign missions? in missions home and colonial? in chapel building? in Sunday Schools? These I should make the main, the necessary, the vital questions.

And so Parker emphasized that such a gigantic union would have to be well watched by every county and every Congregationalist, for it could "either be a great power for good or the greatest engine for mischief we have ever assisted to create". He hoped the Union would never have

great funds to distribute.   The conclusion of the matter
was that the Congregational Churches were first and the
Union second.   " The Churches might possibly do without the Union—the Union could not exist without the
Churches."

Baldwin Brown's Chairman's Address in the autumn
of 1878 stated very effectively the true genius of Congregationalism.   To " the incubus of 'The Church' " he
opposes "the churches", which he describes as "homes
within which the life of the church is a simple, homely,
family life".

> I dread when I hear about "the Church".   I think of
> prelates, priests, tithes, law-books, sacraments, and spirit-
> ual persons and orders.   When I hear about the churches,
> the little households of Christ, my heart is uplifted; I am
> sure that if the Spirit of Christ is anywhere, we ought to
> be able to look for it there.

Hannay had related how "small farms which went to
chapel were being thrown into large farms which go to
church", and there was danger of the same process in Independency.

> God grant that we may never be tempted to make our-
> selves into the Independent Church of England; or even
> to think that American Congregational Councils can do
> much to help the play of our higher life!
>
> But some may ask, Who is conspiring against our In-
> dependency?   I answer frankly, No one.   What I dread is
> the drift of a current, not the action of a will.   There are
> no truer Independents living than the officers of our Union.
> There are no men more in earnest in deprecating centraliza-
> tion than the abettors of the various movements for
> developing more highly the organization of our community.
> But it is well to remember that the corruptions of ecclesias-
> tical society have rarely been the work of conscious intel-
> ligent agents, but rather the result of a drift which appeared
> to be irresistible.   The Franciscans drifted into wealth in
> spite of the most determined protests and struggles of the
> noblest men of the Order.   We live in very busy, anxious,
> burdened times.   It grows daily more difficult to get over-
> worked men to attend systematically to things not close at
> their own doors.   We shall need to watch keenly, lest
> movements begun with the most honest desire to work by
> local nervous centres, as it were, should, by the mere pres-
> sure of the necessities of things in such an age as this, fall

more and more into the hands of those who have time, and whose business it is, to attend to them ; lest, in other words, the body should become all head—voice, limbs, organs, dwindling, with a great head sucking into itself all their life.   The breath of our life is the play of the living Spirit through the free thought and action of our individual Independent churches.   Maintain that in full vigour as the vital core, and then develop and organize as you will.   But we must maintain at all hazards the entire independence of the churches of all but brotherly guidance and influence. Harden into an Independent body, you may look larger and stronger, and may make a more monotonous order in your house of life.   But you may write " Ichabod " on your temples ; your strength has departed, your glory is gone.

II.   Theological Controversy.

The recurrence of theological strife also threatened to disturb the even course of Hannay's policy.   Students of rhythm in history may be inclined to make use of the fact that during the last century the Congregational Churches have turned their attention to theology about once in every generation. The discussions about the Declaration of Faith and Order in 1833, the *Rivulet* Controversy in 1856, the "Religious Communion" discussions of 1877-8, the "New Theology" of the early years of the present century, make it not unlikely that the wheel has come round full circle and another theological debate may be imminent.   It was the "Religious Communion" controversy that crossed Hannay's path.   It can only be rightly understood against the background of the teaching of the evolutionists ; of the theories of Comte and Mill ; and of the growing acquaintance with German philosophy and Biblical criticism. Not without significance, too, was the interest aroused by Keshub Chunder Sen, and by discussions between Congregationalists and Unitarians.   With all these ideas floating in the air controversy was crystallized at Leicester during the Autumn Meetings of 1877 by an invitation to all "who value spiritual religion, and who are in sympathy with the principle that religious communion is not dependent on agreement in theological, critical, or historical opinion" to attend a conference. The promoters, of whom the Rev. J. Allanson Picton was the most prominent, were

endeavouring to discover some common ground on which
Christians of varying shades of thought might meet in in-
dependence of dogma or of Christianity's historical basis.
Picton was the learned and highly respected minister of
St. Thomas's Square, Hackney. Perhaps Waddington not
unfairly summarizes his views thus :

> Mr. Picton was of opinion that Christ was a mere man,
> who performed no miracles, who shared at least *some* of
> the prejudices and errors of His time and nation, and who
> wrought the great revolution traced to Him by appealing
> to and revealing the eternal element in man.

The Conference would, perhaps, not have aroused any
excitement within the Union had it not been that the fact
of its being held during the Assembly week gave rise to the
impression that it was an official gathering, and that the
Congregational Churches were departing from their usual
standards of belief.   The Union Report in May, 1878,
stated that some members of the Union were among those
who called the Conference, which was thus regarded as a
challenge to the Congregational Churches to accept the
principle involved and as a plea for communion "between
those who receive and those who reject what have always
been regarded by Congregationalists as the cardinal facts
and doctrines of Christianity". It was, therefore, felt desirable to appoint a representative committee to consider what
steps had best be taken to relieve the anxiety felt in the
churches.   That Committee's recommendations, accepted
by the Union Committee, and submitted to the May
Assembly in Union Chapel, Islington, included the
resolution :

> That in view of the uneasiness produced in the churches
> of the Congregational Order by the proceedings of the re-
> cent Conference at Leicester on the terms of Religious
> Communion, the Assembly feels called upon to re-affirm
> that the primary object of the Congregational Union is,
> according to the terms of its own constitution, to uphold
> and extend Evangelical Religion.
> That the Assembly appeals to the history of the Con-
> gregational churches generally, as evidence that Congre-
> gationalists have always regarded the acceptance of the
> Facts and Doctrines of the Evangelical Faith revealed in

the Holy Scriptures of the Old and New Testaments as an essential condition of Religious Communion in Congregational churches; and that among these have always been included the Incarnation, the Atoning Sacrifice of the Lord Jesus Christ, His Resurrection, His Ascension and Mediatorial Reign, and the work of the Holy Spirit in the renewal of men.

That the Congregational Union was established on the basis of these Facts and Doctrines is, on the judgment of the Assembly, made evident by the Declaration of Faith and Order adopted at the annual meeting, 1833; and the Assembly believes that the churches represented in the Union hold these Facts and Doctrines in their integrity to this day.

It was a striking coincidence that the Chairman of the Union in 1878 was Baldwin Brown, protagonist in the *Rivulet* affair twenty years before. This added piquancy to the situation, for it was notorious that the Chairman looked on the Union as "the free Parliament of the Churches", and did not agree with the recommendations of the Committee. He believed that a Christianity without definite basis on historic fact would be too vague and nebulous to be an energizing power; but he believed equally strongly that too rigid an insistence on formal and doctrinal orthodoxy would alienate many who could be won for the Kingdom of God. Those no longer in sympathy with the Union in essentials would leave it of themselves; any direct pressure upon them he held to be mistaken. His courage and tolerance were both exhibited in his Chairman's Address in May, 1878. Speaking on "Our Theology in Relation to the Intellectual Movement of our Times", he said there was no doubt about the permanence of Christianity as compared with other religious systems—

> The moon of Mahomet
> Arose, and it shall set,
> While blazoned as on heaven's immortal noon,
> The Cross leads generations on.

There was but one mode of solving the question whether the Independents were evangelical, and that was by being evangelical. He dissented utterly from the course proposed in face of the demand for "religious communion on a basis independent of doctrinal ideas".

Brethren, is it come to this—that the Independents, who suffered in their childhood a long agony for the Gospel, who fought in their young manhood a stern battle for the Gospel, who held the Gospel as in an ark through the weary night of the Nonconformist Exodus, whose great preachers stood shoulder to shoulder with Wesley through that glorious Evangelical revival, whose churches have been for generations the very *foci* of Evangelical influence, and whose ministers are at this moment among the ablest and most successful preachers of the Gospel in our land— is it come to this, that we, of all the great Evangelical Churches, must pray the world to believe that we are loyal to the Gospel, and must hearten our faith by repeating our creed? No, brethren ; do not think so meanly of yourselves in the matter of your loyalty to the truth as it is in Jesus. Be sure that if this resolution would be passed in this Assembly by an overwhelming majority, there is no need to pass it ; you are saying the same thing, and the world hears you, in a hundred nobler and more effectual ways. Think of the touching preface to the Savoy declaration, which notes how our churches, " launched singly and sailing apart and along on the vast ocean of those tempestuous times, and exposed to every wind of doctrine, under no other conduct than that of the Word and the Spirit ", had been kept faithful. Cannot we trust the same spirit to pilot us through the stormy times that are upon us? " O we of little faith, wherefore shall *we* doubt? " . . . Brethren, we are too fearful of our reputation. We have but to work for God and to preach the Gospel, and He will take charge of it. *Qui s'excuse s'accuse* in a matter like this, as the world will see when it reads your resolution.

He further protested against the slipshod nature of the resolution—"such a helpless theological document he had rarely read".

To sum up the whole matter, my conviction is very deep indeed, that if we could see and say that the loyalty of the Independent churches to the great truths of the Gospel which our fathers believed and preached, and to a true spiritual freedom, is too unquestionable to need either affirmation or vindication, it would be all the notice which the Leicester Conference needs at our hands.

But the members of the Union were not convinced by their Chairman's eloquent words. They felt that the suspicion cast on the orthodoxy of the denomination must be cleared,

and Enoch Mellor, not for the first time, defended the
evangelical faith with his customary earnestness and skill.
He moved the resolution of the Committee, and by cate-
gorical questions elicited the views of the Assembly. Dr.
Parker poured scorn on the method of settling deep
problems by loud shouts of *Yes* and *No,* and moved as an
amendment :

> That whilst this Assembly views hopefully every
> honourable effort to extend the terms of personal Religious
> Communion, it is of opinion that theological and co-opera-
> tive fellowship, as between churches and any of their
> organized forms, can be made complete and useful only by
> the acceptance of a common doctrinal basis, and therefore
> the Assembly solemnly re-affirms its adhesion to those
> Evangelical Doctrines which the Congregational Union
> has maintained throughout the whole period of its
> existence.

The discussion took the best part of two days and was
maintained in admirable spirit, though the different views
were both strongly held and strongly expressed. Picton
himself spoke in an earnest and attractive way, much on
Baldwin Brown's lines, urging that they should trust to
the spirit of freedom and that the resolution would cast a
forbidding shadow on the path of those strugglers who
feared to give up their living faith, but had been obliged
to reject its external framework. Eustace Conder said that
either the resolution or the amendment was necessary because Congregationalism was not merely a form of government but involved certain historical beliefs. Alexander
Raleigh said that the Chairman's Address had enunciated
all the items of evangelical faith set out in the resolution.
Why then should he object to the Union doing the same
thing? Dale thought the matter must be dealt with, and
he could not support the amendment as it seemed to give
some approval to the Leicester Conference, and Rogers
said the Conference had thrown down a challenge which
must be taken up. The only layman who spoke favoured
Baldwin Brown's view, and reminded Mellor of the
Declaration of Faith and Order's statement :

> Disallowing the utility of creeds and articles of religion

as a bond of union, and protesting against subscription to any human formularies as a term of communion.

Finally, after many speeches, only a few voted for Parker's amendment, after which the resolutions were carried by an "overwhelming majority", and the Doxology sung.

Whatever be posterity's verdict on the Union's action, all must agree that the freedom of utterance in the discussion was in line with the best Congregational tradition. Baldwin Brown, in his October Address, spoke of the difficult position in which he had been placed, and of the patience and sympathy with which the Assembly had listened to him. He told how, when he had said to Hannay that he shrank from accepting the Chair because some of the things he had to say would cross the convictions of many, he received the reply, "Say them ; we do not want only the echo of our own voices". Brown reiterated his belief that in religion a living Guide was to be preferred to guide-posts, which were helpful mainly to those who had lost faith in the living Guide. While he did not believe that Congregationalism would ever make a new creed or exercise excommunication, he deplored the fact that the May resolutions had put forward the denomination as the body most in peril from doubts and denials, so that eminent preachers in other denominations had patted them on the back about the resolutions and told them they had done very well[1].

Baldwin Brown no doubt had Spurgeon in mind. Writing to Allon[2] the previous November, Spurgeon had said :

> The delightful liberality of some of you truly good men is abused into a covenant with death and hell. The Arianism of the Doddridge time is upon us again. I thank God that the men are mostly beneath contempt, but I am sorry that some of your really solid brethren are the screen behind which they skulk.

[1] For the discussion which raged round the Leicester Conference, see the articles which appeared in the *British Quarterly Review* and the *Congregationalist;* Skeats and Miall, *History of the Free Churches,* which contains a very good summary of the debate ; and the biographies of Baldwin Brown, Dale, D. W. Simon, *etc.*

[2] Peel, *Letters to a Victorian Editor,* pp. 344, 345.

And after the May discussion he wrote to Allon :

> I am heartily glad of the result of your meeting. Many fears are removed, and hopes confirmed. God bless the Congregational Union is my hearty prayer. Your loose fish swam so near the top of the water that they were always visible, but now I trust they will seek deeper waters.
>
> I fear I shall never see your brethren up to my standard, but it is a joy to me to feel that at least the great facts of our religion are heartily believed.

In *The Congregationalist,* Dale vigorously attacked Brown both for using his Chairman's position to propound anti-Committee views, and for reverting to the subject in October. He held that the Chairman's action was entirely unprecedented, and had set a very bad example.

A New Constitution.

Having glanced at the main difficulties which Hannay met, it may be well next to examine the new constitution under which he was to work, the new denominational home in which he was to dwell, and certain other new developments with which he was closely connected.

Although By-laws had been agreed upon in August, 1869, the revision of the Constitution naturally brought every part of the organization under review. A revised Constitution was adopted in October, 1871, Standing Orders in May, 1872, and By-laws (by the Committee) in June, 1872. As these Rules remained practically unchanged, except in regard to the constitution of the Committee and the method of electing Committee and Chairman, until 1896, it is necessary that they should be examined with some care in order to see how the Constitution, already revised in 1852 and 1861, had been changed. The Fundamental Principle was now thus stated :

> The Union recognizes the right of every individual church to administer its affairs, free from external control, and shall not, in any case, assume legislative authority or become a court of appeal,

and the Objects :

> To uphold and extend Evangelical religion primarily in connexion with churches of the Congregational order.

W. J. WOODS   ALEXANDER HANNAY   ANDREW MEARNS

MEMORIAL HALL

JOHN MINSHULL   CHARLES STANCLIFF

D. BURFORD HOOKE

To promote Scriptural views of Church fellowship and organization.

To strengthen the fraternal relations of the Congregational Churches, and facilitate co-operation in everything affecting their common interests.

To maintain correspondence with the Congregational Churches and other Christian communities throughout the world.

To obtain statistics relating to Congregational Churches at home and abroad.

To assist in procuring perfect religious equality for all British subjects, and in promoting reforms bearing on their moral and social condition.

Membership now consisted of :

A. *Representative Members.* The pastor of any church subscribing a minimum of 10s. connected with or recommended by a Congregational Association, and delegates in proportion of one to every fifty members, with a maximum of four.

(At first, there being no London Congregational Union, the London Board was the authority, but with the formation of the London Union the Capital drew into line with the rest of the County Unions.)

" Union churches " were treated as other Congregational churches. Recognized Congregational Colleges or Societies could elect two delegates.

B. *Honorary Members.* Retired pastors whose names were passed by vote of the Assembly on the recommendation of the Committee had all the privileges of Representative Members.

C. *Associates.* Members of churches competent to appoint delegates, and pastors and members of competent churches but which did not contribute, could become Associates on payment of an annual subscription of 5s. Missionaries who had received Congregational ordination, and pastors of Colonial churches when residing in England, were eligible for Associate Membership.

Associates could attend and vote at the Assemblies but not at the Business Meetings. If an Associate Member was elected on the Committee or to office he had the privileges of a Representative Member for the time being.

The Committee was to be elected at the Annual Business Meeting and consist of 72 members, half being ministers

S

and half laymen, half from London and half from the
country. The quorum was 7, and the meetings monthly,
expenses being paid for two meetings annually, the two to
be settled by the Committee according to the importance of
the business. The Committee was to be elected at the
Business Meeting, the outgoing Committee preparing a
ballot paper containing at least 72 names. The Chairman
of the Committee was to be elected by ballot. Three standing Sub-Committees of nine members were to be appointed
annually, three being a quorum. They were :

1. *General Purposes.* To consider matters arising out of
   ordinary Union Business referred to it by the Committee, and to advise the Committee regarding the
   bearing " of public movements and political measures
   on the interests of the churches".

2. *Finance and Publications.*

3. *Literature.* To consider existing or contemplated
   publications referred to it by the Committee, to advise
   the Committee on literary projects, and to advise the
   Editor of the *Year Book.* The *Year Book's* list of
   ministers was to contain only those names furnished
   by Secretaries of Associations or of the London Board.
   Any minister whose name was already in the *Year
   Book,* though not furnished by an Association, was to
   be notified at once by the Editor.

The Chairman of the Union was to be elected at the
Business Meeting for the year beginning 1st January following. Nominations, by at least ten representative
members, were to be sent in by 15th March, those who
had held office during the previous seven years being ineligible. Withdrawals could be made by 31st March. The
names of those nominated were sent to members before-
hand, but ballot papers were supplied only to those entering
the Business Meeting. If there was no clear majority on
the first ballot the lowest name was struck off and a further
ballot held. If the last two names were equal in two successive ballots the senior in age was to be declared elected !

The Assemblies were to be on the Monday and Tuesday
after the first Wednesday in May, and on the following
Friday; the Autumnal Meeting to be at a time and place
fixed by the Committee. Papers were to be not more than

twenty minutes in length, subsequent speakers being allowed ten minutes, though this order could be suspended by the Committee when papers were not meant to open a discussion.   At the request of Local Committees the Committee could make grants in aid of Autumnal Meeting expenses not exceeding one-fourth of the total expenditure or £100.

Subscriptions were to be payable in advance, becoming due on the 1st January, the Secretary being instructed to communicate with all who had not paid their subscriptions before 31st January.   Any church, society, or college failing to pay its subscription for two years in succession was to be incompetent to elect delegates.

Grants of money could only be by vote of the General Committee and could not exceed the amount of the credit balance at the end of the preceding year.   Grants should be made by the Committee in March or April on the recommendation of the Finance Committee,   such recommendations to be stated in the summons calling the meeting.   At least half the sum granted each year was to be for the benefit of " aged and other needy ministers ", while not more than £250 a year could be reserved for literary purposes.

The Report in 1872 said that the hope that churches would enrol under the new Constitution was being fulfilled, 300 churches not previously connected with the Union having joined already, and in 1873 the number was further increased.

This Constitution governed the Union for many years, the only changes made in its general outline being in regard to the elections to the Chair and to the Committee.

1.—There was considerable dissatisfaction about the election to the Chair, and much of it crystallized round the strong personality of Joseph Parker, which aroused both animosity and admiration.   Parker was beaten by Macfadyen by 726 votes to 479 in 1881, and by Fairbairn by 489 to 439 on the third ballot in 1882, but in the following year he secured 665 out of 981 votes cast and so occupied the Chair in 1884.   These figures are a good indication of the size of the Assembly at this time, and also the outward and visible sign of much excitement. In 1881 the Committee were accused of manœuvring to keep Parker out of the Chair, and after a lively debate it was decided that henceforth there should be no nominations but an open ballot. If no one had a clear majority a ballot should then be taken on the first four names. When, under this system, Parker was defeated again (1882) the *Congregationalist* crowed in unseemly fashion :

> As it is, the result of the election must be regarded as having given the death-blow to the allegation that Dr. Parker has been kept out of the chair hitherto by official influence and the jealousy of a London clique . . .
>
> Is it too much to hope that Dr. Parker's friends will see the undesirableness of renewing the conflict? Having tried their strength twice, and having twice subjected him to the pain and humiliation of rejection, it is for them to ask themselves whether it is seemly and for the best interests of the denomination that such a conflict should be prolonged. Of course if they are bent on that destruction of the Union which Dr. Parker has avowed to be his object, and he is to be regarded as the leader of such an enterprise, there is nothing more to be said. The friends of the Union will know how to defend its interests, which are dear to them, not for any selfish purposes they have in view, but because they regard it as one of the great agencies by which the opinion and influence of the Congregational churches can be made to tell powerfully for the advancement of the national life, the strengthening of the churches, and the progress of the kingdom of the Redeemer throughout the world.
>
> Surely it must be clear now that the majority of the representatives of the churches are not prepared to stultify themselves by a vote which would practically be a condemnation of all their past policy. They are not likely to be converted from this view; and if Dr. Parker is ever to secure their suffrages it must be by the adoption of a different course from that which he has hitherto pursued.

This, however, was almost Christian compared with the sentences in which it chronicled Parker's election the following May :

> Dr. Parker having been elected chairman for 1884 by a majority so large as to prove the absence of organized action on behalf of any other candidate, . . .

To put it quite mildly, Rogers did not like Parker! Elections without nominations were, it was clear, unsatisfactory, for if there were no formal nominations, there were certain to be informal ones. As a matter of fact, when letters mentioning certain names appeared in the press, Rogers thought he had better not be left out of it, and used the *Congregationalist* to urge the claims of Edward White; another year it is interesting to find the Rev. J. M. Gibbon advocating the claims of the Secretary, Alexander Hannay! The method was generally deplored, but it held the field for some time; many other schemes were considered and rejected.

2.—The election of the Committee.

In 1884 it was decided that the 72 members of the Committee should be divided into four districts, 36 from the London District, and 12 from each of three others. The nominations were to be in writing by three representative members, and the March Committee was to appoint a special Committee to prepare a ballot paper. This method was not successful, as the next year it was reported that only 7 ballot papers had been sent in, disclosing only 4 new names. Two years later it was again reported that only 7 nomination papers had been sent in.

A New Home.

THE foundation stone of the Memorial Hall had been laid on the 10th May, 1872. The official opening took place on the 19th January, 1875, J. Remington Mills (the oldest Trustee of the old Library), who had contributed £12,000 towards the cost, presiding, the Dedicatory Prayer being offered by Dr. Stoughton. The site had cost £28,000, and with the building the total outlay was about £76,000, Samuel Morley, John Crossley, and Titus Salt giving £5,000 each and the Congregational Union £3,000. Public meetings were held during the opening week, at which addresses were delivered by well-known Congregationalists and other Free Church ministers[1], and the debt on the Hall

1 See *Year Book,* 1876, pp. 73-77.

was practically cleared during the ceremonies. An examination of the Trust Deed makes plain that the Library had first place in the minds of the founders of the Hall, a fact which subsequent Trustees have sometimes overlooked. The Trust further instructs that in letting the building, preference should be given at all times to organizations "connected with the Congregational Union of England and Wales or with some Congregational Church or School or some Association or Ministry connected with the said Congregational Union or with some Congregational Church". It provides that from any profits the sum of £5,000 should be accumulated, after which the Trustees could either continue to accumulate or not at will up to £25,000. Any subsequent surplus was to be applied, as also any money arising from the sale or mortgage of the Hall, to certain objects at the discretion of the Trustees, such as the establishment and maintenance of a theological college, exhibitions in colleges, the liquidation or reduction of any chapel debt, the building or repairing of chapels, and the augmentation of the salaries of ministers. The Trust further lays down that a report and statement of accounts shall be presented each year to the Annual Meeting of the Congregational Union,

> it being nevertheless understood that the presentation of such report is by way of information only and not for the purpose of conferring upon the said Congregational Union or any meeting or Committee thereof any authority, control or right of interference whatsoever in relation to the Hall or the Trust hereby constituted or the management thereof in anywise.

It is sometimes assumed that this proviso arose from some animus against the Congregational Union. This is extremely unlikely. It is to be remembered that most of those instrumental in raising the fund had seen the trouble caused by the Union's association with the Affiliated Societies and with the Magazines, and with that in mind they no doubt desired the Union should be free from any connexion likely to arouse difficulties. It is further to be remembered that the Union was not at this time an incorporated body. The Trustees had to be not more than

36 or fewer than 24 in number. If the names of the first nine of the London and the first nine of the country Trustees are stated it will be sufficient to dispose at once of the notion that they were men moved by any strong suspicion or dislike of the Congregational Union. They are: (London) J. Remington Mills, A. J. Shepheard, Samuel Morley, Binney, Allon, Llewellyn Bevan, Hannay, Raleigh, and Stoughton; and (Country), Balgarnie, Barrett, J. R. Campbell, Cuthbertson, Dale, Pearson, David Thomas, Alexander Thomson, and Charles Wilson. Of these, eight had already been Chairman of the Union, and two were to be elected to the Chair ere long.

The offices of the Union were at once moved to the Hall, and in 1875 both the Assemblies were held in London, the Meetings being held in the Hall and in the newly-opened City Temple, while the newly-formed London Congregational Union provided the hospitality in the autumn.

It was a lamentable fact that some of those who had taken a most active part in the Memorial Hall project had died before the opening day—not merely Joshua Wilson, but also Vaughan, Binney, George Smith, and Thomas James, the latter the younger brother of Angell James, who had been at different times Secretary of the Irish Evangelical Society, the Colonial Missionary Society, Highbury College, and the Memorial Hall Fund.

In 1880, when the Report of the Memorial Hall Trust was presented for information, an amendment was moved which showed that the Assembly was clearly of the opinion that the Hall was not sufficiently useful for the purposes of the denomination. The *Congregationalist* hoped that the Trustees would remove the causes of complaint and make such re-arrangements as would lead to reduced rents for the offices used by denominational Societies. The Report in the following year said that the Committee had interviewed the Trustees and secured alterations which would "make the Hall more serviceable for the purposes of the denomination than it had yet been". The Trustees had been handicapped in various ways, but were now again within "measurable distance" of the extinction of the debt on the Hall. In 1889 the Assembly discussed the relation of the Trustees to the Union, but no action was taken.

In reply to criticism of the administration, Hannay explained that the Hall was not built by the Congregational Union, though proceedings were initiated by that body in 1862 which led to its erection. It was built by moneys subscribed by individual benefactors, in all parts of the country, who appointed a certain body of Trustees to manage the Hall for them for the use of the Congregational body; Counsel's opinion was that the Union could not deal with the Annual Report of the Trust as a document to be accepted or rejected, but the whole spirit of the Trust was that the Trustees should be kept in sympathetic contact with the whole Congregational body as it was represented in the Assembly.

New Societies.

I. *The Congregational Total Abstinence Association.*

An entire change had come over the attitude of Congregationalists to the use of intoxicants since the days when the Union was founded. Then total abstainers, as we have seen, were regarded as fanatics, doing more harm than good. As late as 1840 one of their mentors thus, advised them :

> If, then, the friends of total abstinence would give birth to general confidence in the righteousness of their cause, and if they would not foster a false and ignorant zeal, which must speedily consume itself, and, perhaps, may provoke to fresh and aggravated forms of intemperance, let them principally, if not exclusively, dwell on the moral elements of the question, let them cease to impeach the motives of their neighbours, and let them beware of seeming to make the ordinances of the gospel and the duties of religion merely supplementary to the claims and engagements which arise out of the cause of temperance. It must, indeed, be obvious to themselves that when injudicious means, or rash and violent expedients, are adopted, the end which they contemplate, however desirable and praiseworthy, must be defeated, or, at all events, must be indefinitely delayed,

simply because general opinion becomes enlisted against
them, either as self-conceited mountebanks, or as officious
censors and public aggressors.   If they would study, and
endeavour to reduce to practice, the beautiful philosophy
contained in the fable of the sun and the wind, it cannot
be doubted that fresh accessions would be duly made to their
numbers, and that their cause would be crowned with
triumphs to which it has hitherto been a stranger, and to
which it must for ever remain such, until its friends are
distinguished by more of that charity which "thinketh no
evil", and less of that zeal which is destitute of knowledge,
than has hitherto fallen to the lot of not a few who have
gathered around the standard of total abstinence.

These brief remarks are made, not in the spirit of
hostility, but in that of regret, at finding a cause which has
undoubtedly originated in benevolence, and is destined
hereafter to expand into something commanding and
efficient, crippled and encumbered by the ignorance, rashness, and extravagance of many who profess to be its
friends.   Nor will they have been made in vain, should
they, in the remotest degree, lead to the exercise of more
of the wisdom of the serpent combined with the harmless-
ness of the dove, on the part of the friends of temperance,
and thus tend to give stability to the plans, and secure certain, if not rapid, success to the operations of a Society
whose great principles are evidently in accordance with
the genius and design of the gospel.

Subsequently churches were often divided as a result of
agitation on the question.   Some churches wanted to make
total abstinence a test of membership; in others the use of
wine at Communion caused trouble.   Discussion took place
in the *Congregational Magazine* on what was to be the
attitude of a church to a member who regularly absented
himself from the Communion on temperance grounds.
Slowly but surely, however, the advocates of total abstinence convinced their critics, and the question forced
itself on the notice of the Assembly.   It was in large
measure the new Secretary's enthusiasm for total abstinence
that led to definite action.   A resolution on intemperance
had been passed at the 1860 Assembly, and during the
Assembly at Bristol in 1865 there was a public breakfast
and meeting for the advocacy of temperance principles.   In
his autumn address in 1866, Newman Hall pleaded for

more attention to practical questions, and asked if the time had not arrived for the temperance movement to receive the Union's attention. In May, 1869, the Union,

> deploring the facilities for intemperance offered by the excessive multiplication of public-houses and beershops, and convinced that the main hope of diminishing vice, pauperism, and crime, is to be found in an amended regulation of the liquor traffic, has observed with high satisfaction the unanimous assent of the House of Commons to the principle of the Bill proposed by Sir H. J. Selwyn Ibbetson for suspending, during two years, the licensing power of the Excise; while at the same time, this Assembly expresses the most earnest hope that Her Majesty's Government will, before the expiration of that period, lay before Parliament, and support with all the influence of the Crown, a measure for conferring the licensing power upon some authority amenable to public opinion, and likely to consult the physical and moral interests of the people.

At Wolverhampton, in the same year, a memorial from the local Temperance Society was welcomed and this resolution adopted:

> That this Assembly, cheerfully recognizes the great good which has been accomplished by temperance organizations, [and] heartily wishing them increasing success; and it invites the attention of the members of the Union to any Bills which may be submitted to Parliament for the limitation or suppression of the sale of intoxicating liquors on the Lord's day, and generally to any measures which may have for their object the lessening of facilities for intemperance and its numerous attendant evils, in the hope that they may be able to give them their support.

Temperance resolutions are thereafter common, and in 1873 the Treasurer of the United Kingdom Alliance gave a breakfast during the Autumn meetings at Ipswich, when the formation of a Congregational Total Abstinence Association was mooted. This was duly formed in 1874, Baines being President and Morley Treasurer. Its object was "to extend the principles and practice of total abstinence in Congregational Churches, and to assist in promoting the cause of Temperance throughout the land". The methods to be adopted were "the formation and encouragement of Temperance Societies and Bands of Hope in connexion with the Churches, and sermons, lectures, conferences, and the circulation of temperance literature, *etc.*". Membership was open to ministers and deacons, delegates to the Union, and students of the colleges, who were abstainers. Other Congregational abstainers could be members on payment of an annual subscription of 5s.

At almost every subsequent Assembly there was some mention of temperance. A special Committee was appointed to enquire into intemperance[1]. There were protests against various licensing proposals, and resolutions in favour of Sunday closing. Memorials were received stressing total abstinence and asking for the use of unfermented wine at Communion. At the end of this period three-quarters of the ministers were abstainers and nine-tenths of the students. In 1890 the Union made a grant of £50 on condition that the £250 deficit on the Total Abstinence Society was cleared.

II. *Young People*: *Congregational Guilds*.

At Bristol in 1882 a movement began which was to lead to the formation of a Department for Work Among Young People. It was then decided to appoint a Committee to prepare a plan for examinations for young people in Bible Knowledge and Congregational History and Principles. An elaborate scheme[2] was drawn up and accepted by the Assembly in May, 1883. Candidates must be sixteen ; they could take two of the three subjects—Scripture, History and Doctrine; Christian Evidences; and Ecclesiastical Polity, with special reference to the principles and history of the Free Churches. Essays could also be submitted. The examinations were to be held annually in March. 817 candidates entered in the first year, but only 592 sat, while the following year the number sitting was only 325. Various reasons were assigned for this "comparative failure", and disappointment had to be chronicled in subsequent years.

1 For the "Practical Suggestions" contained in the Report of this Committee see *Year Book*, 1883, pp. 25-6.

2 See *Year Book*, 1884, pp. 14-15.

In 1889 the conduct of the examination was taken over by the National Council of Congregational Guilds, which came into existence in a peculiar way. A Sectional Meeting in October, 1885, asked the Committee to form a Society to promote social purity; the Committee agreed, though pointing out that the resolution of a Sectional Conference did not commit the Union. In 1887 it was suggested that the best way of reaching the desired end was by the formation of Guilds in each church, these being affiliated to a National Council. A strong Guild Committee was formed, including Mr. J. H. Whitley, afterwards to be Speaker of the House of Commons. The Inaugural Meeting of the National Council of Guilds was held in the City Temple on May 11th, 1888, Mr. Edward Spicer presiding, addresses being given by Dr. Macfadyen, the Rev. J. R. Bailey, Dr. Parker, and Dr. F. E. Clark, the founder of the Christian Endeavour Movement. A similar meeting was held at Nottingham in the autumn, Mr. Arnold Pye-Smith presiding, and the Revs. W. J. Woods, R. F. Horton and C. A. Berry speaking. A Constitution was approved in 1889, and during the May Meeting a public meeting was held at which Urijah Thomas, Hirst Hollowell and John Clifford spoke, and after which a number of "Lantern Transparencies, belonging to the Congregational Union, were exhibited and elucidations given by Rev. George Critchley". The Guilds drew up a Handbook, but they did not breathe new life into the examinations, only 223 sitting in 1890, though the Report for the previous year shows that the celebration of the bicentenary of the Revolution of 1688 had increased interest, 3,000 of the textbook, which the R.T.S. supplied at half-price, being sold.

In 1891 quite an elaborate programme was carried through[1]. A yearly letter was now sent to the young people of the churches, and "Occasional Papers" published; experiments were tried in regard to the examination; and in May

---

[1] The Report of the National Council of Congregational Guilds, adopted 14th May, 1891, printed in the *Year Book*, 1892, pp. 22-24, gives a good idea of the Council's activities.

a meeting was held at which Dr. F. E. Clark was again present. Hannay did much to encourage this enterprise, and, in addition to those just mentioned, F. Herbert Stead was extremely active.

Publishing.

It was not until the Hannay *régime* was well advanced that the Union decided to do its own publishing. It had taken the responsibility for a new series of Congregational Lectures, the third of which, Dale's *Atonement,* proved to be a "best seller". Published in 1875, these Lectures were in their fourth edition in the following year, and in their seventh in 1878. Possibly this success suggested that it was just as sensible for the Union to have the entire profits as to share them with an outside publisher. In 1881 a sub-committee was appointed "to consider the desirability of (1) having a book saloon at the Memorial Hall for the distribution of the publications of the Union; (2) appointing a special officer to superintend this department; (3) publishing the works of the Union from the Offices of the Union; and (4) taking any other means to increase the efficiency and circulation of Congregational literature". For a long time the matter hung fire, and it was not until 1888 that the denomination fell into line with other denominations and began to publish, though the book room was still in the future, not being opened until 1894. The Report in 1889 said the Department was giving entire satisfaction.

It was well this step was taken, for the Union was now beginning to branch out and to publish something more than the "Tracts" of the early days. Apart from the Lectures, the most important of its ventures during these years was, without doubt, Dale's *Manual of Congregational Principles*. Since the Jubilee of 1881 he and Rogers had been touring the country on a speaking campaign for Congregationalism similar to that which they had conducted for the Liberation Society shortly before. In his speeches Dale expounded Congregational principles with a fervour and intensity of conviction never before equalled, and, when the institution of Young People's examinations caused a demand for textbooks, Dale was asked to supply both a *History* and an account of the principles of the Congregational Churches. The *History* was not published until long after Dale's death, and then it had grown into far more than a textbook! The *Manual* appeared in 1884, and it at once gave rise to controversy. Dale had included a chapter on "The Sacraments" in the volume; on this subject his views differed from those of the majority of contemporary Independents, and were by some suspected of being sacerdotal. His son's *Life*[1] describes his doctrine of the Sacraments. Rogers analysed it in the *Congregationalist,* while Paxton Hood and Spurgeon attacked it from opposite sides, the latter saying :

> The doctrines of the body would seem to be in a gelatinous condition, and backbone is out of the question. The metal of Independent faith is just now in a fluid state, and may take any form out of a thousand, though at present it shows a preference for the moulds of heterodoxy. There were Independents once; thank God there are some such still.

Considerable stir was created, and eventually it was decided, with Dale's consent, to publish the volume in two forms, one of them omitting the third and fourth books, ("The Christian Sacraments and Christian Worship" and "Some Practical Aspects of Congregationalism").

The story of the Magazines during this period is soon told. Dale edited the *Congregationalist* from 1872 to 1878, though even then he did not escape criticism, some people thinking that his views on immortality, as well as on the Sacraments, made it dangerous for him to be in the editorial chair. His successor was J. G. Rogers. In 1876, after a communication from the Trustees of the *Christian Witness* Fund, the Committee gave a guarantee for that year against loss up to £50, and considered taking over the Magazines once more. A proposal was made to the Assembly to this effect, Allon moving a delaying amendment. Eventually a compromise was, reached on the motion of Hannay and

[1] pp. 354, ff.

Rogers, the question being referred back to the Committee
for reconsideration, pecuniary arrangements being made
with the Trustees in the meantime. The Trustees finally
withdrew their application, making other arrangements
for carrying on the papers; otherwise the Committee had
decided to recommend

> that in the divided state of opinion in the Union on the
> question of taking over the *Congregationalist* and the
> *Christian Penny Magazine,* it is not desirable that further
> steps should be taken.

The *Christian's Penny Magazine* ended its course in
1881, apparently being merged in the *Congregational
Magazine*, the journal of the amalgamated Church Aid
and Home Missionary Society, under the editorship of
the Rev. E. J. Hartland, J. H. Wilson's successor as
Secretary of the Home Missionary Society. In 1883 this
Magazine had a circulation of 18,500. In 1884 the Rev.
D. Burford Hooke was co-editor, and a loss was reported,
though there was a small profit in 1885.

The *Congregationalist* continued to lose money, and it
disappeared in 1886. The *British Quarterly* ended its long
and distinguished course in the same year, and 1887 saw
a new venture, edited by J. G. Rogers, and published by
Fisher Unwin, with the name *The Congregational Review*,
for two years as a monthly, then for two years as a quarterly; this was only short lived, dying in 1890.

Hymn Books.

IN 1871 the Committee reluctantly decided that a *Supplement* to the *Hymn Book* must be prepared, recognizing
that in twelve years "a great change of opinion and feeling
has taken place in the churches with regard to the forms
which the Service of Praise should assume" and that a
large addition had meantime been made in the number of
good hymns. The *Supplement*, published in 1874, contained 281 hymns. It was criticized by Baldwin Brown in
1878 because of "the number of hysterically-sentimental
hymns".

In 1875 an *Abridged Congregational Hymn Book* containing 270 hymns selected from the *Hymn Book* and the *Supplement* was published to replace the *Smaller Congregational Hymn Book*.

In 1879 it was decided that a new Sunday School Hymn Book was required, and the Rev. G. S. Barrett of Norwich was appointed Editor. This was published in 1880 under the title of *A Congregational Hymnal or Book of Praise for the Young*. Barrett's success in this enterprise led to his being entrusted with the preparation of a new *Congregational Hymnal,* the music being in the hands of Dr. E. J. Hopkins and Josiah Booth. There was considerable delay, and it was not until October, 1887 that it was issued. It contained 775 hymns, 147 chants and 85 anthems. The Report in 1888 said that 80,000 copies had been sold during the winter, and this number was increased to 200,000 by the end of the year. The Editors received £550 for their services. Barrett's next task was a *Mission Hymnal,* containing 300 Hymns; this appeared in 1890. In 1891 sales were reported thus :

Hymn Book	...	...	44,000
Hymnal	...	...	68,000
Mission Hymnal	...	...	28,000

A new *Sunday School Hymn Book* was published in August, 1891, and sold to the extent of 40,000 copies by May, 1892.

RELATIONS WITH OTHER CHURCHES.

I. Nonconformist.

In 1871, after E. J. Hartland's paper on "Arrangements with other Bodies of Nonconformists to prevent the Multiplication of Weak Churches", it was resolved to summon a Conference, and in March, 1872, about 200 Baptist, Presbyterian, Methodist, and Congregational representatives met under Morley's chairmanship. The "undue multiplication" of churches in thinly populated areas was deplored and a Committee appointed, but the Union expressed disappointment that so much time was occupied in discussing the points of difference between Baptists and Congregationalists. In 1873 it was agreed that conference

[Photo : Lafayette

W. B. SELBIE

A. M. FAIRBAIRN

P. T. FORSYTH

for religious purposes with other Free Evangelical Churches was desirable, but the Report in 1874 said that such a conference had been, under pressure of other work, necessarily postponed, complaint being made that the resources of the Union did not allow, in addition to the ordinary administration, sufficient margin to carry on the correspondence in regard to Church Finance, Sunday School statistics, and this Conference of the Free Churches.

In 1875 John Kennedy stressed the need for co-operation between Nonconformists, urging that there ought to be colleges with room for Baptist, Presbyterian, Methodist, and Congregational students. In October, 1878, the Committee was authorized to try to arrange a Free Church conference, but they found this too delicate a matter to handle—perhaps the excitement aroused by the Leicester Conference made it so—and they reported that a private individual (Samuel Morley?) was summoning a preliminary meeting. In 1885 the Union co-operated with the London Union in trying to come to a friendly arrangement with the Presbyterians about the church at Tooting, a majority of the congregation of which, in opposition to their Trust Deed, had decided to become Presbyterians. Unfortunately the matter was not settled without recourse to law, and the Union funds eventually suffered to the extent of £500. A set-off against this was the joint Assembly with the Baptists in 1886, in which year a sectional meeting, after a paper on "The Injury to Religion, and the Peril to Free Churches, arising from Denominational Competition" read by the Rev. R. M. Davies, adopted a resolution asking the Committee to summon a conference between the Congregationalists and other Evangelicals to prevent overlapping. A Committee met with the Baptists on this and kindred subjects, but in 1888 it was reported that further conference was inopportune, probably owing to the Down Grade Controversy which was just then causing dissension in the Baptist camp. In 1890 a correspondent having suggested a federal union of Free Churches the Assembly referred the matter to the Committee. In 1891 a resolution was passed saying that

The holding of a Free Church congress, at such intervals as may be thought best, would, in its judgment, be of incalculable advantage. In order to its success it might be necessary that in the first instance it should be a Congress, not of Churches, but of individuals. Its practical utility would, however, be enormously increased if the representative bodies would co-operate in organizing the same. That this Union instructs the Committee to forward this resolution to the representative bodies of other Free Churches and to open negotiations which may lead to the summoning of such an assembly, if possible, in the course of 1892.

Men like Berry and Mackennal played a large part in these schemes, which led to the formation of the Free Church Council.

It is interesting to note as a sign of still wider sympathies that in 1889 the Union sent a message of sympathy to General Booth on the persecution of one of the Salvation Army officers in Switzerland.

II. The Established Church.

IN 1875 the influence of the conciliatory spirit of men like Dean Stanley and Dean Alford was reflected in a Union discussion concerning the desire of some episcopal clergymen to take part in Nonconformist worship. The Assembly reciprocated the fraternal feeling prompting that desire, but it could not

regard any movement in this reform as likely to be successful in the face of the sacerdotal pretensions of one large portion of the clergy, and the assertion of State-Church privilege by another large portion; and it has ceased to hope that a right relation will be established between the several Christian communities in the land until all shall be stripped of distinctive State privileges, and left free to frame their own laws.

In this period deputations of Anglicans as well as of Free Churchmen began to appear at the Autumnal gatherings[1]. In October, 1880, a long resolution cordially responded to the Archbishop of Canterbury's hope that the passing of the Burials Act would improve the relations between Churchmen and Nonconformists, and also to the

---

1 The first was at Bristol in 1882.

liberal sentiments expressed by the Bishop of Peter-
borough, the President of the Church Congress, and other
speakers.

In 1889 the receipt of the Lambeth Encyclical was reported with its desire for corporate reunion on the basis of
the Lambeth Quadrilateral—

> (a) The Holy Scriptures of the Old and New Testa-
> ments, as "containing all things necessary to salvation",
> and as being the rule and ultimate standard of faith.   (b)
> The Apostles' Creed, as the Baptismal Symbol; and the
> Nicene Creed, as the sufficient statement of the Christian
> faith.   (c) The two Sacraments ordained by Christ Him-
> self—Baptism and the Supper of the Lord—ministered with
> unfailing use of Christ's words of Institution, and of the
> elements ordained by Him.   (d) The Historic Episcopate,
> locally adapted in the methods of its administration to the
> varying needs of the nations and peoples called of God into
> the Unity of His Church.

The reply adopted in the Autumn Assembly[1] deplored
the ecclesiastical divisions of the country and welcomed
"every movement towards catholicity of feeling and conduct".   Conference, united worship, common deliberation
on common tasks, were all desirable, but the limitations of
the suggested Conference " to questions touching
ecclesiastical incorporation" deprived the proposal of much
of its value.   Unity in diversity was truer unity than
ecclesiastical incorporation.   The fourth article was "an
insuperable obstacle in the way of conference".   It meant,

> not union with a sister Church, but incorporation into a
> system against which they have been an historical and
> continuous protest.   There is a sense in which we not only
> hold the "Historic Episcopate", but maintain that it is fully
> realized in our midst and by our Churches.   Our pastors
> are bishops, and we strenuously affirm and teach that their
> "episcopate" is at once primitive and historical, i.e., after
> the form instituted of Christ, observed and enjoined by His
> Apostles.   This office our pastors hold by Divine authority,
> and through Divine appointment, their institution being of
> Christ, who acts through the voice and election of the
> Churches, whose one and common Head He is.   This view
> of the Episcopate is our historical inheritance, and we con-

[1] For the full Reply see *Year Book*, 1891, pp. 20-22.

strue it as no mere matter of polity or ritual, but as of the essence or nature of the Church, necessary to its complete dependence on Christ, and involving its no less complete independence of the State. This conception of the Church, held as a matter of deep and settled conviction by Congregationalists, and derived as they believe from the New Testament, is the very thing it is here proposed that they surrender as a condition preliminary to a conference on "Home Re-union". This is a surrender they cannot make; and ought not to be expected to be able to make; and we therefore feel compelled to decline a conference which would allow such a surrender to seem possible.

The Assemblies of Hannay's Reign.

The Assemblies grew in size during the years—at Bradford in 1876 the numbers are given as 1,000. It is strange that Bradford seems to have been so attractive to delegates; in 1892 nearly 1,400 attended the Autumn Sessions there. The increased size made the problem of hospitality in the autumn extremely difficult, and in 1882 the inviting towns were relieved from the pecuniary responsibility for a dinner, and in 1885 hospitality was asked for the minister and one representative from each church only.

The form of the Assemblies was by this time more or less stereotyped, the Colonial and London Missionary Societies having their Sermons and Public Meetings, and the L.M.S. often an evening Valedictory Service for departing missionaries. At Bristol in 1882 there was a morning Communion Service at 8.30. In 1877 the first non-Congregationalist was invited to preach the official Sermon, Alexander McLaren being the appropriate choice. In 1886 a Joint Assembly with the Baptists was held, the Meetings being held in London in April.

In 1877 two laymen, both Members of Parliament, Samuel Morley and Henry Richard, the latter the Secretary of the Peace Society, were nominated for the Chair, and both desired to retire. Richard, who was an ex-minister, was prevailed upon to stand, and was duly elected. This definitely raised the question of the eligibility of laymen for the Chair, and it was decided that as the Union's laws left the matter open laymen were not

debarred from occupying the position.   The Union did
not show any undue anxiety to follow this precedent.   It
was not until 1886 that another layman was elected, and
then Samuel Morley declined to serve, and it was a
minister, Alexander Mackennal, whom the Committee
invited to fill the post.   The election in 1886 definitely dis-
poses of the tradition that Hannay never stood for election
to the Chair.   At that time the election was by open ballot,
and, if no one obtained a clear majority of votes cast, by
further ballot of the first four names.   The result of the
election in this year was :

		Morley.	Hannay.	Mackennal.	Bruce.	Distributed.
1st	...	101	132	150	132	238
2nd	...	188	206	162	151	
3rd	...	262	267	109		
4th	...	345	138			

Allon was called to the Chair for the second time for the
Jubilee Year in 1881, a well-deserved honour and one
which had so far fallen only to Joseph Fletcher, who presided at one of the 1831 sessions and again in 1837.   It was
generally to men in the pastorate that the Assembly turned
for Chairmen, and sometimes competition was keen.

In 1888 a fine tribute was paid to a great missionary,
Griffith John, in far-away China, being elected, but he was
unable to accept office.

The Addresses by the Chairman and others were now
a great attraction, while occasionally they profoundly
moved the Assembly and gave a new turn to policy.   A
masterly speech by Fairbairn at Hanley, in 1885, on "The
Sacerdotal and Puritan Idea" roused the audience to
frantic applause, during which Dale said to Fairbairn,
" There now, you have built Mansfield College, top-stone
and all ".   It is interesting to have Dale's comment on
this speech, for in 1876 he had said that Hannay's effort
in moving the acceptance of the Report of the Finance
Conference, a speech that lasted for an hour,

> was one of the finest ever delivered in the Assembly.   The
> only speech at all comparable to it, so far as we remember,
> was that made by Dr. Vaughan in 1862 on the celebration
> of the Bicentenary of the ejectment of the Two Thousand.

Some of these speeches were of unconscionable length, but we read of the Assembly rising again and again to applaud speakers who had held the floor for an hour and a half! There is only one thing more surprising to the modern student, and that is that people were found to read the speeches when printed. Sometimes in the *Nonconformist and Independent* of this period there are pages of four columns absolutely solid, without the least attempt to aid the reader by paragraphs or headings. One of Edward White's Chairman's Addresses in 1886 occupies 45 pages in the *Year Book*. And this in spite of the fact that when Fairbairn had spoken for an hour and forty minutes in 1883 a correspondent had written to the *Nonconformist and Independent* asking if it would not be wise to take the Chairman's Address as read. Parker immediately went one better in 1884, his Address occupying two hours ten minutes.

At this point just a glimpse must be had of the Assembly's attitude to the work of Congregationalism abroad. Commendation of the Societies forming the " British Missions " was expressed from time to time, both before and after the cessation (1880) of the united appeal to the churches. Great interest was taken in the work of Evangelical Protestantism on the Continent. Pressensé spoke at the Assembly in 1872, and repeated references were made to R. W. McAll's Mission in Paris[1]. In 1885 it was decided to send a delegation to the Synod of the Churches in France, and support was regularly given to the Colonial Society for its work on the Continent. The visits of Dale and Spicer, and of Hannay and Lee, to Australia in successive years did much to stimulate the work of the Colonial Society.

The L.M.S. felt in 1882 that the churches in Jamaica could no longer be regarded as within its sphere, and asked the Union to consider its responsibility for them. A joint deputation was sent to the West Indies, and later an appeal was made to the churches for a fund to help the Congrega-

---

[1] A good summary of this work may be found in the *Year Book*, 1885, pp. 460-461, ff.

tional Unions of both British Guiana and Jamaica, this appeal being backed by the Union and by the L.M.S. In 1890 the L.M.S. again raised the question of churches in the West Indies and the Cape which were now settled and could no longer be regarded as within the enterprise of foreign missions. The hope was expressed by the Union Committee that the International Congregational Council would help to solve the problem created by such churches. The co-operation between the Union and the L.M.S. in regard to Jamaica and British Guiana suggested the possibility of some kind of amalgamation, or at the least, closer co-operation. In October, 1889, the Report of a special committee appointed to confer with the Directors of the L.M.S. on these lines was adopted. It said that

> any change in the title or constitution of the London Missionary Society which would give it an express denominational character would be inexpedient.

Nevertheless, considering that the constituency, the Directorate, and the missionaries of the Society were so largely Congregational, closer working connexion with the churches was esteemed necessary, and it was therefore desirable that provision should be made for direct representation of the County Associations on the Board of Directors and for the representation of the L.M.S. on the County platforms. Devotional Conferences in different parts of the country, arranged by the Union and the Society, should be held from time to time, and the hope was expressed that the Union would see that the claims of foreign missions had a due place in its Assemblies.

Sympathy was expressed in 1883 with the churches of Madagascar in their hardships, and in other ways it was shown that the denomination's concern for foreign missions had not diminished.

It now remains to sum up the resolutions of the Union on public questions, and then to describe Hannay's greatest achievement, the formation of the Church Aid and Home Missionary Society.

Public Questions.

Only a cursory glance can be given at the Union's

manifold activities in these wide fields during two crowded and exciting decades. Loyal messages were sent to the Queen in times of joy and sorrow. Until the Home Rule split similar loyal messages were sent to Gladstone, their tone being exemplified in the resolution on the Affirmation Bill in 1883 :

> That the Assembly hereby records its extreme regret at the reactionary vote by which a majority of the House of Commons has rejected the Affirmation Bill, checked the course of Liberal legislation commenced fifty years ago in the repeal of the Test and Corporation Acts, and carried still further in the Act for Roman Catholic Emancipation and the Relief of Jewish Disabilities, and at the same time expresses gratitude to the minority who were faithful to the principle of religious liberty, and especially to their venerated leader, the Prime Minister, for his exposition and defence of those principles with an eloquence so lofty and in a spirit so eminently Christian.

Strong support was given him during his campaign against the atrocities in the Near East, and vigorous resolutions were passed against Disraeli's policy, and especially the " unnecessary and therefore criminal wars " in Afghanistan and Africa. The result of the 1880 election was acclaimed, and in 1884 the Union sent to the Prime Minister a message " expressive of unabated confidence ". The wide range of the Union's survey of politics may be seen in May, 1885, when, after resolutions on Disestablishment and the new voters, Rogers moved and Parker seconded this motion on behalf of the Reference Committee :

> That this Assembly, meeting at a crisis in public affairs when the nation has reason to rejoice in the brightening prospects of peace, humbly and gratefully magnifies the good hand of God in the removal of the anxieties by which the heart of the people has been oppressed, and devoutly prays that the hopes which have been awakened may be consummated in the honourable and permanent settlement of the differences between this country and Russia, and in the enjoyment of a period of peace abroad, and of progress—social, commercial, political, and religious—at home.
> That this Assembly congratulates the Ministry, and

and Edward Crossley, strongly condemned the Acts.
Ladies were asked to retire during the discussion, and four
of them entered a protest in the papers. One of them referred to the fact that when, three years before, women
members of Congregational Churches desired to present a
memorial on temperance to the Assembly, a member of
the Committee had remarked, "We have nothing to do with
the women", and they had only been allowed to present
the memorial on condition that not a word was spoken in
support.

In 1885 G. S. Reaney and C. Fleming Williams had
given notice of a motion expressing satisfaction at the
passing of the Criminal Law Amendment Bill, and
sympathy with W. T. Stead in his imprisonment, but it
was crowded out. In 1887, at Leeds, a memorial was
adopted without discussion, protesting with astonishment,
indignation, and shame against the introduction of licensed
prostitution into the Indian Empire and various Crown
Colonies. It is to be hoped that the Committee dealt
adequately with some matters that were not considered at
the Assembly for lack of time, as, for example, with the
request of the National Labourers' Union that churches
should be encouraged to allow the Agricultural Union to
hold its meetings in their schoolrooms instead of in the
public-houses to which they were often driven.

In general, however, the period marked a greatly
increased recognition of, and sympathy with, the rights of
the working classes. A public meeting for working men
was held in Ipswich in 1873, and in May, 1874, in urging
arbitration in the Farm Labourers' Lock-out, the Union
expressed " its strong sympathy with the effort of the
agricultural labourers to elevate their moral and social
position ".

In 1885 a message from the Railway Servants' Congress
was received with thanksgiving, and sympathy expressed
with the movement for the limitation of Sunday labour,
and when the same Congress in 1889 asked for help in its
fight for shorter hours and the reduction of Sunday labour
its aims were warmly approved.

Altogether the Union began to show itself concerned with social justice in a way that was quite new. The publication of Andrew Mearns's *Bitter Cry of Outcast London* in 1883 led both to conference with other Free Churches and to Assembly discussions on the Relation of the Churches to the Poor.   In these, G. S. Reaney and C. Fleming Williams were most prominent, and sometimes the vigour with which they urged views akin to those propounded by "Christian Socialists" led to mild "scenes". Nevertheless, although in 1884 the Assembly shirked accepting an amendment which talked openly about "better wages", in May, 1885, this resolution was carried :

> That this Assembly, while deprecating all action that would lessen the sanctions of the rights of property, and recognizing the conditions which at the present time control the markets both of labour and material, affirms it to be the duty of every Christian citizen to seek by all means in his power to diminish the inequalities which unjust laws and customs produce in the condition of those who are common members of the State, to endeavour to bring about such changes in the modes of property in land as shall lead to a fairer distribution of it among the people, to a more profitable employment of it in the production of the common food of the people, to the better housing of the poor, and the relief of the overcrowding of the cities; and, further, that it calls upon every Christian man and woman to remember that the so-called laws of trade and economics are not the only rules which should direct the transactions of manufacturers, traders, labourers, and purchasers.

Support was given to the British and Foreign Anti-Slavery Society, and in 1875 the Admiralty's new regulations on fugitive slaves were strongly condemned, the Opium Traffic was once more denounced, and £105 sent to the Indian Famine Fund.

The question of Home Rule in Ireland split the Union as it split the Liberal Party.   United in abhorrence of the Phœnix Park murders, when matters settled down after the 1885 and 1886 elections it was clear that while the majority of Congregationalists still stood with Gladstone, a considerable minority, led by Dale, were with Chamberlain. Previously, when Congregationalism was almost

entirely Liberal, it had been easy to introduce political
resolutions on the Union platform, but now there were
difficulties. The situation was not made any easier by
frequent references to those Nonconformists who had joined
the Liberal Unionists as " the cream of Nonconformity ",
and it led, most regrettably, not merely to the cessation of
Dale's political activity, but to his withdrawal from active
participation in the work of the Congregational Union.
In 1887 the Assembly decided that there should be a resolution on Ireland, and it was moved in these terms by
Parker :

> That the Assembly, feeling it " a cause of deepest
> regret that in the year of Jubilee there should be so violent
> a discord between Her Majesty's Government and the
> majority of the Irish nation ", records its protest against
> the coercion policy of Her Majesty's present advisers, and
> is of opinion that justice and conciliation would best serve
> to perpetuate the union between the two countries.

Only about 25 voted against this resolution, and when the
previous question was moved on the ground that " as
religious men the Union had nothing to do with the Irish
question ", it was ruled out of order, the proposer's plea
for the severance of religion from politics being utterly
rejected by the Assembly.

The following May Mr. Gladstone appeared at the
Memorial Hall to address a great meeting of Nonconformist ministers.

It was in October, 1888, that Mr. Edward Crossley, in
seconding a resolution on the Royal Commission on
Education, which included thanks to Dale and Richard for
their services, aroused the applause of the Assembly
by saying that the Liberal Unionists were " chained to the
Tory chariot " and had " denied their principles ". At
this same Assembly a special meeting was held, with the
consent of the Committee, to consider a resolution once
more condemning the coercion policy of the Government in
Ireland. In order to avoid repeated controversies in the
Union on questions " on which it was not necessary for
the Union to speak ", Dale withdrew from association with
it. In 1891, while adhering to his resolve, he attended, at

the Committee's request, to speak on the death of Hannay. In 1894, in his final illness, the Assembly sent to him a most cordial telegram of sympathy and of gratitude for all his services, by which he was greatly cheered.

HANNAY'S ACHIEVEMENTS.

Turning now to the main constructive items in Hannay's work, it is necessary to consider—

(1) The formation of the Church Aid and Home Missionary Society;

(2) The International Congregational Council.

(1) *The Church Aid and Home Missionary Society.*

When Hannay came to the Secretarial Chair the question of a Sustentation Fund was under discussion. In 1871 the Committee said that there was nothing to report as a result of communications with the County Associations, and in the following year it was said that the Counties' replies were too general to be of service.

Chronologically the next indication of closer co-operation between the churches is seen in the discussions of the American " Councils of Reference " already mentioned[1]. Some Associations having adopted these, a long discussion took place in the Assemblies of 1872 and 1873, at the end of which it was resolved to give approval to the idea of closer fellowship between the churches, and ask the County Associations for answers to certain specific questions, so that, if thought well, a plan could be prepared for submission to the churches. At this time, as may be gathered from the Report in 1874, there was much pressure of business, and no further steps in the matter seem to have been taken.

In the autumn of 1872 a definite move forward was made. J. Carvell Williams, in a paper on Church Finance[2], spoke not merely of methods by which the churches should maintain their own finances, but argued that the facts and figures showed the need of a Stipend Augmentation Fund by which stipends could be raised 15 per cent or 20 per cent. Referring back to a sugges-

1 p. 246.
2 *Year Book,* 1873, pp. 124-127.

tion of Henry Lee's in 1867, he proposed that a conference of deacons and other laymen should be called to consider the methods of raising funds, and more especially

> for securing such an increase of ministerial stipends as is earnestly called for, with regard both to the present condition of the Congregational body and the circumstances of the time.

At this time there are indications from several sides that Hannay was gathering various strings into his hands. His Report in 1873 gives two pages to " Congregational Societies "—" British Missions ", the English and London Chapel Building Societies, and the Pastors' Retiring Fund—prefixed by the statement :

> The policy of the Union, for many years, has been to give to the Societies, originated at its meetings for express services, an independent existence and management. This the Constitution of the Union necessitates; but the Committee are anxious that while their autonomy is preserved, the several Congregational Societies should be recognized in the meetings of the Union, and in its reports of work done, and that opportunity should be given them from time to time to plead their cause in the Assembly.

This fact, and the suggestion made a little later that the Union should again take over the magazines, seem to argue in favour of the view that Hannay's centralization policy was deliberately conceived.

Be that as it may, he so guided affairs that in December, 1873, the Finance Conference suggested by Carvell Williams met at Birmingham under the presidency of Henry Lee. It consisted of 58 laymen appointed by the County Unions. It presented an Interim Report in May, 1874, and asked that the Union should summon another laymen's conference in June, twice the size in order to make it more representative, although the Warwickshire Union had protested against the exclusion of ministers. The Interim Report dealt with such matters as conscientious giving[1], the regular payment of stipends, and

---

[1] It was in one of the discussions at this time that Edward White told the Assembly of T. T. Lynch's announcement to his congregation : "The collections on Sunday last were two pounds, two shillings, and two pence, and, I might add, too little".

the grouping of small churches, and put the minimum stipend desired at £100 for the country and £150 in towns. New churches were recommended to use the weekly offering system entirely, older churches, where pew rents were an established tradition, to use weekly offerings as far as possible. The enlarged Conference met at Leicester in June and reported in October. Vigorous and animated discussion was aroused, not merely by the two clauses relating to the weekly offering system, which were deferred, but by the further recommendation that a Board of Finance should be formed for supplementing stipends and promoting Congregational Missions. Regarding the existing arrangements as insufficient, the Conference recommended that the Funds at present administered by the several County Associations should be under the control of the Board, which, in order not to weaken local organizations and to secure an impartial administration, should be composed exclusively of representatives of County Associations, 120 in number, two-thirds non-ministerial, the proportion of representation being determined by the number of church members in each Association. In the words of the 1875 Report the principles of the plan were :

1. The consolidation of the funds now raised for Home Missionary operations, and for aiding weak churches, especially those of the County Associations, in one national fund, with the view of providing means by which more efficiently than at present the strong may help the weak.

2. The preservation of the present County Associations as constituents of the organism of the new Finance Body, each county to be a district of the General Association, through which (though not exclusively) moneys would be administered.

3. The constitution of the Board to be strictly representative, and guarantees to be taken against partiality and inefficiency of administration.

On Hannay's motion the plan, after being adopted *nem. con.*, was referred to the Associations for consideration. By the autumn of 1875 nearly all the Associations had reported[1]. There was unanimity about

1 See the long summary of the Associations' returns presented to the Assembly, *Year Book*, 1876, pp. 116-119.

GEORGE S. BARRETT

ALEXANDER HANNAY

the unsatisfactoriness of the present state of things but much divergence about the proposals for improvement, some Associations objecting to the principles of the Scheme, some to the details.

It was the proposal to consolidate existing Funds which naturally aroused most difference of opinion : 23 Associations were more or less in favour, 6 against, and 11 others had not replied or were reserving judgment. It was resolved, again on the motion of Hannay and Lee, to call a still larger conference, again representative of the Associations, but now including ministers and also not more than 12 members of the Union Committee.

Meanwhile, information was being collected in various ways. In 1875 Hannay carried through a tour in the Eastern Counties in order to ascertain at first hand the pecuniary conditions of the ministry. On the evangelistic side Rogers gave several weeks to village and barn services in Berkshire and Oxfordshire.

In 1876, too, a conference of County Secretaries and Treasurers had been called with a view to securing information about the spiritual condition of the thinly populated districts and the extent to which " the provision for a pure and scriptural ministry was lacking ". At Bradford in that year a meeting of County Secretaries was held, and it was decided that an annual meeting of Secretaries should be held on the Friday morning of the Autumn Assembly. The meeting was to be unofficial and not recorded in the Union Minutes. This plan does not seem to have been carried out.

The enlarged Conference, 62 ministers and 71 laymen, met in London in March, 1876, all the counties being represented except Derby and Bedford. There were also present representatives of the Societies for " British Missions " and the English and London Chapel Building Societies. After two days of discussion the Conference adjourned until May, though not before resolving that in consolidating the Funds a new Society should not be formed, but that

the Rules of the Congregational Union of England and Wales should be so altered as to provide within its Con-

stitution for an administrative body, representative of the
County Associations, to which the general fund may be
entrusted.

At Bradford in the autumn Hannay made a great speech
in introducing what some opponents called " Henry Lee's
Consolidation Scheme ". The Standing Orders relating
to the length of speeches was suspended, and what the
Minutes describe as " an animated and lengthened discussion " was continued over two days. A resolution by
Hannay and Lee, accepting the three principles and
referring the matter to the churches and Associations, was
carried[1]. The debate was now transferred to the country,
and that it was lively there is abundant evidence : even the
Union Report warms up. And while the Counties had the
matter under discussion, negotiations were proceeding with
representatives of the Home Missionary Society. Matters
advanced quickly, and the Conference at Derby, September, 1877, was able to draw up a Constitution for the Congregational Church Aid and Home Missionary Society for
submission to the October Assembly without a dissentient
vote. There was a very full debate, relating especially
to the powers that would be given to the central organization, but Hannay was successful in piloting the scheme
through. The *Congregationalist's* description of the
debate is worth printing, as it shows both the objections
to the scheme and Hannay's point of view :

> An organization of such dimensions is sure to get into
> difficulties if it aspire to rival the versatility of power which
> can equally rend an oak or pick up a pin. The picking-up of
> pins will be in danger of becoming the chief burden of its
> thoughts. It was felt by many who were warm friends of
> the scheme as a whole, that to review the grants as was
> proposed, with any thoroughness, would throw an amount
> of routine labour upon the Council which it could never
> overtake, or, if it overtook, would leave it with neither
> time nor energy for weightier matters. This, together
> with the appearance of over-centralization which this par-

---

1 Though Hannay's Minute in the *Year Book*, 1877, p. 134, does not
say so—the sentence has no ending. For the full Report of the Committee
see *Year Book*, pp. 132-134, and for Dale's account of the debate see the
Congregationalist, 1876. Other articles in the *Congregationalist* for the
same year deal with the Consolidation Scheme.

ticular proposal suggested, was the chief cause of the strong opposition which the scheme met with from some of the Northern Associations, and notably in Lancashire and Yorkshire, where the minorities against it were large, and in Cheshire, where it was actually rejected.

It would be difficult to overrate the service which Mr. Hannay rendered to the denomination by the admirable temper and skill with which he met this fire of adverse criticism. All through the winter, at cost of endless labour, he conferred with brethren and Associations in every part of the country, and by his unfailing good-humour and unflinching courage in meeting all attacks, did much to bring the scheme safely through the shoals which at one time threatened to wreck it. Nothing could have been more judicious than the measure adopted by the Committee of the Congregational Union with the view to unite all moderate men on some common ground. Those who had watched public feeling among us for the past few years knew well how swiftly the opinion had grown up that some national united scheme alone was strong enough to meet the necessities of rural Congregationalism; it was also evident that on the main principles of the scheme we were nearly all agreed, and that the bulk of the opposition was based upon points of detail, which could be amended without molesting any principle.

The speech of Mr. Hannay, in introducing the discussion, was in every sense of the word a masterpiece. It showed in every sentence not only the force and fire of the great orator, but oratory made subservient to the wisdom of the statesman and the zeal of the Christian. It lifted the whole subject clean out of the arena of party strife and religious politics, and set it in that serener atmosphere where the great motive forces of the world to come have play, and where men feel that they tread on holy ground. Not a heart among us but responded to the impassioned appeals to love and zeal, and the fear of God and personal service and devotion, which ran through and through the whole speech, and imparted a solemnity and significance most impressive to the act by which the great measure was finally adopted.

Making but slight alterations, the Assembly recommended the scheme to all the organizations concerned. The Home Missionary Society adopted it, and all the Counties gave their assent, though Cheshire delayed for a year.

In the autumn of 1878 Lee read a paper on the Church Aid Society, speaking of it as "an attempt to strengthen our churches where they are weak, and call forth the mental and material resources we possess which have been hitherto unproductive ", and spoke of the challenge it presented

> in the midst of commercial depression, financial derangement, warlike rumours, wasteful expenditure, with the gloomy forebodings thereby produced, the effects of which we, as a community, especially feel, because our resources are mainly derived from trading transactions, and not from funded property or landed estates.

The income of the Society in this year of " unexampled distress " was nearly £30,000.

It is unnecessary to print in full the rules of the new Society[1]. The objects were generally those of the old Home Missionary Society and the County Associations, and are thus summarized :

> (i) To aid the weaker churches with a view to the more adequate maintenance of the ministry, and the increase of their general usefulness.
>
> (ii) To plant and foster new churches where they are needed.
>
> (iii) To provide for the preaching of the Gospel and other evangelistic work in spiritually destitute places.

County Associations, churches, and individuals contributing specified amounts, representatives of contributing Trusts, life members, *etc.*, of the Home Missionary Society were to constitute the new Society. It was to be controlled by a Council of 200 elected by the Associations in the proportion of their church members, plus 25 elected by the Annual Meeting. The Council was to vote a lump sum to the Associations annually, the distribution being entirely in the hands of the Associations. The Annual Meeting was to be held during the May Meetings of the Union and its Report printed with the Union Report.

Wilson retired from the Secretaryship on the re-organization, and Hannay acted as Secretary of the new Society for its first year, after which E. J. Hartland was appointed. Samuel Morley and Henry Lee were the first Treasurers.

The Society's first Report[2] showed that £3,307 more

---

1 They may be seen in the *Year Book,* 1879, pp. 29-32.
2 *Year Book,* 1880, pp. 56-65.

had been expended than by the Associations and Home Missionary Society combined during the previous year, and, in appealing for more support, said :

> The objects of the Society were in danger of being lost sight of in the discussion which preceded its formation touching the principles of organization which it is competent for Independents to adopt. That discussion has happily terminated in the unanimous acceptance of the principles on which the Society is founded, and it now lies with us to prove that the accord and the union of sporadic and isolated agency to which we have attained were not sought at the bidding of the spirit of centralization by which the age is said to be haunted, or out of envy of the elaborate ecclesiastical organizations which are around us, but solely with the view of making English Congregationalism more efficient as a means of extending the Kingdom of Christ in England. We sought what some called " the organization of Independency", but which was really nothing but a plan for the co-operation of Independent churches in promoting the ends for which they individually exist. We have got what we sought, and it becomes us now with one heart, in the spirit of Christ, " leaving the things which are behind ", to do our best to call forth the spiritual power of the united churches in wise and strenuous effort to serve Christ among the masses of the English people.

Stressing the great need, it instanced an Association which needed £2,400 to lift the salaries of ministers to £150, evangelistic pastors to £120, and home missionaries to £80, and it had only been able to provide £1,302.

From the Union the same year £1,000 was granted to the Society.

Such was Hannay's great achievement, motived by an intense desire to make the Congregational Churches efficient for their task. In Fairbairn's words :

> He saw with statesman instinct that rich and potent churches could not live in isolation, that churches poor and scattered and isolated could not live in strength when sapped by poverty and need. His aim and his love and his great desire was to turn the strength of the strong into the support of the weak, and turn the love of the weak into the encouragement of the mighty.

His outlook and policy were thus stated by the *Congregationalist* during his absence in 1880 :

> He is so strong and conscientious a Congregationalist that he is intensely anxious to see the churches which he loves so well doing their full share in the Christian work of the nation; and as he feels that this can only be accomplished by means of united effort, he has laboured with equal earnestness and ability to effect a consolidation of their strength. It would be impossible here to enter into a vindication of his views. Suffice it to say that there is not a man amongst us who is more loyal to the fundamental principle of Congregationalism, or who would resist any attempt to invade the independence of the churches with more determination or with more convincing force. But internal independence is one thing, union for external work is another. As individuals unite in a church, so churches may unite in a County Union, and County Associations in a National Union, and the conditions which govern these several cases are essentially the same. In each the individual retains freedom of action; but in matters affecting the community the will of the majority must prevail. No doubt there may be those who see danger in any organization, and they have a perfect right to maintain their isolation; and this applies alike to churches and to men. But those who take this view have no just ground of complaint against their brethren who see no danger in united action, nor are they entitled to expect the advantages of that union which they on principle repudiate. Union and isolation must be taken for better or worse, and they who choose the one are extremely unreasonable if they repine because they cannot enjoy the blessings of the other. Mr. Hannay has formed decided opinions as to the benefits to be secured by a wise union of English Congregationalism, and he has given himself heart and soul to effect it. Possibly he may have been too sanguine in his hopes and too eager in his advocacy, but these are not grievous faults, and they are certainly the faults of a generous and noble nature.

Afterwards Hannay is said to have concluded[1] that the Church Aid Society had been launched twenty years too soon, the explanation of which judgment Mackennal gave in a letter to the *Examiner*[2]—" the appeal was on the

---

1 See Parker's Address from the Chair in October, 1901.

2 Printed in Macfadyen's *Constructive Congregational Ideals*, pp. 213-219, a volume which gathers together most usefully addresses showing the trend of Congregationalism during the last half of the 19th century.

national scale, the administration was parochial, diocesan ''. Perhaps the comparative failure of the Church Aid Society would have been avoided had Hannay not been absent from England at the time when the arrangements for celebrating the Jubilee of the Union were finally made. In 1879 it had been decided that, to commemorate the Jubilee, the Congregational Lecture in 1881 should consist of 12 addresses by different persons, to be delivered in different parts of the country, and that some Jubilee Fund should be raised with the primary idea of strengthening the Church Aid and Home Missionary work. The Jubilee Fund Committee finally reported that they had been urged to include the following objects in the appeal :

(1) The Liquidation of Chapel Debts ; (2) The Removal of Debts on Colleges ; (3) The English Chapel Building Society ; (4) The Irish Evangelical Society ; (5) The Pastors' Retiring Fund ; (6) The Lewisham School ; and (7) A Project for the Re-publication of some of the Works of the Earliest English Congregationalists.

They had decided to specify two objects only, the Church Aid Society and the Liquidation of Chapel Debts, but to make room for gifts for other denominational purposes at the wish of the donors. The Rev. D. B. Hooke acted as Secretary for the Fund, and Interim Reports were presented from year to year, the Fund not being closed until April, 1888. The expenses of the Fund were covered by a grant of £1,000 from the Union and by interest accrued during the collection, and its total[1] was £434,470 Of this sum £317,764 was recorded by certificates, that is, it was paid to specific objects and reported to the Fund without being actually sent in to the Fund at all. Further, even some of the amounts sent to the Central Fund were earmarked for special purposes. The disbursements were :

	£
Church Aid and Home Missionary Society	40,021
Chapel Debts (including £10,000 raised in Wales)	248,875
Metropolitan Chapel Extension	93,236
Sundry Congregational Societies	5,544
Colleges and Schools	20,218
New Chapels and Sunday Schools	24,372

1 For a full statement see *Year Book*, 1889, pp. 22-28.

Dr. Mackennal's comment on the Fund was that it was " a sorrow instead of a comfort to Dr. Hannay because during his absence . . . it was diverted from national to local objects ". Perhaps the most caustic reflexion that can be made is that in 1887, when these sums were being raised, the Union had an adverse balance on its accounts, the first for many years! It was unfortunate that this came just before the death of James Spicer, who had succeeded Joshua Wilson as Treasurer of the Union in 1874. His successor, in 1888, was Wm. Holborn, of Kensington Chapel, who remained in office until 1894.

Little more need be said about the Fund save to note that (1) When the Union made grants to churches for removal of debts, *etc.*, it was by way of challenge; and (2) Mr. R. S. Hudson, of Chester, died when a large part of the £20,000 he had promised to the Fund was still unpaid; a Deficiency Fund to meet it had to be raised, towards which Morley contributed £1,000 and the Union £250.

The Jubilee did a good deal to stimulate local generosity, while the addresses of Dale and Rogers, whose speaking campaign has already been mentioned, aroused the churches to a sense of the worth of the Congregational witness; but it is clear that it was in many ways a disappointment to many. Manchester gave royal hospitality during the Jubilee Autumn Assembly, when large numbers of American and other Congregationalists were present.

The formation of the Church Aid Society meant, of course, the break-up of the " British Missions " association, with its October collection appeal. On the dissolution the Union blessed the other two Societies and gave them grants, but the plight of the Irish Evangelical continued to be a cause of concern. Due recognition was made of the Jubilee of the Colonial in 1886. That these Societies had not expanded greatly during the fifty years may be deduced from the fact that in the year of Hannay's death the expenditure of the Irish Society was £1,831 and of the Colonial £4,164.

Year by year through the eighties the Church Aid

Society presented reports of its work to the Assembly,
admirable up to a point, but by no means so extensive as
had been hoped. The Report[1] presented in 1885 declared
that a financial crisis was approaching; £9,000 a year had
been spent more than the amounts spent before the re-con-
stitution, but the Jubilee grants were ceasing and the
contributions were nothing like the £35,000 a year needed.

Some of its activities were of an unusual kind. A
" University Towns Committee" was appointed to
consider the provision of special sermons in Oxford and
Cambridge. Men like Allon, Dale, Fairbairn, Reynolds,
and Rogers were on this committee, as well as younger
men like Arnold Thomas, Elkanah Armitage, and C. E. B.
Reed. A special Fund seems to have been raised for this
purpose, and the Report of the Society adopted in May,
1882, related that Caleb Scott, Dale, J. C. Harrison,
Rogers, G. S. Barrett, and Allon were on a list of Select
Preachers at Emmanuel Church, Cambridge, while
attempts had been made to co-operate with the George
Street Church, Oxford, in the search for a suitable pastor.
Doubts were expressed whether this plan should be con-
tinued: the opening of Mansfield solved the problem for
Oxford, but at a later period the Union will be found grant-
ing £25 a year for the expenses of Select Preachers at
Cambridge. In 1881 Hannay received a petition from
Fellows, Graduates, and Undergraduates in Oxford and
Cambridge asking for the delivery of lectures in those cities
by eminent Nonconformists. On the motion of Mr. H. M.
Bompas, Q.C., the matter was referred to the Committee,
conference with the Baptists on the subject being suggested. There was at this time considerable concern
because many Nonconformists in Oxford were drifting
away. In November, 1884, three lectures were delivered in
the new Schools at Oxford by Fairbairn, Richard Glover,
and E. R. Conder, but the Committee, while willing to
arrange similar lectures each term in both Oxford and
Cambridge, felt that this was scarcely the best method of
serving the interests of the Universities and the denomination, and said:

[1] For a six years' Survey see *Year Book*, 1886, pp. 29-37.

The Committee has been greatly encouraged by the discovery that not a few men of eminence connected with the universities, though not themselves Nonconformists, looking not to the interests of Nonconformity but to the interests of the universities as seats of learning, and to the present condition of religious faith in England, are prepared to welcome the teachers of the truth as we hold it. If Nonconformists are wise this desideratum will not long remain.

This expression of opinion presaged the removal of Congregational Colleges to the old Universities.

One other thing the association of the Church Aid Society with the Union certainly did: it resulted in a fresh consideration of the question of statistics. The student of the history of the Congregational Union cannot fail but be bewildered at the varying numbers of churches given in speeches and even in official documents. In the Preface to the *Year Book* of 1880 Hannay said he had tried to distinguish between churches, branch churches, and preaching stations, and had been unsuccessful because the Associations had different ways of recording. In that year his figures are:

	Churches.	Branch Churches.	Preaching Stations.	Evangelists Stations.
England ...	2,013	119	1,004	78
Wales ...	814[1]	36	17	

The problem of the Ministerial Lists also arose from time to time. It was emphasized that the Lists should be new each year, and that only names officially furnished by the County Secretaries should appear. One striking case came up in the Assembly in two successive years, Hannay carrying the Assembly with him in confirming his removal of a name which had appeared in a County List. It was unfortunate that shortly after the " Religious Communion " controversy the London Union should have had to omit Picton's name because he was not a member of the London Board. This led to the charge that he had been excommunicated because of his theology. In the *Congregationalist* Rogers pointed out that the reason for

---

1 Together with 82 English Churches, with 3 Preaching Stations.

exclusion was not theological, for the name of Mark Wilks, who shared Picton's views, was there. It was there because he was a member of the London Board, and despite his theology. Picton was not a member of the London Board, and therefore the rule was against him; he could not be entered just because of his theology! Then he went on:

> Mr. Picton's claim to be returned on the ground of his being a well-known Independent minister, though he refused to comply with the conditions laid down by the committee, was absolutely inadmissible. A rule must be applied without favour, or there will be endless trouble, and in the case of the *Year Book* this had already arisen. The necessity for this stringency may be regarded as one of the disadvantages of "organized Independency", but, at all events, every man that so pleases may be an Independent, and even an Independent minister, without being "organized". The one thing that is impossible is that he can have the freedom from all law which is the privilege of isolation and enjoy the advantages of organization. The Union, which publishes a *Year Book,* has a perfect right to lay down its own conditions for admission into its ministerial list, provided it does not interfere with some antecedent right of individuals. If it professed to keep and publish a complete register of *all* Congregational ministers, any one who could prove himself a Congregational minister would doubtless have just reason for complaint if his name was omitted. But that is precisely what it does not attempt. All that it undertakes is to publish the names furnished by the local Unions, and those Unions compile their lists on terms laid down by themselves.

Hannay also hoped to include a List of Evangelists and Lay Pastors in the *Year Book,* but he was baffled by the returns—and lack of returns—of the Associations.

Papers on the settlement and removal of ministers resulted in the preparation of a pamphlet giving counsel to vacant churches, and in a recommendation that the several County Associations should

> consider the desirableness of appointing a Confidential Committee with which vacant churches and unsettled ministers may correspond; which shall also consider all applications for entrance into the Congregational ministry from men who have not passed through one of our colleges or some recognized institution for ministerial training.

Baldwin Brown protested against this proposal as a breach of Independency. The Union ascertained the views of the Associations, but there was no enthusiasm for the project, indeed the very opposite, the ten Welsh Associations all declaring that " no such expedient was needed within their bounds ". The Union Committee swiftly withdrew the proposal, covering their retreat by saying that no doubt the ventilation of the subject would have served a useful purpose.

Two other subjects considered show the concern of the denomination for evangelization and the prevailing trend towards greater control over the liberty of the individual church.

The demand for increased activity in evangelizing the rural districts and the influence of the Revival movements, especially the Moody and Sankey missions, led to a demand that the Union should appoint special missioners. This suggestion was not approved, whereupon two Yorkshire ministers, Robert Balgarnie and J. F. T. Hallowes, gave up their pastorates to devote themselves to this work.

In 1882 a discussion on lay preaching led to the appointment of a Committee, whose report was accepted in May, 1883. It urged that large churches and groups of smaller churches should have lay preachers' classes, and encourage the use of lay preachers, and that County Associations should have Committees to exercise general oversight, and to encourage the grouping of small churches, even suggesting that all grants to such churches should be made conditional on the Association's grouping proposals being adopted.

The Ministry and the Colleges.

In 1876 the Union asked the County Associations to consider the supply of candidates for the ministry. The following year the Rev. T. Robinson, in a paper on " Desirable Reforms in our College System " read in a sectional conference, said that £250,000 was invested in college property, and £23,000 a year expended in college training, and the system was " so contrived as to obtain the minimum of results for the maximum of outlay".

The Conference recommended the appointment of a special committee to consider " the best steps to be taken in order to secure immediate action " in regard to College Reform (optimists !). The Committee thereupon asked the Colleges to elect 30 representatives to join 15 nominees of the Union in a confidential committee. This Committee duly met, Henry Lee presiding at the first meeting. It appointed Henry Spicer as its Chairman, and Mackennal as Secretary. An Interim Report making admirable suggestions for raising the standard of training, especially by way of making full use of national Universities and Colleges, was presented in May, 1879, and, speaking in October, Henry Spicer said that, while not depreciating the work of the Colleges, it was true to say that the denomination had been standing still in the matter of ministerial education for a quarter of a century, and greater improvements had been made in the two years since Robinson's paper sounded the alarm than in the previous twenty.

A further Interim Report accepted in October recommended the formation of two College Boards, one in the north, the other in the south, to which each College should send ten representatives (Nottingham and Bristol 5 each) to carry out the policy outlined. A *College Calendar* was printed, Dr. Newth himself meeting the cost in the first year, and the Union taking financial responsibility in the second.

The Colleges fell in with the Committee's suggestions, and the two Boards were formed in due course, the Union appointing ten representatives to serve on each. The College Boards set to work[1] immediately " to draw the Churches and the Colleges into better and more mutual association ", and deputations were sent to the different County Associations, while the Churches were asked to observe a day of prayer for the Colleges, and if possible to take a College Collection. The Union granted £100 towards the expenses of the Boards. In 1883 it also received a report from the Senatus Academicus of the

[1] For the full report of the Boards see *Year Book,* 1884, pp. 31-42.

Colleges, instituted four years previously with the aim of raising the intellectual standard of the ministry. An animated discussion followed two papers in the autumn of 1884 on " What the Churches owe to the Colleges ", and " What the Churches expect from the Colleges ". In 1888 some of the immediate action desired ten years before was taken, Airedale and Rotherham joining to form United College. Spring Hill had already moved to Oxford in 1886 to become Mansfield, the Union electing six members of its Council. In 1889 the Board of Education[1] was discharged, with special thanks to Mackennal, and in 1890 the Union urged on the Churches special prayers for the Colleges. In October, 1892, the question again came up for discussion. A resolution moved by Professor A. S. Wilkins and Mr. A. J. Shepheard recognized the services rendered by the Colleges, but suggested the appointment of a Committee representing the Union and the Churches to advise on " some concentration of forces and events " which would increase their efficiency. Two amendments were rejected, but one was passed, recommending the formation of a Committee, and saying categorically that " the Churches expect such concentration ".

The International Congregational Council.

Hannay was well fitted to carry out the arrangements for the first International Congregational Council, the meeting of which he was not permitted to see. From Canada and Australia there came various expression of desire for such a general Council, and Hannay's visit to America and the presence of many American ministers at the Jubilee gatherings had given him personal contacts which inclined him to look with favour on the proposal for a Council. Not, of course, that all those contacts were uniformly happy. Even in British Congregationalism there were two opinions about Beecher, and in 1886 the Union Committee declined to accede to the request of the Norwich

---

[1] It is unfortunate that this term was used in respect of the College Boards : it had previously been employed for the Elementary Education Committee, established in 1843.

Local Committee that he should be asked to preach, though inviting him, and also Noah Porter, to attend the Assembly.   John Hunter, then of Hull, strongly protested in the *Nonconformist and Independent,* and Edward White, then Chairman, and Hannay replied.   The feeling was so strong that the Reference Committee sanctioned a resolution, moved by Hunter and Fleming Williams, declaring the Assembly's regret at not hearing Beecher. Had this been allowed to be put without discussion, the matter might have rested, but Edward White, in a personal word, let slip what some thought was a slighting reference to Beecher.   There was immediate uproar, a suggestion by B. J. Snell that a telegraphic invitation be sent to Beecher at once, and a speech by C. A. Berry, appealing to all to unite in the resolution's expression of goodwill.   White withdrew the offending sentence, Snell his suggestion, and the resolution was carried.

When Beecher addressed the London Board of Ministers in the same year, Hannay carefully left the Memorial Hall an hour or two before the meeting so that he would not be expected to attend.

Many Americans came year by year and were gladly welcomed, and the Union was often represented at the triennial American National Council.   The frequent visits of Dr. Dexter to England proved a strong link between Congregationalists in the two countries.   The Union had co-operated with him in a Memorial to John Robinson, and his death just before the Council was as great a blow to American Congregationalism as Hannay's was to British.

The arrangements for the Council had been carried through largely by Hannay, who had now Burford Hooke as Assistant Secretary, while the Church Aid Society was in the hands of W. F. Clarkson.   On Hannay's death Alexander Mackennal became Secretary of the Council, and, with the approval of world-wide Congregationalism, Dale was nominated as President.   The Council met in London in July, 1891, its cost to the Union being £1,059. This volume can do no more than refer readers to the proceedings of the Council, hailed by the Assembly three months later as a signal success. It stands with the formation of the Church Aid and Home Missionary Society as Hannay's crowning achievement.

It was representative of Congregational Churches throughout the world, and the constitution finally agreed upon was for a Council of 450 members—150 from Great Britain and Ireland, 150 from the United States, and 150 from the rest of the world. Five meetings of the Council have been held as follows :—

Year	Place	Moderator	Preacher
1891	London	Dr. R. W. Dale	Dr. E. P. Goodwin
1899	Boston	Dr. James B. Angell	Dr. A. M. Fairbairn
1908	Edinburgh	Sir Albert Spicer, Bart.	Dr. George A. Gordon
1920	Boston	Dr. J. L. Barton	Dr. J. D. Jones
1930	Bournemouth	Dr. J. D. Jones	Dr. Jay T. Stocking

This is not the place for an examination of the influence of the Council. Reference may be made to the five volumes of the Council Reports, that of 1891, edited by Dr. Mackennal; that of 1899, by the Rev. E. C. Webster; that of 1908, by Dr. John Brown; that of 1920, by the Rev. T. J. Spencer; and that of 1930, by Dr. Albert Peel. For an estimate of the worth of the Councils reference might be made to an article by Dr. J. D. Jones, in the *Congregational Quarterly* (VIII, 325-329). See also an article by the present writer (*Congregational Quarterly*, VIII, 485-489).

Another Summing-up.

As in 1846, the verdict of a discriminating observer of the first years was quoted, so it may be well to take stock half-way through the century. The Union had contained no more judicious and well-balanced mind than Henry Allon, who thus expressed himself during the Jubilee Year in a Chairman's Address the whole of which will well repay reading :

> The union of churches is for the benefit of the individual churches that constitute it. It is their creation, and is subordinate to them. It is accidental; they are inviolable. It can be justified only by its practical recognition of their inviolability. Each Church has an indefeasible right to stand aloof from the Union or to withdraw from it, and

CHARLES A. BERRY

ALEXANDER MACKENNAL

JOHN BROWN

WILLIAM HARDY HARWOOD

every Church joining it is, in virtue of the cardinal principle of Independency, inviolable in its autonomy. All association involves compromise; some exercises of individual liberty are surrendered for the sake of concerted action, but the surrender of Church autonomy is impossible without the surrender of Congregationalism itself.

So long as the Union maintains its character as a voluntary confederation for fellowship and work of independent Churches, it is both unimpeachable and invaluable. Let it in any way put disability upon Churches not belonging to it, impose conditions of Church life and work, assume that membership with it is the criterion of orthodoxy or of moral worth—and these are the natural tendencies of association—and it will invert the true order of its relationship, and become a legislative synod, and that of the worst type, because without its carefully devised safeguards.

Hitherto, the Union has not interfered with Congregational principles. In no way intended to discredit their intrinsic truth, excellency, or sufficiency, it is simply a concert for their broader and more efficient application. It has neither power nor right to put its imprimatur upon either church or minister. A jealous maintenance of individual liberty is really the essential condition of both order and strength.

It is easy, then, to see how the organization of Congregational Churches, constituted upon a theory of individual independence, necessarily involves some of the gravest of ecclesiastical questions. No problem of social life is greater than exactly to adjust the balance of liberty and order, individualism and co-operation, the independence of each and the legitimate subordination of each to the whole.

When, after some tentative and local experiments, the Congregational Union was projected, these problems presented themselves to its projectors with special gravity. They were largely discussed; they are not solved yet; probably they never will be; they are of a character that admits only of empirical, not of scientific, solution.

With the ecclesiastical history of Christendom as a warning, and considering the insidious tendency of association to emasculate and destroy liberty, there was a natural and wholesome jealousy lest the projected fellowship should encroach upon indefeasible rights of independent churches; lest, following the precedents of ecclesiastical history, the Association should become a synod, the synod a legislature, the legislature an autocracy, and thus, by gradual and unintentional encroachments, the parent principle of liberty should be devoured by its own offspring.

v

Under the influence of the apprehension, some of our wisest and strongest men regarded the projected Union with misgivings; by some it was formally and strenuously opposed. This gospel also was preached " with much contention ".

So far from this being cause for regret, it was in every way most wholesome. For the incipient Union itself it was beneficial that it should be subject to the keen scrutiny and criticism of men jealous for the liberties of the churches, and justly deeming no possible precision of action a compensation for any compromise of these. To this wholesome criticism the Union has been subjected ever since—its principles tested, its methods questioned, and its own spirit of freedom kept quick and vigilant.

It will be a disastrous day for our churches when this spirit relaxes. There is nothing that should be more assiduously cherished by us than the spirit of independence —the robust and wholesome integrity of individual responsibility. It is more than a compensation for a hundred practical defects. The most disorderly exercise of liberty were better than its negation. The suppression of liberty is not peace. Maintain a true principle of life, it will be a corrective of all practical defect; surrender the principle and virtue itself is deprived of nobility.

Whatever, therefore, our Congregationalism may lose in precision and force through morbid jealousies of exaggerated individualism, its privation of the responsibilities of individual life would be incomparably more disastrous. Better that our churches were resolved into their primitive constituents than their association should develop legislative authority or even irresistible moral constraint.

These early fears were gradually dissipated, and the Union won the suffrages of its most vigilant critics. From that time to this it has incurred no tangible blame, and has excited only vague and evanescent suspicions. Churches still stand aloof from it. Some, probably, in the mere wantonness of independency; others with unallayed fears concerning the natural tendencies of confederation; but their moral right to do this is fully recognized. They suffer no disability, they are held in unimpaired esteem, save as one judgment necessarily thinks itself superior to another.

It is, I think, in every way advantageous that there should be churches maintaining this witness. The misgivings do not respect Congregationalism itself, but the integrity of it as imperilled by such associations.

Hannay died in 1890. A Memorial Fund was raised, a portrait being painted for the Memorial Hall, and a tombstone erected in Abney Park Cemetery. The remaining capital was invested, and it was fitting that, Mrs. Hannay having received the income from it during her life, it should be added to the funds of the Church Aid and Home Missionary Society.

THE death of Hannay left the Union leaderless, for Rogers, his lieutenant, powerful though he was on the platform, was scarcely the man to fill Hannay's shoes, even had he not been approaching seventy. Those who felt that Hannay had been a Colossus bestriding the narrow world of Congregationalism thought that now was a chance for them to ensure that the Secretary in future should not be of the leader calibre. Conspicuous among them was Joseph Parker, who was not wont or happy to be outshone by any man. On the other hand, there were those who declared, like Rogers, " A *fainéant* administration is the very last thing which the Congregational Churches would regard with satisfaction ". Burford Hooke was Acting Secretary, and a Special Committee was appointed to examine the whole question of the Secretary's duties before proceeding to consider names. They were soon able to agree that Dr. C. A. Berry should be invited to accept nomination. He declined; Alexander Mackennal was the next suggestion, and the Report in May recommended his appointment, as well as the formation of a Committee to discuss all matters pertaining to his office. Parker moved an amendment to the effect that the measure should be delayed until the services the Secretary was expected to render could be considered, and finally a resolution was carried saying that the Secretary must be " a minister holding a leading position in the churches ", and that a Committee should report on the Secretary's duties in the autumn.

There was lively debate throughout the country and in October, at a Session of the Assembly which did no credit to Congregationalism, a long Report which has " Parker " written all over it, was presented. It recommended :

> 1. " That the Secretary of the Union should clearly recognize the idea that Congregationalism is truly Catholic. This may be regarded as a commonplace, or it may be realized as a living and effective inspiration. It

will show itself in the spirit of the man. Under its
influence he will keep the Union in constant touch with all
that is best in Free Church life and service. He will be
more than a Congregationalist. He will avail himself of
every opportunity of promoting honest and useful co-operation with other Christian Communions. The Congregational Union should be more than a Union of Congregationalists. The Secretary will not wait to be plied with
reasons why he should develop the total influence of the
Free Churches and bring it to bear upon common and
public questions, he will himself occasionally take the
initiative in endeavouring to establish larger co-operation.
In other words, the Secretary will be more than a denom-
inationalist. It is impossible at this point to do more than
indicate the spirit in which the office should be administered, but the spirit is of supreme importance, and perhaps
all the more important that it cannot be expressed in
mechanical and final terms."

2. " That the Secretary should have a clear percep-
tion of the natural unity of all our denominational interests,
and should carefully and wisely inquire how far they can
be legitimately consolidated. He should force nothing.
He should adopt a policy of watchfulness, with a view to
the amalgamation (where possible and desirable) of institutions or offices that are practically doing the same work.
This would apply to Colleges, to Charities, to Schools, to
Secretaryships, and to various Societies. In this matter,
as in all others, revolution by evolution should be the
policy. Opportunities cannot be forced but they should be
watched and utilized, and it should be felt that the Secretary is on the side of every lawful amalgamation that will
economize the resources, and at the same time increase the
efficiency of our institutions and our Church life generally.
He should not multiply offices, but concentrate them.
Centralization would be escaped by the Union as a whole
taking a more direct interest in denominational
institutions."

3. " That the Secretary should have faith in the
elasticity and progressiveness of Congregationalism. He
should have an open mind. Inasmuch as the Constitution
of the Union is a starting-point not a goal, he should
always regard its revision as a possible contingency. In
proportion as he recognizes the elasticity and progressiveness of Congregationalism will he feel that it has hardly
yet fully addressed itself to the urgent and critical life of
the immediate age. The best work of Congregationalism
is always before it".

4. [This deals with the use of the Secretary's Sundays, which are to be in the hands of a sub-committee.] " This is vital ".

5. "That the Secretary should be deeply interested in public questions . . . Religious Equality, Temperance, Education, Peace, and Social Reforms in general. The Union must not neglect these questions or the age will leave the Union behind. Struggling men must be made to feel that in the Secretary they can rely upon counsel, protection, and encouragement in carrying out all social reforms".

6. The Secretary " must be great in goodness. He must set small store by mere cleverness in himself or in others. How remarkable soever his powers, unless there be in him the love and the pity of the very heart of Christ, his service will soon become a burden to himself and to the Union ".

7. Income to be £700 a year including *Year Book* editorial fee, with twelve free Sundays.

8. The names of G. S. Barrett, W. F. Clarkson, and J. Hirst Hollowell were suggested.

Barrett withdrew his name. There was an acrimonious discussion, and the Assembly would have none of the Report. They thanked the Committee and snubbed Parker by at once proceeding to appoint Mackennal, at the same time recommending, on the motion of Alfred Sykes, of Huddersfield, that the Special Committee should investigate the possibility of the amalgamation of Congregational Societies with each other and/or with the Union. Mackennal, who would, like Berry, have had general support, declined, though he would probably have accepted had the invitation gone through in May. Barrett was again approached, but with the same result. In February the Committee appointed the Rev. W. J. Woods[1], of Clapton Park, who asked that the appointment should be ratified by the Assembly in May. When May came, Parker, smarting under his treatment in the Autumn, regrettably lent his support to an anonymous attack on the Secretary-elect. On the Saturday before the latter's name was to be presented to the Assembly, an anonymous letter appeared in the *Daily Chronicle,* accusing him of

1 For the terms of Woods's appointment see *Year Book,* 1893, p. 14.

plagiarizing from a sermon of Dr. Oswald Dykes, and Monday's papers announced that Dr. Parker would ask for an explanation, and move a hostile motion.   Little purpose would now be served by recounting the details of the discussion.   The Assembly supported Woods by an overwhelming majority, deeming the explanation he felt constrained to give unnecessary, and desiring to express its feeling that he had been cruelly treated, and its indignation that Parker should have sprung a mine at the last moment instead of communicating with him privately. The audience showed its displeasure very plainly, and not merely by turning down by twenty to one Parker's amendment that the appointment should be by ballot.

For years the minister of the City Temple took no part in the life of the Union : long afterwards he was still bitterly complaining of being hissed off its platform. How strong the cross currents, how violent the winds, during this absence of a captain from the deck, may be realized by a perusal of the periodical literature of the time.   The *Independent* said :

> There was much behind, which went far to justify the clamorous wrath of the meeting.   We could, perhaps, have desired that the Union had shown a greater measure of self-command.   Even righteous indignation needs to be kept under control.   Yet we may not judge too hardly the ebullitions of anger when we remember the provocation which had been received.   We have every desire to let bygones be bygones, but it would not be just to the Union to record the vehemence of its action without indicating at least some of the causes.   For many months the Union has suffered from the open assaults and secret tactics of a few individuals, some of them not even members of the denomination, who essayed to speak in its name.   We have no desire to suggest that Dr. Parker and his associates entered into a deliberate conspiracy in order to humiliate and discredit the Congregational institutions of this country.   But none the less is it true that their action has had that mischievous tendency.   It was also plain that their action was concerted.   They made no secret of their intention to protract the Secretarial crisis as long as possible, with all its unpleasant contingencies.   They assumed the airs of a great Party, and frequently essayed to open negotiations with the duly elected Executive of

the Union as though they were a body of equal standing with it. Their courage was not unrewarded. In a misguided moment the Committee actually succumbed to their pretensions. It is true that the Union took the first opportunity of reversing the capitulation of May, and at Southport turned its late victors to utter rout. But they were not long abashed. The old tactics were resumed. They may not have adopted the deliberate policy of terrorizing every person whom the Committee might nominate for the Secretaryship, but their conduct certainly gave countenance to some such impression . . .

The Union, already exasperated, was in no mood to tolerate this new departure. It was resolved to show no quarter to any persons who would derive support for their policy from such methods. It felt it must put a full stop to the kind of obstruction which had been so long practised. It must free itself from any complicity with autocratic airs and anarchic arts. It was compelled to act in self-defence. It struck, and struck hard. We cannot say the blow was undeserved. Let us hope there may be no need for its repetition.

Hooke, who had rendered good service as interim Secretary, became Editor of the *Independent,* which at that time the Union decided not to take over.

Woods held office for 11 years, serving the churches with ability, ready kindliness, and good will, though he did not pretend to possess the statesmanlike genius of Hannay. It is pleasing to record that before the end of his official career Parker was not merely back in the Union but had been elected its Chairman for the second time, after three ballots, the order in the first being Scott, Parker, Forsyth, Horton, and in the second Scott, Parker, Forsyth. This chapter will cover the years preceding his second Chairmanship.

These comparatively quiet years are marked by increased interest in social questions, and in the welfare of young people. There are signs, too, that the woman is coming to her right place in the denominational life; at Bradford, in 1892, a Women's Conference was held. It was about this time that the first woman delegate was appointed. The honour seems to be Miss Harriet Spicer's, who remembers the difficulty she had in persuading the police that she had any right on the floor of the Assembly.

She was closely followed by her sister-in-law, Mrs. Albert, now Lady, Spicer.

Some examples of the attention now being paid to social reform have already been given. In addition to the usual watchful attitude on education, temperance, and gambling, there is a welcome alertness about industrial and international affairs. Approval was given to F. H. Stead's Old Age Pensions Scheme, and grants of £50 made to Mansfield House Settlement and the Browning Hall. There is a good deal about arbitration and peace, especially in regard to the Czar's proposals, but when the South African War came, the Union, which in its Report in 1898 had proudly said : " The voice of the Congregational Churches ought to speak in trumpet tones, urging a permanent reduction of the armaments of Europe ", found itself " so sharply and miserably divided ", that it was thought " better to keep silence than to speak concerning it ". Personal contacts were maintained with the United States officially by delegates sent to the Triennial Council of the American Churches, and unofficially through such ambassadors as C. A. Berry, and these proved of special help when the Venezuelan question might have led to serious trouble between the two nations. Americans also helped in building the John Robinson Memorial Church at Gainsborough, while arrangements were made for the Second International Council to be held in Boston in 1899.

Notice was taken of public events, the death of Tennyson in 1892, the retirement of Gladstone in 1894, and the Jubilee of the Liberation Society in the same year, when a resolution of thanksgiving was seconded by Mr. D. Lloyd George, who also addressed a Welsh meeting during the Liverpool Assembly in 1894, and a Young People's Meeting in 1898. A delegation came from the R.T.S. on its Centenary, and one was sent to the Jubilee Celebration of the United Free Church of Scotland. Special commemorations of the Tercentenary of the execution of Barrow, Greenwood, and Penry were held in 1893, while a Diamond Jubilee was held in the City

Temple in 1897, the speakers being Rogers, Berry, Mackennal, Parker, and Augustine Birrell. Resolutions were passed on the opium traffic, the Cantonment regulations in India, the persecution of Stundists, the rights of the Matabele, and Lynch Law. In March, 1896, so disturbed was the mind of the churches concerning international affairs, that the Committee sent a circular letter, prepared by Rogers, to all the churches. It dealt with the Venezuelan Question, the treatment of Armenians, and the Transvaal, and said :

> We yield to no body of men in our love for our common country, in our gratitude to God for the liberties which she enjoys, or in our resolution to maintain her rights. But we believe that her greatness depends on the character of her policy rather than on the extent of her territory. We believe that peace is the highest of all British interests, and we therefore venture to urge our Ministers and Churches everywhere, while themselves seeking to inculcate lessons of moderation and forbearance, to unite in constant supplication to the Giver of every good and perfect gift that He would give to this nation a wise and understanding heart, so that it shall see and walk in paths of righteousness, in which will be found enduring peace and prosperity.

Rogers seems to have been employed frequently at this time in the preparation of circular letters. In 1899 he was asked to write one " enunciating Congregational ideas as to the ecclesiastical, the moral, and the political evils of the present Ritualistic Movement in the Established Church".

A new *Sunday School Hymnal* was published in 1891, and an attempt was made " to develop a close and helpful relation between the Union and Congregational Sunday Schools " by the preparation (by W. F. Adeney) of a course of graded lessons. The Guilds were reconstituted and became the Young People's Union[1]. First it was decided that the Guilds' Council should be appointed by the Union Committee, with power to add six members representing work among the young. Then an attempt was made to federate all Young People's Societies, includ-

1 See *Year Books,* 1895, 1897, 1898, 1899, and 1901.

ing the Society of Christian Endeavour, Mr. A. E. Hutton, M.P., being elected the first President, a grant of £100 being given by way of encouragement, and a Handbook being prepared. The Chairman of the Union or some other leading minister continued to write a New Year's letter to young people; this sometimes had a circulation of 70,000. The examinations still continued, but though the sale of textbooks was good, the candidates were few. A clubroom for young Congregationalists in London—the Thomas Binney Institute—was opened at King's Weigh House. Foremost in this Young People's work was the Rev. G. Currie Martin.

Increased interest was taken in the work of Foreign Missions; support was given to the Forward Movement of the London Missionary Society, and the hope expressed that Congregationalists would have a good share in the enterprise of the Students' Voluntary Missionary Union. The question whether a joint permanent Council of the Colonial Missionary Society, the London Missionary Society, and the Union, was not advisable, remitted from the International Council, seems to have been lost in the discussion of the amalgamation of Congregational Societies. Joint action was taken by the three in regard to Jamaica and British Guiana and in other ways. The churches were urged to inform the Colonial Missionary Society of all emigrants, and in 1891 the Union welcomed closer relations with the London Missionary Society, including the invitation to appoint a Director. The Centenary of that Society was commemorated in 1895, in which year Khama and two other African Chiefs were welcomed at the Assembly. Sympathy was expressed with Christians in Madagascar and China in their sufferings under persecution.

Familiar names are now frequent. Hollowell and A. J. Viner peg away at the Education Question, keeping a keen watch on all legislation, and in 1895, on Congregational initiative, the National Educational League of the Evangelical Free Churches was formed. Attractive programmes like a Young People's Demonstration with

J. H. Jowett, R. J. Campbell, B. J. Snell, and C. S.
Horne as speakers, flash before the eyes. J. D. Jones is
now on the Committee; he, R. F. Horton, W. B.
Selbie, and G. N. Ford are extremely active, while J. C.
Meggitt is already showing an interest in the Young
People's Department.

But there were many losses. Henry Allon, whom the
Assembly had stood and cheered on his birthday the year
before, died in 1892, and in 1899 the life of C. A. Berry
was cut short just at the height of his usefulness.

The increased concern with the lives of the people led
in 1891 to the appointment of a special Social Questions
Committee, composed of ten members of the Union Committee and ten others. The following year at Bradford,
during a Conference on " The Church and the Labour
Problem ", Charles Leach attacked Keir Hardie for some
words recently spoken. It was agreed, on the motion of
the Rev. T. Rhondda Williams, that the Labour leader,
who was present, should be allowed to explain. In doing
so he counter-attacked the churches for forsaking the
religion of Christ, and there was considerable uproar.
Eventually Leach qualified the charge he had made.

The following May the Shipping Federation and Seamen's Union, in conflict at Hull, were urged to submit
their dispute to arbitration, and the Social Questions
Committee were asked to report on the relation of Trade
Unions to free labour. In the autumn (1893) a fund was
opened to meet the distress caused by the coal dispute, and
£1,249 contributed[1]. A resolution was moved deploring
" calamitous strikes and lock-outs ", this being amended
by the substitution for non-commital phrases of the
words :

> It desires to bear testimony to the ethical principle
> that the rights of humanity must always take precedence
> of those of property. It declares that alike mining
> royalties and profits made out of the labours of men
> receiving wages inadequate for the support of themselves
> and their families are obviously inconsistent with
> righteousness and fraternity, and it recommends the

---

[1] For a full account of this Fund, see *Year Book,* 1895, p. 80.

submitting of all trade disputes to settlement by impartial tribunals.

The Union Committee and the Social Questions Committee invited Labour M.P.'s to confer with them and with Congregational M.P.'s, and meetings were held in the Memorial Hall on 6th December, 1892, and 8th February, 1893, the Labour M.P.'s present being J. Wilson, J. Keir Hardie, W. Randall Cremer, and W. P. Byles, and the Congregational M.P.'s Wm. Crosfield, A. E. Hutton, John Leng, Mark Oldroyd, C. E. Shaw, Halley Stewart, and J. Carvell Williams.   As a result, the Committee urged the Churches to take part in all efforts at social amelioration and made practical suggestions concerning sweating, insanitary dwellings, better housing, and the closing of unnecessary public-houses. They further pointed out

> that when in industrial disputes the path of right is distinctly seen, but is subordinated to a supposed expediency, then the Christian Churches, and especially their pastors and leaders, are bound to affirm promptly, clearly, and boldly, the paramount authority of righteousness, as being the will of God.

Most attention was, however, devoted to internal affairs during these years, and especially to Church Extension and to the relationships of the denominational Societies to the Union.   While the tempestuous winds of the period of the vacancy had ceased—perhaps because a Jonah had been thrown overboard—it is clear that this decade was the time when the vessel of the Union was amid conflicting currents.   Amid the dry details of the discussion of the Constitution, and of Church Extension, can be clearly seen the divergent opinions and the opposed parties—those who desired to make the central organization powerful, with the disposition of large funds, and those who preferred independence for the Societies and greater power for the local Unions.

Church Extension.

P. T. Forsyth is usually associated with theology rather than with Church Extension, but he combined the

two in a paper which set the Church Extension ball rolling
again in 1892 : its title was " The Duty of Congregationalists to Provide for Church Extension in Our Large
Towns, in View of the Rapid Increase of Population and
the Revived Activity of Sacerdotal Churches ". The
following May representatives of County Unions and
Chapel Building Societies urged the need of a national
movement, and expressed the desirability in certain cases
of securing sites and erecting buildings before a congregation had been gathered. The Committee agreed that
the Congregational Churches were not taking their share
in the provision of accommodation for worship, and the
Assembly appointed a Church Extension Committee.
This Committee made a full and careful survey of the
country, reporting[1] to the Assembly from time to time,
describing " a vast amount of *vis inertiae* " in face of
extension " sadly overdue " in many places, and the
urgent need for a national fund. In the Union Report in
1894 the Committee, referring to the problem caused by
shifting populations, said :

> Excessive provision in one locality is no remedy for
> serious depression in another. If a re-distribution of
> religious accommodation were possible, there are chapels
> enough to meet every existing need. But chapels cannot be
> folded, like tents, and pitched again in some more con-
> venient place : they remain stationary, while the people
> are in motion, and the tendency is for the chapels to be
> without people in the old neighbourhoods, while the people
> are without chapels in the new.

Nevertheless, they were not prepared to launch a national
fund, but hoped that the information disclosed would
stimulate local effort.

This did not satisfy the Church Extension Committee,
who presented a long report in October, 1895, the crux of
which is thus expressed :

> Let us not be misled by a false spirit of undenomina-
> tionalism. We are justified in occupying new districts
> with self-governing churches constituted in loyalty to our

---

[1] These reports, printed in the *Year Books, ad loc.,* are very valuable
and well worth reading.

convictions of the will of Christ. We are justified in doing this systematically with united movement upon a scale commensurate with the duty to be discharged. If Congregationalism has a witness to bear and a work to achieve for God and man, it has a right to existence. If it has a continued existence, it must be through growth. And because the growth of every voluntary society depends upon the self-sacrifice and service of its members, we may boldly say that we Congregationalists are more than justified, are even constrained to seek the extension of our churches wherever opportunity arises. Not to increase is to decrease. Not to advance is to retreat.

As a result it was resolved, on the motion of T. W. Harrison, of Hanley, who did fine work in this and other fields, that a national fund should be started. It was driven home that all other denominations were at work, and Congregationalism must do its part, while co-operating in order to avoid overlapping.

In May, 1897, the Assembly resolved to appeal for at least £100,000 within five years, to be used to stimulate local contributions, and to include donations locally applied. By the autumn £17,000 had been promised, and the Assembly pledged itself to support the effort, giving a collection of £727 as an earnest. Soon plans representing £40,000 were adopted, though Harrison in his 1897 Report spoke of the slow progress of propaganda :

> This is probably in part due to the constitutional distaste for central organization which, amongst Congregationalists at all times, retards response to denominational appeals ; but whatever the causes that make for delay, it is gratifying to note that the urgency of the case for Church Extension is becoming more generally and more clearly realized, and that in various centres there are beginnings of practical work which augur hopefully for the future.

In 1898 the total was £23,000, of which but £5,000 was given to the Central Fund. By May, 1899, when it was resolved to suspend appeals during the Twentieth Century Fund, £29,701 had been received, of which the Central Fund's share was £9,756.

Amalgamation and Reorganization.

The Committee appointed on the resolution of Alfred

Sykes at Southport in 1891 went into the question thoroughly, obtaining evidence from the Baptist Union in regard to their relationship to Baptist Societies.

Meanwhile the position of the Church Aid Society was growing increasingly serious, and in October, 1893, a Resolution was passed urging the Committees of the Union and the Society to discuss : (1) Amalgamation of the Church Aid Society with the Union; (2) Sustentation; (3) Modifications, if (1) or (2) proved impracticable.

The report of this Conference[1], which held three meetings, reveals not merely considerable difference of opinion, but instability too. A proposal in favour of a Sustentation scheme was rejected for one in favour of Augmentation, "without raising the question whether aid should be voted indirectly through the churches or directly to ministers ". A motion by Harrison in favour of amalgamation was withdrawn in favour of reference to the County Unions, this being withdrawn in turn in favour of further consideration.

At the second meeting, " closer co-operation " was just defeated (38—35) by " direct oversight by the Union". This decision was reversed at the next meeting, 34 to 30 deciding for closer union by way of direct representation on each other's Committees, with a day reserved for Church Aid in both Assemblies. The Constitution of the Church Aid Society was then revised. Moneys raised and expended in the Counties were no longer to be regarded as income of the Fund. All County Unions were to be expected to contribute and to be eligible for grants. Unions must have had their rules concerning the admission of members and making of grants approved by the Committee. Eighteen members of the Church Aid Executive were to be representatives on the Union Committee.

Meanwhile the Amalgamation Committee had reported[2]. They were unanimous in finding that there had been an excessive multiplication of Societies, with

---

1 See *Year Book*, 1895, pp. 74-77.

2 *Year Book*, 1895, pp. 64-70.

[*Photo*: *Russell*]   J. D. JONES

JOSEPH PARKER

extravagance, scattering of energy, competition, and too frequent appeals.

> There is an unfortunate competition between different Societies, some of which are in a weak and languishing condition. The frequent appeals to the churches are wearying, and the result too often is to set up a low and inadequate standard of Christian giving. Under these conditions the full development of the aggressive power of the churches is impossible. There is a lack of high ideals, of well-organized plans, and of concentrated force of administration.

Nevertheless, the Union had no power over the Societies, which were jealous for their independence. The Societies were then considered *seriatim* :

(1) *Church Aid.* Amalgamation seemed natural and must be faced if necessary. There were many objections, especially :

    (a) The power of the Secretary of the Union would be greatly increased and might become dangerous.

    (b) Difficulties in administration of the Church Aid Society would embarrass the Union as " British Missions " had done in the past.

    (c) Other Societies would regard with suspicion the preference shown to Church Aid.

The best plan seemed to be representation on each other's Committees.

(2) *Pastors' Retiring Fund and Memorial Hall Trust.* " Both of these were created by the Union itself "[1]. Their separation had been more complete than was intended or was desirable. Amalgamation of administration was suggested.

(3) *Church Aid Society, Irish Evangelical Society, and Colonial Missionary Society.* It was suggested that " a combined administration might be more economical and effective ".

These suggestions were remitted to the Societies, and their replies considered. The advantages and disadvantages of the policy adopted (in 1857 and 1858) of making

---

[1] This statement, frequently made at the time, is not strictly accurate.

w

the Union deliberative only, with independent administrative Societies, were stated, as well as the fact that the Colonial Society was suspending judgment owing to joint consideration with the Union and the L.M.S. about new developments in its work.

The Pastors' Retiring Fund and the Widows' Fund were said to have been " administered with singular efficiency and economy "; their Trustees and those of the Hall were reminded of their denominational origin :

> With reference to the Memorial Hall Trust, this Committee urgently directs attention to the fact that its administrators are not under the control of any constituency, and that consequently there is a possibility which, happily, is not a probability, of its management devolving upon persons no longer in active sympathy with the Union. The mere suggestion is so serious that steps should at once be taken to re-affirm that the Hall was erected by and for the Congregational Churches, and to ascertain that the actual administration is conducted primarily in their interests. The deed under which the trust is held contemplates the establishment of exhibitions in our theological colleges, the liquidation or reduction of chapel debts, the augmentation of ministerial stipends, and similar denominational matters, none of which appear to have been as yet aided by the Trust. It is understood that the erection of the Extension, known as the Memorial Hall Buildings, was a moral necessity, and that the cost of this important addition has greatly taxed the resources of the trustees. The Committee is unanimously of opinion that, as soon as the arrangement can be made without injustice to personal interests, the management of the Pastors' Retiring Fund and the Pastors' Widows' Fund, and that of the Memorial Hall Trust might well be placed in the hands of one Secretary.

(4) The *Irish Evangelical* was recommended to amalgamate with the Irish Union.

(5) The amalgamation of the smaller Societies was not recommended until the demand for consolidation became more evident; in " a common direction of independent efforts rather than in any centralization of machinery " their usefulness lay.

Two years later the Report again referred to closer co-operation, now including the two Missionary Societies

in its purview: " It is believed to be the general opinion
that the self-government of these Societies should remain
undisturbed ". Nevertheless there should be conferences
with them about meetings and all should be on the Union
programme.

The Rev. Alfred Rowland voiced the demand for the
grouping of denominational Funds and Societies to secure
more effective and economic administration in his Chairman's Address in 1898. He went on to suggest that there
was need for Congregationalists to play a more active part
in the work of other Societies to which they belonged.
The Sunday School Union, though practically maintained
by Congregationalists and Baptists, was absolutely independent of them both. They were scarcely ever represented
on its platforms, and their ministers were rarely present at
its meetings.

Even more striking was the relationship to the London
Missionary Society, which was, to all intents and purposes, a Congregational institution :

> Yet how does it stand? Blomfield Street and Farring-
> don Street are independent of each other as Athens and
> Sparta, and occasionally they are at cross purposes, chiefly
> because they know little of each other's plans and appeals.
> It has been already pointed out by *The British Weekly*
> that the *Congregational Year Book,* which consists of 550
> pages, gives less than one page to the London Missionary
> Society, and this inadequate allusion is printed in the same
> small type as that accorded to societies for the help of
> discharged prisoners, female servants, and destitute lads.
> I venture to say that, if this fairly represents the official
> connexion, it does not fairly represent the real connexion,
> and is grotesque in its absurdity.

The Constitution and The Ministry.

Some of these changes necessitated the revision of the
Constitution. This need not detain us long as the form
adopted was to govern the Union for a few years only.
The aim was to make clear that the " National Society
exists for the sake of the individual Church " and not vice
versa, and that "constant co-operation is entirely consistent with happy independence ". Drafted by a Special
Committee, agreed to by the General Committee, the

Revised Constitution came before the Assembly in May, 1895, and May, 1896, being finally adopted in the latter year[1]. The changes introduced were not of great importance. " Pastors' Assistants, and Secretaries of Denominational and Catholic Evangelical Societies " were made eligible for honorary membership, and honorary members were given all representative members' privileges. In place of the Autumn Assembly, two or more Provisional Assemblies could be held. The Committee was to consist of 90 members, half of them ministers; 18 were to be Church Aid nominees; the rest were to be elected at the Annual Business Meeting, but by districts, 8 districts being given an allotted number of representatives. Nine were to be a quorum. The Committees were divided into two classes :

1. To consist of the members of the General Committee only. These were :
   (i) Finance and Publications ;
   (ii) Literature and Statistics ;
   (iii) General Purposes.
2. To include other members of the Union :
   (i) Young People ;
   (ii) Secondary Education.

The duties of these two Committees were :

(i). To promote the education of young people in Congregational principles ; to arrange for meetings of young people in connexion with the Annual and Autumnal Assemblies ; to conduct Examinations in Religious Knowledge ; to maintain a Bureau in London, and where practicable in other large towns, for the purpose of introducing young people from the country to resident pastors or other representative members of churches, including officers of Sunday Schools, Guilds, Christian Endeavour Societies, Christian Bands, and other Young People's societies, and of rendering, in general, such friendly assistance to newcomers as may be deemed desirable ; and to develop and maintain a close and helpful relation between this Union and Congregational Sunday Schools.

---

[1] The proposed Rules and By-laws, with the suggested changes in dark type, are in the *Year Book,* 1896, pp. 66-72, and as finally accepted and put into operation on 1st January, 1897, in *Year Book,* 1897, pp. xv-xxiv.

(ii). To establish such relations between the Congregational Union and the Nonconformist Public Schools as will tend to enforce their claims for support upon the churches by the formation of a Fund for Free Scholarships at the Schools and Exhibitions at the Universities; the circulation of information by means of a Calendar, or in other ways.

The annual maximum for the Publication Department Reserve for publications was increased to £500.

Other minor changes were made, but the one proposal that meant a real change in policy was not accepted. This was moved by Charles Leach and J. Lawson Forster and led to a long debate. It provided that an additional object of the Union should be "to create, maintain, and administer a Sustentation Fund for the Congregational Ministry of the Union ".

Nevertheless, while Sustentation was decisively rejected, this did not mean that no attempts were being made to grapple with the question of ministerial stipends. Mr. Gerard Ford was elected Treasurer of the Church Aid Society in 1894, and at once began to stimulate its work, so much so that in 1897 the Assembly was able to rejoice at the improved position of the Society. Indeed, in that year, the Society was able to make stipends up to the unprecedented figure of £90. At Birmingham, in 1897, W. P. Hartley made an appeal on behalf of the Society, and made a challenge offer of £100, which resulted in £1,065 being raised.

The ministers themselves were also moving, and the suggestion was made that a Ministerial Sick Fund should be created. The Committee wisely said that they would consider such a scheme provided that it was submitted to them by a body of ministers and sanctioned by the Registrar of Friendly Societies. This prevented the Committee from assuming the responsibility for schemes that were not actuarily sound, a decision for which the Union had much reason to be thankful in later years.

During these years attempts were made to make the Memorial Hall of increased service to Congregationalists. The Trustees of the Hall and Union joined in sharing the cost both of necessary structural changes and of maintenance involved. A Reading and Writing Room was provided for members of the Union to consult books, manuscripts, and current periodicals, and arrangements made by which Congregationalists in the country could borrow books from the Library. It was also decided to make regular additions to the Library of works possessing permanent denominational interest. This financial arrangement with the Trustees was continued for many years.

Meanwhile, the Publication Department had been developing, a Book Saloon being opened in the front of the building, this change being reported in 1894. The Department, at this time, was making good progress: the *Hymnal* sales reported in the previous year had been 69,000 copies, while the old *Hymn Book* had sold 35,000 copies. 45,000 copies of the *Sunday School Hymnal* and 32,000 of the *Mission Hymnal* had also been sold. This success enabled considerable amounts to be granted to various Societies: thus, in 1893, the following grants were made:

	£
Church Aid Society	500
London Missionary Society	250
Caterham School for Extraordinary Expenses caused by Epidemic	100
London Congregational Union for special Evangelistic Services	100
Canning Town Women's Settlement	50
Congregational Church, Cambridge, for Special Preachers	25
Improvement of the Congregational Library ...	100
Continental Work	150

Unfortunately the sales of the *Year Book* had been dropping for some time, and it was no longer one of the bright spots in the Union's publications; in 1901 the sale was only 2,761. An interesting code of Regulations drawn up to govern the preparation of the *Year Book* may be found in the issue for 1897, pp. 69-70.

In 1899 a volume of additional Anthems was published, G. S. Barrett again being the Editor.

In this year too the Congregational Historical Society was founded, its first officers being Dr. McClure, President; the Rev. G. Currie Martin, Secretary; and Mr.

W. H. Stanier, Treasurer. The purposes of the Society were thus stated :

> 1.—To encourage research into the origins and history of Congregationalism.
> 2.—To issue transactions giving the results of and discussions on such research.
> 3.—To print MSS. and documents, and to republish rare books and tracts.

In the *Year Book* for 1899 for the first time there appeared a list of complete statistics giving the number of Church Members, Teachers, Scholars and Lay Preachers. Woods felt that this deserved a special preface, which is worth reading as it shows once more the attitude of the denomination to statistics. The summary given, which is for the year 1898, is as follows :

	Churches, Branch Churches, and Mission Stations	Sittings provided	Church Members	Scholars	Teachers	Lay Preachers
England ...	3,326	1,222,750	236,616	465,703	46,617	4,674
Including Wales, Monmouth and Channel Isles	4,569	1,634,327	377,339	614,742	54,135	4,981

The Twentieth Century Fund.

In 1899 an attempt was made to help all the Societies by the Twentieth Century Fund, which aimed at half a million guineas. The objects, after revision, were as follows :

		£
1.	Foreign Missions	80,000
2.	Colonial Missions	20,000
3.	Church Buildings	150,000
4.	Church Debts	50,000
5.	Aid to Weaker Churches	50,000
6.	Aid to New Pastorates	50,000
7.	Aged Pastors	50,000
8.	Memorial Hall Debt	25,000
9.	Colleges, Schools, Settlements, *etc.* ...	25,000
	and Working Expenses	25,000
		£525,000

The Fund was first suggested by a letter by Mr. A. G. Hooper in the *Independent*. Rogers seized on the idea, and in February, 1899, a draft Scheme was submitted to the Churches and the County Unions, and the proposal to raise half a million pounds was adopted in May, after a discussion in which various speakers urged special claims —more adequate stipends, greater allocations for Church debts, and Church Extension. A special Council was appointed for the raising of the Fund, with Albert Spicer as Chairman, Rogers Chairman of Executive, and Mr. James Rutherford, of Birmingham, as Organizing Secretary, Birmingham being made the Headquarters for the Fund. The Council decided to recognize as part of the Fund moneys not sent to the headquarters but raised by Churches or Districts for Church Extension or the relief of Chapel Debts in their own neighbourhoods. This was called the "Supplemental Fund". Where Churches contributed wholly to the Central Fund, their contributions were divided *pro rata* among all the objects; where they contributed partly to the Central Fund and partly to the Supplemental Fund, their contribution to the Central Fund was divided among the objects exclusive of Extension and Debt.

The money for Foreign Missions was to be paid to the London Missionary Society; for Colonial Missions to the Colonial Missionary Society; for Extension and Debt to the Church Extension Committee; for the Memorial Hall Debt "to the Trustees in order that the rent to Congregational Societies be reduced".

In the distribution of the amount for "Aid to Weaker Churches", and "Aid to New Pastorates", the money was to be paid in equal proportions to the Church Aid Society for those Counties now receiving aid from that Society (the Church Aid Society having readily consented to regard the grant for New Pastorates as available for the whole country); and to the County Associations direct in the case of self-supporting Unions, *pro rata* to the contributions from these areas. The grant for Aged Pastors was to be equally divided between "The Pastors' Retiring Fund" and the New Superannuation Fund, if, after three years, that Fund should be in active operation, the income meanwhile being paid to the Congregational Union.

The method of earmarking and the "Supplemental Fund" did not work well from the point of view of the central organization. The Supplemental Fund amounted to £287,570 for Church Extension, and £120,241 for the Debts—a total of £407,811. For the Central Fund £83,121 was contributed, but even of that over £7,000 was earmarked.

The final disbursements from the Central Fund were (£'s only, which accounts for the slight discrepancies in the totals) :

	£
London Missionary Society	18,319
Colonial Missionary Society	4,126
Pastors' Retiring Fund	6,404
Reserved for Superannuation Fund	5,000
Pastors' Widows' Fund	5
Pastors' Insurance Aid Society	25
Memorial Hall Trustees	5,000
Church Aid Society for Weaker Churches ...	5,458
Church Aid Society for New Pastorates ...	5,000
County Associations for same objects ...	10,694
Church Extension Committee for Debts ...	1,955
Church Extension Committee for New Buildings distributed *pro rata* to County Associations	6,520
Church Extension (Old Fund)	1,646
Church Extension, South Wales	880
Church Extension, North Wales	100
Schools, Colleges, Settlements, *etc.* ...	5,499
	£76,635

	£	s.	d.	
Caterham School for Ministers' Sons	700	0	0	
Milton Mount School for Ministers' Daughters	700	0	0 +	£1 earmarked
Silcoates School for Ministers' Sons	300	0	0	
Blackheath School for Missionaries' Sons ...	92	0	0 +	£104 earmarked
Sevenoaks School for Missionaries' Daughters	240	0	0	
Cheshunt College ...	100	0	0	
Hackney College	300	0	0 +	£6 earmarked

Lancashire College	...	100	0	0
Mansfield College	...	100	0	0
New College		100	0	0
Nottingham Congrega-tional Institute	...	400	0	0 + £235 earmarked
Western College		400	0	0
Yorkshire United College		250	0	0
Bangor College		10	10	0
Browning Settlement	...	100	0	0
Lancashire College Settle-ment	... ...	100	0	0
Mansfield Settlement	...	100	0	0
Mansfield Women's Settle-ment	... ...	50	0	0
Mansfield Medical Mission		100	0	0
Middlesbrough Settlement		50	0	0
Broad Plain Settlement ...		50	0	0
Ministers' Home at Moor-hill	... ...	100	0	0
Ministers' Home at Mort-hoe	... ...	100	0	0
[1]Berry Memorial Scholar-ship Fund	... ...	500	0	0
Evangelical Continental Society	... ...	100	0	0 + £3. 3 earmarked
Irish Home Missions	...			£3. 3 earmarked
Medland Hall	... ...			£4. 4 earmarked

The organizers of the Fund claimed that it had been a success, and that is true in so far as it had stimulated generosity and sacrifice and developed interest in the work at home and abroad. Perhaps the main credit for the fund is due to Rogers, but there were many strenuous helpers whose names appear in the Final Report[2], which shows that 1,441 churches contributed. But the result was extremely disappointing to many people, and especially to the Church Aid Society, which had hoped for a large increase in its Central Fund, to the Missionary Societies, and to those who had a concern about ministerial superannuation. That there were grounds for the disappointment is evident when the amounts received by these Societies and interests

---

[1] This Scholarship, open to all Free Churchmen, is tenable at Mansfield College, Oxford.

[2] Separately printed 1902.

are put side by side with the sums aimed at. It remains to be noted that Congregationalists in Wales, Ireland, Australia, South Africa, and Jamaica all started parallel funds. These were massed together under the name Affiliated Funds, so that the final Report gave the following details :

					£
Central Fund	...	...	...	...	83,121
Supplemental Fund	...	...	...	...	407,811
Affiliated Funds	...	...	...	...	219,791
					£710,724

Meanwhile, demands were being made for some scheme to assist the removal and settlement of ministers. From 1845 on, when John Angell James and John Campbell advocated a Central Committee in London for this work[1], this demand continually recurred. In the *Christian Witness* in 1861 a correspondent wrote :

Some while ago there appeared in your columns a letter on the subject of Ministerial Removals, showing the desirableness of some means or machinery of promoting them in many cases, without the difficulty, violence, or odium too frequently felt and witnessed. Many ministers, whose term of labour has ranged between ten and twenty years, in trying parts of the vineyard, anxious, care-worn and dispirited, would, at sixty years of age and upwards, removed to a new sphere, be fresh as a daisy and blithe as a lark for further exertion and usefulness, and thereby effect a great saving of the Retiring Pastors' Fund.

But, as things now stand, how can such beneficial changes be effected? Numerous churches would be glad of the services of such men, and would greatly prefer them for the experience they have had. But how can these parties become acquainted with each other? This important work might be most beneficially effected by a body of right-minded gentlemen in London, ministers and others, who, becoming acquainted with the circumstances of the different places where ministers are needed, could introduce to them many likely to be suitable ; those chosen might be both happy and useful for many years to come, while their vacated places might be occupied by new men of life and power, and prosperity be the result of the movement on every hand.

1 Above, p. 158.

At Bristol in 1882, as we have seen, a proposal for such a Committee was very strongly opposed and emphatically rejected.

In 1899 a Resolution was passed authorizing the Committee to prepare a Scheme, but in 1900, the Assembly, finding itself unable to express any opinion on the "advisability or otherwise of attempting to frame any Scheme", deemed the subject of such grave importance that it authorized a special Committee to be formed to consult with the County Unions and present a Report, with power to proceed further and present a Scheme should the County Unions prove favourable.

Thus, when Joseph Parker was elected to the Chair for the second time in 1900, everything was more or less in the melting pot. Ministerial sustentation and superannuation, the training, supply, and removals of ministers, the relation of the Societies to the Union, all were matters of keen debate. It remained for Parker to fuse them together.

XV. IN DRY DOCK, 1900-1905.

THE new century seems to have released a great amount of
denominational energy.   It was inaugurated by a joint
Assembly with the Baptist Union held in London in April,
1901, when Mr. W. H. Brown entertained the 2,300 united
delegates to lunch in the Holborn Restaurant.

Then the Union settled down to consider a large number of subjects. The County Unions were asked to accept
an Interim Report in regard to ministerial removals and
settlements, and the Colleges were asked to state their views
on it and on proposals for sustentation. Anxiety was already beginning to be felt about the Education policy of
the Government.   Concerning the war a resolution was
passed advocating "the adoption of a magnanimous and
conciliatory policy".

Everything else, however, was thrown into the shade by
the Address of the Chairman. Nobody reading what
Parker had to say about organized Congregationalism in
1876 could have foreseen that in 1901 he would be the pro-
pounder of a scheme for a United Congregational Church.
But Parker's movements could never be foretold with any
certainty.   In 1889 he had invited a large number of ministers and laymen to a Conference[1] on "The Present and
Future Prospects of Congregationalism", when he said
that "there was no platform on which a capable man could
secure a fairer hearing than the platform of the Congregational Union—the Assembly was sufficiently discriminating to put down any man who wished to waste its time".
At the turn of the century he produced this grandiose
scheme.   In committee he moved a resolution, "That the
Congregational Church of England and Wales *be and is
hereby established"*, the fate of which it is easy to imagine.
Nevertheless, both his Chairman's Addresses dealt with the

---

1 It was at this Conference that J. P. Gledstone said : "Independency
has had enough of Congregationalism. County Unions were at first offered
for every brotherly fellowship and mutual aid—now, woe to the man who
is not a member of the County Union ! It means leaving his name out of
the *Year Book,* and that, in many cases, means ruin".

same subject and they brought definite proposals before the denomination. He argued that Congregationalism was too much organized or too little. It needed not repairing but reconstruction, not pottering but consolidation. A United Congregational Church would have a Sustentation Fund, and some way, or some one of several ways, of receiving and recognizing ministers. It would preserve the central principle of Congregationalism, and would extend and complete the fabric started in County Unions. This fabric he thus outlined :—

(i) The County Union is the point of equipoise between isolation in which sympathy is dead and centralization in which responsibility is wrecked.

(ii) The poor districts would be helped by the rich. That was the first idea of Hannay, "the most capable leader that has appeared in Congregationalism", but its application had not been equally strong all round.

(iii) It would make the best use of all its resources, a representative and responsible Assembly allowing no waste.

In looking at these resources Parker examined all the denominational organizations in turn. He glanced at the Colleges and asked whether three Colleges at Oxford, Cambridge, and Durham, would not be sufficient. He wondered whether the "many charities, funds, and trusts", scheduled in the *Year Book,* could not be consolidated, and whether denominational Societies could not be brought together "so as to cut down their expense without impairing their efficiency". He asked whether the almost abandoned chapels in great cities could not be turned into Central Missions, or sold and two or three serviceable chapels erected with the proceeds. All this could not be done by an individual; it could be done by a United Congregational Church.

Other resources of which such a Church would make use would be a lay agency, women's work, and the press.

Our relation to our own literature has often been simply contemptible—we want our own paper and we want that paper to be the well-supported organ of the United Congregational Church.

He was constrained to ask the fundamental question,

What are the 2,866 Congregational ministers in England and Wales doing? What are the 400,000 Church members doing? Not only what they are doing, but what under the encouragement of holy emulation they might do. To what use are the 1,600,000 church sittings being put? For what noble testimony do the 4,600 Congregational churches, chapels and mission stations unitedly and co-operatively stand?

With his Address an epitome of the scheme was presented.

In the autumn, at Manchester, Parker returned to the scheme. He said that all detailed proposals—"sustentation funds; superannuation funds; Board of ministerial settlements; and the like"—were summed up in this policy. The Union was not in a satisfactory position when these official figures with which he had been furnished could be quoted :

> The actual number of self-sustained Congregational Churches and Branch Churches in England and Wales is 2,342. The actual number of churches connected with the Congregational Union varies from year to year. . . . The actual number of churches which have this year subscribed to the Union is 1,278, which is practically little more than half the possible number ! Yet some people talk of the Union going on just as it is ! This is not my view at all. I want to interest the whole of the churches in the great work of Congregationalism; to do this the churches want an Ideal, some great uniting policy, some noble and sovereign principle. I think they will find it in the United Congregational Church.

An energetic, far-reaching policy was wanted, a move forward like that which was made in 1831. The United Congregational Church would bear a distinct relationship to all its ministers, to all its Colleges, and to all its Societies. He did not urge that it should have any creed. He had recently been at a committee meeting where

> a skeleton doctrinal trust-deed was discussed. One speaker described certain words as participles, another declared they were nouns and not participles at all, a third pointed out exactly where the whole Nicene Creed came in by implication, and a fourth averred that the submitted skeleton was hardly more than the baldest Unitarianism. In that conversation I could see the beginning of endless lawsuits, indeed one vigilant solicitor who was present

quite beamed, and broadly smiled as if he saw the "fields already white unto the harvest". Describe your doctrine as that of Congregationalism, and if difficulty should unhappily arise let living witnesses be called to testify what that doctrine has always been. It is the glory of Congregationalism that it has no Creed, yet it is the still higher glory of Congregationalism that it has a vital and imperishable Faith.

Therefore at the beginning of a new century he suggested this outline of a new Congregationalism :

(1) A simple but pregnant name—The United Congregational Church; (2) a vital and sympathetic relation of all Congregational institutions to one central and governing purpose and discipline; (3) perfect harmony between autonomous churches and a consolidated and representative Congregationalism; (4) a self-assessing and autonomous Independency contributing to the general good of all the churches; (5) a Ministry carefully guarded, well supported in service, in retirement, and in old age; (6) a profound doctrine and an aggressive policy; (7) a creedless but potent and ever-enlarging Faith; (8) an eager brotherliness of spirit towards all other communions and a not less eager spirit of brotherliness towards one another.

The Address made such an impression that the Assembly, on the motion of Barrett and Rowland, without committing itself, directed the Committee to take immediate steps to bring the whole subject before the churches and County Unions and to report at the earliest possible date.

At the same Assembly a long discussion took place on a motion favouring the re-organization of the Union, with the County Associations and not the churches as units. This was withdrawn, probably because it was realized that it was but part of the reconstruction which would take place were Parker's proposals accepted. To those proposals the widest publicity was given, 30,000 copies of the Address and 50,000 of an explanatory circular letter being issued. In 1902 it was reported that of replies received from County Unions[1], not one expressed absolute agreement with the scheme, but 6 expressed general approval, 10 asked for closer federation without committing themselves to any scheme, and 7 "declared for organic association with the

---

1 See *Year Book*, 1903, pp. 75-78.

[Photo : Swaine] SIR JOHN McCLURE

[Photo : Elliott & Fry] J. C. MEGGITT

SIR A. A. HAWORTH

County Unions". It was difficult to tabulate the returns from the churches, 642 of which had replied, though 252 churches with 28,748 members had declared for the proposal, and 168 with 30,419 members against it : 75 gave it "general approval", 80 voted for "closer federation without committing themselves to any scheme", and 69 favoured an amalgamation of the County Unions with the National Union. In general the larger churches did not favour the scheme, though they seemed to lean in the direction of closer federation. 164 churches approved the title "The United Congregational Church", 352 disapproved, and 161 "declared their positive preference for the present title". The smaller churches in general seemed to favour the scheme, as did the churches not yet in the Union.

In face of these figures and of the prevailing sentiment in the churches it was clear that there could be no formal acceptance of Parker's proposals. They had their effect, none the less, in the discussions then raging about sustentation, superannuation, ministerial settlements, and the Constitution, while three County Unions drew up schemes of their own for the reform of the Union.

To the different strands of reform proposals attention must now be directed.

Superannuation.

In 1901 the Committee reported that the total amount of funds for superannuation, either in the Pastors' Retiring Fund or in local funds, had not kept pace with the growth of the denomination. They appointed a Committee

> to consider the various proposals for a Ministers' Superannuation Fund, to invite consultation with managers of the Pastors' Retiring Fund, and to ascertain how far amalgamation of or combination with any existing provident funds is possible in order to secure its object.

In October of that year a Ministerial Conference declared itself

> strongly in favour of supplementing existing benevolent funds by means of contributions from ministers and Churches, and meanwhile urges the consolidation of all British funds.

In 1902 the Report incorporated the Report of the Sub-Committee, which had collected very valuable information[1], having discovered that there were 20 purely Congregational Societies, 7 partly Congregational and partly Baptist, and 6 in which the two were associated with other Free Churchmen. The strictly Congregational funds had a capital of £321,025, and it was shown that at least £25,000 went annually to the relief of Congregational ministers. Only four of these Societies were willing to consider a scheme of amalgamation. The Committee, remembering the failure of the attempt to create a Ministerial Assurance Society because of lack of numbers in 1834, had been negotiating with Assurance Societies through whom they suggested insurances should be effected. They outlined a scheme on an equitable basis, the principle being that each payment secured an annuity whether or not future payments were made. The rate of contributions suggested was 5 per cent, half of which should be paid by the minister, half by the church. The Assembly received the report with satisfaction, and ordered the Committee to bring it into operation. Eventually the Prudential Assurance Company was made the office through which insurances could be effected, and the scheme passed the Assembly in May, 1903, in which year the tables, printed for the first time in the *Year Book* for 1904, p. 70, were issued to ministers.

Ministerial Settlements and Removals.

The Interim Report of this Committee, mentioned above[2] and presented in 1901, spoke of the different ways of admission to the ministry. In regard to the Colleges, it suggested that the Arts course should be taken in a University, if possible, and that amalgamation of Colleges should be considered. With reference to ministers without special training, a three years' course of reading, with examinations at the end of each year, was proposed. Each County Union should have a Consultative Committee to deal with ministerial vacancies, and these confidential Committees should communicate with a Central Committee in London. Rules

1 See *Year Book*, 1903, pp. 55-56.
2 p. 348.

were also drawn up regarding the recognition of ministers
and churches. The whole of this Report was remitted both
to the County Unions for their approval and to the Colleges
for their comments.   In 1902 the replies of the Colleges
were received[1].   The Assembly, in accepting this Report,
accepted also the suggestion of Mansfield College to constitute "some of its gravest members a special committee"
to enquire into College training and make recommendations, and also into the desirability of forming a central
College Board. The Report for 1903 stated that this
"Colleges' Committee" had been established, consisting of
40 members, 20 appointed by the ten Colleges and 20
chosen by the General Committee, 15 from its own number
and 5 from outside.

The County Unions through their representatives also
adopted the "Rules relating to the Recognition of
Churches and Ministers[2]".

These laid it down that a minister must present creden-
tials from his College or from a County Union, and, if he
came from another denomination, not merely produce
evidence as to character, status, etc., but have been a member of a Congregational Church for at least six months.
They gave instructions to County Secretaries how to prepare lists for the *Year Book,* enjoined that aided churches
must not even invite a minister to preach with a view to the
pastorate without the consent of the County Executive, and
required that no Ordination or Induction should take place
without the presence of a County Union representative.

Men without college training who were invited to pastorates, in addition to furnishing evidence *re* character, *etc.,*
must have been recognized by a County Union as
Evangelists or Lay Pastors for three years, and must take a
three years' course of study, with examinations.

The Constitution.

The Superannuation scheme had been adopted, the
County Unions had practically all accepted the suggested

1 The *Year Book,* 1903, pp. 72-75, summarizes them.
2 See *Year Book,* 1903, pp. 70-1.

"Rules for the Recognition of Ministers and Churches", and a "Colleges' Committee" had been appointed. Meanwhile, in May, 1902, another Committee had been formed "to prepare a scheme which may serve to unite Congregational churches more closely for common purposes". This Reconstitution Committee, of which Dr. George Barrett was Chairman, was one of the most important the Union ever appointed. It held prolonged meetings, and finally beat out a new Constitution, which, adopted in September, 1904, still, with some additions and minor alterations, governs the Union's proceedings. Before being accepted it was sent down to the County and District Unions and the churches, considered in several Assemblies, and approved by the Church Aid and Chapel Building Societies, which expressed their willingness to come under the administration of the reconstituted Union. The first Assembly to be held under the new rules was that in the autumn of 1905, although the first meeting of the newly constituted Council was held in May of that year. The new Constitution opened with this Preamble :

1.—Certain powers and duties belong to the individual Church in self-government under the Headship of the Lord Jesus Christ, due regard being had to the interests of other Churches of our own and other denominations. For example : The reception and dismissal of members ; the discipline necessary to preserve purity of communion ; the election of pastor and deacons ; the order of worship ; financial arrangements ; and all that concerns the internal administration of the Church.

2.—Certain duties and responsibilities concern Congregational Churches as a whole, and these can be most effectively fulfilled by a union of Churches. For example : Congregational Church extension, and the promotion of missionary work at home and abroad ; the assistance of Churches needing support ; the introduction to the ministry of properly qualified and suitable men ; the support of Congregational Colleges in the training of Ministers ; the admission of none but worthy persons to the privileges of the Denomination and of the Union ; the provision of facilities for the settlement and removal of Ministers ; the adequate support of the ministry ; the assistance, when necessary, of Ministers of good standing disabled by age or infirmity ; the bringing of Congregational societies and institutions into closer connexion with the Union and with each other, and the brotherly co-operation with other Christian denominations in the extension of the Kingdom of God.

This Preamble is not exhaustive, and it should be interpreted in the widest sense. The aim of this Constitution is to enable Congregational Churches collectively to fulfil their responsibilities in relation to such questions as are indicated in the second paragraph[1].

The Union was said to be "a federation or Union of Congregational churches which are connected or associated with the County Unions of England and Wales or with the Union of Welsh Independents". The objects of the Union were now increased in number to 13, as follows :

(1) To extend and realize the Kingdom of Christ, primarily through Churches of the Congregational Order.

(2) To promote New Testament principles of Church fellowship and organization.

(3) To strengthen the fraternal relations of Congregational Churches, and to facilitate co-operation in everything affecting their common interests.

(4) To help such Churches as need assistance, and to stimulate and support efforts for Church Extension and Evangelization.

(5) To increase the usefulness of the County Unions, and to co-ordinate their operations.

---

1 Morlais Jones in his Address from the Chair in 1896, put the contents of the Preamble much more picturesquely :

We must realize its solidarity, and share in the larger life of the denomination. You have read Von Moltke's stirring story of the Franco-German war ; the calm old soldier's pride in the regiments of Prussian, Bavarian, and Saxon soldiers marching to battle side by side to the thrilling strains of the *Wacht am Rhein*. Its own special territory was dear as life to each of them, but this grand march made them one. The *Wacht am Rhein* was the duty of every one of them. They fought each under his own flag, but every one fought for that. *We* have our *Wacht am Rhein*. There is a work given to Congregationalism to do, not as isolated churches, but as a banded whole. The city church must march side by side with the village church, the rich by the side of the poor, the suburban church side by side with the panting, half-defeated church in the crowded district, where it is supposed Christ is not wanted because the rich have removed to suburban villas. Our hymn, the soul of our *Wacht am Rhein*, must be that a free, absolutely independent church, controlled and hampered by no synod nor conference, shall live to do its full tale of work in bringing the health and power of the gospel, the genius of Christ, to bear upon village and alley. And let no one be able to say, when wealth recedes from a neighbourhood, "Congregationalism can live no longer here ; let the chapel become a mission hall ; Methodism may live here, the Salvation Army may thrive, but the mission of Congregationalism is done".

(6) To secure a common standard of admission to the privileges and fellowship of the denomination.

(7) To develop and organize the work of Lay Preachers.

(8) To aid in the extension of Sunday Schools, Guilds, and Institutes for Young People.

(9) To prevent the alienation of Trust property[1] belonging to Congregational Churches, Societies, and Institutions.

(10) To maintain correspondence with Congregational Churches and other Christian communities throughout the world.

(11) To obtain information relating to Congregationalism, and to extend its influence at home and abroad.

(12) To promote Christian unity ; especially to co-operate with the Free Churches in the maintenance of their principles and traditions, and in collective action for their defence and support.

(13) To secure perfect religious equality and moral and social reforms.

The Union's business was now placed under the Council, which appeared for the first time in the Union's history. It was to consist of 300 members in the main elected by County Unions, but including 15 co-opted members (including representatives of the two Missionary Societies, and the Total Abstinence Association). At least one-half, and where possible, two-thirds, of the County Union representatives should be non-ministerial, and the County Unions had to contribute ten shillings annually for each representative. It is unnecessary to detail the duties of the Council, which essentially had to prepare business for the Assembly, to initiate movements necessary to promote the progress of the denomination, and to secure uniformity in the rules of the County Unions, as well as

> to consider the relation of various Congregational Societies, Colleges, and other Institutions and Trusts to The Union, and to secure their united and effective co-operation, and, where desirable, their ultimate amalgamation with The Union. Also, to confer with the Trustees of Beneficiary Funds connected with the denomination with a view to promoting the more advantageous distribution of those funds.

The Administration Committees were now to be—

---

[1] No doubt an echo of the Tooting case (above, p. 289).

1.—General Purposes.
2.—Church Aid and Home Missions, Lay Preaching, Sustentation, and Superannuation.
3.—Church Building and Extension.
4.—Literature and Statistics, including the *Year Book*.
5.—Finance and Book Room.
6.—Ministerial Settlements and Removals.
7.—Sunday Schools and Work Amongst the Young.
8.—Primary, Secondary, and Collegiate Education.
9.—Temperance.
10.—To co-operate with other denominations re Overlapping.

Regulations were also made in regard to the Assembly and the Chairman of the Union. The Chairman was now to be nominated by the Council, or the annual meeting of a County Union, or 25 members of the Assembly. New by-laws were made for the Assembly, the Council, and all the Committees.

One or two miscellaneous points of interest about the Assemblies may be noted. The Autumn Assemblies in 1901 and 1902 were held in conjunction with the Congregational Unions of Scotland and Ireland, that of 1901 being in Manchester, that of 1902 in Glasgow. In 1903 centenary deputations from the British and Foreign Bible Society and the Sunday School Union were welcomed. In 1904 the custom began of reading the names of ministers deceased during the previous year and of recruits to the ministry. In that year a resolution of sympathy was passed with the United Free Church of Scotland in the grave crisis produced by the recent legal decision about its property. In 1905 the Leeds Meetings included a mass meeting for women addressed by Mrs. Bramwell Booth.

In the 1902 Report, mention was made of the Union's 70th birthday, and its work during the period outlined. The catalogue began, perhaps not quite accurately :

> It has established the Colonial, the Evangelical Continental, the English Chapel Building, the Church Aid, the Pastors' Insurance Aid, and the Total Abstinence Society. It created the Memorial Hall Trust, the Pastors' Retiring Fund, the Pastors' Widows' Fund, the Young People's Union. . . .

And it ended :

> if last, yet certainly not least, it has diminished the isolation

which obtained among our churches when it was formed, and has greatly promoted their fraternal feeling.

Some attention was paid during the period to the development of lay preaching. The Church Aid Society suggested that the Union should foster an Association of Lay Preachers, and form local associations into a national federation[1]. The Church Aid Society raised a special fund of £500 to support the movement. Special conferences were arranged in many of the counties to stimulate lay preaching, arrangements were made for training classes, and weekly notes by Dr. Garvie were published in the *Examiner,* which had succeeded the *Independent* in 1900 and was, in the words of the 1902 Report, "rapidly becoming the recognized organ of our churches". The *Examiner* was the property of a keen group of Congregationalists, the "Congregational Publishing Company", who had bought the *Independent,* and unwisely changed its name. Many of the leading men in the denomination worked hard for it, but the few years of its existence were a continual struggle.

In November, 1902, the Union became an Incorporated Body, and in the same year it was reported that a Model Trust Deed had been drawn up, with and without a doctrinal schedule. The Publication Department continued to flourish, the sales on various hymn books in that year being 154,000. The total sales were £11,421, and the balance at the end of the year £814. It was well that the Department showed a measure of prosperity, for while salaries were £2,017, the annual subscriptions only produced £916. Further demands continued to be made on the Union from many sides. In 1903 the Revs. Alfred Rowland and J. D. Jones, Dr. Lambert, and Mr. Edward Smith visited the Canadian churches. They found them staggering under the weight of chapel debts amounting to £40,000; the home churches endeavoured to raise £4,000 to help them, and £250 was granted from the profits of the Union by way of encouragement and challenge. The following year, when

---

[1] For the development of the lay preaching movement, see the long report on Lay Preaching in the *Year Book,* 1904, pp. 65-70.

the London Missionary Society informed the Colonial
Society that it was withdrawing from the 1894 agreement to
support the West Indian churches, a joint conference was
convened, at which the three parties agreed to furnish a total
sum of £1,500 in equal shares during the next five years.

Woods had a very severe illness in 1899-1900, and from
it he never fully recovered. He resigned in February, 1903,
and died suddenly a month later before he had laid down his
work. The Rev. G. S. Barrett, of Norwich, who had taken
"a leading and very useful part in the drafting of the Constitution, . . . could probably have served the Union
more efficiently than anyone else[1]", but his age no doubt
prevented his nomination. The Special Committee cast
envious eyes on C. Silvester Horne, but it was intimated
that he would not accept the office. Finally the Committee's
vote resulted in the secretaryship being offered to the Rev.
W. Hardy Harwood, of Islington, but he too declined to
accept nomination. After further consideration an invitation was given Principal J. A. Mitchell, of Nottingham
College, who accepted and began his duties in January,
1904. He had merely given a taste of his powers during
the Assembly's discussions on the Constitution when he
died, in April, 1905. His successor was the Rev. R. J.
Wells, of Havant, the Secretary of the Hampshire Union,
who held office until his death in 1923.

1 Mr. G. N. Ford's memoranda.

XVI. EDUCATION AGAIN, 1872-1931.

AFTER the storm aroused by the Education Act of 1870 there was comparative calm, though watch was kept continually upon educational proposals and on the administration of the Act. When the Royal Commission on Elementary Education was appointed in 1885, the keenest scrutiny of its proceedings took place, both officially and through Dale and Richard, who were members of the Commission. Protest was made against some of the evidence and against signs that the Commission approved a reactionary policy, and when the Majority Report showed that these apprehensions were justified, a strong resolution was passed, in October, 1888, coupled with thanks to Dale and Richard for the stand they had made. It was this resolution which had such unfortunate consequences, for in seconding it Mr. Edward Crossley, M.P., attacked the Liberal Unionists. To avoid having to reply, Dale left the Assembly, and in order that the divisions on Home Rule should not cause controversy in the Union, withdrew from participation in its activities. Disturbed by the Majority Report the Union summoned a Conference of "the friends of a true and equitable system of National Education". This led to the formation of the National Education Association, to which a donation of £50 was made "as a mark of goodwill". In May, 1890, the Assembly put on record its opinion—

> that a free and efficient education should be secured for every child ; but at the same time calls upon all Liberals and Nonconformists to insist that free education shall be accompanied by popular representative control of all schools aided from the public funds.

The following year gratification was expressed[1] at the proposal to provide for Free Elementary Education, with the reservation that the Assembly

> at the same time affirms its conviction that the grant for the

---

[1] See the resolution passed at the Assembly, 12th May, 1891 (*Year Book*, 1892, p. 16). In face of this resolution the statement in A. W. W. Dale's *Life of Dr. Dale*, p. 579, that "the Nonconformists as a body resisted the measure" seems out of accord with the facts.

purpose should appear on the Annual Estimates, and that increased grants of public money to Denominational Schools should be conditional on their being subjected to the control of Managers appointed by the public; and also that there should be Unsectarian Schools, managed by School Boards, within reach of the children of every locality.

As a result of a Sectional Meeting in Manchester in 1881, a Committee was formed to inquire into middle class education. It sent out a schedule of questions[1] to County Union Secretaries about the Schools in their areas. Nothing more was heard of this inquiry, but attention seems to be diverted to the denominational secondary schools, addresses on behalf of Lewisham, Silcoates, and Milton Mount being delivered in the Assembly. In May, 1890, "Secondary Education among Nonconformists" was one of the subjects on the programme, and a Committee was appointed to ascertain how Nonconformist Secondary Schools might be more widely supported and their usefulness and effectiveness increased. The Baptists do not seem to have accepted an invitation to co-operate with this Committee, which in June conferred with the Headmasters, Headmistresses, and Managers of the Schools, Mill Hill, Taunton, Tettenhall, Bishop's Stortford (Boys and Girls), Blackheath, Caterham, and Milton Mount being represented. As a result the Committee recommended the establishment of a Standing Committee of Secondary Education

> in connexion with the Congregational Union, the objects of which shall be to further the interests of Nonconformist Public Schools, and to establish closer relations between them and the parents of our young people.

Further, the Committee was asked to consider the raising of a Scholarship Fund and the preparation of a *School Calendar,* and to survey the whole position with a view to extension, amalgamation, and the provision of new Schools, especially one in or near one of the Universities.

In May, 1891, on Fairbairn's recommendation, the

---

1 *Year Book,* 1904, pp. 57-58.

Council on Secondary Education was established, its purposes being thus stated :

(a) To attempt to secure the recognition and operation of the principle of religious equality in all the public schools and throughout all departments of the secondary and higher education of the country.

(b) To endeavour to secure the liberal and impartial administration of the local grammar schools of the country, and to aid in the creation of a public spirit favourable to their free government and efficient management.

(c) To secure the better organization and equipment of schools created to meet the special needs of Nonconformists.

(d) To promote the success of such schools by awakening a keener and more practical interest in their work.

(e) To raise a fund to be administered by the Council for providing scholarships and exhibitions at schools which the Council shall hereafter determine to be Nonconformists' public schools, and from such schools, at the Universities.

(f) To seek co-operation with the representatives of other Free Churches in order to carry out any or all of the foregoing purposes.

The Council was also asked to discuss the provision of hostels for Nonconformist pupils in public schools.

Throughout the last decade of the century, and especially after the accession to power of the Unionist Government in 1895, the Union's educational watchdogs were on the alert, and the other Free Churches were invited to join in the National Education League of the Free Churches in 1896. That there was abundant reason for vigilance was made plain when the proposals which became the Education Act of 1902 were revealed to the country. Then the value of the spade-work done by Hollowell, Viner, and others was plainly seen.

The introduction of the Bill rallied the Free Churches as they had not been rallied for a long time. When Dr. Caleb Scott was unable to take the Chair in 1902, Dr. Fairbairn, who substituted, spoke on "Congregationalists and the Education Question", and every Assembly for some years had a resolution recording "emphatic condemnation" of the "iniquitous" Act, with its provisions "which encourage hypocrisy, restrict liberty, and perpetuate political

injustice". Silvester Horne, Ryland Adkins, John Massie,
A. E. Hutton, and many others led the fight against the
Bill, while it is interesting to note that in 1902 a rider was
carried which said :

> The Assembly desires, in accordance with solemn
> declarations made in years past, to give expression to its
> conviction that there can be no final solution to the religious
> difficulty in national education until the State lays aside all
> claim to interfere, either by support or control, with
> religious education, and freely leaves to parents and
> Christian churches the responsibility and opportunities for
> the provision of the same.

Again and again the basic principles that public control
should follow the expenditure of public money, and that
there should be no religious tests for teachers, were pro-
claimed. Sympathy was expressed with the passive
resisters who refused to pay the Education Rate and whose
goods were distrained upon or who went to prison. When
the Act was passed its administration was carefully
scrutinized, special conferences on the subject being held
both in May and September, 1904. The considered view
of the Assembly may be stated in the resolution passed in
May, 1905 :

> That this Assembly affirms the conviction that any
> system of Schools, Primary, Secondary, or Technical, main-
> tained by public funds, if it is to be acceptable to the con-
> stituents for whom the Congregational Union is entitled to
> speak, must embody the following principles :
>
> 1.—The efficient preparation of the scholars for the
> performance of the duties of British citizens should
> not be subordinated to the interests of a religious
> denomination.
>
> 2.—No teaching in religion should be given at the
> expense of the Education Authority, and the school
> curriculum should be so framed as not in any way to
> violate religious equality.
>
> 3.—All teachers should be appointed solely on
> grounds of educational and personal fitness, without
> being required to submit to religious and sectarian
> tests, or to comply with any ulterior conditions of
> service.
>
> The Assembly further affirms its conviction that the
> Education Acts of 1902 and 1903 have failed to secure
> effective local self-government in the matter of education.

The Education Authority should be open to all persons without distinction of class or sex; its members should be freely elected, and directly responsible to those who elect them; its meetings should be open to the public; and it should be required by statute to secure for all the children under its administration a free, unsectarian, and efficient system of education. The area administered by the Education Authority should be such as will best admit of effective popular control.

Finally, it once more expresses its profound sympathy with all those who have felt themselves bound by conscience passively to resist the demands of the law, and it rejoices in the contention of the Welsh people for effective public management of all rate-supported schools, and believes that the action of both has done much to produce a national conviction that the Education Acts must be amended as soon as possible.

The indignation aroused by the Act and the powerful opposition of men like John Clifford and Silvester Horne had much to do with the Liberal victory in 1906. This was probably the last occasion on which the denomination as represented by the Union stood solidly behind the Liberal —or, indeed, any other—Party.

But those who believed the unprecedented Liberal majority in the House of Commons would speedily bring about the millennium were as speedily doomed to disappointment. Already, in May, 1906, strong objection had to be urged against an obnoxious clause in an Education Bill that was generally approved, while in November a Special Assembly was held to denounce the House of Lords for its amendments to the Bill.

The Assembly watched with concern the further attempts of the Liberal Party to solve the education problem. The main principles on which their contentions were based were repeated so often that they almost became wearisome, while occasionally an awkward jar would be given to the Assembly when a delegate would ask about the acceptance of State grants by denominational Secondary Schools. In 1910 the Report said that the Education Committee was opposed to the reception of State aid by the Schools and suggested better financial support, regretting that the Central Fund Campaign made an appeal for them impossible.

A manifesto, presenting the case of the Schools, was sent out to the County Union Secretaries. At a later date a list of Secondary Schools recommended to Nonconformist parents was drawn up.

In 1914 the Council represented to the Government

the growing disappointment of Nonconformists at the continuance of the injustices and anomalies of the Education Laws, and the Council, whilst recognizing the attempts which have been made by successive Ministers to deal with these matters, and the enormous pressure of public business with which legislation is hampered, welcomes the promise of a Bill during the present Session, and in view thereof expresses its opinion that no measure will be satisfactory which does not secure :

1.—Effective public control of all Schools maintained from public funds.

2.—The abolition of sectarian tests for State-paid teachers ; and

3.—The exclusion of all sectarian formularies and catechisms from publicly supported Schools.

This Council further urges that provision should be made in the promised legislation for a generous statutory grant in relief of capital charges, thus expediting the erection of new Council Schools, more especially to meet the needs of Single School areas, and facilitating the transfer of all denominational Schools in such areas to the Local Authority.

Further, this Council re-affirms its opposition to what is known as "Right of Entry" into Council Schools.

In 1918 approval was expressed of the educational advance shown in the Bill of the President of the Board of Education, Mr. H. A. L. Fisher, although a deputation to him made clear that the sense of grievance in regard to the 1902 Act still remained. This position was also taken up in a Resolution passed in November, 1919, which read :

The Assembly cordially welcomes the endeavours made by the Rt. Hon. H. A. L. Fisher, Minister for Education, to improve the educational system of the nation, and hopes that the appointed day may soon be fixed for the abolition of half-time, the raising of the school-leaving age to fourteen, and the institution of the Continuation Schools. The Assembly, however, records its deep and especial disappointment that under the present Government nothing has been done to remove the long-continued injustice under which Free Churchmen and Free Churchwomen suffer in being shut out from appointments in a multitude of Elementary Schools that are maintained from public funds. The Assembly demands that in the interests alike of education, of civil liberty and of religion, all positions on the Teaching Staff of Elementary Schools maintained from public funds shall be open to teachers of ability, training and good character without respect to ecclesiastical relationships or theological belief.

When it seemed clear, two years later, that the schools were to be the first to suffer under the economy campaign, Mr. Fisher was informed,

That the Council of the Congregational Union of England and Wales desires to impress upon the Board of Education that, in considering modes of reducing the National Expenditure it will be false economy to starve the Schools or even to restrict carefully devised means for the advancement of education, and that denominational school buildings should still be maintained, altered and improved, apart from public funds, with the exception of damage due to fair wear and tear.

At the end of 1921, at the instance of the Chairman of the Union, A. J. Viner, an attempt was made to put an end to the dual system in elementary education. Representatives not only of the Free Churches, the Unitarians, the Church of England, and the Jews, accepted the invitation to a Conference, but also of the National Union of Teachers, the Association of Education Committees, the National Education Association, and the County Councils' Association, the Roman Catholics alone declining on the ground that

the whole Catholic body regard it as essential that Catholic children should be given Catholic religious instruction in Catholic schools by Catholic teachers under Catholic oversight.

Some slight approach to an understanding seemed to be made at first, but eventually the Conference broke down, as it was impossible to accept the conditions laid down by the Anglican representatives.

In 1925 the Council Report showed considerable anxiety about new demands being made by the Anglicans in regard to their schools, while in 1929 the Council expressed

ROBERT ASHTON

J. A. MITCHELL

R. J. WELLS

W. J. WOODS

its profound concern at the reply of the Board of Education
to the Dorset Education Authority, suggesting as it does a
clear evasion of the Cowper-Temple Clause; that whilst
welcoming the transfer of Denominational Schools to the
local Education Authority, it consents to such transfer only
on the condition that the religious education in the transferred Schools shall be that of an agreed religious syllabus.
It, therefore, expresses its strongest disapproval of the
right of entry into the Council's Schools.

In 1930 and 1931, though there was every sympathy with
the proposals for re-organization arising out of the Hadow
Report, strong opposition was expressed to the demand of
the voluntary schools for building and re-conditioning
grants without public control.

XVII. FITTING NEW ENGINES.

THE SECRETARYSHIP OF R. J. WELLS,
1905—1923.

It is interesting to compare the Secretaryships of Hannay and R. J. Wells. Their terms of office were almost the same in length, and they both started with the advantage of a new Constitution. Hannay, as we have seen, was a statesman with wide outlook and a strong personality, exceptionally powerful in debate and in his management of Assemblies. Wells's gifts lay along other lines. He did not shine in discussion or on the platform, nor had he the power to conceive great changes of policy. Nevertheless, the changes in the life of the Union were much greater during the years 1905 to 1923 than between 1870 and 1890. There are probably as many opinions as there are delegates to the Union about the reasons which contributed to this remarkable result. Some would say it was merely due to the fact that the tide which turned towards centralization in Hannay's administration was now running far more strongly, that the undercurrent of the early period had now become a stream in spate. Some would give the credit to Wells, who had the power of securing his ends none the less effectively because he worked in unobtrusive ways. Some would say that the change was to be ascribed to the influence of J. D. Jones, who was looked upon as the " power behind the throne " and the director of the Union's policy. There is no reason why all these causes should not have contributed at one and the same time. Certainly the current towards centralization was running strongly; Wells's gifts are well described in an article written in the *Congregational Quarterly* in 1923 by Dr. Jones; and there is no doubt at all that the latter, as will shortly be seen, had a great deal to do with denominational developments during this period.

These developments must next be described.

The Constitution of 1904 governs the Union to this day.

It has, of course, been expanded as the organization has developed, and made to incorporate the Moderatorial System, Army Chaplains, and additional Committees, notably,

1915. Committee for Women's Work;
1917. Special Committee of 9 (to deal with questions of ministerial status, *etc.*);
1920. New Superannuation Committee;
1920. Board of Moderators (incorporating the Ministerial Settlements and Removals Committee);
1924. Publication Committee or Independent Press.

Other changes were the inclusion (May, 1922) of associate or personal members, who had the right to attend the Assembly, but not to vote (minimum subscription of £1, life membership £21); the adoption of the system of the alternative vote in the Election of Chairman (1919), the explicit statement that a woman could be Chairman, or two ministers who had held a joint pastorate[1]; the increase of the Council by the inclusion of General and Departmental Secretaries and Moderators, and of the number of co-opted members from 15 to 25. The affiliation fee was raised to 7s. 6d. per 50 members in 1922, and then to 17s. 6d. in 1924.

On the whole the new Constitution has worked well. It has secured extremely useful service from many laymen, especially those called to the Council Chair. These have been :

1907. Rt. Hon. Sir Albert Spicer, Bt.
1908. Sir J. Compton-Rickett, D.L., M.P.
1910. Mr. C. W. Toms, J.P.
1911. Sir Arthur A. Haworth, Bt.
1912. Mr. Alfred J. Shepheard.
1913. Sir Arthur A. Haworth, Bt.
1914. Mr. C. W. Toms, J.P.
1916-1918. Mr. Alfred J. Shepheard.
1919-1920. Mr. John Massie, M.A., D.D., J.P.

---

[1] This addition was made to meet the specific case of the Revs. Bertram Smith and Francis Wrigley, who after a life-long ministry at Salem Chapel, Leeds, were elected to the Chair for the year 1928-29.

1921.　　　　Sir Arthur A. Haworth, Bt.
1922-1924.　Mr. J. C. Meggitt, J.P.
1925-1927.　Sir Alex. Glegg, J.P.
1928.　　　　Mr. E. Hindle, J.P.
1929-1931.　Mr. F. N. Tribe, J.P.

It has been found, however, that the Council is too large for an executive body.

The March Council, held at some provincial town for two or three days is, perhaps, the most important Union gathering of the year. The Union's work has developed at such a rate that the Council's Agenda is now considerably overloaded, and often the Reports of important Committees have to be rushed through without adequate consideration. Recently, too, the practice has been adopted of appointing Commissions to deal with special subjects like " Terminable Pastorates ", " Church Membership ", and " Church Unity ". These Commissions have presented valuable Reports which have been discussed in the Council, but sometimes it has been at the expense of the Reports of the ordinary Committees. A likely and useful reform would be the " starring " for special discussion of certain Reports each year, so that, in the course of three or four years, every Department would have its affairs thoroughly ventilated in turn.

But a Constitution, no matter how carefully thought out, is of no value without adequate means of maintenance. The task of the Treasurers—Mr. William Crosfield from 1894 and Mr. R. Murray (afterwards Sir Murray) Hyslop from 1910—was by no means an easy or a pleasant one during these years. While the Publication Department continued to do well the nakedness of the land was concealed, but apart from its profits the resources of the Union were slender indeed. In 1906 subscriptions of £1,602 had to meet salaries of £2,224, while the expenses of Committees were £514. The invested funds of the Union, not including a small amount earmarked for Staff Superannuation, were only £7,219.

Altogether there appears to have been a deplorable reluctance to grapple with the financial situation during

this period.   Experience might have shown that the
Union's finances rested in large measure on the sale of its
hymn books.   With that in mind it is scarcely credible that
it was eight years from the beginning of the preparation of
a new hymn book to its actual publication.   The Report of
1908 said that the Counties were being consulted about the
advisability of a new book, and in 1909 a Committee was
appointed to prepare the book, under the chairmanship of
Dr. J. D. (afterwards Sir John) McClure.   Of course, on
this announcement the sales of the *Hymnal* almost ceased,
as the Council Reports several times admit.   Nevertheless
there was delay after delay.   The Rev. T. G. Crippen was
called in to help, and Mr. Josiah Booth made Musical
Director, but it was not until 1916 that the *Congregational
Hymnary* was published.   It contains 771 hymns, 116
chants, and 117 anthems, and still has a very considerable
sale.   It is to be hoped that now at any rate the Union will
have learnt a lesson, and that the production of the
Hymnary's successor will be a much more expeditious
process.

The sales of publications, which had been more than
£11,000 in 1905, dropped below £7,000 in 1912, and the
Union accounts ceased to show a credit balance in 1909,
while the Report in 1916 said that there had been a deficit
of nearly £1,000 a year for several years (the exact figures
from 1916 backwards are : £855, £814, £726, £1,290, £943,
£977).

The publication of the *Hymnary* in 1916 checked this
descent to a financial Avernus for a time, but with the
additional heavy expense incurred by the Moderatorial
Scheme the approach to it was rapidly accelerated.   In
order to finance this scheme Dr. Jones collected large
personal subscriptions, but they by no means met the
charges involved, and "appalling" is the only term that
can be applied to the accounts presented in 1922.   The loss
on trading (the two accounts had again been separated from
1919) was £777, the loss on the General Account £4,471.
Of this, £2,001 was due to the Moderatorial System, the
special donations providing £2,499 towards an expenditure

of £4,500. Salaries were now £2,133, Departmental Salaries £850, and salaries in the Trading Department (where the sales had now been swollen, largely by *Hymnaries,* to £18,718) £2,908. The Union's capital had dwindled to £4,677, while there was a Bank Loan approximately equal to the value of the stock. A loss on the General Account of £4,283 in the following year, against which there was a profit of only £91 from trading to set, reduced this capital to £580.

It was clear that drastic measures would have to be taken to set the Union's financial house in order.

One Scheme, it is true, had been tried. It bore the name of " A Shilling a Member Scheme ", and suggested a direct subscription of at least a shilling a year from every Congregationalist. In advocating the Scheme in 1916 the Council pointed out that a general acceptance of this proposal would not merely clear up the financial morass, but would enable the Council

1. To take the work of its Committees under more immediate control and so be free to effect changes of administration, thereby avoiding financial waste and obtaining better departmental work.

2. To secure a sufficient retiring allowance for aged ministers, including those that are already too old to avail themselves of any equitable insurance provisions.

3. To initiate and co-ordinate local efforts at Church Extension.

For some reason the Scheme never " caught on ", and not in this period was the problem of maintaining the Union's work solved.

In 1922 the Memorial Hall Trustees came to the Union's aid and promised an annual grant of £200, but they were unable to maintain this for long.

It is now necessary to see how this lamentable state of affairs had arisen.

I. First there were some general causes :

1. *The appeals of the London Missionary Society had been allowed priority.*

Through all these years the Union gave wholehearted support to the L.M.S. It noted special anniversaries, like

that of Livingstone's birth, took great interest in the World
Missionary Conference in 1910, and in 1913 deprecated any
retirement on the Mission-field before there had been an
appeal to the churches.   In 1914 it delayed a Finance
Scheme so as not to jeopardize this L.M.S. appeal.   There
can be no doubt that the continual drive for money by the
L.M.S. during these years had considerable influence on the
Union's finances; it was made in the main in the Congregational Churches, and people naturally would give to the
romantic and adventurous rather than to the comparatively
prosaic work at home.

No student of the period can fail to wonder whether it
would not have been well to bear Samuel Morley's contention[1] in mind : make your home churches and your County
Unions strong, with church extension scientifically planned
in new districts, and then your foreign missionary income
will inevitably increase.

2.   *The appeal for the Central Fund* no doubt had some
influence, as special appeals invariably have, in attracting
certain sums from the ordinary income of the Union.

3.   *The War.*   The drain on the man-power of the
churches, and the powerful appeal of war charities, could
not but have its effect from 1914 to 1918, while afterwards the increased cost of living tightened the purse
strings of individuals and churches.

II.   The primary cause was domestic, however, and not
external.

It was the fact that the work of the Union was developing on every side, without corresponding efforts being made
to sustain new enterprises, which was in large measure
responsible for continually recurring deficits.   The increase
in the number of Committees, and especially of Departmental Secretaries, meant a steady increase in expenditure.
Very often enthusiasts for some particular form of activity
would provide the means to begin new work, but gradually
subscriptions dropped off, and the Union was saddled with
the permanent maintenance of the Committee and its Secretary.   Such a process has been frequently repeated in the

1 See above, pp. 236, f.

Union's recent history. Some of these developments must now be described.

1. *Social Service.* In 1910 it was decided that there should be a Departmental Secretary for the Social Service Committee which had been formed for

> the collection and study of social facts, and the discussion of social problems and theories from the Christian standpoint in order to educate public opinion and to promote social progress.

Each County was asked to form a Social Service Committee which should encourage study circles, *etc.* The following year the Council made an appeal for contributions towards the extra £200 a year which the appointment of the first Secretary, the Rev. Will Reason, would involve. This Committee presented full accounts of its work, but in 1914 the Council Report said that both the Social Service and the Young People's Departments were held up for lack of funds, just as was the provision of adequate superannuation. Both departments were engaged in trying to stimulate County Union activity in their respective spheres. In 1919 some economy was effected by the appointment of a joint Secretary to the Temperance and Social Service Committees.

2. *The College Board.* The planning of the Central Fund resulted in the creation of the College Board in 1910. All the Colleges approved and sent representatives, and the first Union delegation consisted of Dr. Barrett, the Revs. R. Veitch, A. J. Viner, and R. J. Wells, and Mr. (afterwards Sir) A. A. Haworth. The Board at once set to work to bring the procedure of the Colleges into harmony with the new rules for admission into the ministry.

3. *Committee for Women's Work.* In 1915 the Council fell in with the suggestion of its women members that a Committee be formed to promote and stimulate women's work in the churches and to keep in touch with the various Leagues and Guilds of Congregational women throughout the country. In 1919 this Committee formed a Congregational Women's Training Institute for those who wished to train for Christian service, especially as deaconesses. Such women were to be attached to some Congre-

gational Central Mission or similar institution, and to attend classes at New College, London. The response to this laudable experiment was very disappointing.

The first full-time Secretary of the Committee was appointed in 1921.

4. *Young People's Department.* In 1906 it was reported that an enquiry was being made by the Rev. W. Melville Harris into the Sunday Schools of the denomination. This was published in 1907 under the title *Our Sunday Schools as they are and as they might become,* the expense being borne by Mr. J. C. Meggitt. The interest aroused by this survey caused the allocation of a whole day to a discussion of Sunday School problems in the Assembly in 1908. Not only so, but it was decided to re-organize the Young People's Union and form a Young People's Department, to include Sunday School work in the sphere of its activities, Mr. Harris being its first Secretary. The examinations continued to be conducted by the department, which also gave help to schools by means of lectures and by a Teachers' Library.

In 1915 an interest was acquired in " Teachers and Taught ", both the journal and the textbooks which go under that name, and an active interest was taken both in the steps which led to the opening of Westhill, Birmingham, and in the early years of its activity. In 1918 the Rev. A. Hallack succeeded Mr. Harris as Secretary.

The report presented by the Committee in 1922 was perhaps the most important in the history of the department. Not only did it announce the appointment of a Commission on Christian Education, the entire acquisition of " Teachers and Taught ", and the formation of the Congregational Young People's Fellowship, but it stated that a hymn book suitable for modern Sunday Schools was in preparation.

The other side to these manifold activities is the fact that the Department was now in receipt of a grant of £400 a year from the Union funds.

5. *Settlements and Removals Committee and the Moderatorial System.* After the revision of the Constitu-

tion this Confidential Committee soon settled down to work. It obtained information about the administration of the Congregational Board of Pastoral Supply in New England, asked the Counties to form Confidential Committees, and made Mr. A. A. Haworth its Chairman. There were only two other laymen on the Committee, and it is refreshing to find Fairbairn urging that the number should be increased. Soon yearly statements were presented of the number of introductions of ministers to vacant churches that had been effected, and the number of invitations that had been extended.

The task proved too difficult for the Committee, however, and in 1917 we find the Secretaries of the Lancashire and Yorkshire Unions (A. J. Viner and E. J. Saxton) carrying a resolution in the Assembly

> that in view of the need for some adequate scheme for effecting such changes from one pastorate to another as may be desirable, the Council of the Union be requested to take the matter into its consideration and report.

Meanwhile proposals were under discussion which would attempt a solution of this problem in conjunction with others allied to it. As early as 1907 in his Autumn Address from the Chair Sir J. Compton-Rickett had argued that County Union divisions should no longer necessarily follow ancient geographical divisions, and urged a system of paid County Secretaries to devote the whole of their time to the development of Congregationalism.

This suggestion of Compton-Rickett's was combined with another attempt to solve the problem of ministerial settlements and removals in the Scheme for Provinces and Moderators, which was thoroughly discussed for several years in Committee and the Council, and then sent down to the County Unions for consideration. This scheme was finally adopted in May, 1919. It provided for the division of the country into nine provinces :

North-West : Lancs, Cheshire, Westmorland, Cumberland.

North-East : Northumberland, Durham, Yorks.

East : Cambs, Essex, Herts, Suffolk, Norfolk.

East Midland : Derby, Lincs, Leics, and Rutland, Notts, Northants, Hunts, Beds.

West Midland : Staffs, Salop, Warwick, Glos. and Hereford, Worcs, Oxford, Bucks, Berks.

South : Kent, Surrey, Sussex, Hants.

West : Cornwall, Devon, Somerset, Dorset, Wilts.

London : The area of the London Congregational Union.

Wales and Monmouth.

Each of these Provinces was to be served by a Moderator appointed by the Assembly of the Union on the nomination of a Committee of nine nominees of the General Purposes Committee, plus five representatives of the Province concerned. The Scheme was to be administrated by the General Purposes Committee of the Union, and the Moderators were to be appointed for periods of five years. Crucial clauses in the Scheme are these :

I. That larger Provinces be formed by the grouping together of County Unions, and that to such Provinces Moderators should be appointed. It is hoped that such Provinces will as soon as possible become administrative areas.

II. The general duties of such Moderators shall be :—

(a) To stimulate and encourage the work of the Denomination within their own Provinces, and to act as friends and counsellors of ministers and churches.

(b) To act as superintendents of Church Aid and Central Fund Committee Administration.

(c) To assist churches and ministers in all matters connected with ministerial settlements and removals by personal action and by constant and regular conference with one another.

There were many difficulties in regard to a Scheme of this kind. At no time in the history of the Union has suspicion of centralization been stronger than during the period of the Great War. Especially was the feeling between London and the North extremely pronounced. This seems to have broken out periodically throughout the century. In the early days of the Union it was, so Guinness Rogers in his *Autobiography* calls it, " one of mutual suspicion rather than of hearty co-operation ". He found the cause then largely in politics, pointing out that at the

time of the Corn Law agitation London was generally
Conservative and the North Radical. Halley at this time
wrote to John Blackburn a letter which reflects the feeling
between North and South :

> When I heard that you imagined that I had become an
> agitator, it was quite time for me to disclaim the suspicion.
> I do not wish to take any pains to set other persons right,
> as there are not a score of Londoners besides yourself to
> whose opinion I pay any regard.

Henry Lee, at the time of the Consolidation Scheme in
the seventies, said that Lancashire had evaded the discussion of the Scheme, and Yorkshire had not condescended
to notice it. It is not difficult to understand the position of
the Northern Unions. They are strong enough to stand
alone, and are sometimes apt to suspect London domination
when it does not exist, especially when economy dictates the
appointment of a majority of members of committees from
in or near London. They have, too, their own whole-time
County Secretaries, and their affairs have been in the hands
of very efficient leaders. It was here that one of the main
troubles of the Moderatorial proposals arose, the London
Union, which also had a full-time Secretary, not feeling the
difficulty as acutely as Lancashire and Yorkshire, which
were not disposed to allow the intrusion of another officer
into their areas who would be performing functions much
the same as those previously performed by the County
Secretaries. A resolution which meant the rejection of the
scheme was only defeated in the Lancashire Union because
it was not well presented, and an amendment was carried
demanding that the election of the Moderator should be by
the Committee established under the Scheme for each
Province. In the National Assembly this amendment was
not accepted, but words were introduced which made it
clear that members of the Provincial Committees had equal
powers with the nominees of the Union in the nomination
of Moderators. The situation was further complicated by
the fact that to the area of the Lancashire Union the
Cheshire County Union was tacked on, and to that of
Yorkshire the Union of Durham and Northumberland,

Eventually the Scheme was accepted, though concessions had to be made to the larger Unions.

There was much suspicion of these new " bishops " in many parts of the country, but the men appointed were highly respected for the service they had rendered in their pastorates, and opposition became less vocal as the years went by. The first Moderators were :

North-West Province	Rev. A. J. Viner.
North-East Province	Rev. E. J. Saxton.
Eastern Province	Rev. H. Ross Williamson.
East Midland Province	Rev. H. H. Carlisle, M.A.
West Midland Province	Rev. D. Lincoln Jones, B.A., B.D.
Southern Province	Rev. F. H. Wheeler, D.S.O.
Western Province	Rev. E. P. Powell, M.A.
London Province	Rev. W. L. Lee.
Wales and Monmouth Province	Rev. David Walters.

In 1924, when new Moderators were to be appointed, changes were made in the Scheme. Sections I and II were now made to read :

I. That Provinces be formed by the grouping together of County Unions and that to such Provinces Moderators, either ministerial or lay, be appointed. The question whether any Province is to become an administrative area is left to the judgment of the counties concerned.

II. The general duties of Moderators shall be :

(a) To stimulate and encourage the work of the Denomination within their own Provinces, and to act as the friends and counsellors of Ministers and Churches.

(b) To act as advisers with regard to all financial assistance from denominational funds.

(c) To assist Churches and Ministers in all matters connected with Ministerial Settlements and Removals by personal action and by constant and regular conference with one another. This is not to be understood as excluding other means of effecting changes of pastorates, but it is desirable that the Moderators should be kept informed of any introductions effected so as to avoid overlapping.

N.B.—Whereas it may be considered fitting that the Moderator attend the Ordination, Induction, or Recognition Services in his Province, his presence shall not be deemed essential, nor shall he preside *ex officio,* but only when invited to do so.

The appointment was still to be by the Assembly on the nomination of a Committee consisting of not more than 14 Provincial representatives and not more than nine representatives of the Union. Stipends were now to be provided by the Provinces and the Union jointly, but the Provinces' proportion was represented by an increase in the affiliation fee from the churches of 7s. 6d. per 50 members. To meet the cases of Lancashire, Yorkshire, and London it was stated that Unions with a whole-time Secretary may be deemed Provinces for the purpose of the Scheme and may nominate their own Secretaries for recognition as Moderators, in such cases the Province being entirely responsible for its Moderator's stipend.

Into the detailed adjustments of Counties under the Scheme it is unnecessary to go. After ten years it is becoming possible to estimate the value of the new enterprise. There is no doubt at all that the Moderators have done much for the churches, especially in the country districts, serving to encourage and inspire, and to keep the churches in touch with the larger life of the denomination; they have been extremely useful in settling troubles and disputes within churches; they have helped to dignify Ordination and Induction Services; they have presented to the Council reports on various aspects of the denominational life. It cannot be said that they have succeeded in solving the problem of ministerial settlements, but the fault for that does not lie at their door; it is largely due to the ease with which unsuitable men have obtained admission into the ministry. It is clear, too, that the Provinces are far too large, while there are those who would claim that with the course of years too much power accumulates in the hands of the Moderators, and so the liberty of the individual church and minister is endangered.

The Central Fund.

It is now necessary to return in order to describe efforts made to cope with the problem of ministerial maintenance.

At the meeting of the Council in October, 1908, Dr. Wardlaw Thompson moved and Mr. G. N. Ford seconded this resolution :

> This Council having received the report of the Church Aid Committee, while convinced that the time has arrived when immediate steps should be taken to grapple in some practical way with the whole question of ministerial support, recognizes that this problem is closely bound up with questions of ministerial status and the grouping of churches. It is mindful also that other great questions intimately connected with the growth and spirit of Congregationalism are occupying the minds of many in the denomination. It resolves therefore that the report now received be referred to a Special Committee, such Committee to take into consideration these other questions, and to report to the Council in March of 1909.

A representative Committee drew up a scheme on the lines of this resolution, and it was finally adopted by the Assembly in May, 1909. After referring to Dr. Parker's plea for a United Congregational Church and to the new Constitution of the Union, it said that the most urgent of the denomination's problems gathered round the question of the ministry, and it was therefore necessary

> to concentrate upon the fundamental question of ministerial status and support, for only when that problem was solved would the seriousness of other denominational difficulties be largely relieved.

It was resolved to raise a Central Fund for ministerial support amounting to £250,000, the aim being to secure an adequate minimum stipend for all ministers, not fixed, but variable according to cost of living in town and country. This minimum having been reached, the Fund could be used in grants to ministers out of charge or for superannuation grants. Only the interest of the Fund, which was to be vested in the Union, was to be used. The Scheme aimed at a minimum of £120 a year, but immediately desired to secure an income of £100 and to make such further provision for ministers in cities and in towns as might be required. The ministers eligible were to be those on a list known as List A, this including the names of ministers duly returned by the County Unions in accordance with the regulations. Only List A ministers could receive grants from the Central Fund; List B was to contain the names of evangelists and lay pastors. It was further required that a minister receiving a grant of not less than £10 should, if below 40 years of age, contribute 2½ per cent of his total income as premium of insurance to the Congregational Superannuation Fund; if over 40 either to that Fund or to the Pastors' Retiring Fund. A church seeking a Central Fund grant had to satisfy the Committee that it was raising an adequate proportion of the minister's stipend, and had to fall in with any scheme of grouping required by the County Union. The adoption of this scheme made it necessary that the Rules relating to the Recognition of Churches and Ministers should be revised. The revision was adopted by the Assembly in May, 1909, and revised in May, 1912. These Rules were printed in the *Year Book,* and special notice should be taken of the following:

" In the interest of the Aided Churches it is required as an absolute condition of grant that no invitation be given to any person to accept the pastorate, or even to supply the pulpit with a view to the pastorate, without the approval of the Executive of the County Union ".

It was also suggested that no Ordination or Recognition of ministers should take place without the concurrence and approval of the County Union expressed by the presence of its appointed representatives.

The Central Fund campaign was conducted by the Rev. J. D. Jones of Bournemouth, who gave himself without stint to propaganda for the Fund, both in public addresses and by securing private gifts. As the Council Report in 1913 says:

> His advocacy of the Scheme assured its acceptance, and by his untiring and self-denying labours he has carried it through to completion; he has shirked no task, and he has grudged no sacrifice, and your Council can do no other than place on record its gratitude and appreciation of his splendid services on behalf of our ministry and churches.

The Fund was completed in 1913, when a thanksgiving demonstration in the Albert Hall was presided over by the

[Photo : Russell

GERARD N. FORD

ALBERT SPICER

JOHN CARVELL WILLIAMS

J. COMPTON RICKETT

Right Hon. J. H. Whitley, M.P., addresses being delivered by Sir Albert Spicer, Sir Arthur A. Haworth, the Revs. J. D. Jones, C. Silvester Horne, and J. M. Gibbon, and a thanksgiving prayer offered by Dr. R. F. Horton.

While the Fund was in process of collection stipends were raised to £100. In 1916 the Church Aid and Central Fund Committees were combined, being empowered to request the attendance of County Secretaries where necessary. The capital value of the Central Fund at the end of 1930 is £270,189, of the Church Aid £41,922.

The Fund proved, and still proves, the greatest boon to churches throughout the country. It merely needs a reference to the grants made in the *Year Book* in any year to realize the difference that the Fund has made to many churches and ministers.

The Support and Superannuation of the Ministry.

The greatly increased cost of living pressed very heavily on ministers with small stipends, and in 1919 the churches were asked to increase this minimum by at least 25 per cent, the Central Fund giving £2,000 in challenge grants.

In November, 1919, a Laymen's Commission was appointed in order to give practical effect to this plea for an increased minimum stipend. They recommended that this minimum be fixed at £220 for the country and £250 for towns, and asked the County Unions to appoint Committees of laymen to urge this throughout their areas. Some of the Committees carried through the recommendations speedily, Hertfordshire leading the way. The Chairman of the Commission was Sir Albert Spicer, who gave to it much time and thought.

These Commissions continued their useful work for some years, coming to the conclusion that

> with the help of the Central Fund and the Church Aid Committee, together with the action and continuous co-operation of the County Executives and Laymen's Committees, an annual visitation of the Churches, a better system of raising the income, and a more generous giving in proportion to increased earnings by the congregation, the minima salaries of £220 and £250 for the Ministers of Aided Churches is

z

within the means of our people throughout the country in agricultural as well as industrial districts.

Meanwhile the question of superannuation was pressing heavily on the minds of many. Arrangements had been made, under a new Finance Scheme, to devote part of the Union's income every year to superannuation, and the Report for 1918 said that a Ministers' National Provident Society had been inaugurated on an equitable basis to afford facilities for ministers to assure for themselves with their own denominational Society an annuity at the age of 65[1]. A. J. Viner[2], the Secretary of the Lancashire Union, and the Union Chairman in 1921, was specially desirous of putting the Superannuation Scheme on a satisfactory basis. He hoped to celebrate his year of office by raising the sum of £150,000 for this purpose, which made a great appeal to the heart and conscience of the churches, for it was generally recognized that most ministers did not receive sufficient income to enable them to make much provision for old age, and that the annuity of £32 10s. granted by the Pastors' Retiring Fund was altogether inadequate. It was realized, too, that this state of things meant that many ministers retained their pastorates long after they were able to do effective work, and so the witness of the churches suffered.

It was agreed, therefore, that the Union should be responsible for superannuation, and that, to be eligible, ministers in youth should themselves begin to contribute to some Society to provide for superannuation. It was found that a Capital Account of £150,000, together with the capital from the Pastors' Retiring Fund, would probably enable the annuities at present given to be doubled. The Scheme for raising the £150,000 was finally merged in a wider Scheme for raising a Fund of half a million pounds for denominational purposes, the first charge to be the £150,000 for superannuation. This new

[1] See *Year Book,* 1919, p. 31 for details. The motive behind this Society was to afford ministers in counties where there was no local Provident Society an opportunity to make provision for old age through a denominational institution.

[2] Viner's Chairman's Address on " Our Ministry " in 1921 deals very effectively with the question of superannuation,

Central Fund was to be called the Forward Movement Fund, and the Assembly committed itself to it in May, 1921.   The objects of the Fund were :

£150,000 (to be the first charge on the Fund) for Ministerial Superannuation,

£50,000 for the assistance of the Widows of Ministers,

£50,000 for the Schools, Milton Mount, Caterham, Silcoates,

£40,000 for the maintenance and extension of the work at Headquarters,

£50,000 for the Moderators, if continued, or such purpose as the Union may determine,

£20,000 for the Superannuation of Evangelists in List B,

£25,000 Colonial Missionary Society,

£75,000 London Missionary Society.

Dr. J. D. Jones was again the leader of the campaign for raising this Fund.   In this case a new method was adopted.   Instead of all moneys being sent direct to the Central Office, Forward Movement Commissioners were appointed in different areas, and in this way many laymen were drawn into service and a good deal of hidden talent discovered.   Further, the all-important decision, based on previous sad experience, was taken not to allow earmarking. From the point of view of the Fund this was undoubtedly wise, as there was strong criticism, especially in Lancashire and Yorkshire, where it was often claimed that the less popular and more controversial parts of the Scheme (the endowment of Headquarters and of the Moderatorial system) were being carried over the stream of disapproval on the back of a Superannuation appeal which everybody welcomed. In reply to these criticisms the words "if continued, or such purposes as the Union may determine" were added to the clause referring to the Moderators.

For the completion of the Forward Movement we must wait until the next chapter.

We now turn to the attitude of the Union towards War, and the influence of the Great War of 1914 to 1918 upon its activities.

The War.

In 1909 the Assembly welcomed resolutions passed by representatives of the Christian Churches in the United Kingdom and Germany gathered in London in 1908, and in Berlin in 1909. In 1911 the Council expressed thankfulness for

> world-wide movements that are evident, and which in spite of much to the contrary herald the dawn of a day wherein Peace among the Nations shall be enthroned, and the grinding burdens of armaments and the ghastly horrors of war shall become impossible.

They went on to welcome Sir Edward Grey's response to President Taft's overtures, hoping they

> foreshadow a Treaty of absolute and unreserved arbitration between ourselves and our great Sister Country, the United States of America, and point the way to a world-wide peace between all Nations, and to relief from the crushing burdens of armaments.

In 1912 the Council observed with

> the greatest satisfaction the growing desire both in Germany and England for a better understanding between the two peoples.
>
> To the Council it seems inconceivable that two great Christian Nations so near akin and whose interests are so closely interwoven should for any lengthened period remain estranged.

In May, 1913, when addresses on "The Cultivation of National Peace, particularly as between England and Germany" were given by Dr. Gensichen and Dr. Moore Ede, the Assembly passed a strong resolution against the increase of armaments and the growth of militarism, and urged the Government to insist on The Hague Conference being held in 1915. The War broke out in August, 1914, to the surprise and dismay of all Christian people. The Autumn Assembly in 1914 was not held, but the following May the Assembly carried the resolution :

> That this Assembly of the Congregational Union of England and Wales desires to express its profound sorrow at the outbreak of the present calamitous war; it believes that the awful suffering caused by the war and the heroism evoked by it together present a great challenge to all the

churches to re-consecrate themselves to the task of discovering and declaring the will of Christ for human society, recognizing that on all who bear His Name lies the responsibility of transforming through His Spirit the relations between men and peoples. While there are individuals among us, for the sincerity of whose convictions we have respect, who believe that war is never justifiable in the light of Christianity, our Assembly as a whole is of opinion that in view of all the facts now before the nation no other course was open consonant with national righteousness save that pursued by His Majesty's Government, and it would assure His Majesty's Ministers of its loyal and prayerful support. It is united in regarding with admiration and reverent gratitude the ready and sacrificial response of the manhood of the country, including tens of thousands associated with our Congregational churches, to the call of duty, and commends them and the cause for which they are fighting to Almighty God. It would further place on record its abhorrence of the treatment meted out to Belgium by Germany and the brutal disregard of all the usages of civilized warfare[1] by the German authorities. And this Assembly would extend to all the suffering and bereaved, both in our own land and abroad, its heartfelt and sorrowing sympathy.

A letter was sent to the churches suggesting how they might best render service during the War, and steps were taken to secure that the spiritual interests of Congregationalists in the Services were cared for. Eventually it was arranged that the Baptists, Congregationalists, Primitive Methodists, and United Methodists should form the " United Board ", with its own chaplains—eventually 300 chaplains and 1,000 " officiating ministers " were appointed, besides large numbers who served with the Y.M.C.A. at home and abroad.

In 1917 there was no March Council, the meeting being held in May, and the Annual Assembly in London in October. In May, 1918, the Assembly urged that the institution of a League of Nations should be put in the forefront of the peace terms, and recorded its judgment

that a first essential to a World Peace as the outcome of the World War is the general disarmament of all the nations, except in so far as is required for the maintenance

1 " Civilized warfare " !

of an international force sufficiently strong to enforce the will of the League.

In the same year the Council reported that it had appealed to the Government to forbid the sale of intoxicants during the war and demobilization, protested against its indifference to the moral welfare of the troops, and against the unjust treatment of " many who have, however mistakenly, claimed exemption on conscientious grounds from military service ".

Resolutions were frequently passed urging support of the League of Nations and of the World Alliance for Promoting International Friendship through the Churches, and satisfaction was expressed at the calling of the Washington Conference.

A Memorial to Congregational Chaplains and Ministers killed in the War was unveiled in the Memorial Hall Board Room in May, 1921, in which year the Council noted with pleasure the fact that

> permanent Chaplaincies will be allotted under an agreed Scheme to the United Navy, Army, and Air Force Board. Thus we shall now for the first time secure permanent Chaplaincies in the Navy, both ashore and afloat.

In May, 1922, a message was sent to the Prime Minister, Mr. Lloyd George, at the Peace Conference at Geneva, and a resolution passed rejoicing at the success of the Washington Conference and affirming

> its whole-hearted belief in, and advocacy of, the League of Nations, in a policy of drastic International disarmament by land and sea, except for police purposes, in the supersession wherever possible of methods of secret diplomacy by wise publicity and open parliamentary discussion of international problems, and in a just revision of the Versailles Treaty.

These convictions were re-affirmed in October, 1922, when special thanks were accorded to Lord Robert Cecil. This last resolution was moved by Dr. J. H. Jowett, whose peace campaign at this time was strongly backed by the Assembly, as was Dr. F. W. Norwood's a few years later. Right down to the present, resolutions in favour of the League of Nations, disarmament, the Kellogg Pact for the outlawry of war, and arbitration have been regularly passed.

The failure of the churches to keep the world at peace gave rise to much searching of heart among their members, as well as to scornful criticism from without. One of its results was the appointment, in March, 1923, of a Commission, whose duty it was to carry out the terms of the following resolution :

> That in view of the need and growing desire in our churches for clearer and more definite guidance upon the problem of the attitude of the Christian individual and the Christian community to war, and in view of the widespread desire of the Ministry to find a common Christian policy that they can unitedly recommend, and in view of the urgent need for quiet thinking before passions are aroused by the possibility of another conflict, the Council do at once proceed to appoint a representative Commission to consider and report upon this matter without delay.

This representative Commission, on which the diverse points of view were represented, met at frequent intervals during two years, and finally presented its findings in a volume[1] under the editorship of its Chairman, Dr. Peel. The Commission acknowledged with sorrow that its members had not been able to arrive at agreement. In their Report they set out the different opinions and then outlined what might be done by the churches in the present circumstances to bring the nations into a peaceful commonwealth.

Attempts have been made at times to commit the Assembly to pacifism, but without success, the War Commission Report aptly illustrating the cleavage in the denomination on the subject. This was plainly evident at Norwich in 1929, when six addresses on " War and Peace" (afterwards published[2]) were delivered.

Among the many casualties caused by the War was the weekly paper that was serving the Congregational churches. In 1906 the *Examiner* had become the *British Congregationalist,* and attempts were made to make it a

---

1 *The Christian and War,* 1925.

1 *Christianity and War.* By B. L. Manning, E. J. Price, C. H. Dodd, Leyton Richards, G. Shillito, and H. C. Carter, 1929.

strong denominational journal. At the Council Meeting in 1907 the increasing value of the paper as a denominational organ was recognized, and this resolution passed :

> That this Council, recognizing the necessity to Congregationalism of a strong denominational newspaper, pledges itself to support the *British Congregationalist* by every means in its power, and urges upon the Churches and upon Congregationalists generally the duty of giving to the paper the necessary financial assistance, and of increasing its circulation and influence.

At this time W. B. Selbie was rendering valuable services as editor, and for a time the circulation increased.

The Report in 1909 announced the decision to take over the paper providing satisfactory terms could be arranged. The following year it was reported that a temporary agreement had been made with the Directors, the Rev. Frank Johnson being appointed Editor. £100 was contributed to the support of the journal in 1909, and large use was made of its pages to urge the Central Fund and publish lists of subscribers. £300 was granted from the General Fund, and £500 from the Central Fund in 1910; and in 1911 £825 given from the latter fund. In this year the Directors reported to the Council that the sales were disappointing and the financial position difficult. An endeavour was made to increase the circulation, and in the following year £300 again granted. Sir Arthur Haworth made valiant attempts to save the paper, and there were other loyal supporters in a most discouraging campaign. In his address from the Chair in October, 1915, Sir Arthur reported that much of the appreciation expressed had been only "lip service", and continued :

> The support of the paper has been wholly inadequate, and the dead weight of inertia and supercilious neglect has still to be lifted. The generosity and loyalty of some of our most eminent men has been beyond all praise, and our churches owe a deep debt of gratitude to them. I doubt if any paper of standing ever received so much voluntary service as *The British Congregationalist*. The time has now come, however, when it must receive adequate support or be abandoned. To discontinue it would, I believe, be disastrous, and the Union and all the churches be weakened and handicapped in their endeavours.

A. J. VINER

A. E. GARVIE

[*Photo: Laugfier*
ROBERT F. HORTON

Members of the Assembly were asked to guarantee £10,000 over five years, but their promises were inadequate, and in 1916 the paper came to an end. Attempts to establish a journal to serve both Baptists and Congregationalists failed. The desirability of a denominational paper was strongly emphasized from time to time, but the Council insisted that the Assembly should secure pledges of financial support from the churches before they would recommend another venture. In 1919 an attempt to secure such guarantees was made, and the Literature Committee seemed to think the response from 253 out of 1,600 churches circularized encouraging.

Some miscellaneous features of the life of the Union during this period must not be overlooked :

Publications.

There is little in the way of publication to record in these years, Dr. P. T. Forsyth's Congregational Lecture, *The Person of Christ* (1909) being the outstanding feature. The 250th Anniversary of the Ejectment of 1662 and the Tercentenary of the Sailing of the *Mayflower* produced a crop of historical literature.

In 1920 a publication of an unusual kind was the *Book of Congregational Worship,* which contained ten Orders of Service for ordinary worship and also Orders for Baptisms, Holy Communion, Marriages and Funerals. The *Ten Orders of Service* were afterwards separately printed with a view to their use in the pew, but very few churches seem to have adopted them.

Colleges.

The question of the Colleges was thoroughly considered in the years following 1921 by a College Commission, which included representatives of the College Board. The terms of reference of the Commission were :

(a) Whether the needs of the Congregational Churches cannot be adequately met by fewer Colleges ;

(b) Whether an amalgamation of some of the Colleges would or would not increase efficiency and promote economy ;

(c) Whether it would be possible to secure a greater variety of type in the training given to the students preparing for the Congregational ministry;

(d) How an adequate supply of suitable candidates for the ministry could be secured.

The Commission presented Reports in October, 1922, and March, 1923, recounting the failure of attempts at amalgamation between Lancashire and Yorkshire Colleges, on the one hand, and Paton College, Nottingham, and Western College, Bristol, on the other, while the amalgamation of Hackney and New Colleges had been previously planned by their authorities. The Commission came to the conclusion that " the training of the ministry is being carried on with as much economy and as great efficiency as the actual conditions allow ". The churches were urged to give better support to the Colleges and to have a College Sunday. The Commission also discussed the shortage of candidates for the ministry and of College-trained men.

The " New Theology " Controversy.

In the first decade of the century the churches were disturbed by what was known as the " New Theology " Controversy, which arose through the teaching of the Rev. R. J. Campbell, of the City Temple. Mr. Campbell afterwards withdrew his book from circulation, and it is unnecessary here to discuss the elements of his teaching which were thought by many to forsake the essentials of the Christian faith. Violent attacks were made on Mr. Campbell, and many people rallied to his defence who by no means agreed with his opinions. The controversy only concerns the history of the Union because, especially after an attack on Mr. Campbell by Dr. P. T. Forsyth, of Hackney College, demands were made in some quarters that he should no longer be recognized as a minister by the Union. The Union Committee took the position which it had taken in the case of Allanson Picton[1]. Mr. Campbell was a minister whose name was sent up by the London Congregational Union, and over his recognition as a minister the

---

[1] See above, pp. 266ff.

Congregational Union of England and Wales had no jurisdiction.   The bitterness of the attacks on Mr. Campbell
finally culminated in a personal statement made by him in
the May Assembly in 1910, in answer to which the then
Chairman, Silvester Horne, merely stated the constitutional position.   The Union Minute altogether disguises
the intensity of the feeling during the speeches in the
Memorial Hall on the occasion.   It reads :

> By permission of the Assembly, on the understanding
> that no resolution was put to the vote, the Rev. R. J.
> Campbell, M.A., made a statement largely of a personal
> character.   The Chairman of the Union, the Rev. C. S.
> Horne, M.A., M.P., replied, and the incident closed.

Excitement afterwards died down, and some years later
Mr. Campbell resigned the pastorate of the City Temple
and joined the Church of England.

Church Unity.

(a) The Federal Council of the Free Churches.

The tendency toward increased unity between the
denominations was marked in these years.   It was mentioned by Dr. J. D. Jones in his Chairman's Address on
" Catholic Independency " in 1909.   In 1910, when the
Autumn Assembly was held at Hampstead, a striking
public meeting was addressed by the Master of the Rolls,
Canon Hensley Henson, the Rev. J. H. Shakespeare, and
the Union's Chairman, the Rev. C. Silvester Horne.   In
1916, after addresses from representatives of the Free
Church Council, the Assembly appointed ten representatives on a Committee to consider the possibility of a Free
Church Federation.   Dr. P. T. Forsyth spoke on " Congregationalism and Christian Union " in May, 1918, when
the proposals for a Federal Council of the Free Churches
was approved, and in 1919 29 representatives were
appointed on that Council.   One of its first Reports, presented to and accepted by the Assembly, was in regard to
overlapping, while it was urged that efforts should be made
to secure minimum stipends of £220 in the country and
£250 in the towns.

(b) The Anglican Community.

In regard to wider union some definite approaches were made during these years. Anglicans and Free Churchmen were coming to understand one another better and seeing more of each other, although the Union was constrained in 1919 to register its opposition to the Enabling Bill. Preparations had already begun for a World Conference on Faith and Order, and unofficial conferences of Anglicans and Free Churchmen to discuss union were being held.

In 1920 the " Lambeth Appeal " was issued from the Lambeth Conference, and the Assembly at once welcomed its brotherly and eirenical spirit, while declaring that the conditions suggested for union were such as loyalty to fundamental matters of faith would prevent Congregationalists from accepting. The following May an evening was given to the discussion of the Appeal, and a long resolution passed insisting that union was " only possible on the basis of a frank acknowledgment of the validity of one another's ministries ", and emphasizing that Congregationalism's " historic witness in favour of the continuous guidance of the Spirit and the consequent freedom of faith" made it difficult to accept the insistence upon a formulated creed, to assent to the necessity of the Episcopate, or agree to any form of Church Establishment.

XVIII. STEAMING AHEAD.

S. M. BERRY, SECRETARY, 1923-1931.

FOR a successor to Wells the Union turned to one of the most important churches in the country, Carrs Lane, Birmingham, whose ministers, Angell James, Dale, and Jowett, had all taken a prominent part in the life and work of the Union. Its pulpit was now occupied by the Rev. S. M. Berry, son of Charles A. Berry who had been invited to the Secretaryship of the Union thirty years before. The new Secretary was in the prime of life and happily and successfully at work in a very influential pastorate, and it was only a strong sense of duty and opportunity which led him to leave this charge for the leadership of the Union. To some the change from the pastorate to the Secretarial office seemed a step down, but any office is what a man makes it, and Sidney Berry has made the Secretaryship of the Union the vehicle of as wide a service to the Kingdom of God as any man might desire.

His coming at once breathed a new spirit into every part of the Union's activity. Dr. J. D. Jones, who had been elected Honorary Secretary in 1919, continued to act in the same capacity, and the two made an irresistible combination. Perhaps Berry's main achievement is that he has managed to make the Congregational ministry into a family, and a happy family at that, and at the same time to make even the Memorial Hall into something approaching a home.

Of course, while the main credit for the improved prospects of the Union is due to its Secretary, it has to be shared with others, both ministers and laymen. Berry took office when all kinds of new proposals were in the air and when at long last a real attempt was being made to grasp the financial nettle.

Finance.

The Report of a strong Finance Commission was accepted by the Council in 1924. Some economies it effected at once, others it was unable to carry out because certain arrangements were in the way of legacies, "relics of the time when . . . the Chapel Building and Church Aid Societies were wholly independent of the Union". An increase in affiliation fees was recommended, and also the enforcement of a rule that in order to be eligible for grants churches must be affiliated with the Union. The appointment of an independent Publication Committee was recommended, and also of a Finance Secretary to bring under one control the finances of the Chapel Building Society, the Church Aid and Central Funds, the Pastors' Retiring Fund, and the Pastors' Widows' Fund. *Teachers and Taught* was not to be continued without a guarantee against loss. The Finance Committee should be strengthened, and a number of ministers included[1]. In time most of the recommendations of this Commission were carried into effect. The Commission also made a direct appeal to the churches for a collection to meet the deficit on the Union's funds and received £1,086 in response. The Chairman of the Council, Mr. J. C. Meggitt, backed by Sir Albert Spicer, the senior ex-Chairman of the Union, made a special effort to remove the accumulated debt of the Union, finally receiving £12,844. Meanwhile, £12,000 had been received on account of the Bowdler Bequest for poorer ministers and churches, a bequest which finally will probably bring at least three times that amount to the Union, and which is already rendering great help to the Church Aid and Central Funds.

In 1924 the Publication Committee was converted into a Private Limited Liability Company, the Union or its representatives holding all the shares, the first Directors being the Rev. T. H. Darlow (Chairman), Sir R. Murray Hyslop (Treasurer of the Union), Dr. Albert Peel, Mr.

---

1 Perhaps at no time had the Finance Committee had a minister on it save Union Secretaries, probably under the double and equally strange assumption that ministers should not concern themselves with material things and that no minister could be a man of business! A precedent was made in 1922 by the appointment of the present writer on the Committee. Afterwards the suggestion of the Finance Commission was acted upon, and other ministers added.

Stanley Unwin (Managing Director of Messrs. George
Allen & Unwin), Mr. Thomas Young (Chairman of the
Directors of Messrs. Cassells), Mr. James O'Hanlon, Dr.
J. D. Jones, and Dr. S. M. Berry. From that point the
Independent Press has not looked back. It accepted
£7,500 as its proportion of the Union's bank overdraft, and
it has not only wiped this out and made provision for the
superannuation of its staff, but also paid a handsome divi-
dend to the Union year after year.

Altogether the administration of the finances of the
Union, under a Committee strengthened by the addition
of several professional accountants, became extremely
efficient. The churches, too, responded, and affiliation fees
in 1926 actually brought in over £5,000, while the number
of personal members was considerably increased. A long-
standing reproach was removed by the establishment of an
adequate Contributory Staff Superannuation Fund,
although there was strong opposition in the Assembly to
the inclusion of Moderators in this scheme on the part of
those who felt that it would be well for Moderators to rank
with their brother ministers in this regard rather than as
Union officials. Soon the Union's accounts began to show
an excess of income over expenditure year by year, and it
became possible to make annual grants to funds like the
Superannuation Fund.

Forward Movement.

Much relief also came to the finances through the success
of the Forward Movement appeal. From the Fund the interest on £50,000 is available for the administration of the
Moderators' Scheme, and on £40,000 for the Headquarters'
Account of the Union.

The Forward Movement Fund was finally completed
in May, 1925, when at a Thanksgiving Meeting at the
Albert Hall, addressed by Sir John Simon, Mrs. Alderton,
Sir James Carmichael, Dr. Jones, and Dr. Berry, it was
announced that over £500,000 had been obtained. Subsequently the value of some shares included in this total
was written down, and in May, 1931, the total amount produced by the Fund is stated as £481,157 16s. 2d.

To the Commissioners in the Counties, and to the Rev. A. G. Sleep, who organized the Fund in the concluding stages, much credit was due, but again it was by Dr. J. D. Jones that the lion's share of the work was done. Testimony has been borne in many ways to the services he has rendered to the denomination. His Majesty the King made him a Companion of Honour in 1927, he was elected a second time to the Chair of the Union for the year 1925, during which year his brother ministers presented him with an oak bench and desk for use in the chancel of his church, and in 1930 world-wide Congregationalism elected him Moderator for the Fifth International Congregational Council held in Bournemouth.

By the success of the Forward Movement the ministry benefited in many ways. The income on £50,000 was used for scholarships for their children, available at Caterham, Silcoates, and Milton Mount the income on another £50,000 went to pastors' widows; on £161,041 (increased from £150,000) to the superannuation of ministers on List A; and on £30,000 (increased from £20,000) to superannuation of evangelists on List B. In 1925 the new Superannuation Fund was formed by the merging of the Pastors' Retiring Fund with the £150,000 already collected under the Forward Movement. Thanks to the invaluable advocacy of Mr. Owen Kentish, to whose actuarial skill the Union has been continually indebted in recent years, a Contributory Ministerial Superannuation Fund (The Congregational Ministers' Friendly Society) has been added to the Superannuation Fund just mentioned. Through this Friendly Society ministers under 50 paying £3 10s. 0d. yearly (plus £3 10s. 0d. from their churches) secure an annuity of £50 at the age of 65. Through the Superannuation Fund annuities of amounts varying according to length of service are secured to ministers over 65 under certain defined rules, while there is an income limit of £150 a year[1].

No part of the Forward Movement Fund has been more useful than that for ministers' widows. A Pastors' Widows'

1 See *Year Book*, 1931, pp. 19-26 for these Societies.

[Photo: Russell

ALBERT PEEL

C. SILVESTER HORNE

J. H. JOWETT

Fund had been started as early as 1871, but even in 1920 all that a widow could hope to receive from the Fund was from £8 to £10 a year.

It will be appreciated that the Union has now under its control large funds. The last Statement of Assets and Liabilities showed assets amounting to £988,208, the main Funds represented being[1] :

	£
Headquarters for Administration and Moderators	107,117
Staff Superannuation	17,757
Schools	51,500
Church Building	35,648
Special Church Extension	10,174
Central	270,189
Church Aid	41,922
Bowdler	29,246
Pastors' Superannuation	324,093
Pastors' Widows	93,733

These Funds are administered by the Finance Department of the Union and make a contribution towards administration. In addition the Union is now Trustee of many Funds belonging to churches and societies throughout the country.

A few figures from the last Income and Expenditure Account will show the growth of the Union :

Income.

	£
Affiliation Fees	5,401
Personal Membership	1,005
Contributions from Societies and Funds toward Administration	1,490
Dividends	6,965
Congregational Insurance Company	105

Expenditure.

	£
Salaries, Staff Superannuation and Pensions	4,624
Moderators	4,740
Grants, mostly for Departments	1,871
Postages and Stationery (including *Year Book* expenses, £207)	701

The excess of Income over Expenditure was £1,331.

1 This is exclusive of capital in the Friendly Societies.

AA

These developments in the sphere of finance are balanced by corresponding progress in other sections of the Union's work. In 1922 the Union decided to make still another venture in the way of periodical publications. It was resolved to publish a quarterly journal under the editorship of the present writer. In 1923 the *Congregational Quarterly* made its appearance, and to the surprise of everybody, editor included, it made a considerable profit in its first year. It has continued to pay its way down to the present time. The Editorial Board at first consisted of Dr. W. B. Selbie, the Rev. Arthur Pringle, and Mr. H. B. Shepheard, to whom Mr. B. L. Manning and the Rev. E. J. Price were subsequently added.

In the following year the editor of the *Congregational Quarterly* and the Rev. A. G. Sleep planned a monthly magazine with a view to its use by Congregational churches as an inset. They invited the Union to assume responsibility for this journal, but this was the time when great attempts were being made to put the Union's finances on a more satisfactory footing, and the authorities therefore were not disposed to take any risks. The inset was at once adopted by many churches, and it has proved of great value to the Union. It provides direct means of communication by which the Secretary, who has the use of the first two pages each month, can speak to the individual Congregationalist. It should be mentioned too, that since 1929 he has also been in a privileged position in regard to the *Christian World* (a weekly paper always owned by Congregationalists, and now the property of the Rev. A. G. Sleep), of the Editorial Board of which Dr. Berry became a member in 1929.

Teachers and Taught, though having to be subsidized from time to time, is rendering useful service to teachers in graded schools under the management of the Young People's Department, but there is no doubt that the best piece of work that Department has so far done has been through *School Worship,* published in various forms in 1926, which is by far the best hymn book obtainable for the modern Sunday School. The Department also published

A Scheme of Christian Education, containing the findings of a Commission in 1922, which has proved a valuable guide to many schools throughout the country. For some years, too, the Union published the *Concise Guides,* only losing this connexion through the departure of the editor, Mr. E. H. Hayes, to the Sunday School Union. The examinations are now an established and successful part of the Department's work.

Closer co-operation has been secured during these years with the Missionary Societies. From 1928 the two Societies have presented a Joint Report to the Council each year in March. An attempt was made in 1925-26 to secure a common headquarters for the London Missionary Society and the Union. Efforts to sell the Memorial Hall proved impossible, and it was found equally impossible to adapt the Hall so as to accommodate the two organizations. There is a movement which seems to be increasing in force for a still closer union between the Union and the Missionary Societies which represent the Congregational churches. In 1930 the Union responded to the invitation of the L.M.S. to appoint representatives on a Joint Commission formed to advise the South India United Church in regard to the South India Scheme of Church Union, while in 1931 the Society submitted to the Union the Report of its Survey Committee, which is to be considered in the Assembly in May, 1931.

This may be the time to note that considerable alterations have been made in the Memorial Hall. Mr. J. C. Meggitt placed panels behind the platform of the Great Hall on which the names of the Chairmen of the Union were inscribed. Sir James Carmichael generously redecorated the Council Chamber and made it worthy of the denomination. By his generosity too, the Union has been able to send to the County Unions annually for some years circulating libraries for the use of ministers.

In some Departments progress of the Union's work has been checked. The great demand for Church Extension, and especially the need for new places of worship in extensive new areas, has unfortunately coincided with a period of intense and prolonged industrial depression. In some localities there have been praiseworthy efforts to cope with the situation, but, despite some generous gifts to a Central Extension Fund to be used in the way of challenge grants, that Fund has not received any great addition. Mr. Halley Stewart's gift of £10,000—£2,500 each for London, Surrey, Kent, and Essex, on condition that each county Union raises £7,500—has already been taken up in some of the Counties, while his own County of Hertfordshire has raised £15,000 in order to qualify for a challenge offer of £5,000 from him.

The Chapel Building Society has continued to perform its work in steady fashion. The number of cases it has helped during the 77 years of its life is 1,758, during which time the advances paid and promised have amounted to £348,462, of which £264,017 has been by way of loans and the remainder in grants.

The Union has sent representatives to various International Conferences during these years. At the Stockholm Conference on Life and Work in 1925 the following representatives were appointed : Dr. J. V. Bartlet, the Rev. W. Blackshaw, Dr. A. E. Garvie, Sir R. Murray Hyslop, the Rev. Henry Knowles, Mrs. A. MacGregor Morris, Mr. Arthur Porritt, the Rev. Will Reason, the Rev. Malcolm Spencer, Miss Stafford, and the Rev. James Beeby ; and at Lausanne in 1927 it was represented by the Drs. J. Vernon Bartlet, Berry, Garvie, and Peel. It ought to be said that a leading part has been played in all the international contacts of the Union by Dr. Garvie, who was Deputy Chairman of the Lausanne Conference. The Reply of the Union to the Report of the Lausanne Conference happily revealed the strength of the traditional Congregational conceptions of the Church and the ministry. The Committee having allowed to enter its Report to the Assembly a statement that "the ministry is essential to the Church", a statement entirely opposed to Congregational teaching, at Mr. G. N. Ford's instance the Report was sent back that the offending sentence might be removed and other alterations made.

The Assembly watched with considerable anxiety the progress of negotiations subsequent to the Lambeth Conference between bishops and Free Church leaders, fearing lest in their desire to conciliate and to secure the manifest unity of the Churches, those belonging to the denomination might be inclined to make compromises which would entail the abandonment of fundamental principles. No tangible result came from these Conferences[1] except mutual respect and acknowledgment of conscientious differences, and the Lambeth Conference Report of 1930, to the analysis of which Dr. F. W. Norwood devoted one of his Chairman's Addresses, showed how far the bishops were from making any real concessions to the Free Church point of view.

In 1928 the Council had made its position plain with regard to the revision of the Prayer Book, protesting that the permission given to the practice of Reservation seemed to involve of necessity the Roman Catholic conception of the Sacrament and was therefore incompatible with the position of the Church of England established as a Protestant Reformed Church. They expressed the belief that the House of Commons, in rejecting the Book, had rightly interpreted the feelings of the great majority of the British people, and did not feel that the changes proposed when presenting the Book a second time met the objections raised.

The churches were drawn into closer fellowship in many ways during these years. In Mr. J. C. Meggitt's year of Chairmanship he arranged a visitation scheme in conjunction with the County Unions, whereby leading ministers visited many of the smaller churches in the different Counties. Still later, in a period of acute distress in the mining areas, a fund was raised by which the ministers of churches in those areas and their people were substantially helped by gifts of money and of shoes and clothing. The Women's Committee (Secretary, Mrs. J. G. Stevenson) has regularly had as part of its work the assistance of needy ministers and their families by the provision of clothing, etc.

---

[1] See G. K. A. Bell, *Documents on Church Unity*. Oxford Press.

It is impossible to describe the various developments of the Union's many-sided work. The Social Service Committee, under the leadership of the Rev. Malcolm Spencer, has worked in association with the Social Service Committees of other denominations, and especially in "Copec" and the newly-formed Christian Social Council. The Temperance Committee (Secretary, the Rev. T. Eynon Davies) is affiliated with the Temperance Council of the Christian Churches, and has urged that Council's " Three Point " Programme.

With the establishment of the Central Fund and the various Funds for Superannuation, there is no doubt that there has been an inevitable stiffening of the regulations regarding the ministry. Since the revision of the "Rules for the Recognition of Ministers and Churches" in 1912, those Rules have been revised and supplemented in 1917, 1922, 1923, and 1930. Altogether there is more rigidity than was the case at the beginning of the century, the policy being to secure a definite standard of admission to the ministry, and also to raise the status of evangelists and lay pastors, and to bring the churches, colleges, and County Unions within a well-defined scheme. The Rules now in force are to be found in the *Year Book* for 1931, pp. 51-54, together with the Regulations about the Examinations. With them should be considered the "Regulations for the Preparation of the *Year Book*", pp. 57-59.

In the course of these revisions it has been made clear that nothing prohibits the recognition of women ministers who have fulfilled the regulations, and there are several women ministers on List A.

The Terminable Pastorates Commission, of which mention has been made above, concluded that terminable pastorates were undesirable "except in cases of men of advanced age and of churches not in the full sense Congregational, such as mission churches or stations under the oversight of a County Union". Specially important in the Report of the Commission was the reference to the colleges.

The Union, now assisting to maintain ministers in work
and in retirement,

> cannot decline the corporate responsibility of determining
> who shall be admitted into the ministry. The time has come
> when we should take steps to secure such a degree of co-
> ordination between the now independent, and too often
> competing, Colleges and the whole body of the Churches
> through the Union, as will enable us to exercise this
> corporate responsibility.

The discussion of their Report led to a resolution that
the Moderators be asked to consult with the College
principals as to the best way of giving effect to the Report's
suggestions dealing with the admission of men to the
ministry. This discussion finally led to the formation of
a Ministerial Training Committee, which has superseded
the College Board.

It would not be fitting to close this record without men-
tioning the devotion of many of the Union's servants. The
Rev. W. Mottram in the Temperance Department; the
Rev. J. E. Flower and Mr. W. W. Hancock in the Church
Aid Society; Mr. A. W. Dorling in the Chapel Building
Society; Miss B. M. Woods (daughter of the Rev. W. J.
Woods) who for many years has been private secretary to
the Secretary of the Union; Mr. Henry Thacker, Mr. C. F.
Garrood, and Miss Stancliff in the Publication Department,
have all rendered long and faithful service. Deserving of
special mention are Mr. John Minshull, who was in the
service of the Union for 37 years and the head of its financial department for 25 years, and Mr. Charles Stancliff who,
coming as a youth in 1878, became Chief Clerk and Editor
of the *Year Book,* retiring with tokens of appreciation from
the Assembly in 1926. With Mr. Stancliff's retirement and
the changes resulting from the acceptance of the Finance
Committee's recommendations, the personnel of the staff
changed considerably. A minister, in the person of the
Rev. Maldwyn Johnes, Secretary of the Hampshire Union,
was appointed Assistant to the Secretary of the Union, and
an accountant, Mr. H. Simpson, Financial Secretary. Mr.
Stancliff continued to edit the *Year Book* until 1930, the
editor of the 1931 Book being Mr. J. B. Gotts, O.B.E.

EPILOGUE.

THIS chronicle should serve in itself to answer the question how far the Congregational Union has carried out its aims. Certainly it has promoted evangelical religion and cultivated brotherly affection and co-operation. Certainly it has established fraternal correspondence with Congregational churches and other Christians. It has not addressed an Annual Letter to the churches, but it has in other ways kept in communication with them. It has obtained "statistical information" from the churches, though perhaps only an optimist would consider that information to be invariably "accurate". It has given due consideration to the building of churches and the securing of funds for their building. It has "maintained and enlarged the civil rights of Protestant Dissenters". All these are quoted from the objects contemplated in the original "Plan of Union". Perhaps discussion is most likely to arise on the question whether in carrying out all these varied aims the Union has managed to preserve "the scriptural right of every separate church to maintain perfect independence in the governing and administration of its own particular affairs". The possession of large Funds for the maintenance and superannuation of the ministry and for the aiding of churches tends to destroy in some measure that independence which the Congregationalists of 1831 held to be "their own distinctive principle", and there are some who would urge that while the administration of these Funds is kindly and well disposed, nevertheless its effect is, in the long run, the reverse of beneficial.

The problem of combining entire freedom with the full advantages of union is not yet solved. Some Congregationalists lean toward closer organization and an idea of the church and ministry that may perhaps be labelled Presbyterian. Others still believe in complete independence for church and minister alike. For a hundred years the Congregational Churches have been trying to discover how to unite freedom and fellowship and keep the advantages of both. They have probably approached nearer to this difficult ideal than any other social organization, political or religious. They have shown how a church and County Union can have a very large measure of freedom and yet be affiliated to a central body that exists to stimulate and help the whole. Whether the lessons they have learned in the process will enable them to work out a complete solution, the future must show.

Two facts encourage the belief that the liberty and independence which Congregationalists cherish will never be forsaken. One is the way in which the churches frequently recognize the services of men who have been by no means strong supporters of a central organization. They have often elected to the Chair ministers and others whose work has largely been confined to their own churches or their own locality. It is a striking thing that a minister could be elected who could say, as Morlais Jones said from the chair in 1896:

> Let me make a confession to you. I have no right to criticize Congregationalism. Of all men here I have been the poorest Congregationalist. I have lived far from denominational movements. I am on no denominational committee except one, and I never attend that. I have always had a suspicion of the Memorial Hall. I was born with the instinct to fight all secretaries. I turn every circular that comes to me with a secretary's name on it round and round, and always suspect that he is trying to get the better of me.

Then, there is a growing freedom of utterance on the Union platform. In 1887, commenting on a theological paper, Guinness Rogers said:

> Of course, there were things said with which we did not ourselves agree, but one of the superstitions relative to the Union and its meetings, of which it is necessary to get rid, is this idea that everybody is to agree with everything that is said or done.

That superstition was long in dying. Not so very long age there seemed to be the same strange fear abroad, a desire that we should all say the same things and say them together, a suspicion of those who did not take the official

view, and an impatience with minorities. Now we seem
to have arrived at a stage when it is recognized that within
the wide bounds of Congregationalism it is possible for
men to have diverse views on matters of theology, organization, and policy, and yet be of one mind and heart in their
love for Christ and His Church. In this fact one hope for
the future lies.

Perhaps no better prayer can be offered for the Congregational Union than that which John Ely offered on his
death-bed in 1847, even though it is coloured by the controversies of his day :

> May you have in your assembly, and in all your pro-
> ceedings, the wisdom that is from above—pure, peaceable,
> gentle, easy to be entreated, and full of mercy and good
> fruits. Keep to great principles, and on no account
> abandon or compromise them. I hope all our churches will
> adhere faithfully to the principles we have solemnly and
> publicly avowed, and that none of them will ever take a
> fraction of the public money,—not a fraction of Govern-
> ment money—for the purposes of religion and education.
> Discussions will necessarily arise; court discussion, but
> avoid all bitterness. God, I trust, will guide and bless you.
> The God of love and peace be with you !

APPENDIX

CHAIRMEN.

For list of Chairmen and places of Autumnal Meeting, see the *Congregational Year Book*. This is incorrect in some details which will be corrected in the 1932 *Year Book*. Especially should it be noted that Joseph Fletcher was Chairman on one day of the Assembly in 1831, and that there was no Autumn Meeting until 1839.

SECRETARIES:

Rev. Arthur Tidman, D.D., 1832-33.
Mr. Joseph Turnbull, 1832-34.
Mr. Joshua Wilson, 1832-36.
Rev. Wm. Stern Palmer, 1833-52.
Rev. John Blackburn, 1834-47.
Mr. Joseph Wontner, 1836-42.
Rev. Algernon Wells, 1837-50.
Rev. George Smith, D.D., 1851-70.
Rev. Robert Ashton, 1852-70.
Rev. Alexander Hannay, D.D., 1870-90.
Rev. D. B. Hooke (provisional), 1891-92.
Rev. Wm. J. Woods, B.A., 1892-1903.
Rev. James A. Mitchell, B.A., 1904-05.
Rev. Richard J. Wells, 1905-23.
Rev. J. D. Jones, C.H., M.A., D.D. (Honorary Secretary), 1919—
Rev. Sidney M. Berry, M.A., D.D., 1923—

Treasurers.

Benjamin Hanbury, 1831-64.
Joshua Wilson, 1864-74.
James Spicer, 1874-88.
William Holborn, 1888-1894.
William Crosfield, 1894-1909.
Sir R. Murray Hyslop, 1909—

HYMN BOOKS, *Etc.*

(published by the Union).

1836. *The Congregational Hymn Book,* edited by Josiah Conder. 620 hymns.

1859. *The New Congregational Hymn Book.* 1,000 hymns.

1866. *The Smaller Congregational Hymn Book* (selected from the *New Hymn Book* and sometimes called *The Cottage Hymn Book*). 150 hymns.

1867. *The Congregational Sunday School Hymn Book.* 302 hymns.

1874. *The Supplement to the Congregational Hymn Book.* 281 hymns.

1875. *The Abridged Congregational Hymn Book* (selected from the *New Hymn Book* and *The Supplement*). 270 hymns.

1880. *A Congregational Hymnal or Book of Praise for the Young,* edited by G. S. Barrett. 378 hymns.

1887. *The Congregational Church Hymnal,* edited by G. S. Barrett, E. J. Hopkins and Josiah Booth. 775 hymns, 147 chants, 85 anthems.

1890. *The Mission Hymnal,* edited by G. S. Barrett. 300 hymns.

1891. *Congregational Sunday School Hymnal,* edited by G. S. Barrett and J. Barnby. 500 hymns (incorporating the 378 hymns in the 1880 book).

1899. *Additional Anthems* to the *Congregational Church Hymnal,* by G. S. Barrett. 35 anthems.

1916. *The Congregational Hymnary,* edited by J. D. McClure and Josiah Booth. 771 hymns, 116 chants, 117 anthems.

1920. *A Book of Congregational Worship.*

1923. 10 *Orders of Service* from the *Book of Congregational Worship.*

1926. *School Worship* (in various forms for different Departments). 404 hymns, with Orders of Worship, Psalms, and Prayers.

1929. *101 Hymns.*

OFFICIAL PUBLICATIONS.

Name of Publication.	Dates.	Editor.
Congregational Calendar.	1840-48.	J. Blackburn.
Congregational Year Book.	1846-47.	J. Blackburn.
	1848-49.	A. Wells and W. S. Palmer.
	1850-51.	R. Ashton and W. S. Palmer.
	1852-78.	R. Ashton.
	1879-88.	A. Hannay.
	1889.	D. B. Hooke.
	1890.	A. Hannay and D. B. Hooke.
	1891-92.	D. B. Hooke.
	1893-1902.	W. J. Woods.
	1903-30.	C. Stancliff.
	1931.	J. B. Gotts.

OFFICIAL PERIODICALS.

The Christian Witness. (Editor, John Campbell) 1844-1857 (continued unofficially until 1871).

The Christian's Penny Magazine and Friend of the People. (Editor, John Campbell) 1845-1857 (continued unofficially until 1881).

Teachers and Taught. (1915——; Editor, A. Hallack, 1924—), (the Union acquired an interest in the paper in 1915, and took the management at the end of 1920, and entire control in 1924).

Teachers of To-day. 1921-1923.

The Congregational Quarterly. (Editor, Albert Peel) 1923—

UNOFFICIAL PERIODICALS

(in close connexion with the Union).

The Congregational Magazine. 1818-1845.
The Biblical Review and Congregational Magazine. 1846-1847.
The Biblical Review. 1847 (July)-1850.
Christian Witness. 1858-1871.
Christian's Penny Magazine and Friend of the People. 1858-1881.
The Congregationalist. 1872-1886.
The Congregational Review. 1887-1890.
The Congregational Church Monthly. 1924—

The Home Missionary Society published its own journal before its amalgamation with the Union, under the title, *The Home Missionary Magazine*. For some years after the amalgamation its periodical was called *The Congregational Magazine and Church Aid Journal*.

Influence was also exercised on the *Evangelical Magazine* and the *Eclectic Review*. In addition, Congregationalists had a greater or less connexion during the period with weekly journals like the *Patriot; British Banner; British Standard; Nonconformist; Nonconformist and Independent; Independent and Nonconformist; Independent; Examiner; British Congregationalist; Christian World*. There was the widest variety in the connexion of organized Congregationalism with these journals, both in regard to proprietorship and editorial. It was closest in the case of the *Examiner* and *British Congregationalist*.

There is nothing more difficult to discover than the exact facts in regard to the religious periodical literature of the nineteenth century. There is nothing for which the student would be more grateful than a list of periodicals with facts about their editorship and ownership. This *History* is not the place for it, but a conspectus of the periodical literature connected with the denomination from 1793 to 1931 is in preparation.

SOME OUTSTANDING DATES.

1818. *Congregational Magazine* started.

1831   Opening of Library.

1831   First Meeting of Union.

1832   Union officially formed.

1833   Declaration of Faith and Order.

1836   First Hymn Book.

1836   Colonial Missionary Society formed.

1838   First Legacy.

1839   First Autumn Assembly.

1843   Congregational Board of Education.

1844   First Periodical—*Christian Witness*, with its Fund for Aged Ministers.

1853   Chapel Building Society.

1856-7 *Rivulet* Controversy.

1857-8 Separation of Societies and Magazines from Union.

1859   Pastors' Retiring Fund.

1862   Bicentenary Fund.

1872   First Investment.

1872   New Constitution.

1874 Congregational Total Abstinence Association formed.

1875 Memorial Hall opened.

1877 Leicester Conference and Religious Communion Controversy.

1877 Church Aid and Home Missionary Society formed.

1881 Jubilee Fund.

1891 First International Congregational Council.

1899 Twentieth Century Fund.

1901 Parker's United Congregational Church proposals.

1904 New Constitution.

1908 Young People's Department formed.

1909-13 Central Fund.

1910 Social Service Department formed.

1910 College Board.

1915 Women's Work Committee.

1919 Moderators First appointed.

1921-25 Forward Movement.

1924 Independent Press formed.

INDEX.